MANAGING FAMILY JUSTICE IN DIVERSE SOCIETIES

The aim of this book is to explore what response the law has or should have to different family practices arising from cultural and religious beliefs. The issue has become increasingly debated as Western countries have become more culturally diverse. Although discussion has frequently focused on the role Islamic family law should have in these countries, this book seeks to set that discussion within a wider context that includes consideration both of theoretical issues and also of empirical data about the interaction between specific family practices and state law in a variety of jurisdictions ranging from England and Wales to Bangladesh, Botswana, Spain, Poland, France, Israel, Iran and South Africa. The contributors to the 17 chapters approach the subject matter from a variety of perspectives, illustrating its complex and often sensitive nature. The book does not set out to propose any single definitive strategy that should be adopted, but provides material on which researchers, advocates and policy makers can draw in furthering their understanding of and seeking solutions to the problems raised by this significant social development.

Oñati International Series in Law and Society

A SERIES PUBLISHED FOR THE OÑATI INSTITUTE
FOR THE SOCIOLOGY OF LAW

General Editors
Rosemary Hunter David Nelken

Founding Editors
William L F Felstiner Eve Darian-Smith

Board of General Editors
Carlos Lugo, Hostos Law School, Puerto Rico
Jacek Kurczewski, Warsaw University, Poland
Marie-Claire Foblets, Leuven University, Belgium
Roderick Macdonald, McGill University, Canada

Recent titles in this series
The Legal Tender of Gender: Welfare Law and the Regulation
of Women's Poverty
edited by Shelley Gavigan and Dorothy Chunn

Human Rights at Work
edited by Colin Fenwick and Tonia Novitz

Travels of the Criminal Question: Cultural Embeddedness and Diffusion
edited by Dario Melossi, Máximo Sozzo and Richard Sparks

Feminist Perspectives on Contemporary International Law:
Between Resistance and Compliance?
edited by Sari Kouvo and Zoe Pearson

Challenging Gender Inequality in Tax Policy Making: Comparative
Perspectives
edited by Kim Brooks, Åsa Gunnarson, Lisa Philipps and Maria Wersig

Emotions, Crime and Justice
edited by Susanne Karstedt, Ian Loader and Heather Strang

Mediation in Political Conflicts
Soft Power or Counter Culture?
edited by Jacques Faget

Criminological and Legal Consequences of Climate Change
edited by Stephen Farrall, Tawhida Ahmed and Duncan French

For the complete list of titles in this series, see
'Oñati International Series in Law and Society' link at
www.hartpub.co.uk/books/series.asp

Managing Family Justice in Diverse Societies

Edited by

Mavis Maclean

and

John Eekelaar

Oñati International Series in Law and Society
A SERIES PUBLISHED FOR THE OÑATI INSTITUTE
FOR THE SOCIOLOGY OF LAW

·HART·
PUBLISHING
OXFORD AND PORTLAND OREGON
2013

Published in the United Kingdom by Hart Publishing Ltd
16C Worcester Place, Oxford, OX1 2JW
Telephone: +44 (0)1865 517530
Fax: +44 (0)1865 510710
E-mail: mail@hartpub.co.uk
Website: http://www.hartpub.co.uk

Published in North America (US and Canada) by
Hart Publishing
c/o International Specialized Book Services
920 NE 58th Avenue, Suite 300
Portland, OR 97213-3786
USA
Tel: +1 503 287 3093 or toll-free: (1) 800 944 6190
Fax: +1 503 280 8832
E-mail: orders@isbs.com
Website: http://www.isbs.com

British Library Cataloguing in Publication Data
Data Available

ISBN: 978-1-84946-400-0

Typeset by Hope Services (Abingdon) Ltd
Printed and bound in Great Britain by
MPG Books Group Ltd

Acknowledgements

The editors would like to express their gratitude to the General Editors of the Oñati International Series in Law and Society, Rosemary Hunter and David Nelken, and to Malen Gordoa and the staff at the IISL in Oñati for their impeccable organisation of the Workshop leading to this volume, and their help with preparing the materials for publication. The contributors brought a wide range of experience and expertise to the meeting, and all went on to develop their papers with the benefit of the robust discussion there; we fully appreciate their scholarship and commitment to this important debate.

Richard Hart and his staff have taken the book smoothly and skilfully through the production process, for which we are most grateful.

Contents

Contributors

Farrah Ahmed obtained a DPhil having attended Lincoln College, University of Oxford, UK and joined Melbourne Law School, Australia, in 2012.

Waheeda Amien is Senior Lecturer at the Faculty of Law, University of Cape Town, South Africa.

Samia Bano is Lecturer in Law and Deputy Director of Research at the University of Reading, UK.

Benoit Bastard is Directeur de Recherche at COS, Centre National de la Recherche Scientifique, Paris.

Farah Deeba Chowhdury is Associate Professor (on leave) at the Department of Political Science, University of Rajshahi, Bangladesh and Adjunct Faculty at the Department of Gender Studies, Queen's University, Canada.

Yasmine Debarge is a PhD student at Ecole Normale Supérieure of Cachan and Research Assistant at the Institut des Sciences Sociales du Politique, Paris.

Norman Doe is Professor of Law and Director of the Centre for Law and Religion, Cardiff University, Wales.

Gillian Douglas is Professor of Law, Cardiff University, Wales.

John Eekelaar FBA is Emeritus Fellow of Pembroke College, Oxford, UK, and Co-Director of the Oxford Centre for Family Law and Policy. He is a Fellow of the British Academy.

Pascale Fournier is University of Ottawa Research Chair in Legal Pluralism and Comparative Law, and Associate Professor.

Małgorzata Fuszara is Director of the INSS, Institute for Applied Social Studies, University of Warsaw, Poland.

Nazila Ghanea is University Lecturer in International Human Rights Law, Department of Continuing Education, University of Oxford, UK.

Sophie Gilliat-Ray is Reader in Religious and Theological Studies, Director for the Centre for the Study of Islam in the UK, Cardiff University, Wales.

Anne Griffiths is Professor in the School of Law, Edinburgh University, UK, currently Senior Research Fellow at the IGK International Research Centre on Work and the Human Lifecycle in Global History, Humboldt University, Germany.

Jagbir Jhutti-Johal is Lecturer in Sikh Studies, Department of Theology and Religion, University of Birmingham, UK.

Asma Khan is Research Assistant, Norah Fry Research Centre, University of Bristol, UK.

Jacek Kurczewski is Professor of Sociology of Custom and Law at the University of Warsaw, Poland. From 1991–93 he was Deputy Speaker and member of the Polish Parliament and from 1997–98 he was Director of the International Institute for Sociology of Law in Onati, Spain.

Merissa Lichtsztral is a graduate of the J.D. National Program, Faculty of Law, Common Law Section, University of Ottawa, Canada.

Pascal McDougall is a graduate of the LL.L. Licence en droit Program, Faculty of Law, Civil Law Section, University of Ottawa, Canada.

Mavis Maclean CBE is Co-Director of the Oxford Centre for Family Law and Policy in the Department of Social Policy and Intervention, University of Oxford and a Senior Research Fellow in the Faculty of Law. She is former President of the RCSL, a Fellow of the IISL and academic adviser to the Ministry of Justice.

Ann Phoenix is Professor of Education and Co-Director of the Thomas Coram Research Unit at the Institute of Education, University of London.

Teresa Picontó-Novales is Profesora Titular de Filosofía del Derecho and Sociología del Derecho (Lecturer of Legal Philosophy and Sociology of Law) at the University of Zaragoza, Spain.

Jordi Ribot is Professor of Civil Law, Institute of European and Comparative Private Law, University of Girona, Spain.

Russell Sandberg is Lecturer in Law, Cardiff University, Wales.

Prakash Shah is Senior Lecturer in Law, Queen Mary, University of London.

Marjorie Smith is Professor of the Psychology of the Family and Co-Director of the Thomas Coram Research Unit at the Institute of Education, University of London.

Introduction

MAVIS MACLEAN AND JOHN EEKELAAR

I T IS NOT surprising that the law which regulates family matters in any
jurisdiction generally enshrines the values of the dominant elements in that
society, whether they are defined by factors such as wealth, status, age and
gender or by culture, ethnicity and religion. The ways in which the less powerful
groups relate to the state family justice system depend on many factors. As societies become more diverse in culture, religion and ethnicity, there is a growing
interest in the impact of these influences on the individual's experience of family justice. The question of how the family practices of distinct cultural, ethnic
and religious minority groups are accommodated within the legal framework of
the wider society of which they are a part has been attracting increased theoretical attention since the beginning of the twenty-first century, though not as
yet accompanied by sufficient empirical research activity. The issue has been
presented as a particular difficulty for Western liberalism because of the tension
between the liberal values of respecting difference and the autonomy-enhancing
features of individuals identifying with particular cultures, and the autonomy-
restricting aspects of cultural membership, including the apparently illiberal
practices of some cultural groups, for example, with respect to gender equality
in family law. Furthermore, in human rights discourse, the rights of the individual to respect for his cultural and religious beliefs and practices may conflict
with the rights to equality of treatment, personal safety and autonomy.

In addition there is a question of social solidarity. Fears that multicultural policies are creating a divided society have been expressed in Europe (Joppke 2004;
Kepel 2005; Pfaff 2005; Meer and Modood 2009) and have been voiced by the
chair of the English Commission for Racial Equality (Phillips 2005). In October
2010, the German Chancellor, Angela Merkel, went so far as to say that multiculturalism in Germany had failed, and that minority groups must do more to integrate. In England, these concerns were exacerbated when the Archbishop of
Canterbury, the senior primate of the established Church, suggested in 2008 that
Islamic law was already recognised in some circumstances and argued that it
might need to be treated as a system supplemental to and running in parallel
with the state law if proper respect was to be given to people's religions (Williams

2008). In Canada, the question whether the procedure under the arbitration legislation in Ontario should be used to allow disputes to be resolved in accordance with Islamic law has caused much controversy (Aslam 2006).

The issue has been expressed as being not about negotiation with, but about the 'accommodation' of minority group norms. Jeremy Waldron (2010: chapter 7) distinguishes between two types of accommodation. One is by granting minorities certain exemptions from majority norms; another is by permitting minority norms to have legal effect. Either case, Waldron notes, can raise tensions with the rule of law. However, sometimes such accommodation may be held to be 'reasonable'. It is obvious that what is considered to be reasonable in this context could be difficult to agree. One problem, Waldron observes, is whether the exemptions or permissions in themselves cause injustice. But then conceptions of justice may vary between groups. The only solution he suggests is that the minority's views should feed into the 'general mix of democratic debate'.

Academic debate is part of democratic debate. And this collection is part of that debate, presenting a variety of views and a range of empirical studies. We begin by questioning how actively and in what circumstances the state needs to take a view on the family practices of subordinate or minority groups, whether defined by race, culture or ethnicity. We fully acknowledge the salience of other characteristics such as age or gender, but these have been considered elsewhere and are not the primary focus here. We emphasise the need for better information about the social norms and behaviour of all groups which form part of the wider society. We end by questioning how much law we need to regulate the family as an institution, and take as an example of family behaviour the physical punishment of children, presenting empirical evidence which has implications for considering the range of recent legal responses.

We wish to set the currently widely discussed question of the tension between 'state' law and norms within religious or ethnic groups in the context of a more general tension that is common between the law and society. Law does not always attempt to create a monolithic code of practice for everyone. The law itself may legitimate a variety of practices. For example, the recent addition of civil partnerships in England and Wales and in other jurisdictions alongside heterosexual marriage can be seen as the law itself legitimising a wider diversity of lifestyles than formerly. In Israel, the law requires people who wish to marry to do so according to certain recognised religious norms. Other types of practice may not attract specific legal recognition, but do not attract disapproval either. The widespread practice of cohabitation outside marriage, especially in Western Europe, is an example. This allows diversity, but in a different way. But some behaviours, such as polygamy or forced marriage, may attract social disapproval, which may be expressed through the operation of the law. These then are no longer viewed by the state as features of social or cultural diversity, but become defined by the legal response as forms of deviance.

The role of law in marking out the distinctions between social acceptance and social disapproval is particularly acute with regard to family behaviours, as it feeds into existing concerns about the interrelationships between family norms in the wider society and those of primary communities within families (Maclean 2005). This volume not only discusses theoretical issues underlying any approach to the question, but looks at actual examples supported by empirical evidence and considers what practical action might be taken to respond to it. To illustrate the international scope of their occurrence, the examples are drawn from a variety of national jurisdictions ranging from England and Wales to Poland, France, Israel, Iran and South Africa.

Theoretical and ideological issues which underlie strategic approaches to these issues are dealt with primarily in part one. In chapter one, John Eekelaar sets out a view consistent with Western liberal values that cautions against communitarian approaches that imply that communities may justifiably use coercive means through law to place the interests of the community (or a particular conception of the community) above those of its constituent members. He argues that while submission of individual interests to a particular form of community can have value, that value primarily lies in the voluntary nature of any such submission. He argues that an approach which sees individuals within their cultural context and permits them to choose to follow either the norms of their group, or general state norms, could provide a way of promoting diversity among individuals within a geographical polity. Eekelaar calls this approach 'cultural voluntarism' whereby the state resists conferring state-backed legal authority on minority group institutions, but nevertheless accepts that members of such groups may follow their own rules, enforcing them where they coincide with its law, always allowing group members access to its law, including human rights protection and prohibiting behaviour only where it causes harm or contravenes ordinary criminal law. The chapter raises the question that if the interests of individuals to experience the support and stability of participation in cultural norms are being met there may generally be no need for the state either to incorporate norms of any particular ethnic or religious group into state law or to confer on the institutions of the group express authority to exercise legal jurisdiction over its members. Any attempts to do so might raise problems regarding the identification of the applicable norms and their compatibility with human rights and inhibit the fluidity of individual movement between groups and cultures. He supports the view that no one can escape living within a culture or cultures, but no one culture should be allowed to capture any individual.

This approach implies giving significant value to personal autonomy, and is further explored by Farrah Ahmed, in chapter two. Ahmed challenges the view that group autonomy necessarily restricts individual autonomy. She considers forms of Alternative Dispute Resolution (ADR) which are based in religious beliefs and questions the view that Religious Alternative Dispute Resolution (RADR) necessarily enhances group autonomy at the expense of individual autonomy in ways which challenge liberal values. She argues that, under certain conditions, the use of RADR has the potential to *enhance* individual autonomy as the institutions of RADR provide contexts for expressing freedom to practise religion, and could even provide opportunities for individuals to influence the nature of the religion and its norms by which they live, either through their representatives or by participating in modes of group deliberation. It is important to note that Ahmed does not argue that RADR does not or cannot restrict autonomy, only that it does not necessarily do so, and under certain conditions can enhance it. This raises important questions about the approach states should adopt towards RADR. It suggests this should not be rejected out of hand and, if approached in certain ways, may be consistent with core liberal values.

We record here with appreciation the contribution made by Maleiha Malik at the 2010 Onati Workshop, where, focusing on law for the family, she outlined the historical role of Sharia in providing a remedy for individuals who want resolution of their disputes primarily in accordance with the norms of their faith rather than in the public sphere of state legal systems. She also emphasised the dynamic nature of Sharia and the difficulty which this can cause both for British law and state structures. Malik developed these themes in a report published by the British Academy in 2012, *Minority Legal Orders in the UK: Multiculturalism, Minorities and the Law*. This reviews the options available to liberal societies with regard to minority legal orders within them. In particular, it develops the idea of 'cultural voluntarism' and shows how it can coexist with a degree of 'mainstreaming', whereby elements of minority legal orders are absorbed within the state law by way of special provisions or exemptions.

The next two chapters in this section go on to develop a robust critique of the liberal approach presented in chapters one and two. Prakash Shah, in chapter three, challenges the use of a liberal framework within which these questions of accommodating minority laws within a legal system are discussed. The liberal values may not be shared by all minority subjects, and could be viewed by them as Eurocentric and oppressive. He questions the assumptions made when human rights are expressed as being in opposition to group values. In opposition to 'cultural voluntarism', he argues for a more active approach which would recognise the need of each individual to have his own system of values reflected in the legal system in which he lives, and for those concerned with policy development to pay close attention to the socio-legal reality of the bargaining processes employed not just between, but within legal minority groups.

Samia Bano, in chapter four, sets the issues within the context of Alternative Dispute Resolution, in particular, religious ADR as used by Muslims in contemporary Britain. Bano stresses the diversity of local Shariah councils, indicating that 'the socio-legal reality of Muslim communities in Britain can be presented as a complex scenario of a multiplicity of state laws and personal laws which challenge the assumed uniformity of state law (as superior, monolithic and homogeneous) and instead points to a postmodern analyses of law and legal relations which highlights 'a diversity of laws' and 'interlegality'. As a result, Muslims have reconstructed personal law systems of law within localised Muslim communities.

Bano describes the emergence of a 'national' Muslim Arbitration Tribunal, and considers its possible role in family issues in the context of legislative moves that appear to be directed at prohibiting religious arbitration in family and criminal issues. There is a clear tension between what people may fear to be the restrictive and discriminatory features of religious arbitration, which could lead to punitive attempts to prevent it, and its role in enhancing community cohesion and fulfilling the sense of identity of both men and women users. Bano's research suggested that, while some women indeed had criticisms of the process, their attitudes were complex, and 'several' appreciated the contested nature of some Islamic perspectives put forward by religious scholars. The women should not necessarily be considered to be unable to exercise genuine agency. Until more is known of these matters, Bano cautions against either recognition or accommodation of these processes.

Bano's comments on the complex nature of the relationship between religious arbitrators and users, and between both and the state, leads us into part two, which is concerned with detailed examination of instances of state action to regulate the interaction between religious, cultural and state norms in a number of jurisdictions. The first three chapters look at what can be achieved in practice through legislation – whether dealing with specific issues or taking a broader approach – and the fourth chapter looks at the state's use of the courts to deal with an issue of child protection.

In chapter five, Pascale Fournier and colleagues report the initial results of a research project examining the working of recent Israeli legislation intended to help the *agunah* wives who seek divorce but remain married under Jewish law because their husbands refuse to initiate the necessary religious process. These wives are unable to remarry, and any children of a new union are illegitimate and excluded from Judaism. To combat this problem, Israel enacted a Sanctions Law in 1995 giving the rabbinical courts the right, in certain cases, to deprive men who refuse to seek the religious divorce (*get*) of certain privileges, such as the right to leave the country, or hold a driving licence and even to send them to prison. In their responses to the interviewers, the *agunah* demonstrate that religious subjects do not always wait for, or desire, the benevolence of a secular state or a declaration of human rights to make their lives better. Instead, Fournier describes the women as struggling from within the religion to shape and influence religious institutions, seeing the new law as 'a helpful, albeit imperfect, legal instrument'. This is seen as a religious solution to the *agunah* issue, which can be activated through the agency of the women themselves. Nevertheless, the Sanctions Law itself was an enactment of the State of Israel, directed at the activities of a religious community. Its implementation is very inconsistent, being heavily dependent on the attitudes of specific rabbis, many of whom are concerned that its enforcement could be inconsistent with the principle that a *get* could (retrospectively) be pronounced invalid if it had not been granted freely. These uncertainties prevail in a context where obtaining the *get* has become the occasion for bargaining between the parties over the property and financial consequences of the divorce, and even the arrangements regarding the children and thus contribute further elements to the bargaining process.

This research illustrates how an aspect of a religious regime to which the parties hold themselves bound can become an element in a negotiation process that will affect their eventual legal rights. Bargaining can, of course, be an element in any divorce settlement, and negotiating parties will place their own value on the matters up for negotiation. But there could be a question whether the general law should *allow* one party to use his (it is usually his) superior position over the other according to their religious law as part of the bargaining process in relation to their civil law rights. English law appears to be content to do so.[1] Courts could refuse to uphold such bargains, but since they cannot require a religious body to grant a divorce that would be contrary to its religion, to do so would also deprive a wife of what she wants: namely, the divorce. One way (perhaps the only way) of avoiding (or reducing) this outcome is to legislate to bring the religious norms within the jurisdiction of the civil courts, as is proposed in the Muslim Marriages Bill (MMB) in South Africa, discussed by Waheeda Amien in chapter six. But as this major step would retain most features of Islamic family law that maintained gender inequality, the Commission for Gender Equality drafted an alternative, the Recognition of Religious Marriages Bill (RRMB). This alternative allows religious communities to follow their own norms regarding marriage, but permits the secular law and process of divorce to apply to religious marriages. This provides gender equality at this point, but allows the religious norms to operate alongside it. Under the MMB, however, Muslim marriages would not simply be *recognised*; they would be *regulated* by the state courts. Thus many features of Islamic family law, including regulation of polygyny, matrimonial property, forms of divorce and maintenance obligations would be incorporated into the law applied by state courts. Yet the degree to which this would redress imbalances between the parties would depend on the character of the religious norms applied by the courts, and that in turn could depend on the orientation of the judiciary (much for example would depend on whether Muslims appointed as judges followed conservative or other traditions) and of the experts advising them. Questions would also arise regarding the interpretation given to the reach of the provisions of South African constitution with regard to protecting human rights, in particular, gender equality. While the RRMB would be ineffective in protecting women against discriminatory application of Islamic family law, at least, outside the divorce context, the MMB 'codifies' such discriminatory features into the state system. One the other hand, such codification provides a means of regulating those features in a manner that offers more protection to Muslim women than they currently have, and holds out the prospect of developing Islamic family law in accordance with the equality norms of the Constitution, which could be said to be the basic objectives of Islamic law in any case.

The third example of a legislative response comes from the United Kingdom, and concerns an extreme form of marriage involving coercion, usually known

---

[1] *X v Y (Y & Z Intervening)* [2002] 1 FLR 508.

as 'forced marriage', a practice or strategy for survival based not in religious belief but in the local customs in certain areas from which immigrant families have come to the UK. Forced marriage clearly falls within the category of a human rights issue under UK state law. Marriage has long been subject to the influence of the wider community for reasons ranging from the need for diplomatic alliances or title to the ownership of land, or the need to provide for widows and children without a breadwinner. The choice of a marriage partner by the parties for emotional reasons in the UK is a relatively recent development, as readers of Jane Austen will appreciate. But although in Britain some degree of parental influence on the choice of a marriage partner may still be the norm, and the practice of assisted marriage where parents help to find a suitable partner is quite widespread, serious concerns arose about the occurrence of forced marriage where refusal to cooperate with parental choice has led to maltreatment and even the death of some young women in some Asian communities. Pressure from the public for legislation grew, and the government response and its limitations in practice are described by Mavis Maclean in chapter seven. An evaluation of the Forced Marriage (Civil Protection) Act 2007, which sought to protect the persons at risk without criminalising the perpetrators, was published by the Ministry of Justice in 2009 and showed that those working in the courts found its procedures to be workable, and valued by the police in preventing further honour-based violence. The primary remedy involves separating young women and some men thought to be at risk of being coerced into marriage from their families. But there remains a serious problem in making this form of protection known in the communities most affected, and some reluctance by some public authorities to risk disturbing their developing relationships among the minority communities by taking action. Perhaps the hardest problems arise after the legal intervention and concern how to offer long-term support to the young women who have a protection order but are then cut off from their family and community without educational qualifications or employment opportunities. Legislation which is so far removed in its values from the accepted practices of a tightly-knit community is hard to implement, and where it is used, can give rise to further problems for the members of that community. The limits of legislation as an effective remedy are clear.

The next chapter in this section (chapter eight) concerns a different form of governmental intervention through the use of the criminal courts to deal with parents thought to be endangering their child through adherence to their religious beliefs, even where the child protection legislation gives the state a clear power and duty to intervene. Teresa Picontó Novales presents the case of a 13-year-old boy in Spain who died after refusing a blood transfusion as a result of his religious beliefs. The case was complicated by the fact that, because of those beliefs, the boy rejected the treatment in such a 'state of terror' that the doctors felt unable to carry it out. The parents were charged with attempted murder for failing to try to persuade him to accept the treatment. But how could they have done so given their beliefs? Picontó Novales suggests that earlier intervention, involving removal of the child by the welfare authorities, would have been possible and would have obviated placing any such duty on the parents that would have conflicted with their religious freedom. But the state authorities were sensitive to the need to respect religious beliefs and reluctant to intervene until matters were sadly beyond remedy for this child.

Similarly, sensitivities regarding intervention, but in relation to a rather different problem of a cultural rather than religious nature arise in Poland with respect to underage marriage among the Roma described by Jacek Kurczewski and Małgozata Fuszara in chapter nine. The age for marriage accepted by the entire Roma community, despite many tribal and local variations in other customs and practices, is lower than that permitted by state law in Western countries and, while not necessarily problematic for the young people themselves, contravenes state law and triggers intervention by often reluctant public authorities. So here we have the state acting reluctantly at the insistence of those concerned with child welfare to enforce a law where neither the minority group nor the state finds the practice particularly problematic. Kurczewski and Fuszara expand their discussion to the general question of state recognition of minority norms, pointing to the 2003 UNESCO Convention on Protection of Intangible Cultural Heritage, and the earlier multiculturalism of the one-time Kingdom of Poland and Lithuania. However, the discussion focuses on the feasibility of recognising Roma marriages in the same way as other religious marriages are recognised in Poland, and Kurczewski and Fuszara argue that it should be possible to reach an accommodation with Roma communities (despite their diversity) on condition that registration requirements are complied with, and the consent of the parties (though possibly not their adulthood) is assured. This would be similar to the way in which Jewish and Quaker marriages have long been recognised in England and Wales, and which could be extended to other minorities.

There appears to be a consistency in the nature of these very different forms of government intervention in family life, demonstrating caution, a reluctance to intervene except in extreme circumstances and certainly no urgent desire to actively mould different forms of family life into a single uniform model through top-down intervention. However, government intrusion can occur differently, in the form of a strongly proactive policy that ignores (at least officially) its impact on minority cultures. In chapter ten, Yasmine Debarge and Benoit Bastard describe what happens when immigrant families from a different cultural and religious background come into contact with the welfare services of a strongly secular nation state. In France, though 'Child Access Services' are intended for all separating parents and their children, ethnic minority families are over-represented among the users, most of whom are directed to the centres by the courts. Because the 'republican' ideology of the state disregards cultural or religious difference, cultural matters are marginalised (to the extent of disallowing use of any language other than French) and the major professional concern is to promote child–parent bonding, in particular, maintaining bonds with the family lines of both the child's parents. The agendas of the state and of these parents may be very different, and there is little dialogue between them. Debarge and Bastard describe the various ways cultural factors are negotiated in that setting, distinguishing four approaches: approving, acknowledging, ignoring and refusing.

In part three, the contributors turn away from governmental actions to community behaviour, including the role of community-based institutions, and look at ways in which mechanisms have developed in order respond to the issue of inter-penetration of social norms between communities. This part begins in chapter eleven with a description by Gillian Douglas and colleagues, based on empirical research, of the English way of arranging the relationship between religious and state courts concerned with marriage and divorce. It might be termed a 'middle way' between the Israeli conferment of jurisdiction on rabbinical courts and the proposals in the South African Muslim Marriages Bill to bring aspects of Islamic law within the jurisdiction of the civil courts. Under the English arrangement, as regards divorce and annulment, the members of religious institutions who wish to do so accept the authority of those institutions, but the decisions made are not treated as having legal standing by the general law except insofar as they may satisfy the requirements of that law, for example, under the law of contract or arbitration. Douglas describes this as a 'cohabitation' model and presents findings from an empirical study of three religious tribunals in England and Wales, the Birmingham Shariah Council, the London Beth Din of the United Synagogue and the National Tribunal for Wales of the Roman Catholic Church. Douglas describes the workings of these institutions, and their interaction with the secular law, in detail. All three institutions strongly encourage parties seeking dissolution of a marriage to have obtained civil divorce (the Roman Catholics go so far as to require it) so that they will not need to dissolve or annul marriages that remain intact according to civil law. There appeared to be no desire within the religious institutions that the state should grant legal recognition of their determinations: they seemed to understand and accept the demarcation between the religious and the secular authority. Douglas emphasises the fact that the primary focus of these institutions is on the marriage itself, since they can enable applicants to remarry in a manner that is compliant with their faith. So, whether recognised by the state or not, the decisions of these bodies are of great significance for the parties, and it is hard to see reasons for disallowing this, although it is possible (and common) for related matters, for example, regarding children and finances, to be dealt with (also) under the civil law. In this way the civil and religious legal systems 'cohabit'. However, Douglas et al, noting that state law recognises religious marriages in certain circumstances, see no reason why that law should not also recognise divorces performed according to religious procedures, especially as the civil law of divorce is moving even more strongly towards simple administrative notification, thus, in this context, following an 'integration' model.

In chapter twelve, Jagbir Jhutti-Johal describes how parties to Sikh marriages (where divorce is not recognised) use and are influenced by the norms of their religion when engaging with the secular law of divorce. Sikh marriage (*Anand*

Karaj) is not only a physical legal or civil contract which can be dissolved, but a sacred contract recognised and ordained by God. Since separation was regarded as bringing dishonour on the family, families intervened strongly to prevent this. It is still the case that family 'mediation', by parents, other family members or a middleman, plays a strong part in marital disputes, and has a strongly directive character. But research by Jhutti-Johal showed that the younger and better-educated generation of Sikhs are less likely to be directed by the older generation as they interact with the dominant culture around them.

A similar process of cultural evolution, this time modifying legal norms in favour of a traditionally disadvantaged group, is described by Anne Griffiths in chapter thirteen. Griffiths shows how changing social attitudes towards women in Botswana have led to informal modifications of the application of customary law concerning the acquisition of property through inheritance, traditionally dominated by the privileging of male offspring and in particular the eldest son in recognition of his responsibilities as head of the family. An examination of Land Board records shows a marked increase in land holdings by women. The chapter provides an important illustration of how non-state law can adapt and evolve in response to wider social developments, in this case the growing confidence and higher expectations of women. While acknowledging the influence of the actions (including legal developments) of the state and of NGOs in this process, Griffiths observes that this evolution is generated from the 'bottom up' as much as from the 'top down'. Like others in this collection, she urges that in considering the role of the state, close attention should be paid to socio-legal reality 'on the ground'.

This process of social impact on legal regulation can be much more difficult, though not impossible, when state law is the target and it is supported by powerful and repressive elite groups. In chapter fourteen, Nazila Ghanea describes the impact of civil activism to improve – or at least prevent further erosion of – the position of women in Iranian family law. There are limitations in that since this has resulted from a strategic and reluctant response to advocacy the successes are fragile and at risk of reversal. Family law in Iran is only a part of the gender laws, relating to women's role in the wider society, which remains strictly controlled and can be very discriminatory. For example, Ghanea states that 'blood money penalty or "*diyeh*" payment offered on the killing of a Zoroastrian, Christian or Jewish man' was equalised to that payable on killing a Muslim man in 2004, but payment for 'killing a Zoroastrian, Christian, Jewish or Muslim woman is half, and no payment for killing men or women belonging to other religions (such as Bahá'ís) or beliefs is required'. However, Ghanea reports a number of remarkable indications that the official positions are not necessarily reflected in people's behaviour. Hence, despite reduction in the official age of marriage, women's age at marriage is in fact rising. Despite official easing of a husband's right to enter polygamous marriages, the number of single women is increasing. Despite official ideology of restricting women to the home, the numbers of women in education have grown. So this is another example of bottom-up change. Ghanea discusses the kinds of processes that might influence such change.

Chapter fifteen, however, suggests that resistance to change does not always result from coercive measures from state or other institutional authorities, but may reside in the population itself. Farah Deeba Chowdhury argues that, given its recent political history, secular attempts to impose gender equality in Islamic Bangladesh will not succeed, and gives the example of inheritance law. In strong contrast to the position in Botswana, described by Griffiths (chapter thirteen), Chowdhury observes that women are not able to exercise the limited property rights they already have, so are unlikely to be able to enjoy increased inheritance rights were equality to be granted. It would be better, she implies, to work through Islamic law, which does provide protections for women, and secure the rights they should have under that law, than attempt to impose norms that are inconsistent with that law.

The book concludes in part four by revisiting the original question of how legal systems have accommodated and are now responding to pressure for change in the relationship between different family behaviours arising from cultural and religious beliefs and state systems of family justice. The two chapters look first at law and then at family behaviour. In chapter sixteen, Jordi Ribot asks a question fundamental to the whole debate: how much family behaviour should the law seek to regulate anyway? For to the extent that such behaviours fall outside the remit of the law, it matters less (within limits of course) what norms the family members follow. Ribot therefore considers what it is that family law seeks to achieve. He is sceptical about the capacity of family law to mould social behaviour according to predetermined conceptions of society. Instead, he sees it as a tool for responding to 'the individual's request for justice within family relationships'. This echoes the individualised approach, as set out by Eekelaar in chapter one. Ribot emphasises that the quest for fairness must take into account the social context, including the cultural context of any regulation. Giving examples drawn from a wide range of issues in family law, Ribot suggests that the result could be a hybridisation of the law, in which various active and changing cultural elements would be incorporated into the resolutions applied by the general law on an individualised basis, subject to limits to ensure that the results do not 'jeopardise individual self-determination or result in gender discrimination'.

For the last word, we step outside the sociology of law to the sociology of the family. Marjorie Smith and Ann Phoenix, in chapter seventeen, describe evidence about the use of corporal punishment of children by parents. They remind us of the range of responses the law can make to a common form of behaviour in families, but also of the variety of such behaviour, demonstrating the range of social norms in play. Although there are, or may be, variations between ethnic groups, these are complex. For example, the same kind of behaviour that may be indicative of some form of dysfunction (deviance) in one group (thus associated with negative outcomes for children) may be consistent with a well-functioning relationship (and thus positive outcomes for children) in another. The evidence also shows the capacity of these norms to fluctuate over time and between generations. All this highlights the care needed in attempts to legislate regarding the inner workings of families, a lesson underlined by problems of interpretation of data exemplified in the description of an interview with an Afro-Caribbean mother in London. The mother was asked about punishment. She said that when her daughter behaved badly, she beat her. When the interviewer asked what she beat her with, she replied: 'With words, of course with words'.

REFERENCES

Aslam, J (2006) 'Judicial Oversight of Islamic Family Law Arbitration in Ontario: Ensuring Meaningful Consent and Promoting Multicultural Citizenship' 38 *International Law and Politics* 876.

Joppke, C (2004) 'The Retreat of Multiculturalism in the Liberal State: Theory and Policy' 55 *British Journal of Sociology* 249.

Kepel, G (2005) 'Europe's answer to Londonistan': www.opendemocracy.net/conflict-terrorism/ londonistan_2775.jsp (24 August 2005).

Maclean, M (ed) (2005) *Family Law and Family Values* (Oxford, Hart Publishing).

Meer, N and Modood, T (2009) 'The Multicultural State We're In: Muslims, "Multiculture" and "Civic Re-balancing" of British Multiculturalism' 57 *Political Studies* 473.

Pfaff, W (2005) 'A Monster of Our Own Making' *The Guardian* (21 August 2005).

Phillips, T (2005) *Sleepwalking to Segregation* (London, Commission for Racial Equality).

Waldron, J (2010) 'Questions about the Reasonable Accommodation of Minorities' in R Ahdar and N Aroney (eds), *Sharia in the West* (Oxford, Oxford University Press).

Williams, R (2008) 'Civil and Religious Law in England: A Religious Perspective' 10 *Ecclesiastical Law Journal* 262.

Part I

Theories, Ideologies and Strategies

1

Law and Community Practices

JOHN EEKELAAR

I GROUP LOYALTY AND INDIVIDUAL RIGHTS

ANY EXAMINATION OF the laws of groups raises the issue of the obligations individuals may have towards different groups to which they may belong. This tension is as old as recorded literature. Sophocles' *Antigone* provides the paradigm case of a conflict between sets of obligations deriving from the community of family and obligations deriving from the state. Family loyalty compels Antigone to bury the body of her brother, Polyneices. That conflicts with her duty to her ruler, Creon. Which duty should she follow? If the primary justification for imposing the duty is the benefit performing it brings to the group, the conflict can be resolved only by Antigone's choice between the groups to which she owes loyalty. The point of allegiance to a community is that allegiance is owed to that community, to the exclusion of others. This conflict is not very different from that recounted in the Indian epic *Mahabharata* discussed by Amartya Sen (2009: 23–24; 208–17).

But what if justification for the norms lay elsewhere than in communal allegiance? What if there was a justificatory basis that transcended communal loyalty? There was. For Sophocles it lay in an appeal to a higher loyalty to the laws of the gods, binding on both Antigone and Creon, which condemned leaving the dead unburied (except that Creon could not see it, for which he was duly punished). Now Antigone need not choose between the groups to which she owes loyalty. She follows the higher duty. In our world we do not have such ready recourse to the laws of the gods. But we have the idea of individual rights and these may transcend duties owed to either group. It is possible that individual rights may be fulfilled better through group norms than state norms, or better through state norms than group norms. They may be best fulfilled in some cases by allowing people to choose between the two sets of norms.

The idea of individual rights includes the proposition that the justification for placing people under coercive duties (apart from those that concern the interests of beings, whether human or non-human, outside the community) is found in the benefit performing them brings to individuals within the community. It is not sufficient to claim only that a norm sustains a particular form or shape of community, without regard to its effect on the individuals within it. This is important because the historical record shows that duties to promote the interests of the community as a whole above those of its individual members have frequently masked the fact that such duties have been imposed by persons or elites within communities in order to advance their own interests or ideologies under the guise of the interests of the community. I do not mean to say that individuals ought never owe legal duties to the community. Specifically, they could attach to the holders of certain public roles (such as the police, judges and ministers). I recognise that people may assume that the wellbeing of the group implies the wellbeing of its members, and indeed that is often the case. But in such cases, the claim that fulfilling the responsibility to the group is beneficial to the community's members must be open to critique and evaluation. Whether legal norms enhance individual wellbeing raises complex and contested issues of evaluation, justice, legitimate authority and no doubt others, and these must be subject to constant reappraisal and debate (Eekelaar, 2011a). Nor do I maintain that group participation has no value; quite the contrary. But demands based *solely* on loyalty, tradition, the honour of the group, or national or religious affiliation, should generally not be reinforced by legal sanction, but should rely on commitments voluntarily given. Their great virtue lies primarily in the voluntary nature of those commitments. Indeed, it is my contention that the most significant role legal processes have is in *protecting individuals against the effects of such demands*. Indeed, such protection is impossible without law. (For a fuller discussion of the theoretical basis of this position, grounded in a conception of an 'open society', see Eekelaar 2007: especially chapters 1, 6 and 7).

Since families are groups, obligations within them reflect a power structure within the group. That is one reason to be cautious about clothing the norms operating within operating families with the force of law. Another is that the enforcement of law is inevitably a bureaucratic process, with little sensitivity to the nuances of personal relationships. Furthermore, it risks imposing dominant ideologies upon the intimate lives of individuals, giving them little space to develop lifestyles that suit them best. I have elsewhere (Eekelaar 2010) suggested that the nature of state regulation of family behaviour might be expressed in terms of three models:

1. The 'authorisation' model, wherein the state expressly or tacitly gives the force of state law to norms and decisions made within families.
2. The 'delegation' model, wherein the state prescribes and gives legal force to the norms to be followed within families so that families can be seen as delegates through which state law and policy is applied.
3. The 'purposive abstention' model, wherein moral or social obligations within families are not normally given the force of law, unless their failure threatens community interests, or to achieve justice when families fall apart. However,

the general law of the state, including human rights norms, remains always applicable, and states are free to influence family behaviour in other ways.

For the reasons given, it is suggested that the third model is to be preferred and that states should exercise restraint in the extent to which they seek to convert the norms that operate within families into legal norms (Eekelaar 2011b). Similar arguments may be used in favour of restraint in the state legal regulation of group norms that apply to relationships between individuals and families within minority groups. It must be emphasised that these 'models' are intellectual constructs, paradigms, intended to highlight core features of possible *approaches*, or *strategies*, and are not meant as socio-legal descriptions of any particular historic or contemporary system, and that any real system is likely to reflect features from each of them. In this chapter I want to examine more closely the implications of each of those models in the multicultural context, and conclude by offering some reflections on the 'right to cultural identity'.

II THE 'AUTHORISATION' MODEL

The authorisation model in the multicultural context corresponds to the Ottoman 'millet' system, described by Will Kymlicka (1995) as a 'federation of theocracies' and Ayelet Shachar (2001) as 'religious particularism'. It may be viewed as promoting diversity, but it is not diversity within a group, but rather a *diversity of groups* within a geographical polity. It comes at a cost. Although it has been applied in a very limited way in England where for many years marriages conducted in accordance with the practices of Jews and Quakers have been recognised,[1] that recognition is confined to the formation of marriage and does not extend to any consequences of the marriage, or to its dissolution. If the law was to go further and recognise the norms operating within minority groups exclusively as having the force of law, the model presents significant problems and has been twice rejected at government level (Poulter 1998: 210–12). The problems include the following:

1. Cultural and religious groups are seldom totally homogenous with regard to normative practice. The state would therefore need either to identify which norms are to be given the necessary recognition or (more probably) which authority within the group to recognise as authoritative. It may need to recognise multiple strands within the group in this way, finding a method of resolution where they clashed in particular cases.[2]

---

[1] Marriage Act 1949, s 26(1) (and other provisions).

[2] See Bano (2008) on different traditions within the UK. As an example, see the clash of 'experts' on Islamic law in the South African case of *Rylands v Edros* 1997 (2) SA 690 (C), discussed by Fishbayn (1999: 160–63). For a discussion with regard to Pakistan, see Ali (2002: 317). In India the potential growth of Islamic and Shariah courts in parallel to the official courts, and of caste 'pachayats' (village councils) exercising powers along caste lines, has been challenged: see Malhotra and Malhotra (2007). The problem is endemic in states which formally recognise customary law as

2. Conflict could arise between the group norms and the state's commitment (whether in its constitution or through its international obligations) to human rights norms.
3. Conferring such powers upon religious or cultural authorities is likely to make it more difficult for individuals within such groups to exit from the group. Farrah Ahmed (2010) has argued that even if individuals become subject to such norms on an opt-in basis, pressures felt by many group members to conform reduces their autonomy. Problems may arise as to the definition of membership of the group to whom the group norms apply.
4. Shachar (2001: 60–61, 84) has worried that conferring jurisdiction on groups to administer their own norms could in some circumstances entrench 'reactive culturalism' whereby the groups become defensive about their distinctiveness and less open to adaptation.
5. Transferring significant legal power for communities to regulate themselves could reduce the incentive of the state to perform protective and supportive roles towards individuals within those communities, for example, in the areas of child care and elder care.

Shachar put forward a modified version of this strategy in the form of a mechanism of 'joint governance' that she called 'transformative accommodation' (2001: chapters 5 and 6). The Archbishop of Canterbury regarded this with favour when he referred to the possibility of creating a 'supplemental' jurisdiction which could apply Islamic law to members of that community (Williams 2008). That idea depends on a concordat between the state and group authorities under which various segments of law (Shachar gave examples from family law, immigration law, education law and criminal justice) can be applied *as law* either by the state or by the group, according to the option of individuals. Once having opted for a particular system for one purpose (for example, entry into marriage) it would be possible for an individual to reverse the option at 'reversal points' agreed between the state and the group authorities (for example, at the point of exit from the marriage, or when an issue concerning allocation of property arose). The hope is that both the state and the groups (but particularly the latter) will be encouraged to adapt their norms by way of accommodation with the other in order to minimise the risks of individuals choosing to transfer out of their system to the alternative regime.

Such a scheme raises the concerns similar to those referred to earlier:

1. The state would need to identify the appropriate authorities in the group with whom to negotiate. Putting such arrangements into place with regard to all possible groupings would require legislating for an elaborate pattern of legally enforceable regimes, resulting in possibly excessive legal complexity.

---

part of their (plural) legal system. This is because 'tradition' can be constantly undermined by emerging practices. Writers can only appeal for transparency and dialogue to resolve conflicts (Stewart 1998: ch 13; Schmid 2001).

2. It is not clear how readily groups would permit a member to have recourse to secular law and maintain membership of the group, and, even if this was allowed, whether they would easily agree what the 'reversal' points should be. Problems would arise where one individual wished to opt in and another did not. The risk of reinforcing 'reactive culturalism', which Shachar feared for the 'religious particularist' model, seems present here, too, and the objections raised by Ahmed (2010) with regard to autonomy would remain.

However, Shachar (2008; 2010) has later suggested a more nuanced approach, 'regulated interaction', which will be considered below.

III THE 'DELEGATION' MODEL

In the 'delegation' model, the state takes over the legal regulation of the group. It expects the group to act as its delegate, enforcing norms as defined by its own institutions. It may be regarded as treating any degree of diversity as a form of deviance. Its extreme form appears in totalitarian (or theocratic) societies where the state expects all groups to follow the norms dictated by the state. Beck and Beck-Gernsheim (2001: 10) cite an example from a German marriage register in the early 1940s: 'Marriage cannot be an end in itself, but must serve the greater goal, the increase and survival of the species and race. Adolf Hitler'. Yet even democratic societies can take on this tinge when they insist, for example, that all recognised family relationships must follow one particular state-approved, civil, form, with only the legal consequences stipulated by the state. State law will, after all, reflect its own values and these may diverge sharply from those of some minority groups.

The model may take a more concealed form, where the state itself applies the minority law through its institutions as part of state law. This manifestation may not be best captured by the expression 'delegation', for the state seems rather to incorporate the group's norms into general law. To the extent that state law reflects the values of minorities groups, and, as a result of the legislative process, or application of human rights norms, recognises group practices as having legal consequences (such as marriages according to Jewish and Quaker usages), the model can operate in a benign and positive way. However, if state institutions determine and interpret issues related to minority practices, this could be seen as expecting the group to follow the state's version of their law, and to lack legitimacy in its eyes.

The dangers in this approach are perhaps most clearly seen in the hostile reaction to the attempt by the Supreme Court of India to pronounce on Islamic law in *Mohammed Ahmed Khan v Shah Bano Begum*.[3] On one possible interpretation,

---

[3] *Mohammed Ahmed Khan v Shah Bano Begum* AIR 1985 SC 945, discussed by Shachar (2001: 81–83).

this may have occurred in the English case of *Uddin v Choudhury*.[4] The husband refused to pay deferred *mahr* to the wife after a short Muslim marriage, not recognised by English law, had been dissolved by the Islamic Shariah Council. Apparently the bride and her family had taken items valued at some £25,500 from the groom's house, refused to return them, yet still demanded payment of £15,000 promised as deferred *mahr*. The judge held that items were gifts and not returnable (though there was much doubt as to their real value) and that the agreement to pay the *mahr* was enforceable. This was upheld on appeal. Mummery LJ said that what determined the case was

> the expert evidence from Mr Saddiqui on Sharia law and that, *as a matter of Sharia law* in the circumstances of this marriage and its dissolution, the gifts were absolute, not returnable, not deductible from the dowry, and the dowry was payable notwithstanding the failure of the marriage (para 14, italics supplied).

If this was the true basis for the Court's decision (though it seems it was not, see below), this would have been a case arising solely within England, with no 'foreign' element, in respect of a marriage not recognised by English law, in which an English court determined, and enforced, a litigant's obligations created under the community's religious law. Presumably, if there had been disagreement among experts as to the content of that law, the Court would need to have chosen between them. Courts make such choices when deciding between experts on the content of foreign law. That is considered a finding of fact because the law the court is applying is its own conflict of laws rules, according to which the foreign law is a matter of fact. The court's decision on that fact has no legal effect in the foreign jurisdiction. But where the 'foreign' law is one that operates within the court's jurisdiction, the court's choice between different interpretations of that law looks much more like a determination of the law that is to be applied within its jurisdiction. So the minority group has a version of its law, as interpreted by the state system, imposed on it.

Another difficulty that arises if state courts seek to apply aspects of a minority's legal order is that the application may ignore the wider cultural context in which the outcome was intended to take effect. Pascale Fournier (2010: 66–70) has demonstrated the dangers of Western courts attempting to resolve issues of Shariah law outside their proper religious context. For example, in *Nathoo v Nathoo*[5] the British Columbia Supreme Court awarded the wife a share in family assets under the provincial provisions on allocation of family assets *and also* enforced payment of agreed *mahr* as being a religious obligation, almost certainly over-compensating the wife.

It may be possible to mitigate – or perhaps even avoid – these dangers by incorporating authorities from minority groups into the state judicial structure, as Waheeda Amien (2010; and chapter six of this book) suggests for South Africa with respect to Islamic law. That could be an attractive solution, since it

---

[4] *Uddin v Choudhury* [2009] EWCA Civ 1205.
[5] *Nathoo v Nathoo* [1996] BCJ No 2720 (SC).

seeks the benefits of the authorisation approach without its problems. But will it completely avoid those problems? Even if the personnel who make the decisions are drawn from that group, they would be acting as officials of a state institution, which may have no legitimacy to interpret and develop the religious laws of the group. Furthermore, the courts are (subject to any constitutional restraint) constitutionally subject to the authority of the political legislative body, to which they must give precedence over any religious source recognised by the group. There must also be concern that the state could be accused of imposing its own version of the group's law through manipulation of the judicial process. In a state with a variety of minority groups, selection of appropriate representative and their incorporation into the judicial process could be difficult. While it may be possible to overcome these problems, it will not be easy.

A more thoroughgoing form of mainstreaming has been proposed in Uganda through the incorporation of Khadi (Islamic) courts into the state court structure (Mujuzi 2012). At one stroke this gives full state recognition to the areas of Islamic law within the jurisdiction of those courts (in this case, over family matters) while at the same time imposing a measure of state control over those courts, for example, with regard to qualifications for appointment to judicial positions in them, and compliance with the norms of the constitution. These could be points of friction, and other matters that would seem to flow from such incorporation, such as state responsibility for their funding and performance, the handling of appeals within the state system, conflicts between the application of Islamic and state law and the implications for other minority legal orders, need to be confronted.

IV THE 'PURPOSIVE ABSTENTION' MODEL

The model that I favoured was based on an approach that, applied to families, I called 'purposive abstention', and applied to cultural and religious groups, 'cultural voluntarism' (Eekelaar 2010; 2011b). I argued that, within certain parameters, which could be strictly drawn (for example, the requirement of consummation of a marriage and spousal fidelity), there was a strong element in English family policy (in contrast to that of civil law jurisdictions) that deliberately refrained from prescribing through law the way family members should behave towards one another. I called this 'purposive' abstention because the non-intervention was not necessarily a result of indifference, but was intentional, and had certain beneficial consequences. This was earliest seen in regard to testamentary behaviour, and intra-familial duties of support. In more recent times it extended to division of labour, authority between family members and intimate behaviour. In such cases families were free to follow (or not) prevailing social norms. However, the law *did* recognise, and in various ways gave effect to, the *consequences* of such actions insofar as this could be done under standard legal doctrines. I noted that this policy would not be followed when family life was seriously disrupted, and particularly where such disruption threatened wider social stability, including, of course, where the family broke up entirely. In such cases a form of the delegation model was applied: legal norms were laid down for family members to follow. These families had become, to some extent, deviant. Legislation has also intervened in other matters where the ways families behave has wider social impact, such as education of children or with regard to certain health measures.

In commending this approach, to remove possible misunderstanding, it must be emphasised that the restraint is only with regard to constructing legal obligations between individual family members; it does not urge restraint with regard to compliance within the family with the general law. In particular, child protection laws and other legal and social protections against harmful behaviour, should always apply. Nor does the approach imply that the state should be neutral to what occurs within families. State action that supports family relationships, or various forms of such relationships, or discourages others, is perfectly consistent with it.

V 'CULTURAL VOLUNTARISM' (CV)

Applied to cultural and religious groups, the model recognises that individuals can experience considerable benefits from the operation of intra-group support mechanisms that give groups a certain solidarity and self-sufficiency. It also recognises the role of group norms in supporting the sense of self-identity of certain individuals. Specific institutions that apply between families, such as the Islamic *mahr* (involving a payment from the husband or his family to the wife) can operate beneficially for individuals within the context of the general practices of a group, inhibiting divorce and providing a means for compensation should it occur. Some group institutions, such as the Islamic Law Shariah Council described by Shah-Kazemi (2001), can provide effective avenues for resolving conflict, and safeguarding the interests of parties, which are accessible to group members. They may do so according to group norms that may be regarded as a form of law by members of the group. These are good reasons for states to stand back and allow individuals within groups considerable freedom to follow their own family and inter-family practices.

But, as in the case of families, *this need not involve conferring power on the groups to make and apply norms that would be enforced in the state courts* (as under the 'authorisation' model). As noticed above, such an approach lends state support to power structures within the group, enhancing the risk of subjecting individual wellbeing to group interests. It fragments the national polity into separate communal groups. Conversely, the delegation model risks conferring excessive power on state institutions to modify religious or cultural norms that individual members of minority groups' value. Instead, under, CV the state allows individuals to follow the norms of their group should they so wish, and gives effect to the outcomes of transactions made according to those norms. In effect, it promotes *diversity among individuals* within the general community, but it does so only insofar as the general law allows. Where benefits have been conferred in performance of religious or cultural obligations, there seems little reason to regard their retention as unjust unless the transaction contravened the normal principle of duress and lack of capacity (Burrows 2002: 48–51). Similarly, there seems no reason why contractual obligations should not be recognised even if they arise in a religious or other cultural context, but they would be recognised on the same basis as any other contract would (or would not) be in the relevant family context. So it would not follow the Ontario court in *Kaddoura v Hammoud*[6] where the Court refused to enforce an agreement to pay deferred *mahr* simply because the agreement was part of a religious institution (Fournier 2010: 76–79). Disputes as to the content of the contract would be determined as a factual matter relevant to the parties' intentions, and not as a ruling on the religious law. It could be that this was the real ground of decision in *Uddin v Choudry* because Mummery LJ also said:

> As a matter of contract, arising out of the agreement which the parties had made, I think that the judge was entitled in law to say that this was an enforceable agreement, and therefore he was right to grant judgment on the counterclaim (para 13, italics supplied).

Of course, in all such cases the entire cultural and religious *context* would be relevant to the application of the general law, such as in determining the intentions of the parties to a contract.

Fournier (2010: 94–97) gives other examples:

1. A German court refused to enforce payment of *mahr* in full because this would have been inequitable for the husband; instead it was 'translated into alimony and its amount adjusted based on fairness considerations'.
2. A Quebec trial court, 'embracing egalitarian considerations in the interpretation of contract law', enforced an agreement to pay *mahr* in circumstances where Islamic law would have disallowed the claim because the wife had initiated the divorce (a *khul* divorce). Not to have done so would have been improper discrimination. (The decision was reversed on appeal.)
3. Quebec and German courts declined to enforce *mahr* on the grounds that it would bring about unjust enrichment of the wife.
4. A Nova Scotia court refused to apply *mahr* on the grounds of 'substantial injustice' and instead (on the basis of its own private international law principles) applied the German law of property division.

In none of these cases did the courts purport to decide the content of and apply Islamic law. Where payments were ordered, they were done according to local

---

[6] *Kaddoura v Hammoud* (1998) 44 RFL (4th) 228.

doctrine: contract, alimony, division of family assets. Enforcement was refused where that doctrine would disallow it.

Another option would be to treat determinations by group institutions as arbitrations, enforceable by the state courts. This raises the problem that the state courts could be enforcing decisions based on non-state norms in matters arising solely within their jurisdiction, whereas CV requires that state courts apply only state law (or agreements according to which parties compromise their rights under that law). This is important because state law is subject to human rights standards, and is (at least theoretically) also subject to the democratic legislative process.

For this reason, once invoked, state law would apply according to *its* principles. There would be no need to pre-arrange 'reversal points'. State law could, for example, uphold payment of *mahr* unless vitiated by those principles, or take its payment into account when considering post-divorce financial and property arrangements, or delay granting divorce to a husband who does not grant his wife a religious divorce.[7] Since abstention is not complete immunity, the state could intervene even without invocation where this presently occurs with regard to families, for example, in child protection cases (Brophy, Jhutti-Johal and Owen 2003). Some practices might be forbidden completely, such as when the Indian state intervened to prevent the payment of dowry among Hindus, since this was seen to encourage extortion by husbands and their families, exposing wives to cruelty and even death (Karanjawala and Chugh 2009).

VI OBJECTIONS TO CULTURAL VOLUNTARISM (CV)

A CV would Tolerate Hardship experienced by Individuals

Under the model, some hardship may be undergone by individuals who choose to follow the group norms rather than invoke state norms. Yet it needs to be accepted that perceptions of justice by group members may not be the same as that of the state, or that group members may be prepared to put their religious commitment above any apparent hardship. An *agunah* (a wife who remains 'chained' to her husband because he refuses to grant her a divorce under Jewish law) or a Roman Catholic, who requires an ecclesiastical annulment to be free to re-marry, may be prepared to accept hardship if the husband does not grant the divorce or the tribunal does not grant the annulment. Such decisions could be expressions of the chosen self-identity of the individuals concerned. Such practices would be tolerated under CV, but at all times the state legal system and its norms would be available to any person who chose to invoke them.

---

[7] Divorce (Religious Marriages) Act 2002. Another method is to impose a financial penalty if the (husband) does not comply: *A v T (Ancillary Relief: Cultural Factors)* [2004] 1 FLR 977.

Shachar (2008; 2010: 127–32) argues that such non-intervention could trap vulnerable people between religious norms disadvantageous to them and the benefit of state norms. She considers two 'promising' alternatives. One is 'democratic deliberation' which promotes intercultural dialogue. That is perfectly consistent with CV. The other is enforcing agreements designed to discourage religious barriers to remarriage, such as an agreement that a husband should seek a *get*. This might be enforceable in the civil courts by an award of damages.[8] This too is consistent with CV. More significantly, Shachar suggests that religious authorities might be 'licensed' to make arbitration awards if they met conditions involving training and compliance with due process, including assuring parties received legal advice and applied certain basic equality norms in their decisions. The trade-off is that compliance with such conditions would make their decisions enforceable in the state courts. Such 'regulated interaction' is designed to promote dialogue and modify religious norms.

For reasons already given, CV holds that in cases arising entirely within its jurisdiction (that is, where there is no foreign element) only state norms, or acceptable compromises over those norms, should be enforced in state courts. However, CV is an approach, not a rigid doctrine, and if the norms are sufficiently close to those of the state, it would not be opposed to such a process. But it would expect strict conditions to be imposed. It would be an empirical question whether this strategy was more likely to win acceptance and assist in accommodation between minority and majority norms, or whether it would encourage 'reactive culturalism'. Where agreement could not be reached, CV would not seek to impose norms on the minority group, but nor would it accord the groups' norms legal recognition, except in so far as they might be expressible in terms of the civil law.

B CV Rests on an Unrealistic Conception of Autonomy

Of course it is not difficult to point to a certain artificiality of the concept of voluntariness in this context: the idea of purely voluntary behaviour is an abstraction (Raz 1986: 155). Nevertheless, degrees of voluntariness of behaviour are real. Individuals may not consciously choose the culture (or religion) into which they are born, but they do often modify, or even abandon, their original identification. To the extent to which opportunities to do this are restricted, to that extent we can say that an individual's scope for voluntary action is diminished. Conversely, to the extent that such restrictions are absent, we may say that the culture is voluntarily chosen, or at least voluntarily maintained.

It does not follow that commitment to voluntariness demands ever-expanding opportunities to encounter new cultures. Pragmatic considerations arise. As Isaiah Berlin (2006: 169–70) observed with regard to freedom:

---

[8] As is *Bruker v Marcovitz* [2007] 3 SCR 607.

The question of whether it is better to have many purposes, with relatively little defence against adverse factors which might interfere with them, or fewer purposes with better chance of fulfilment, is no doubt a perfectly real, practical, problem and arises at all levels. This, though, is not the problem of freedom, but a quasi-utilitarian problem of calculating factors in the empirical world for the purpose of obtaining as much of what one wants as one can.

So it would not be right to think that an individual living in a mono-cultural society with no, or few, external contacts, cannot be acting voluntarily. Holding to what you have is a form of choice. But if alternative cultural norms are not available, individuals may nevertheless wish to modify those *within their culture*. Since no one knows whether an individual may wish to do this or not, restrictions on opportunities to do this diminish voluntariness. As a minimum, therefore, respecting voluntary behaviour requires that institutional means, supported by, but not identical with, the state be readily available to allow the individual voice to be heard against group interests, whatever they may be, and to adjudicate the competing claims. The legal system and the legal profession are part of this.

C The 'Right of Exit' would be Impracticable

Resort to the state system under 'purposive abstention' may not always be easier for an aggrieved party than it would be under Shachar's joint governance mechanism. But it seems less dramatic. Taking advantage of a 'reversal point' – even one agreed between the group and the state – could have the appearance of a more explicit rejection of the group norm than resorting to legal principles that have always been available to the group member, as to all citizens. Social pressures to conform will always reduce the scope for voluntary behaviour. But, by refraining from conferring state-recognised legal power on any particular group structure – even on the basis of negotiated exit points – CV, unlike 'transformative accommodation', focuses on individuals and accepts the value which the application of cultural norms may have for them. It is therefore prepared in principle to permit such practices and recognise their consequences, without in any way withdrawing the jurisdiction and applicability of state law, to which any individual may have recourse at any time. By not reaching 'deals' with any particular element within groups, it recognises the fluidity and malleability of group practices, making it easier for them to evolve through their own internal dynamic. It is important that social policies reduce barriers that inhibit individual members of minority groups from having recourse to the civil law.

D The State's Norms would not necessarily Uphold Individual Rights

It is true that CV in itself does not guarantee that state law itself will necessarily respect individual rights: it may reflect oppressive norms of the majority community. But a discussion such as this can only take place within the current national legal and political climate, which by and large, at least in its rhetoric, accepts individual wellbeing as a significant criterion for the evaluation of law and policy. In so far as norms fall short on this account, they are subject to criticism. In any event, the practice of CV inherently values individual wellbeing in so far as it is premised on giving as much space as feasible for adults to follow norms they believe instantiate their interests, even if the state may assess those interests differently. But at the same time, it applies its evaluations of individual interests to all citizens who wish to use them.

VII CULTURAL VOLUNTARISM AND THE 'RIGHT TO A CULTURAL IDENTITY' (RCI)

Might it be argued that, although CV respects minority cultural practices, it fails to provide sufficient support for them? Does the emphasis on voluntariness, and holding open the ever-present possibility of use of state norms by minority members, provide insufficient protection to the norms of minorities that see the value of their identity in terms of insulation from state norms and conservation of their traditions?

Arguments of those kinds have been developed by Avishai Margalit and Moshe Halbertal (2004) in a discussion of Ultra-Orthodox Jewish culture and Arab culture in Israel, and by Andrea Cassatella (2006). Both are critical of Will Kymlicka's defence of multiculturalism in terms of the value of culture in enhancing autonomy. That, they say, privileges liberal culture above others, and gives too little weight to the value of culture in promoting and preserving 'self-identity'. In particular, the claim is that people have a right to maintain a *particular* culture, not just any culture. The argument has been developed by Meital Pinto (2010) with regard to the issue of offences to feelings. Pinto believes that the interest to be protected against behaviour that is culturally offensive is not the injury to people's feelings, but to their right to express their identity through their culture, that is, the right to cultural identity (RCI). In particular, she argues that the extent of weight to be afforded to the right should be related to the vulnerability of the particular community in wider society. She calls this the 'Vulnerable Cultural Identity Principle'. Insults to a majority community would be less in need of protection than those made to minorities. It follows from both arguments that states should be willing to devote sufficient resources to enable minority cultures to flourish because the individuals that constitute them have a right to their maintenance.

Since the RCI claims the perpetuation of a culture is a 'right', its recognition as a right explicitly requires that it needs state protection unless outweighed by some other right. Cultural Voluntarism stops short of this, and may be inconsistent with it. The RCI (together with the 'Vulnerable Cultural Identity Principle') might be seen as commending the 'authorisation' (or 'religious particularist') model as being that which the members of the culture believe best protects its survival. That could imply requiring support for measures that insulate group members from the values of, or even contact with, other cultures, including the majority culture. This would not be consistent with the position of CV that the general state norms should be always available and accessible to members of all community groups.

The position taken by Cultural Voluntarism is defended on the following grounds:

1. While individuals' sense of self is importantly developed by social interaction, the RCI as understood here fails to confront the multiplicity of social forces that affect individual identity. Are *all* of these to be given special protection? In fact, it focuses on those cultures or cultural practices that stand out more visibly from others, especially if they have a religious basis. There seems no reason to hold that, simply because of their higher visibility, or religious foundation, the perpetuation of these cultures should have special protection over other aspects of people's cultural identities. (For example, people may have both a religious and a regional identity: on what basis should one be considered more important than the other?)

2. Insofar as the RCI ignores the fact that those claiming its exercise claim it not just for themselves but for future generations, seeking to perpetuate their identity and beliefs into the future, and to restrict opportunities for their successors to seek different identities, they are making a claim not for themselves but for others. (See for a fuller discussion in the context of multicultural families, Eekelaar (2004)). There is no reason why any such claims should be given special consideration.

3. Proponents of RCI perhaps underplay the extent to which individuals are able profitably to adapt and combine identities.

4. RCI effectively confers a group right. This raises issues about who has power to represent the group and define its interests.

5. Arguably the RCI could inhibit any form of criticism of the group if that criticism might lead to self-questioning within the group and thereby the weakening of the culture. To permit this would intrude unacceptably on the values of the majority liberal society.

6. Excessive emphasis on cultural identities tends to highlight differences between people rather than what people have in common. In many cases this can sow discord and lead to physical harm to individuals.

7. One of Franz Schubert's most beautiful songs[9] sets a text of Friedrich Schiller:

> Schöne Welt, wo bist du? - Kehre wieder,
> Holdes Blüthenalter der Natur!
> Ach, nur in dem Feenland der Lieder

---

[9] *Die Götter Griechenlands*, D677.

Lebt noch deine fabelhafte Spur.
Ausgestorben trauert das Gefilde,
Keine Gottheit zeigt sich meinem Blick,
Ach, von jenem lebenwarmen Bilde
Blieb der Schatten nur zurück

Beautiful world, where are you? Return once more
Fair springtime of Nature!
Alas, only in the enchanted world of Song
Does your fabled Memory live on.
The deserted fields are in mourning,
No gods appear before me.
Ah, of all those life-warming Images,
All that remain are Shadows.

The faint echo of a culture, once a reality, now forever lost, conjured by Schubert's music has a deep pathos. We know, of course, that culture is important for individual wellbeing, and people express themselves through culture. Actions taken to maintain cultural beliefs and practices can therefore have value, and may deserve support from general community resources. Individuals have the right not to have their cultures oppressed. The individual right to manifest religious beliefs can be reasonably extended to cultural practices. But (and the distinction is important) none of that demands that any *particular* culture and belief system is *entitled, as of right, to continue* in perpetuity. It is salutary sometimes to take a long-term view which shows that social organisations and world views that may seem indispensable and immutable to their present participants are not fixed. All cultures change over time. This is often because of changing patterns of power, but may also be because of internal evolution, perhaps as a result of interaction with other cultures, geographic mobility, technological change, advances in knowledge or other reasons. In his magisterial account of defunct European polities, Norman Davies (2011: 5) writes,

> transience is one of the fundamental characteristics both of the human condition and of the political order. Sooner or later, all things come to an end. Sooner or later, the centre cannot hold. All states and nations, however great, bloom for a season and are replaced.

We can only evaluate these changes through the lens of our current cultural perspective. The more tolerant, culturally diverse twenty-first century British culture is different from the more monolithic, imperialist culture of its nineteenth century equivalent. Schiller evokes nostalgia over the lost imaginative world of the ancients, but would we want to return to its discrimination and slavery? Cultural change can bring sadness, but it could also be a cause for celebration.

Proponents of the RCI do not maintain that the right prevails over all other rights. That of course is true about nearly all rights. But accepting the interest as a right elevates the status of the interest when considered in competition with other interests that might also be rights. In some versions, the state has to adopt a neutral stance to such interests in deciding which are to prevail in cases of conflict. CV does not presuppose a neutral state; it requires the state to respect the voluntary decisions people make about their cultural affiliations and to permit the practices of the culture provided they are consistent with the general law. It does not, however, see the maintenance of any culture as an end in itself. While it upholds the right of individuals to practise their culture, and should not attempt to undermine a culture through denigration or humiliation of its members, whether it supports a culture may depend on contingent judgements of its value: it need not consider all of them as being worth promoting or beyond criticism. It is legitimate (indeed important) for the state to encourage openness and toleration within the community, but that does not require it to sustain cultural practices into the future for no reason other than that people practise them today or to defer to attempts by contemporaries to compel subsequent generations to act in the same way as they do.

REFERENCES

Ahmed, F (2010) 'Personal Autonomy and the Option of Religious Law' 24 *International Journal of Law, Policy and the Family* 222.

Ali, SS (2002) 'Testing the Limits of Family Law Reform in Pakistan: A Critical Analysis of the Muslim Family Laws Ordinance 1961' in A Bainham (ed), *The International Survey of Family Law*, 2002 edn (Bristol, Family Law).

Amien, W (2010) 'A South African Case Study for the Recognition and Regulation of Muslim Family Law in a Minority Muslim Secular Context' 24 *International Journal of Law, Policy and the Family* 361.

Bano, S (2008) 'In Pursuit of Religious and Legal Diversity: A Response to the Archbishop of Canterbury and the "Sharia Debate" in Britain' 10 *Ecclesiastical Law Journal* 283.

Beck, U and Beck-Gernsheim, E (2001) *Individualization: Institutional Individualism and its Social and Political Consequences* (London, Sage).

Berlin, I (2006) *Political Ideas in the Romantic Age* (ed Henry Hardy) (London, Pimlico).

Brophy, J, Jhutti-Johal, J and Owen, C (2003) *Significant Harm: Child Protection Litigation in a Multi-Cultural Setting* (London, Lord Chancellor's Department).

Burrows, A (2002) *The Law of Restitution*, 2nd edn (London, Butterworths).

Cassatella, A (2006) 'Multicultural Justice: Will Kymlicka and Cultural Recognition' 19 *Ratio Juris* 80.

Davies, N (2011) *Vanished Kingdoms: The History of Half-Forgotten Europe* (London, Allen Lane).

Eekelaar, J (2004) 'Children between Cultures' 18 *International Journal of Law, Policy and the Family* 178.

—— (2007) *Family Law and Personal Life* (Oxford, Oxford University Press).

—— (2010) 'From Multiculturalism to Cultural Voluntarism: A Family-based Approach' 81 *The Political Quarterly* 344.

—— (2011a) 'Evaluating Legal Regulation of Family Behaviour' 1 *International Journal of Jurisprudence of the Family* 17: heinonline.org/HOL/Page?handle=hein.journals/ijjf1&id=1&collection=journals.

—— (2011b) 'Self-Restraint: Social Norms, Individualism and the Family' 13 *Theoretical Inquiries in Law* 75.

Fishbayn, L (1999) 'Litigating the Right to Culture: Family Law in the New South Africa' 13 *International Journal of Law, Policy and the Family* 147.

Fournier, P (2010) 'Flirting with God in Western Secular Courts: Mahr in the West' 24 *International Journal of Law, Policy and the Family* 67.

Karanjawala, T and Chugh, S (2009) 'The Legal Battle against Domestic Violence in India: Evolution and Analysis' 23 *International Journal of Law, Policy and the Family* 289.

Kymlicka, W (1995) *Multicultural Citizenship: A Liberal Theory of Multicultural Rights* (Oxford, Oxford University Press).

Malhotra, A and Malhotra, J (2007) 'Hindu Law and the Uniform Code' in B Atkin and F Banda (eds), *The International Survey of Family Law*, 2007 edn (Bristol, Family Law) 107.

Margalit, A and Halbertal, M (2004) 'Liberalism and the Right to Culture' 71 *Social Research* 529.

Mujuzi, J (2012) 'The Entrenchment of Qadhis' Courts to deal with Muslim Marriage, Divorce and Inheritance in the Ugandan Constitution' 26 *International Journal of Law, Policy and the Family*, issue 3 (forthcoming).

Pinto, M (2010) 'What are Offences to Feelings Really About? A New Regulative Principle' 30 *Oxford Journal of Legal Studies* 695.

Poulter, S (1998) *Ethnicity, Law and Human Rights: The English Experience* (Oxford, Oxford University Press).

Raz, J (1986) *The Morality of Freedom* (Oxford, Clarendon Press).

Schmid, U (2001) 'Legal Pluralism as a Source of Conflict in Multi-ethnic Societies: The Case of Ghana' 46 *Journal of Legal Pluralism and Unofficial Law* 1.

Sen, A (2009) *The Idea of Justice* (Cambridge, MA, Belknap Press).

Shachar, A (2001) *Multicultural Jurisdictions: Cultural Differences and Women's Rights* (Cambridge, Cambridge University Press).

—— (2008) 'Privatizing Diversity: A Cautionary Tale from Religious Arbitration in Family Law' 9 *Theoretical Inquiries in Law* 573.

—— (2010) 'State, Religion and the Family: The New Dilemmas of Multicultural Accommodation' in R Ahdar and N Aroney (eds), *Sharia in the West* (Oxford, Oxford University Press).

Shah-Kazemi, S (2001) *Untying the Knot: Muslim Women, Divorce, and the Shariah* (London, The Nuffield Foundation).

Stewart, JE (1998) 'Why I Can't Teach Customary Law' in J Eekelaar and T Nhlapo (eds), *The Changing Family: International Perspectives on the Family and Family Law* (Oxford, Hart Publishing).

Williams, R (2008) 'Civil and Religious Law in England: A Religious Perspective' 10 *Ecclesiastical Law Journal* 262.

2

Religious Norms in Family Law: Implications for Group and Personal Autonomy

FARRAH AHMED*

I INTRODUCTION

FAMILY LAW CAN accommodate religious norms in a variety of ways. John Eekelaar (chapter one) indicates the breadth of options available. Religious groups in particular are accommodated in some jurisdictions through *millet* or personal law systems. Under a *millet* system, religious communities are governed in some matters by a religious leadership recognised by the state (Kymlicka 1992). In a personal law system, the state itself applies a version of religious doctrine to citizens who it identifies as belonging to different religious groups (Galanter and Krishnan 2000: 103; Ahmed 2010). While the *millet* and personal law systems are important modes of accommodation, this chapter will focus on another mode. In many Western jurisdictions, the form of accommodation that is frequently proposed is religious alternative dispute resolution. Religious alternative dispute resolution ('RADR') has appeared as a proposal in the debates on the accommodation of religious norms in family law in Canada (Ryder 2008: 87; Farrow 2006; Bakht 2006; Weinrib 2008: 239), Australia,[1] the

* I would like to thank Nazila Ghanea, Leslie Green, Joel Harrison, Jarrod Hepburn, Tarunabh Khaitan, Jane Norton and all the participants of the Workshop on Families: Deviance, Diversity and the Law at the Onati International Institute for the Sociology of Law.

[1] See, eg, Australian Federation of Islamic Councils Inc, *Submission No 81 to Australian Parliament Joint Standing Committee on Migration* (Parliament of Australia 2011): www.aph.gov.au/house/committee/mig/multiculturalism/subs/sub81.pdf; T Soutphommasane, 'Avoid the Hysteria but Reject Sharia' *The Australian* (21 May 2011): www.theaustralian.com.au/news/opinion/avoid-the-hysteria-but-reject-sharia/story-e6frg6zo-1226059621354; P Karvelas, 'Imam Wants Sharia Law Here, but A-G Says No Way' *The Australian* (18 May 2011): www.theaustralian.com.au/national-affairs/imam-wants-sharia-law-here-but-a-g-says-no-way/story-fn59niix-1226057823890; 'Even Muslim Jurists are Divided about what Sharia is' *The Australian* (23 May 2011): www.theaustralian.com.au/news/opinion/letters-to-the-editor/story-fn558imw-1226060688189.

United Kingdom,[2] the Netherlands (Berger 2006), Europe generally[3] and the United States.[4]

By RADR is generally meant arbitration, mediation or conciliation conducted according to religious norms, agreed to by the parties in a contract and recognised and (if appropriate) enforced by the state. The importance of this mode of accommodation is reflected in the extensive literature devoted to its evaluation. This literature often assumes that RADR necessarily harms autonomy,[5] possibly because of the belief that women and other vulnerable people are often coerced into RADR (Boyd 2004: 50–51; Bakht 2004: Art 7; Shachar 2008: 588–90; Gaudreault-Desbiens 2005/06) and the worry that the norms used in RADR disadvantage women.[6] This chapter, however, challenges the assumption that religious arbitration necessarily harms personal autonomy. It will argue that RADR in fact has the potential to enhance personal autonomy through its positive implications for religious group autonomy. In the course of this argument, we will also have the opportunity to challenge another common assumption in the literature on multicultural accommodation: that granting greater autonomy to religious groups necessarily diminishes the personal autonomy of group members. While the focus of this chapter is RADR, the arguments made here might also be applied to other modes of accommodation. To be clear, the purpose of this chapter is not to provide an all-things-considered evaluation of RADR. Nor does it aim to discover whether RADR always or generally promotes (or harms) personal autonomy. Its only aim is to consider whether the common assumption that it harms autonomy is *necessarily* true – that is, whether there are in fact circumstances where it does not harm, and perhaps promotes personal autonomy.

The next section of this chapter will introduce the concepts of personal autonomy and group autonomy which will be used and elaborated on in subsequent sections. Section three then outlines four circumstances in which religious

---

[2] Poulter (1990) 147–66; R Williams, 'Archbishop's Lecture – Civil and Religious Law in England: A Religious Perspective' (2008): www.archbishopofcanterbury.org/articles.php/1137/archbishops-lecture-civil-and-religious-law-in-england-a-religious-perspective#Lecture; Lord Chief Justice Phillips, 'Equality before the law' (East London Muslim Centre, 3 July 2008): www.judiciary.gov.uk/Resources/JCO/Documents/Speeches/lcj_equality_before_the_law_030708.pdf.

[3] M Rohe, 'Alternative Dispute Resolution in Europe under the Auspices of Religious Norms' (January 2011) Religare Working Paper No 6: www.religareproject.eu/content/alternative-dispute-resolution-europe-under-auspices-religious-norms.

[4] E Volokh, 'May American Court Appoint Only Muslim Arbitrators, Pursuant to an Arbitration Agreement?' (*The Volokh Conspiracy*, 3 January 2011): volokh.com/2011/01/03/may-american-court-appoint-only-muslim-arbitrators-pursuant-to-an-arbitration-agreement; Oklahoma Constitution art VII §1-C; Estin (2004).

[5] R Gupta, 'One Law for All rally' (21 November 2009): www.onelawforall.org.uk/november-21-a-successful-day-against-sharia-and-religious-laws: 'accommodating alternative systems of justice is not about choice or tolerance in a pluralistic society; it is not about Muslim women's autonomy. These demands emerge from fundamentalist politics – however they are dressed up'. See Gaudreault-Desbiens (2005/06: 160, 162–65).

[6] Critics of religious arbitration might point to religious norms that deny women equal inheritance rights; eg, under Islamic inheritance law, male heirs in the same relationship to the deceased as female heirs inherit more: Fyzee and Mahmood (2008: 316).

group autonomy can enhance personal autonomy. It also considers whether each of these four circumstances applies to RADR such that RADR can be said to have the potential to enhance personal autonomy by enhancing religious group autonomy.

II PERSONAL AUTONOMY AND GROUP AUTONOMY

This chapter evaluates RADR against the value of personal autonomy. But there are many disagreements about the nature of personal autonomy, its preconditions, what diminishes it, whether it is valuable (Kukathas 2003: 15, 16, 36) and why it is valuable.[7] Many liberal political and legal philosophers, however, have a shared understanding of at least the core of the concept of personal autonomy.[8] Joseph Raz, in the *Morality of Freedom,* largely appeals to this core, shared understanding of personal autonomy (McCabe (2001: 494–95, fn 5). This chapter broadly adopts Raz's approach to the concept of autonomy because of its ecumenical (though not universal) appeal, its plausibility and its resonance with the issues raised here. On this account of personal autonomy, an autonomous person is the helmsman (May 1994), the author (Raz 1986: 370), the creator (ibid) or the governor (Mele 1995: 155–56) of her own life. In other words, personal autonomy is the ideal of giving shape to one's own life. The preconditions for personal autonomy include familiar factors such as the absence of coercion (Raz 1986: 407–08), the absence of manipulation (Waldron 1989: 1117–120) and the availability of an adequate range of valuable options (Raz 1986: 370ff, 375; Hurka 1987: 366–71). A life in which one is coerced and one's actions and decisions are the product of manipulation is not an autonomous life. Nor is a life where one's options are few, trivial or unappealing an autonomous life (Raz 1986: 373). But further details on this account of autonomy will emerge in the course of the argument that follows.

With that brief outline of personal autonomy in mind, we can proceed to the concept of group autonomy. While there are clearly disanalogies between group autonomy and personal autonomy, autonomy is a notion that can be applied both to individuals and groups. Its application to groups is historically prior – this is the sense in which we talk about autonomous regions or national groups (Dworkin 1996: 19–26; Levey 1997: 239). The features of personal autonomy roughly apply *mutatis mutandis* to group autonomy. Group autonomy is diminished when a

---

[7] For an outline of these debates, see S Buss, 'Personal Autonomy', *The Stanford Encyclopedia of Philosophy* (Fall edn, 2008): plato.stanford.edu/entries/personal-autonomy/#2; Waldron (1989); McCabe (2001).

[8] '[I]n neither *The Morality of Freedom* nor the later essays does Raz provide such an account ["a clearly articulated account of autonomy"] . . . My sense is that Raz does not provide a highly detailed account of autonomy . . . because he quite reasonably takes it for granted that, in its overall features, the notion of autonomy relevant to debates over liberalism is fairly non-controversial and well understood': McCabe (2001: 494–95, fn 5). Buss, above (n 7) also notes the overlaps between prominent accounts of autonomy.

group is coerced or dictated to by an outside force such as the state, a person or another group.[9] An autonomous group, like an autonomous person, has the capacity and the opportunity to make choices between a range of valuable options. If the idea of groups making choices seems strange, consider Denise Réaume's account of this:

> A group's path is formed through a complex social process in which the choices of individuals play a part but no one choice is decisive. The process is deliberative. Growth and development, change or reaffirmation of tradition arises out of debate and reflection within the group about the best forms of life for the members of the group. A path is set, even if there is no decisive moment of the sort that constitutes the paradigm case of choosing. With each question that arises for discussion within the group about the adequacy of its social forms the community faces a deliberative enterprise very similar to that engaged in by an individual assessing her life plan. There is more than one way socially to organise familial relationships or the workplace or the case of the aged, or to recognise the spiritual dimension of human experience. . . . Thus a decision can be right for this group, because of its history, that would not be right for – certainly would not be the outcome of an organic process of decision-making within – another group (Réaume 1995: 133).

It might seem that the description so far of an autonomous group presupposes that the group is democratic. While a group does not need to be perfectly democratic in order to be autonomous, it does need to be minimally representative and deliberative. It is difficult to describe a group which is controlled by a small group of leaders who are unresponsive to the views of other group members as autonomous. The group in this case is not controlling itself, but rather is being controlled by 'its' leadership. In other words, then, group autonomy is 'something that can be exercised by a collective *as a whole*, rather than individually by persons in a group' (Wellman 2003: 273). Dictatorial leadership could also be viewed as an internal constraint on a group's autonomy. Autonomy is diminished when the individual or group has internal obstacles to self-governance, even if they are free from external interference. In the case of individuals, this could be because they are insane, lack minimal will-power, or are in the thrall of an addiction. In the case of a group, it could be because the group is controlled by a dictatorial leadership, rather than by group members.[10]

A group could achieve the minimal representativeness and deliberative quality necessary for group autonomy in this sense by using decision-making processes which are reasonably transparent to group-members and which are sensitive to members' views, by allowing (even if not encouraging) deliberation among group members on the direction the group should take, and by ensuring a right to exit for members (as exit or non-exit by members is itself potentially expressive of their views). None of this implies, though, that group autonomy requires free and fair elections or an idealised public square for democratic deliberation.

[9] For a similar definition, see Wellman (2003: 266).
[10] A different internal constraint on group autonomy would be if the group is in chaos or has no way of steering or governing itself.

'Group autonomy' in this chapter refers therefore to a religious group having a level of freedom from external (usually state) control, as well as the ability to govern itself through minimally democratic institutions of governance. A few points of clarification should be made here. Given the context of this discussion, an autonomous group need not be autonomous with respect to all matters, but must be autonomous at least with respect to family matters. 'Groups' here mean, roughly, groups sharing a religion and a common sense of religious identity. It is assumed that these groups will be smaller than the group of all citizens; that is, the groups are smaller than the state as a whole. The arguments which follow assume that the alternative to group autonomy is decision-making at the level of the state.[11]

III COULD RADR ENHANCE PERSONAL AUTONOMY BY ENHANCING GROUP AUTONOMY?

There is good reason to think that RADR has the potential to enhance the autonomy of religious groups. It is significant that religious *institutions*, such as the Muslim Arbitration Tribunal in the UK and the Islamic Institute of Civil Justice in Canada, played a large part in the debates on RADR in those jurisdictions. These institutions might form the locus of a religious group with some amount of autonomy.[12] While most jurisdictions would place limits on who can act as an arbitrator, mediator or conciliator,[13] the general principle is that this is the decision of the parties (Ahmed and Luk 2011: 297). Equally, while there are limits to the religious norms that the parties can use to govern the dispute (ibid) this too is the parties' decision. This means that religious groups can set up arbitration councils which can resolve a dispute on family matters brought to it by consenting parties. Thus the religious group can have a fair degree of control over both the norms which it will apply to its members as well as who ultimately settles the dispute. When a religious group has members that consent to these RADR arrangements, it can be said to govern itself, or be autonomous at least over family matters.

Assuming then that RADR has the potential to enhance group autonomy, the question becomes whether it has the potential to enhance the personal autonomy of group members through its enhancement of the autonomy of the group. This requires a consideration of the effect that group autonomy has on personal autonomy, more generally, which has not been completely mapped in

---

[11] 'Groups' based on other criteria such as culture or ethnicity might be alternatives to religious groups and the arguments that follow might apply to such groups as well. This is, however, beyond the scope of this chapter.

[12] This is not to say that the institutions *as they exist now* preserve personal autonomy. This is just to indicate that religious groups are already starting to form institutions around RADR, which has the potential to preserve personal autonomy.

[13] The rule against bias would be one such common limit.

the literature.[14] The most prominent of the claims about the connection is that group autonomy diminishes personal autonomy. The idea here is that '[p]ower, under such circumstances, becomes a zero-sum game, where the more power government grants to religious and cultural groups, the more difficult it will be for an individual religionist to access the fundamental rights granted by the state'.[15] That is, when groups have greater autonomy (vis-à-vis the liberal state), they have more power over their members. This leaves the members with less power over themselves, and thus less religious autonomy.

This relation between group autonomy and personal autonomy is plausible and probably true of many religious groups. However, what follows shows that it is not *necessarily* true and that the converse – that group autonomy supports personal autonomy – is also true under certain circumstances. This is important because, once we know if and when group autonomy promotes personal autonomy, we can consider whether RADR meets these conditions. The sections that follow are not an exhaustive list of how group autonomy can enhance personal autonomy, but rather an attempt to highlight some key connections between the two. They draw on democratic theory and the literature on subsidiarity for this purpose. They will outline four circumstances in which group autonomy can enhance personal autonomy. These are four circumstances in which individuals have more personal autonomy if they are members of an autonomous group than if they are simply citizens of a state, or if they are citizens who are members of a non-autonomous group. (It is important to keep in mind that references here to personal autonomy being enhanced by group religious autonomy are thus implicitly comparative to a state of affairs where the agent is not a member of an autonomous religious group.) Each of these sections then considers whether each of these four circumstances applies to RADR, such that RADR can be said to have the potential to enhance personal autonomy by enhancing group autonomy.

A Religious Practice and Religious Group Autonomy

One way that group autonomy could promote personal autonomy is by enhancing religious freedom. Giving religious groups greater autonomy might promote the religious freedom of individual group members. Religious freedom is commonly defended on the grounds that it is necessary for, or at least contributes to, personal autonomy.[16] In other words, the option to practise a religion is likely to

---

[14] The connection between culture, recognition of cultural groups, accommodation, respect for culture and personal autonomy has been commented on at great length. Here we are referring only to the study of group autonomy (as a type of autonomy) and its relation to personal autonomy.

[15] MA Helfand, 'Religious Arbitration and the New Multiculturalism: Negotiating Conflicting Legal Orders' (2011) 86 *New York University Law Review* 1231, 1276. See also Tamir (1999) 47–53; Shachar (1998).

[16] Sandel (1989: 611) notes: 'in contemporary liberalism . . . religious liberty *serves the broader mission of protecting individual autonomy*'; *Syndicat Northcrest v Amselem* [2004] 2 SCR 551; Laycock (1996); Tribe (2000: 1284–1300); Greenawalt (2006: 3–4).

be an autonomy-enhancing option. The sphere of religion is considered so important by those who are religious, and religion can have such a great impact on those who engage in it, that it would be difficult to imagine a plausible notion of autonomy that did not include the option of religious practice. It would be difficult to describe someone without religious freedom as having an autonomous life.

Group autonomy might promote religious freedom because it might be necessary for certain religious practices. For instance, some religious practices might require that the religious group as a whole, or representatives of the group, perform certain actions.[17] Closer to our topic, 'religious courts' or 'religious tribunals' also perform religious functions. Religious courts are bodies, comprised of members of a religious group, which claim authority (and are recognised by group members as having authority) to solemnise religious marriages, grant religious divorces or resolve disputes based on religious norms.[18] These religious courts are controversial because of worries relating to women and vulnerable persons.[19] However, they clearly serve important religious functions including performing rituals and ceremonies necessary for religious marriage and divorce. Autonomous RADR institutions could similarly facilitate religious practice by resolving disputes based on religious norms. It is not difficult to see how dispute resolution according to religious norms, by persons belonging to (or holding a particular status) within a religion, might be regarded as an aspect of religious practice (Shippee 2002). Their existence therefore facilitates, and in the case of some religions is possibly necessary for, religious practice (Norton 2011: 244–45).

But could these religious functions performed by the group or its representatives not equally be performed by a group which is *not* autonomous? A priest or imam leading prayers or a religious tribunal or court, it might be argued, could perform the same service for group members regardless of whether the group is autonomous or not. It is true that there may be circumstances where an *autonomous* religious group, as opposed to a non-autonomous one, is not necessary to perform functions which facilitate religious practice. But as the recent controversy about the Chinese Government's efforts to appoint Catholic bishops demonstrates,[20] if a group is not autonomous because it is controlled by the state, or a large corporation, or a different religious group, it seems unlikely that

---

[17] eg, the Eucharist must for many Christians take place in a communal setting and it must be received from an authorised person: Volf (1998: 32–39). The Jewish festival of Passover might similarly be seen as a communal affirmation of identity: Bokser (1984: 138). Congregational prayers on Fridays are an important part of Islamic practice: Esposito (2011: 35–36). I thank Joel Harrison for suggesting these examples.

[18] See generally, G Douglas and others, *Social Cohesion and Civil Law: Marriage, Divorce and Religious Courts* (Cardiff, Cardiff University, 2011) 24–40: www.religionandsociety.org.uk/uploads/docs/2011_07/1310467350_Social_Cohesion_and_Civil_Law_Full_Report.pdf.

[19] S Bano, 'Islamic Family Arbitration, Justice and Human Rights in Britain' (2007) 1 *Law, Social Justice & Global Development Journal*: www.go.warwick.ac.uk/elj/lgd/2007_1/bano.

[20] 'China and the Vatican: Your Billion or Ours?' *The Economist* (London, 20 August 2011): www.economist.com/node/21526402.

it truly can serve its members in the same way that an autonomous religious group can. If priests, imams, Battei Din or Muslim Sharia councils were known to be stooges of the state, it seems unlikely that the communal worship they lead, the marriages they solemnise, or the decisions they come to will have the same quality for group members that they would have if the group were autonomous and free from such control. There is thus reason to think that religious group autonomy facilitates religious practice. Since the option of religious practice is an aspect of personal autonomy, this marks one way in which group autonomy enhances personal autonomy. This is not to deny the genuine concerns that autonomous religious groups could also interfere with the religious freedom of members by, for instance, coercing them in religious matters. But given the purpose of this chapter – to discover any potential positive implications that RADR might have on personal autonomy – these concerns are not relevant here.

B Representation and Religious Group Autonomy

In this section, another way in which group autonomy might enhance personal autonomy is considered. Group autonomy, it is suggested, facilitates representation of individual group members, which in turn enhances their personal autonomy. When a decision affecting a person has to be made, excepting special circumstances, it is best for their autonomy that they make that decision themselves. Sometimes, this is not possible. In such circumstances, perhaps the second best option is for someone to act on their behalf. On representative accounts of democracy, this second best option is adopted because we live in a society where decisions have to be made collectively. Does this second best option – political representation – preserve to some degree the personal autonomy of those who are represented? An analogy is easily drawn between a political representative and an agent acting for the principal in her business or personal affairs (see, eg, Ptolke 1997). Such agents can enhance autonomy: they allow you to transact multiple points of business at more than one place at once. That is, they broaden the sphere of your influence. Moreover, agents are accountable to you for their actions, and you can revoke your agency agreement if they do not act appropriately. The terms of the agency agreement keep a check on the danger that they will do something that you did not authorise.

Doubtless, this analogy between a business agent and a political representative is rough. A political representative in the modern state represents not one, but many constituents. She must take into account *general* public interest, and not just the interests of her constituents. She was, most likely, chosen to represent the constituency by only some constituents, perhaps not even a majority of them. Moreover, she has interests of her own besides those of her constituents.[21]

---

[21] cf, Edmund Burke, 'Speech to the Electors of Bristol' (3 November 1774): press-pubs.uchicago.edu/founders/documents/v1ch13s7.html.

Few would say that the autonomy of a member of society is not (in some sense) constrained by laws which she might otherwise prefer to live without. But given certain facts about her life – that she lives in a community, that decisions affecting the community must be made in some manner and that there are advantages to living in a community – there appears to be good prima facie reason to think that the representative aspect of democracy goes some way towards preserving her autonomy.

There are of course several problems with this picture of life in a democracy. There is one of particular concern to us: what if a member of a democratic society is governed by those from whom she is so alienated that they cannot truthfully be described as her delegates, representatives or agents? This alienation might result from the fact that her culture or values are completely at odds with those claiming to represent her, or that her political representative does not think of himself as representing *this class of citizen*. The view of her relationship with her representative which allows her to retain some autonomy breaks down.

This worry about alienation is exacerbated when decisions on matters within the sphere of religion must be made. This is where greater religious group autonomy would decrease the likelihood of alienation.[22] If religious individuals feel alienated from their state representatives, RADR might give them the opportunity to be governed instead, at least in family matters, by those who they feel represent them better – their co-religionists. Group members and their leaders share a religion, and therefore (one might expect) some values, goals and cultural attributes. So RADR, by enhancing group autonomy, might improve the representation of individual group members in family matters relating to their religion.

RADR institutions have the potential (but only the potential) to benefit their members through better representation at two levels. The first is at the level of the religious group as a whole. That is, RADR facilitates each group that can be identified as a religious group – eg, Muslims, Buddhists, Sikhs, etc – to form a RADR institution, which could later develop into an institution of governance. For instance in India, the All India Muslim Personal Law Board, which initially was concerned only with the preservation of Muslim Personal Law, has developed into a powerful lobbying group on general issues relating to Indian Muslims.[23] The group's representatives in these institutions might give group members the opportunity to be governed, at least in some matters, by those who share their values, have more in common with them, and who therefore represent them better. When collective decisions have to be made, at least about family matters, RADR therefore might preserve personal autonomy by giving those affected better representation on matters that concern their family lives.

[22] This is arguably a virtue of subsidiarity in general: Philpott (1995).
[23] Not to say that this is a good model. This board has been criticised precisely as being unrepresentative, leading to the development of the All India Muslim Women Personal Law Board, AIMWPLB, 'About Us': muslimwomenpersonallaw.com/aboutus.html.

RADR also has the potential to provide better representation at a second level. Each of these religious groups comprises competing sects, schools and interpretations. Each group is large and diverse. It might be true that someone with Christian values might represent Christian constituents better than anyone else. But, extending that reasoning, someone affiliated with not just the Christian religion but the same denomination or church of her constituents, would represent these constituents even better. RADR makes this possible. Anver Emon, a commentator on the Ontario debate, for instance, offers a proposal for how RADR can be used to allow Muslims to develop new and heterodox forms of Sharia:

> Imagine a political spectrum of Muslim family service organizations. Those on the left might critically engage the Islamic legal tradition, concluding, for instance, that the Sharia can accommodate same-sex marriage and divorce and offer those services to gay and lesbian Muslims. Those on the right might instead follow a more traditional or even patriarchal Sharia law regime. Other Muslim family service organizations might advocate positions between these poles. Ultimately, Muslims who desire religiously-based family law services would have different organizations to choose from, thereby giving them a choice between competing visions of Islamic law (Emon 2008: 423).

Emon's proposal, of course, could equally be applied to other religious groups. RADR can thus allow religious persons to be governed (at least in family matters) by religious institutions whose values closely fit their own. So giving greater autonomy to these RADR institutions would have the potential for better preserving the personal autonomy of group members than would leaving them to be governed by the state.

C Deliberative Participation and Autonomy

One way, described above, of preserving autonomy in collective decision-making is to have those in power being representative. Another way is through deliberative decision-making, in which 'people routinely relate to one another not merely by asserting their will or fighting for their predetermined interests, but by influencing each other through the publicly valued use of reasoned argument, evidence, evaluation and persuasion that enlists reasons in its cause' (Gutman 1993). There are many competing accounts of why this kind of deliberation preserves autonomy, but the details of these debates are not essential here.[24] The important point is that there seems to be a fair degree of consensus that making decisions by deliberating with the person affected preserves autonomy to some degree.

---

[24] Cooke (2000). Even those who disagree with deliberative accounts of democracy are likely to agree that deliberation goes some way towards preserving autonomy.

Because of this consensus, only a few reasons why deliberation protects autonomy will be sketched here. First, there is something to be said for the idea that when decision-making is deliberative, even the person who has lost the argument, and who has to abide by a decision that she might disagree with, retains more autonomy than someone who was not consulted at all. The first-mentioned person at least had an input into the decision-making process. She therefore had at least some power to affect what happened to her. Secondly, attempting to persuade her by drawing her attention to the applicable reasons implies that she is considered capable of responding to such reasons (Cohen 1999). Attempting to persuade her suffers less, then, from the insult that coercion might otherwise carry: that the coerced person is unable to reason or take care of herself.

Moreover, deliberation might even enhance autonomy. The ability to respond to reason and the ability to draw attention to the reasons that others have would be sharpened by participation in the process of deliberation. The first ability is a necessary condition for autonomy because a person who cannot respond to reason cannot see the world as it truly is. As such he cannot navigate his way through it autonomously. Most accounts of autonomy make some level of rationality necessary for autonomy because it is undeniable that a person without the ability to reason will be unable to effectively translate their will to action.[25] The second ability is a kind of power. Wielding it well enables a person to have the kind of power over others which is consistent with respect for their autonomy. Such a power contributes to the autonomy of the person who wields it.

This is, again, not to say that collective decisions that are deliberative necessarily *completely* preserve personal autonomy (Nedelsky 1989). Rather, they go some way towards mitigating the harmful effects of collective decision-making on autonomy. One argument, then, in favour of greater group autonomy is based on the potential that it has to make deliberation more effective at preserving personal autonomy. If deliberation protects personal autonomy by giving those affected a say in the decision, having fewer people at the metaphorical table might give each person *more* of a say. Further, as suggested in the section above, religious group members are less likely to feel alienated from their group than they do from the state. If the goal is for people to influence each other 'through the publicly valued use of reasoned argument, evidence, evaluation

[25] Raz (2000: 1); J Christman, 'Autonomy in Moral and Political Philosophy' *The Stanford Encyclopedia of Philosophy* (Fall edn, 2009): plato.stanford.edu/entries/autonomy-moral; Christman (1988); Berofsky (1995: 199); Buss (above n 7); Raz (1986: 372–73). For example, say Peter wants to send his daughter to the best school in his area. A rational person might go about making enquiries from friends or colleagues, consult school rankings, visit various schools in his area. He might estimate the accuracy of all the resulting information, assign a certain weight to opinions depending on their source, consider factors specific to his daughter and then come to a decision based on a comparison of the available schools. The better Peter is at reasoning, the better he will be at this process. Equally, his ineffectuality may cause us to question whether he is in fact autonomous.

and persuasion', this might be easier in a religious group than in the state at large (Gutmann 1993: 141). The kinds of groups we are concerned with share values, goals and norms. Those affected by a decision can appeal to common reasons in defence of their position based on these shared values, goals and norms.[26] As one writer says about a common nationality, it 'facilitates the com-· munications, confidence, and mutual respect that are necessary or desirable in a democracy' (Whelan 1983: 30). This might also apply to shared values, goals and norms of a group and might lead to better participation among group members in deliberation.

Many of these considerations apply to RADR institutions. RADR institutions could serve as forums for effective deliberation among group members within groups with shared values, goals and norms. They could enable the group to make collective decisions about the content of the norms by which they will be governed, whether and how these norms should be enforced and who these norms will be enforced by. In short, RADR institutions could facilitate the kind of deliberative decision-making that results in a group making a decision collectively, as described in the quotation from Réaume above. It might therefore be argued that RADR, by increasing group autonomy over family matters, improves the quality and effectiveness of deliberation and thereby helps preserve personal autonomy.

D Individual Political Autonomy and Religious Autonomy

A fourth way in which religious group autonomy can enhance religious autonomy is by enhancing what will be referred to here as 'individual political autonomy'. By political autonomy is meant the kind of freedom that Benjamin Constant described as the 'liberty of the ancients' – the freedom to

> exercis[e] collectively, *but directly,* several parts of the complete sovereignty; in deliberating, in the public square, over war and peace; in forming all instances with foreign governments; in voting laws, in pronouncing judgments; in examining the accounts, the acts, the stewardships of the magistrates; in calling them to appear in front of the assembled people, in accusing, condemning or absolving them (Constant 1997: 66, emphasis added).

The literature on personal autonomy perhaps neglects to emphasise as much as it should the contribution that the exercise of this political freedom can make to personal autonomy. If an autonomous person is part-author of her life, *direct* partial authorship of the politics of her religious group – a significant part of the context in which her life is probably lived – will only give her more autonomy. This is why the influence that a member of a democracy might have on political decision-making is one reason why political freedom supports autonomy.

---

[26] Of course the values themselves might be contested or subject to interpretation.

Participation in politics is also likely to hone other qualities that enhance autonomy. A sense of responsibility for the fate of their society might habituate people to a sense of responsibility for their actions more generally. This sense of responsibility bears an intimate relation to autonomy (Raz 1986: 381–85). Earlier, autonomy was described as self-authorship or self-creation of one's life. No-one can claim to be the author of her own life, unless she takes responsibility for her actions, unless she claims them as her own. If she is alienated from her actions, if she disclaims them, then she cannot be the author or creator of those actions. If individual political autonomy promotes habits of responsibility, it also nourishes the capacity for personal autonomy.

Constant was right to note that this liberty was probably enjoyed to a greater degree in the smaller democratic societies of the past where each participant in politics was much more influential than one voter in the large states of today (Constant 1997: 68). It is true that exercises of political freedom continue today through street protests, 'occupations' of landmarks, lobbying, voting, petitions and even the formation of virtual groups in support of 'causes' on social networking websites, even if not every citizen has the right to speak in a legislative body as in some societies in the past. But Constant's ideal is that of *direct* influence on political events. This is clearly easier to achieve in smaller political communities than larger ones. If some matters of government – the regulation of family life for instance – were devolved to religious groups, individual political autonomy might thus be more easily achieved and more effective in these (smaller) religious groups, than in the state at large.[27] These groups can serve as a stage for individuals to influence the politics of their religious groups. This is especially true given the concerns expressed above over the alienation of people from their government.

In any case, if individual political autonomy is to be achieved in a religious group, this religious group must be autonomous. If it is not, ie, if the group does not govern itself and if it is not free (to some degree) from external control, then the agent cannot claim to part-author her political context (ie, the religious group). She cannot claim to have individual political autonomy. If RADR institutions can form the locus of a religious group with some amount of autonomy,[28] their smaller size might provide a more conducive forum for Constant's kind of political autonomy (Constant 1997). But the smaller size of these religious groups will not promote individual political autonomy if group members are not given an opportunity to influence group norms, play a role in their execution, choose group leaders and hold them to account. There has been a wave of recent interest in how RADR institutions work.[29] Regardless of how they actually do

---

[27] No effort is made here to try to estimate how large these groups might be. Certainly they are smaller than a state, and likely small enough that direct influence can be felt.

[28] This is not to say that the institutions *as they exist now* preserve personal autonomy. This is only to indicate that religious groups are already starting to form institutions around RADR, which has the potential to preserve personal autonomy.

[29] See, eg, Douglas and others above (n 19); Bano (2008); Shah-Kazemi (2001).

work, it is clear that unless members are allowed to participate, they cannot be said to enhance political autonomy. The fact that RADR allows group norms and leaders to be chosen and developed by the groups means that RADR has the *potential* at least for enhancing personal autonomy by granting individuals greater political autonomy in their religious groups. So one defence of RADR might be that it enhances group autonomy, thus providing an appropriate context for the exercise of individual political autonomy (at least over some matters); this in turn enhances personal autonomy.

IV CONCLUSION

It is important to be careful about what conclusions we draw from the discussion above. This chapter does *not* prove that group autonomy promotes or preserves personal autonomy in general. It does prove that, given the alternative of state authority, group autonomy promotes or preserves personal autonomy in cases where greater group autonomy leads to enhanced religious freedom, better representation, enhanced deliberation or greater political autonomy. This chapter does not prove that that RADR *necessarily* enhances any of these. But it does establish that, contrary to common assumptions made in the literature, RADR has the *potential* to enhance personal autonomy. We cannot conclude from this that RADR overall is good for personal autonomy. There are many more considerations including the nature of the religious norms, the nature of members' consent to RADR and the possibility of exit that have to be considered before the larger question of the effect of RADR on personal autonomy can be answered. However, the conclusions of this chapter are significant because of the key role played by RADR in current debates on religious accommodation in family law, especially in Western jurisdiction. Moreover, the argument made here might be applicable to other modes of accommodation as well; whether it is will be left for future research.

REFERENCES

Ahmed, F (2010) 'Personal Autonomy and the Option of Religious Law' 24 *International Journal of Law, Policy and the Family* 222.

Ahmed, F and Luk, S (2011) 'Religious Arbitration: A Study of Legal Safeguards' 77 *Arbitration* 290.

Bakht, N (2004) 'Family Arbitration Using Sharia Law: Examining Ontario's Arbitration Act and its Impact on Women' 1 *Muslim World Journal of Human Rights* Art 7.

—— (2006) 'Were Muslim Barbarians Really Knocking on the Gates of Ontario? The Religious Arbitration Controversy – Another Perspective' *Ottawa Law Review* 67.

Bano, S (2008) 'In Pursuit of Religious and Legal Diversity: A Reply to the Archbishop of Canterbury and the "Sharia Debate" in Britain' 10 *Ecclesiastical Law Journal* 283.

Berger, M (2006) 'Sharia Law in Canada – Also Possible in the Netherlands?' in P van der Grinten and T Heukels (eds), *Crossing Borders: Essays in European and Private International Law, Nationality Law and Islamic Law in Honour of Frans van der Velden* (Kluwer) 173.

Berofsky, B (1995) *Liberation from Self: A Theory of Personal Autonomy* (London, Routledge).

Bokser, B (1984) *The Origins of the Seder: The Passover Rite and Early Rabbinic Judaism* (Berkeley, CA, University of California Press).

Boyd, M (2004) *Dispute Resolution in Family Law: Protecting Choice, Promoting Inclusion* (Ontario, Ministry of the Attorney-General).

Christman, J (1988) 'Constructing the Inner Citadel: Recent Work on the Concept of Autonomy' 99 *Ethics* 109.

Cohen, J (1999) 'Reflections on Habermas on Democracy' 12 *Ratio Juris* 407.

Constant, B (1997) 'The Liberty of the Ancients Compared to That of the Moderns' in D Boaz, *The Libertarian Reader* (New York, The Free Press).

Cooke, M (2000) 'Five Arguments for Deliberative Democracy' 48 *Political Studies* 957.

Dworkin, R (1996) *Freedom's Law: The Moral Reading of the American Constitution* (Oxford, Oxford University Press, 1996).

Emon, AE (2008) 'Islamic law and the Canadian Mosaic: Politics, Jurisprudence, and Multicultural Accommodation' 87 *Canadian Bar Review* 391.

Esposito, JL (2011) *What Everyone Needs to Know about Islam*, 2nd edn (Oxford, Oxford University Press).

Estin, AL (2004), 'Embracing Tradition: Pluralism in American Family Law' 63 *Maryland Law Review* 540.

Farrow, TCW (2006) 'Re-Framing the Sharia Arbitration Debate' 15 *Constitutional Forum* 79.

Fyzee, AAA and Mahmood, T (2008) *Outlines of Muhammadan Law*, 5th edn (Delhi, Oxford University Press).

Galanter M and Krishnan, J (2000) 'Personal Law and Human Rights in India and Israel' 34 *Israel Law Review* 101.

Gaudreault-Desbiens, J-F (2005/06) 'Constitutional Values, Faith-Based Arbitration, and the Limits of Private Justice in a Multicultural Society' 19 *National Journal of Constitutional Law* 155.

Greenawalt, K (2006) *Religion and the Constitution: Free Exercise and Fairness* (Princeton, Princeton University Press).

Gutmann, A (1993) 'Democracy' in R Goodin and P Pettit (eds), *A Companion to Contemporary Political Philosophy* (Oxford, Blackwell Publishers).

Hurka, T (1987) 'Why Value Autonomy?' 13 *Social Theory and Practice* 361.

Kukathas, C (2003) *The Liberal Archipelago: A Theory of Diversity and Freedom* (Oxford, Oxford University Press).

Kymlicka, W (1992) 'Two Models of Pluralism and Tolerance' 14 *Analyse & Kritik* 33.

Laycock, D (1996) 'Religious Liberty as Liberty' 7 *Journal of Contemporary Legal Issues* 313.

Levey, GB (1997) 'Equality, Autonomy, and Cultural Rights' 25 *Political Theory* 215.

May, T (1994) 'The Concept of Autonomy' *American Philosophical Quarterly* 133.

McCabe, D (2001) 'Joseph Raz and the Contextual Argument for Liberal Perfectionism' 111 *Ethics* 493.

Mele, AR (1995) *Autonomous Agents: From Self-Control to Autonomy* (Oxford, Oxford University Press).

Nedelsky, J (1989) 'Reconceiving Autonomy: Sources, Thoughts, and Possibilities' *Yale Journal of Law and Feminism* 7.

Norton, J (2011) 'Law and Religious Organizations: Exceptions, Non-interference and Justification' (DPhil thesis, University of Oxford).

Philpott, D (1995) 'In Defense of Self-Determination' 105 *Ethics* 352.

Poulter, S (1990) 'The Claim to a Separate Islamic System of Personal Law for British Muslims' in C Mallat and J Connors (eds), *Islamic Family Law* (Richmond, Graham and Trotman).

Ptolke, D (1997) 'Representation is Democracy' 4 *Constellations* 19.

Raz, J (1986) *The Morality of Freedom* (Oxford, Clarendon Press).

—— (2000) *Engaging Reason: On the Theory of Value and Action* (Oxford, Oxford University Press).

Réaume, D (1995) 'Justice Between Cultures: Autonomy and the Protection of Cultural Affiliation' 29 *University of British Columbia Law Review* 117.

Ryder, B (2008) 'The Canadian Conception of Equal Religious Citizenship' in R Moon (ed), *Law and Religious Pluralism in Canada* (Vancouver, University of British Columbia Press).

Sandel, M (1989) 'Religious Liberty – Freedom of Conscience or Freedom of Choice' 33 *Utah Law Review* 597.

Shachar, A (1998) 'Group Identity and Women's Rights in Family Law: The Perils of Multicultural Accommodation' 6 *Journal of Political Philosophy* 285.

—— (2008) 'Privatizing Diversity: A Cautionary Tale from Religious Arbitration in Family Law' 9 *Theoretical Inquiries in Law* 573.

Shah-Kazemi, S (2001) *Untying the Knot: Muslim Women, Divorce and the Shariah* (London, The Nuffield Foundation).

Shippee, R (2002) 'Blessed are the Peacemakers: Faith-Based Approaches to Dispute Resolution' 9 *ILSA Journal of International & Comparative Law* 237.

Tamir, Y (1999) 'Siding With the Underdogs' in SM Okin and others (eds), *Is Multiculturalism Bad for Women?* (Princeton, Princeton University Press).

Tribe, LH (2000) *American Constitutional Law*, 3rd edn (New York, Foundation Press).

Volf, M (1998) *After Our Likeness: The Church as the Image of the Trinity* (Grand Rapids, MI, WB Eerdmans).

Waldron, J (1989) 'Autonomy and Perfectionism in Raz's *The Morality of Freedom*' 62 *Southern California Law Review* 1097.

Weinrib, LM (2008) 'Ontario's Sharia Law Debate: Law and Politics under the *Charter*' in R Moon (ed), *Law and Religious Pluralism in Canada* (Vancouver, University of British Columbia Press).

Wellman, C (2003) 'The Paradox of Group Autonomy' 20 *Social Philosophy and Policy* 265.

Whelan, F (1983) 'Prologue: Democratic Theory and the Boundary Problem' in J Pennock and J Chapman (eds), *Liberal Democracy* (New York, New York University Press).

3

Shadow Boxing with Community Practices: A Response to Eekelaar

PRAKASH SHAH

T HIS CHAPTER IS written as a response to John Eekelaar's chapter (chapter one) in this book. In his chapter, Eekelaar presupposes a basic-ally liberal ethical framework through which to view the dilemmas of accommodating minority laws within a legal system. It is constrained by the demands of that framework which also limits its methodological flexibility. Eekelaar presumes, without saying so openly, that his audience accepts a liberal perspective, and that the minority subjects about whom he speaks are amenable to their legal issues being confined to that liberal ethical framework, even if they may not share it.[1] This lack of an explicit acknowledgment implies that liberal values are above contestation and self-evidently universal; as such we are not required to assess their reasonableness in plural contexts. Still less, one assumes, should those liberal values be brought into juxtaposition with the ethics found in other, specifi-cally non-Western, traditions, a position which Parekh (2011) has recently argued to be typical of the failure of liberals to engage in intercultural dialogue.[2]

Eekelaar accepts the liberal legal order the way it is. It seems also that we are asked to accept that there are no real problems in subsuming a variety of different communities under an overarching legal order with its liberal presuppositions, and that we need not problematise the potentially violent, oppressive, or absurd consequences of applying such a framework to non-liberal communities, that is, communities that do not operate from within a liberal ethical framework.

---

[1] Among the various strands in Western thought, I refer only to liberalism here. This is further justified not only because Eekelaar adopts a liberal position, but because, as Ahdar and Leigh (2005: 38) have noted in their work, 'liberalism is the principal philosophical foundation for law in modern liberal democracy'.

[2] This sort of non-questioning in light of globalising and pluralistic ('superdiverse': Vertovec 2007) realities, and a consequent denial of the intellectual heritage of others, switches off many bril-liant students, acts as a block to deeper investigation and is thus a massive blow to intellectual life. The much-heralded 'rise of Asia' leaves Europeans as largely disabled from being able to cope with the global power shift that that entails, while Asians are much less willing to take lectures on 'supe-rior' Western ethics or anything else from Europeans. See, for a sustained argument, work by Mahbubani (2008, among other writings).

Eekelaar's framework is Eurocentric. One could ask what the problem is in being Eurocentric, since we are in Europe, and should accept the premises on which Europeans have learned over time to formulate their own conceptions of ethical and legal order, and that newcomers should learn to adapt to them as quickly as possible. Indeed, this demand seems to be a part of the European common sense. To accept this, however, we also have to accept the foundational role that liberalism, which was brought forth within Western culture's now-occluded Christian religious structures, plays in culture, ethics and law, although there is no reason why we should do that since it is neither self-evident that agreement will be arrived at about *what* founds society nor, indeed, that societies need *founding* on *anything*.

I focus my comments on Eekelaar's tripartite structure of models, namely the 'authorisation', 'delegation' and 'purposive abstention' models, with more attention to the first two. Given the dominant framing of Eekelaar's arguments within a liberal framework, I presume that the very possibility of thinking of those models, and about them, also emanates from within that framework. Meanwhile, Eekelaar's examples mostly derive from their embedding in non-Western traditions, either in jurisdictions outside Euro-America or within diaspora communities of non-Western origins in Europe. The logic of Eekelaar's framework means that they are so divorced from their cultural embedding that they are severely distorted, and for the first two models this unwittingly achieves the result that Eekelaar wishes, which is the nullification of any value they may have as exemplars.

I THE 'AUTHORISATION' MODEL

Eekelaar's 'authorisation model' presumes a top-down methodology, viewing the state as the authorising body, and groups (or leaders, etc) as its authorisees. It raises the question why he does not consider taking a bottom-up approach in a socio-legal sense regarding problems that might need resolution by the state or any sector of society, either on a case-by-case basis or by providing some general, though group-specific mechanisms by which individuals may have recourse to state law. This would have required some empirical research evidence, which Eekelaar largely fails to bring to bear. Although Eekelaar intends to discuss the utility of the authorisation model for contemporary contexts, its main exemplar is the so-called Ottoman *millet* system. He presents what is in my opinion an inaccurate, stereotypical and basically Orientalist view of Ottoman legal pluralism. In other words, he presents versions of the Western experience of it, referring to Kymlicka's 'federation of theocracies' and Shachar's 'religious particularism'.[3] Although it is not widely acknowledged,

---

[3] Edward Said's work is the seminal text of the critique of Orientalism (Said 1979). However, I rely here on the clarification provided by Balagangadhara and Keppens (2009) of Orientalism as an account of how the West experienced the Orient and as the structuring of that experience.

because of the amnesia regarding legal history, before the Enlightenment and the introduction of uniform state laws, European legal orders exhibited comparable arrangements, as demonstrated by the long-standing situation of Jews who had their own laws but who were then subtly (England: see Freeman 1981, Finestein 1993) or more strongly (France: see Schechter 2003, Schwarzfuchs 1979) brought under a regime of uniform state laws.

The Ottomans recognised many different jurisdictions. They were not only focused on recognising the authority of religious courts, but allowed other forms of self-regulation, eg, in the Kurdish areas (Bayır 2013). They lived in a complex segmented state with many internal variations. Eekelaar assumes (or at least does not divulge any awareness) that the Ottoman context did not manifest some interplay between state, the communities and their religious norms. Oftentimes *sharia* courts were also required to enforce the *kanoon* (state law, legislation). Further, it did not necessarily follow that individuals were 'confined' to their own theocratic jurisdictional boxes. Studies of Ottoman courts and of other places where Muslims were politically dominant show evidence of 'forum shopping', both among Muslim courts of different types and across the religious divide, eg, Christians seeking divorces in Muslim courts because their own canon laws would not allow it![4] A contemporary manifestation of the phenomenon is found with Muslim women in Britain who are approaching Sharia councils for religious divorces and the 'secular' official courts for financial claims.

The alleged problem relating to the non-homogeneity of groups, as cited by Eekelaar, is a non-argument, for seldom is homogeneity regarded as a precondition to the recognition of various types of jurisdiction, while heterogeneity does not prevent recognition in different ways. Maintenance of a uniform legal order on the ground of the non-homogeneity of the social field may, in practice, mean a legal order based on the dominant cultural formation. In terms of examples where non-homogeneity does not lead to uniformity in the legal order, one could point to the more than ten different Christian communities recognised under Syrian law today, an inheritance of the Ottoman era, an overlooked pluralist solution that may be threatened in the current tussle for power in the country. Contemporary India exhibits a situation where various types of Muslim law, among other orders, are recognised.[5]

Eekelaar is evidently correct when he points out, albeit in a footnote, that competing non-state jurisdictions continually emerge to challenge the state's interpretation of law. This argument relates to the state's co-optation of the norms of some communities which then continually raises the issue of disjunction between

---

[4] See, eg, Al-Qattan (1999) for non-Muslims' use of a Muslim court in Damascus. For a study on Muslim courts in western India, where similar processes of inter-jurisdictional shopping are evident during the period of Mughal ascendancy, see Hasan (2004).

[5] References to custom in Indian legislation, for instance in the Hindu Marriage Act 1955, demonstrate that, in practice, state officials will be paying attention to a huge diversity of local and familial practices.

living and official versions of customary or religious laws; or, as noted, the availability of different options to litigants makes recourse to more than one field attractive. This 'problem' never goes away in any jurisdiction, no matter what legal arrangements are adopted officially, as law is a dynamic phenomenon and no state can control everything or expect to freeze society at one point. Indeed, any state needs to adopt the attitude, and have appropriate mechanisms in place, to continually respond to the changes in the social field, and correspondingly be able to negotiate with its constituent groups. While states such as Britain have generally attempted to keep such modalities in place, responses to non-dominant groups have generally been slow and often based on priorities determined through a dominant cultural framework.

It is not quite clear what Eekelaar is thinking of when speaking about the conflict between human rights norms and various types of authorisation models, and on what basis he assumes that there would be such a clash. I agree that there can be clashes, but to what extent are they the consequence of approaching the interpretation of human rights in a Eurocentric and thus universalising or homogenising fashion? Or can human rights only be Eurocentric? It is true that human rights and liberal values emanate from the Western Christian religious tradition (Ruston 2004; Pera 2008) and, to that extent, clashes do arise from the culture-specific character of different ethical traditions. In the process, one would have to provide reasonable grounds for why human rights norms – based as they are on the European Christian and liberal tradition – should outtrump other traditions followed in a community, rather than be imposed unilaterally. Certainly, there often arises a need to ameliorate the oppressive effects of certain activities within society and one must respect the internal plurality within any group right down to individual level. The state could hold out some offer of protection for such people, assuming that it is competent, not jurisdictionally, but in terms of having the knowledge and cultural adeptness to do so. Can our states promise such adeptness? Much evidence rather points in the other direction, and reading Eekelaar's account does not make me more confident that we have yet developed the know-how to be able to deal with problems that might arise. In fact, it reinforces my view that Western state officials and spokespersons working through official legal systems very often have no real idea about how best to address individual concerns, but are often working on the basis of stereotypes or pursuing other agendas. The evidence proffered by Mavis Maclean (chapter seven of this book) worryingly bears this out, as legislation that ostensibly relies on civil law mechanisms to protect victims of forced marriages turns out to be enforced primarily by the crime control agencies, and the actual criminalisation of forced marriage appears to be on the legislative horizon in England.

I also question how real the issue of exit is. Eekelaar in particular and liberals in general are certainly preoccupied with it. Do members of communities, because they object to some practice, effectively demand exit from the group in which they have been reared and socialised? The issue of exiting and opting-in seems to be a fantasy of liberal ethical theorists demanded by their individualism and attachment to rational choice (again with its Christian underpinnings), and not on a study of the socio-legal evidence. From a different viewpoint, the performance of law occurs at a daily level, as 'living law' (Ehrlich 1936), precisely because of the effects of socialisation and considerations of appropriate behaviour inculcated over time, not as a matter of opt-in or opt-out. So, the problem of exit seems to have a fictitious and social-scientifically illiterate premise. Indian law provides many examples of opt-in laws. For instance, in the case of marriage laws there is a possibility of opting into a 'secular' framework instead of marrying under one of the personal laws.[6] However, this may or may not have implications for 'exit' or group membership. In fact, some evidence – mainly seen within legal practice in immigration and in other cases with a transnational dimension – reveals that individuals have simultaneously opted in to different types of marriage law in India and elsewhere for a variety of reasons ranging from dodgy legal advice or for immigration purposes.[7] This causes real problems for British officials and judges, while the individuals concerned regularly get penalised because British functionaries are bedazzled or really want to penalise such people. In all this, can one derive the conclusion that choosing to formalise a relationship according to one state norm entails the abandonment of one's inherited legal order?

Eekelaar also worries about his authorisation model leading to a reduction in incentives for the state to perform protective and supportive roles with respect to, say, elder or child care. On that point I would return to my observation earlier that a growing amount of evidence in Britain appears to indicate state ineptitude in dealing with the families who often resent intrusions by the state. Less state intervention might actually be more, not less, welcome and could enhance the willingness of community members to take on their share of familial responsibilities. In most countries around the world it is assumed that these are not the state's function but the responsibility of families and social groups. In fact, such social policies are presumed in, or aided through, the adoption of specific legal stances taken by the state and its judges (see Menski 2001a for India). The state-centric view seems more specific to Western countries.

Eekelaar addresses various positions taken by Shachar, whose book *Multicultural Jurisdictions*, is a sustained discussion, with reference to comparative material, of the ways in which Western states could arrive at sharing jurisdictional competences with leaders of what she calls *nomoi* groups. Relying on Shachar, Eekelaar is concerned that conferring jurisdiction on groups to administer their own norms could entrench 'reactive culturalism' whereby the

---

[6] See the Special Marriage Act 1954. Also see Juvenile Justice (Care and Protection of Children) Act 2000 (as amended) for adoption under the general law rather than the Hindu personal law.

[7] My knowledge of such cases derives mainly from being asked to act as an expert witness on foreign law in legal proceedings within British courts and tribunals. Such cases often do not get reported and the generality of legal researchers and practitioners will not get to know of them. For an account of some of my experiences as an expert witness, see Shah (2011: 35–52).

groups become defensive about their distinctiveness and less open to adaptation. Despite some cautionary remarks, it might be useful to bear in mind that Shachar's thesis is that, on balance, groups which are *denied* their cultural autonomy engage in 'reactive culturalism' while those who have it recognised, she argues, are presumed to engage in the process she refers to as 'transformative accommodation', with commensurate changes in *nomoi* group leaders' and state behaviour. This type of accommodation occurs within communities anyway, even where there is a policy of general non-recognition of *nomoi* group norms or practices as exemplified by Western jurisdictions (although with some exceptions, eg, for first nation's peoples). Studies of diasporic minority groups' adaptation show a gradual building in of the dominant legal order to their own routines, although they may not necessarily abandon their own group ways while so adapting. Rather, they will engage with the state system for the benefits it provides to them. Menski's evidence regarding what he terms *angrezi shariat* (Pearl and Menski 1998: 58–59; Menski 2001b), which has even been taken notice of in the British Parliament, is precisely this kind of development, although Eekelaar overlooks it completely.[8] Muslims may also shop internally as the evidence for Sharia councils cited by Gillian Douglas (chapter eleven of this book) shows. Studies of Sharia councils and Jewish *batei din* indicate (and again Douglas' study shows) that, even without formal recognition, they are aware of operating 'under the shadow of state law', providing further indications of transformative accommodation on the part of non-state groups.[9]

It seems therefore that the main attraction and added value of Shachar's untested and largely hypothetical model is that it is the *state* which would then have incentives to mould its behaviour in favour of recognition so as not to lose the support of members of minority *nomoi* groups or its leaders. However, the state does not necessarily act in that direction as the Ontario example demonstrates. In Ontario, the state, and the more vocal sections of the wider society, reacted *against* the minimal recognition which was operating through the mechanisms regulating family arbitrations, thus driving matters further into the informal sphere.[10] The Arbitration and Mediation Services (Equality) Bill, which had its first reading in the British Parliament on 7 June 2011, makes an even stronger statement in that it attempts to drive Sharia councils out of business altogether. Some American states have also moved to pass legislation to prevent courts paying heed to *sharia* based claims. Shachar (2010) now refers to such examples as indicative of the trend towards 'privatised diversity', with a wall of separation between state and religion.[11] While this is often the starting

---

[8]   Lord Lester, House of Lords Debates, 30 Jun 2000, cols 1246–47.
[9]   See also Taş (2012), a study of the 'secular' Kurdish Peace Committee in London, which reveals a similar picture.
[10]   See the Family Statute Law Amendment Act 2006 of Ontario, stipulating that only family arbitration decisions made in accordance with Ontario and Canadian laws may be enforced in courts.
[11]   Shachar may be drawing on the discourse on the 'wall of separation' between religion and the state often referred to in the United States, and generalising it to Western jurisdictions, but it may also be read as a cloaked reference to the building of an actual wall to keep communities apart in her

point for most Western jurisdictions, recently reinforced by some reactionary legislation and judicial decisions, many states have been developing consultation mechanisms despite the contention that diversity makes that process excessively complex. This already happens with respect, say, to the UK Government's consultations with the Muslim Council of Britain (MCB) or Mosques and Imams National Advisory Board (MINAB) or by individual or groups of MPs or House of Lords Members with, for example, Dalit organisations[12] or with more specific issues like the establishment of religious schools and so on. This is not to suggest that the 'take me to your leader' phenomenon is not without problems, but it is, after all, part and parcel of managing complex societies. A future research agenda would more deeply analyse the ways in which states choose to 'listen' to certain lobby groups while ignoring other voices.

Eekelaar's assumptions about groups controlling their members result in his thinking that groups (or presumably some 'leaders') decide for their members whether to allow the latter to have recourse to official laws. This does not seem really grounded in socio-legal reality but it would be interesting to know about evidence of the contended-for scenarios. There could be obstacles placed in the way of some people, as with women (or a seemingly increasing number of men) who face domestic violence by other family members, or because of their own unwillingness to engage authorities, especially when their bargaining power is less strong, for instance, because of the danger of losing immigration status.[13] However, the more interesting hypothesis here is that people use state law selectively, and often to enhance their bargaining powers at other levels of the socio-legal matrix. This requires some real study, but cannot be accomplished within Eekelaar's framework which, because of its constraints, skirts around socio-legal evidence. As to the question about one party 'wanting in' while the other objects, surely it is not outwith the capacity of clever judges to manage, although there may be issues of compliance with court orders and the effectiveness of state law as some preliminary evidence among British judges, and also research of family courtrooms in Belgium, is showing.[14]

---

native Israel, which was found to be contrary to international law by the International Court of Justice. See its Advisory Opinion in the Legal Consequences of the Construction of a Wall in the Occupied Palestinian Territory, 9 July 2004.

[12] The campaign to include caste as a ground of discrimination in the UK's Equality Act 2010 was orchestrated by Dalit Christians and Buddhists in alliance with sympathetic British parliamentarians, with British Hindu groups not being consulted at all, thus evidencing the contemporary persistence of the colonial construction of Hinduism and the 'selective hearing' that law-makers often display.

[13] See, for instance, the observations of the immigration judge cited in *Ishtiaq v Secretary of State for the Home Department* [2007] EWCA Civ 386 to the effect that conditions imposed by the Immigration Directorate Instructions undermined the purpose of the domestic violence policy (offering exemption from compliance with the 2-year probationary period for spouse immigrants) and discriminated against Asian women who could not communicate effectively in English and who were unable to act independently.

[14] For complaints by an English judge of the Family Division of the High Court that 'the population do not generally take our decisions seriously enough and do not obey the orders promptly and fully', see Coleridge (2010).

II THE 'DELEGATION' MODEL

In the 'delegation model', Eekelaar conflates a large number of different sorts of legal systems, ranging from the Western uniform law model to the personal law type of system as adopted in India. For Eekelaar, the common thread seems to be that the state is the main actor whether interpreting a uniform law or doing the same with a set of state-defined personal laws. The focus is therefore on a variation of what Chiba (1986: 5–6; 1989: 139) calls 'official law' whereby the state enacts or sanctions various laws. However, the sheer variety of legal systems brought under the delegation model by Eekelaar means that it is not obvious that the cases he selects necessarily fall together as a class, although this is somewhat occluded because of the rather de-contextualised manner of citing and discussing the cases.

Eekelaar's citing of the *Shah Bano* case from India and the more recent *Uddin* case in the English Court of Appeal merits some further comment to illustrate the problem.[15] Briefly, in the former case, the Indian Supreme Court held that Muslim divorcing husbands have an obligation to maintain their ex-wives for a reasonable period beyond the stipulated *idda* (three menstrual cycles) period *as a matter of Muslim law*. Eekelaar warns against the potentially 'hostile reaction' to state interference in its personal law by a group or its leaders as indeed occurred in India where Muslims launched mass protests. However, the aftermath of that judgment has often been interpreted incorrectly whereby it is assumed that the Indian legislature gave in to the protests by restoring the situation prior to the Supreme Court's decision. In fact, the opposite is true. The legislation which followed the *Shah Bano* case, the Muslim Women (Protection of Rights on Divorce) Act 1986, actually reinforces the authority of the Indian courts to order maintenance and provision which is reasonable and fair, and case law from Indian states sees it vigorously applied (Menski 2001a: 231–94). This is not to argue that interference in the affairs of a community might not result in protests and even 'hostile reactions', especially in the case of Muslims, where personal law issues can be a quite sensitive matter. In that sense, the *Shah Bano* protests in India may well provide a warning of things that might come to Europe in future, while various other events like the *Satanic Verses* and the Mohamed cartoons affairs already indicate the potential. However, 'hostile reactions' may occur whether or not there is a perceived state-directed interpretation of personal law and the issue should probably be considered as part of a wider problem of how any state meets the concerns of a non-dominant community.[16]

---

[15] *Mohd Ahmed Khan v Shah Bano Begum*, AIR 1985 SC 945 (India); *Uddin v Choudhury* [2009] EWCA Civ 1205 (England).

[16] Could we, for instance consider the riots in England in the summer of 2011 in the same light? More broadly of course the riots are not an isolated event but are part of what is seemingly a global protest movement against excessive state-focused positivism and authoritarianism which definitely has legal dimensions.

The discussion of the *Uddin* judgment by Eekelaar also begs some questions. The Court of Appeal's decision was a refusal to appeal to itself although, effectively, it upholds the county court's judgment. The case concerned a very short marriage between two Bangladeshis who had not registered their marriage. Certain money and jewellery was given to the woman and some had allegedly been taken by her and her mother and the issue was whether it should be returned. While the Court of Appeal took cognisance of the fact that a Sharia council had dealt with the case and of the evidence of the '*sharia* expert', it is not clear that it was 'enforcing' the Sharia in the way it seems contended by Eekelaar. In fact, one could even say the opposite. The complainant man was being told: 'you had an unregistered *nikah* marriage, and went to the Sharia council, so now you have to accept it'. The county court did not know how to deal with the issue of Muslim law and obtained a specific interpretation of the facts and applicable Islamic position from Shaikh Siddiqi who, typically for many *sharia* scholars, sidestepped the social considerations surrounding payments on marriage. This in turn begs the following questions: should what is basically a non-marriage in which the parties did not like each other, probably never had sexual relations, and could have been forced into marrying, lead to enrichment by thousands of pounds? And what precisely is the role of the expert? So the failure of the official courts to ask these questions meant an unjust result but the courts accepted the story as recited by the 'expert', Shaikh Siddiqi, sided with the 'downtrodden' Muslim woman, and nobody was any the wiser. I read this case as one where Muslim legal politics is being played out before our very eyes and we (and the courts) do not know what to do; or are maybe purposely silent, hiding behind fictional walls of separation! Perhaps Eekelaar is correct then if he is suggesting that we play with Muslim law without acknowledging it. The Indian courts, by contrast, demonstrate their awareness of the consequences of what happens in a non-welfare state context when Muslim women are thrown out on the street with nothing except some remaining *mahr*, raising questions about who will look after them. So the decision by the Indian Supreme Court was arguably the right one, as with the legislation which followed (although misinterpreted by most writers, including Shachar), and the one by the county court and Court of Appeal in England is arguably wrong![17] This could be an object lesson about the ignorance of the British courts and how the whole Sharia question needs a lot more study and work if official organs are to obtain a socio-legally realistic picture of Muslim legal practices anywhere in Europe.

Overall, Eekelaar is concerned that, in the state's choosing to impose law, there arises a disjuncture between the state's version of religious or customary law and the actual living versions. In fact, socio-legal work shows that this is an

---

[17] I do not think that Eekelaar is ignorant of the issue, however, as his reference to the British Columbia case of Nathoo [1996] BCJ No 2720 (SC) (as cited by Fournier) makes evident. What is not clear is why he does not apply the same criticism of 'over-compensation' to the wife in Uddin.

ever present dilemma. In India, the *Shah Bano* case and its statutory reinforcement seems to have led to a new movement for non-state Sharia councils, to provide the *ulema* (learned men, scholars) with a platform through which to find ways to avoid state interference as directly as occurred in *Shah Bano*, but how could they prevent women seeking the help of state courts? In fact, the Indian developments may also have had an impact in influencing the setting up of Sharia councils in Britain, Canada and elsewhere, which might indicate that in a globalising environment state jurisdictions are less and less in control of such trans-jurisdictional developments. Lest it be understood that erecting walls of separation are only a Western liberal fantasy, one might add that the steering away from state jurisdictions by many Muslims may also be indicative of objections to Hindu or secular, Christian and Jewish judges ruling on Muslim law matters.

III THE 'PURPOSIVE ABSTENTION'/'CULTURAL VOLUNTARISM' MODEL

Finally, and briefly, I turn to the 'purposive abstention/cultural voluntarism model' which seems to be preferred by Eekelaar. This model seems basically reflective of the status quo. It reinstates the wall of separation between religion and state law and entails the application of state norms, adapted in so far as they might offer room for the accommodation of minority norms. The state could, however, intervene in the private sphere where there are issues of harm to human rights of individuals. Most of the discussion in that section then acts as a justification for intervention in minority groups and questions the right to cultural identity as providing a defence to the protection of minority group norms. Basically, it looks as though Eekelaar regards culture as not worth defending, although it is unclear whether he is thinking of particular cultural practices or culture in general and what his theory of identity is. I do not say much here about Eekelaar's defence of the third model as, again, he raises some chimerical ethical problems only to diminish their force. The more important point here has to be the fact that his approach is rather status quoist and basically supports the retention of the hegemony of the dominant cultural community in a state.

As noted, Eekelaar seems to assume that every addressee agrees with this liberal approach which pits individuals as being against their groups, rather than as embedded and socialised within their communities. This basically follows the liberal and Eurocentric logic of individualism and implicitly says that those who do not like it can lump it! Eekelaar's discussion hardly takes us forward in helping to think more creatively and with a more socio-legally informed perspective about the ways in which minority accommodation can be thought through. While advocating purposive blindness to the everyday self-regulatory mechanisms within communities, he would support state intervention only on grounds of harm to human rights. This would be unsatisfactory for all concerned since, even if we are to focus just on the minority cases that pop up in the official sphere, there is much more at stake than issues of harm. Rather, close and continued attention to socio-legal reality and bargaining processes within minority groups should remain on the agenda. The positing of false problems with which to shadow box in the make-believe world of liberal legality seems quite passé.

REFERENCES

Ahdar, R and Leigh, I (2005) *Religious Freedom in the Liberal State* (Oxford, Oxford University Press).

Al-Qattan, N (1999) 'Dhimmis in the Muslim Court: Legal Autonomy and Religious Discrimination' 31 *International Journal of Middle East Studies* 429.

Balagangadhara, SN and Keppens, M (2009) 'Reconceptualizing the Postcolonial Project: Beyond the Strictures and Structures of Orientalism' 11 *Interventions* 50.

Bayır, D (2013) *Minorities and Nationalism in Turkish Law* (Farnham, Ashgate).

Chiba, M (ed) (1986) *Asian Indigenous Law in Interaction with Received Law* (London and New York, KPI).

—— (1989): *Legal Pluralism: Toward a General Theory through Japanese Legal Culture* (Tokyo, Tokai University Press).

Coleridge, PJD (2010) 'Let's hear it for the child: Restoring the authority of the Family Court, blue skies and sacred cows', speech given at the Association of Lawyers for Children, 21st annual conference (Southampton, 25–27 November 2010): www.judiciary.gov.uk/Resources/JCO/Documents/Speeches/speech-coleridge-j-assoc-lawyers-for-children.pdf.

Ehrlich, E (1936) *Fundamental Principles of the Sociology of Law* (Cambridge, MA, Harvard University Press).

Finestein, I (1993) *Jewish Society in Victorian England* (London, Valletine Mitchell).

Freeman, MDA (1981) 'Jews and the Law of Divorce in England' 4 *The Jewish Law Annual* 276.

Hasan, F (2004) *State and Locality in Mughal India: Power Relations in Western India, 1572–1730* (Cambridge, Cambridge University Press).

Mahbubani, K (2008) *New Asian Hemisphere: The Irresistible Shift of Global Power to the East* (New York, Public Affairs).

Menski, W (2001a) *Modern Indian Family Law* (Richmond, Curzon).

—— (2001b) 'Muslim Law in Britain' 62 *Journal of Asian and African Studies* 127.

Parekh, B (in conversation with R Jahanbegloo) (2011) *Talking politics* (New Delhi, Oxford University Press).

Pearl, D and Menski, W (1998) *Muslim Family Law* (London, Sweet & Maxwell).

Pera, M (2008) *Why we should Call Ourselves Christians: The Religious Roots of Free Societies* (New York, Encounter Books).

Ruston, R (2004) *Human Rights and the Image of God* (London, SCM-Canterbury Press).

Said, E (1979) *Orientalism* (London, Routledge and Kegan Paul).

Schechter, R (2003) *Obstinate Hebrews: Representations of Jews in France, 1715–1815* (Berkeley and Los Angeles, California, University of California Press).

Schwarzfuchs, S (1979) *Napoleon, the Jews and the Sanhedrin* (London, Routledge).

Shachar, A (2001) *Multicultural Jurisdictions: Cultural Differences and Women's Rights* (Cambridge, Cambridge University Press).

—— (2010) 'Faith in Law? Diffusing Tensions between Diversity and Equality' 36 *Philosophy and Social Criticism* 395.

Shah, P (2010) 'The Indian Dimension of An-Na'im's *Islam and the Secular State*' in M-C Foblets and J-Y Carlier (eds), *Islam and Europe: Crises are Challenges* (Leuven, Leuven University Press).

—— (2011) 'When South Asians Marry Trans-jurisdictionally: Some Reflections on Immigration Cases by an "Expert"' in L Holden (ed), *Cultural Expertise and Litigation: Patterns, Conflicts, Narratives* (London, Routledge).

Taş, L (2012) *Kurds in the UK: Legal Pluralism and Alternative Dispute Resolution*. PhD thesis, School of Law, Queen Mary, University of London.

Vertovec, S (2007) 'Super-diversity and its Implications' 30 *Ethnic and Racial Studies* 1024.

4

Muslim Dispute Resolution in Britain: Towards a New Framework of Family Law Governance?

SAMIA BANO

I INTRODUCTION

TODAY, THE CHANGING nature of resolving disputes in matters of commercial, civil and family law generates much discussion and debate. Questions regarding the emergence and type of new methods of dispute resolution have led to an unprecedented rise in the number of scholarly and policy orientated initiatives that seek to both promote and critique such developments (see Genn 1999). Such debates fall within the wider discussions on promoting access to justice for all citizens and to better understand the relationship between cultural and social norms that may underpin such forms of dispute resolution. Indeed the contemporary landscape of civil and family justice is part of a renewed recognition by the state to build on mechanisms of Alternative Dispute Resolution (ADR) mechanisms that are evidenced by the increasing use of arbitration, mediation, conciliation and initiatives developed by practioners such as collaborative law. As part of these contemporary developments issues such as cultural diversity and the necessity to accommodate community needs also underpin such initiatives. We have therefore seen the rise of cross-cultural mediation mechanisms that have come to the fore in determining both the use and delivery of services and the desire to accommodate the needs of all users. In essence, then, we see not only the emergence of new forms of legal cultures, but the ways in which new forms of informal and formal adjudication in all their complexity emerge and develop within groups, communities and networks. This increasing privatisation of disputes takes shape both outside the traditional adversarial framework of family law but also seeks to resolve matrimonial disputes in conjunction with state law process and practice.

More importantly, it raises a number of fundamental questions relating to citizenship, personhood and agency and the extent to which the privatisation of ADR mechanisms may undermine traditional conceptions of justice, 'equality before the law' and 'common citizenship'. A further question relates to the ways in which ADR mechanisms may in fact increase citizen participation in civil society and the effect on changing patterns of state governance in resolving family law disputes. Over the years legal scholars and practioners have recognised the role played by culture and more recently religion in the ways in which matrimonial and family law disputes are resolved.

In Britain, we have seen the emergence of community and family mediation mechanisms that seek to resolve matrimonial disputes both outside the framework of state law and in conjunction with state law mechanisms. For example, the work of Shah-Kazemi (2001) and Bano (2007) illustrates the emergence of Sharia councils within diasporic Muslim communities that act as mechanisms to resolve matrimonial disputes within the family, home and local communities. This development has been followed by the emergence of the Muslim Arbitration Tribunal (herein referred to as 'MAT') which operates as a civil law mechanism under the auspices of the Arbitration Act 1996 to produce decisions that may be enforced and relied on in the civil courts. Within British Muslim communities we therefore currently have a three-tier approach to resolving matrimonial disputes: state law, unofficial community mediation (Sharia councils) and the new Muslim Arbitration Tribunal.

This chapter draws on existing scholarship and original empirical research to consider the nature of Muslim dispute resolution in Britain today and questions the use of religious dispute resolution mechanisms by Muslim women. In doing so it cautions against the increasingly polarised debates between those who call for the recognition of religious bodies in matters of family law and those who seek to monitor their practice and ban their use altogether.

II WHAT IS MUSLIM DISPUTE RESOLUTION IN BRITAIN?

In the 1990s, the legal anthropologist Werner Menski (1997; 2001) first published a series of articles based on his research which documented the ways in which South Asian Muslims practised, utilised and perceived 'law' in Britain. Drawing on the work of Masaji Chiba (1986) he described this new understanding of law as a complex process of legal and cultural practice that drew on Islamic and English legal precepts of law (mixed in with cultural norms and values) to form a new hybrid understanding of legal practices in Britain which he broadly described as 'Angrezi Sharia'. He went onto to develop his work to illustrate both the dangers and problems associated with what was then largely described as 'ethnic minority laws' practised under the rubric of state law. In particular, he argued that state ignorance of such practices left vulnerable parties with little if any legal protection and allowed some individuals to circumvent the law in order to promote personal interests at the expense of more vulnerable parties. More importantly, perhaps, he argued that the consequences of this had led to privatised unofficial and de-regularised systems of religious laws operating in the private sphere which undermined both the authority and recognition of state law. And while promoting the principle of diversity in law and the diverse ways in which individuals seek to resolve matrimonial disputes, he argued that the law must evolve to recognise multiple systems of dispute resolution that more specifically include rather than exclude personal systems of family law. In this way the universal principles of liberal legality, justice, equality before the law and common citizenship then have real meaning to all in society, applicable to all irrespective of differences in ethnic, cultural and religious backgrounds (see Pearl and Menski 1998).

This work provided the impetus for a whole new scholarship in Britain (see Shah Kazemi 2001; Yilmaz 2002, 2005). In 2005, I completed postdoctoral research based on the experiences of a group of Pakistani Muslim women using Sharia councils to obtain a Muslim divorce certificate in England. This study (Bano 2007) produced some insights into the workings of a small number of Sharia councils in England and focused on the experiences of British Muslim women using these bodies to resolve matrimonial disputes. My interest in this area was both personal and professional. On a personal note as a British Muslim Pakistani woman I was intrigued to find out why my peers had chosen to use a Sharia council to resolve matrimonial disputes on family and relationship breakdown. More importantly, what were the personal consequences, if any, for these women in their use of these bodies? Were the rights of Muslim women in effect being eroded in the private sphere outside the protection of state law? Was the emergence of Sharia councils the impetus to introduce a parallel legal system in Britain whereby Muslims would be encouraged to use religious bodies to resolve family law type disputes simply on the basis of their religious identity and belonging to a particular Muslim religious community? Why do some British Muslim women choose to use the services of religious bodies which may seem (at least to some outside and within the community) as patriarchal in nature and unequal in their protection of the rights and interests of Muslim women? Was this a clear-cut example of social coercion and the exertion of family and community pressure some women may experience in being compelled to use these services? Theoretically such new explanations of dispute resolution were being frequently discussed under the rubric of multiculturalism in theoretically informed ways across disciplines, in particular politics and history. For example, the rise in theoretical debates in liberal political theory, crudely summed up today as the Okin-inspired debate (1999) of 'Is multiculturalism bad for women?' with its focus on conflicts between community and individual rights (see Taylor 2007), questioned the increasingly tenuous relationship between the rights of the individual and moves to accommodate group rights in the name of culture and religion, with little analyses on protecting vulnerable members of the group, most often women. These debates also mirrored a theoretical re-examination by legal scholars drawing on a postmodern analysis of law which sought to better understand the practice of cultural and religious systems of law at times in opposition to state law. Some of this analysis drew on the practice of multiculturalism in Britain and the idea of cultural rights that were based on fixed notions of religious and cultural norms, values and practices and understood as essential and homogeneous in nature: in other words such scholarship seemed to make clear that you either belonged to your community or you did not, the traditional insider versus outsider debates. Yet I began to wonder whether individuals actually experience identity and law in such a fixed and structured way. More importantly, I was aware that decades of sociological research had given us plenty of data to reveal that identity can never be understood in a fixed or essential way but actually is always in flux, challenged and fluid. Of course this is not to deny that individuals, communities, groups and networks cannot and do not operate along fixed structures and boundaries that can be based on fixed notions of belonging in order to maintain group loyalty, cohesion and commitment (in what they may perceive as a challenge to their survival). But in reality, sociologists have also drawn our attention to the fact that for many individuals living within cultural and religious communities, identity is far more fragmented, messy, complex and contested. And furthermore, Islamic scholars point out that this idea of identity as one based on personal and group contestation also underpins Islam and Islamic thought, a process in which choice and belonging to a Muslim community then becomes more autonomous and consensual rather than being predicated exclusively on group membership and belonging; in the case of Muslims, belonging to the Muslim Ummah. So how can Muslim dispute resolution in family law matters be understood in Britain today? And why do the debates continue to be framed in the context of those who belong to the community and seek the recognition of religious councils in Britain and those who do not?

A What is Muslim Family Law?

The term 'Sharia' in classical Muslim law refers to 'definition of practice'. As Wheeler (1996: 34) points out, the Sharia 'determines how certain aspects of everyday life are to be practiced according to the model provided by the canon'. This model is established in the key sources of Islam, the Qu'ran and Sunnah and revelation contained in the text of the Qu'ran is interpreted through the medium of the *sunnah* to indicate the contents of the Sharia. In Islam there are two main groups of Muslims – Sunni and Shia – and these groups subsequently developed their different *madhhabs* of *fiqh* or schools of law.

Islamic history illustrates how the development of Muslim jurisprudence has led to different interpretations of Islamic law. The principles of jurisprudence are referred to as *usul al-fiqh* and the methodologies for understanding and applying the Sharia are consensus (*Ijma*), critical reasoning (*Ijtihad*) and analogical reasoning (*qiyas*). Muslim scholars point to the tensions between the Sunnah and Qu'ran as the primary source of authority for the Sharia. In Sunni Islam there are four schools of legal thought and jurisprudence, namely, Shafi,

Maliki, Hanafi and Hanbali and in Shia Islam there are three schools. While each recognises the others' parameters and orthodoxy, tensions persist between them. As Abdullahi An-Naim (1990: 33) observes, far from being 'a single logical, whole, the Sharia reveals a diversity of opinions not only across schools but within them as well'.

Despite these differences, An-Naim (1990: 31) also comments that all the schools of thought concur that men and women are not to be treated equally and that even though 'Islam is probably the most uncompromising of the world's religions in its insistence on the equality of all believers before God . . . to the jurists it did not follow from the equality of "all believers" before God that men and women should be equal before the law'. Scholars also document that there is enormous literature on the nature of the conflicts generated between the different schools of Islamic jurisprudence. In this regard the growth of divergent opinion on what was understood as Islamic law was deemed as dangerous to the power and authority of Allah and led to consensus and the closing of the gates of *ijtihad* (Nasir 1986). Thus, uniformity across the four Sunni law schools was deemed necessary to safeguard the development of Islamic thought and practice. Esposito (1982: 9) however, points out that other extra-textual sources also played a key role in the implementation of Sharia law.[1] Asma Barlas (2006: 12) and An-Naim argue that the development of Muslim legal norms must be understood in the historical context in which they evolved. For example, An-Naim (1990: 26) remarks that, in spite of its 'assumed religious authority and inviolability', the Sharia is 'not the whole of Islam' but an 'interpretation of its fundamental sources as understood in a particular historical context'. Not only was the method for deriving it a 'product of the intellectual, social and political processes of Muslim history' but the 'Sharia was constructed by its founding jurists'. In the process, some jurists tried to reconcile it with what they perceived to be the community's best interest at that time; others 'simply disregarded reality and addressed themselves to an ideal situation in theorizing on what *ought* to be the case'.[2]

B Sharia Councils

Over the past few years, scholars have explored the nature of Sharia councils in Britain, drawing on the experiences of Muslim women using their services to resolve matrimonial disputes (see Shah-Kazemi 2001; Bano 2007; Yilmaz 2005). Still, very little is known about *how* Sharia councils operate as ADR mechanisms

---

[1] There are three key principles: *Istihan*, the principle of juristic preference that comes into play when analogical reasoning seems to rigid to ensure equity; *Istislan*, the principle of public interest that comes into play in cases where public interest is not 'textually specified'; and *Istishab*, the principle of presumed continuity that bases rulings on antecedents deemed valid unless proven otherwise.

[2] The codification of Shariah in different countries has led to extensive discussion among scholars on the interpretive methodologies used to develop Shariah: An Naim (1990: 37).

in Britain. One particular point of dispute is the number of Sharia councils operating in England and Wales. In the report, *Sharia Law or 'One Law for All'* Denis MacEoin (2009) argued that at least 85 'courts' are known to exist in the United Kingdom. This figure was derived from an internet search of mosques and community organisations, many of which may not in practice operate as Sharia councils. Therefore, bearing in mind the obvious methodological limitations to such research, this figure must be considered with some caution. In 2010, the Ministry of Justice commissioned a report entitled 'An Exploratory Study of Sharia councils in England with respect to Family Law' which identified 30 Sharia councils operating in England. The aim of this project was to learn more about the nature and scope of Sharia councils in England, with a particular focus on their administration. The project also looked more generally at the feasibility of further research in this sensitive area (forthcoming).

We do therefore have some literature with divergent opinions among scholars as to the reasons for the emergence and establishment of Sharia councils in contemporary multicultural Britain, but there remains little substantive discussion on the ways in which these bodies facilitate state law mechanisms in relation to resolving matrimonial disputes (Shah-Kazemi 2001). Scholars point to the fact that Sharia councils must be understood as part of the British socio-legal fabric of family governance and very much a product of British multicultural society as they have failed to emerge in the same way in other European countries. And therefore attempting to understand this process of dispute resolution as *the* Islamic approach to resolving matrimonial disputes is not only a difficult task, but suggests that there is some kind of unified understanding of what constitutes Islamic law, rather than understanding the patterns of Muslim dispute resolution as descriptions of an Islamic legal culture influenced by the social, political and economic context in which it is placed.

In Britain, the emergence of Sharia councils can be traced to a diverse set of social, political and religious developments in civil society. The formation of Islamic religious organisations and their engagement with the state has been characterised by the practice of multiculturalism and the development of 'multicultural' state policies to accommodate cultural and religious 'difference'. And, in the past two decades, a growing number of scholars has explored the changing and contested nature of this relationship which has revealed a new discursive space of engagement, contestation and negotiation between minority ethnic communities and the state. One way of viewing this new relationship has been the claim that cultural and religious communities actively seek to avoid interaction and possible conflict with the secular state and hence retreat to the privatised sphere of local Muslim community where matrimonial disputes are resolved according to principles of Muslim family law.[3]

---

[3] Steve Vertovec (1996) suggests that multicultural policies have created specific conditions for the emergence of ethnic governance in the UK. The literature on migration provides an interesting insight into the conditions under which ethnic, cultural and religious difference is accommodated by the state and which has led to forms of 'ethnic governance'. Such organisations are fragmented, and

Sharia councils operate as unofficial legal bodies specialising in Muslim family law and providing advice and assistance to Muslim communities on these matters. They are neither unified nor represent a single school of thought but instead are made up of various different bodies representing the different schools of thought in Islam.[4] Many Sharia councils are closely affiliated to mosques[5] and this reflects developments in Islamic religious practice in Britain.[6] In his study of Muslims in Bradford, Lewis (1994: 66) argues that the socio-political establishment of Muslims in Britain via mosques and community organisations such as Sharia councils indicates a shift 'within the migrants self-perception from being sojourners to settlers'. Indeed, there has been much academic discussion and contributions to our understanding of citizenship and identity and national belonging within minority ethnic communities.[7]

In essence, a Sharia council has three key functions: issuing Muslim divorce certificates, reconciling and mediating between parties and producing expert opinion reports on matters of Muslim family law and custom to the Muslim community, solicitors and the courts. It is also significant that, in addition to providing advice and assistance on matters of Muslim family law, Sharia councils have also been set up to promote and preserve Islam within British society (Bunt 1998: 104). Subsequently, the socio-legal reality of Muslim communities in Britain can be presented as a complex scenario of a multiplicity of state laws and personal laws which challenge the assumed uniformity of state law (as

---

in opposition to competing financial demands often shift their strategies in response to local and state politics, which shapes their development and their engagement with the state. Vertovec concludes that minorities have their own reasons for choosing their 'idioms of mobilization' as well as 'their own orientations, strategies and levels of experience that affect the kind of state liaisons which they foster and maintain'. More recently, discussions on multiculturalism and narratives of national belonging illustrate the ways in which privatised forms of dispute resolution can be perceived as a challenge to existing constructions of national belonging. Indeed, it seems that one of the most pressing questions today is whether Muslims have become a politically effective diaspora that challenges the national polity. See Soyal (2000). The development of Shariah councils in Britain offers a unique opportunity to better understand the dialectical relationship between settlement patterns, community formation, religious practice and state law relations in a multi-faith, multi-ethnic society.

[4] The four ancient Islamic schools of Sunni thought can be broadly categorised as Hanafi, Maliki, Shafi'i and Hanabali. For an in-depth analysis on the historical development of these schools see Coulson (1969).

[5] *The Times* (1 April 2008) headline, 'No more Mosques' says synod Member. Prominent evangelical member of Church of England general synod called for a ban on building any more mosques in Britain. Copy of the report can be found at: www.timesonline.co/uk/tol/comment/faith.

[6] Many are based within mosques but have their own distinctive approach to dispute resolution. Mosques are classified as charitable organisations and are essentially free to develop their own policies within the framework of existing legislation. In particular, mosques play a significant role in Shariah councils by reinforcing the significance of Islamic religious practice, a significance often underpinned by the role of imams who act as a linkage between mosques and Shariah councils. For example, imams often lead religious prayer at mosques and also act as mediators in resolving marital disputes within Shariah councils. This relationship is clearly important in its emphasis on Islamic beliefs and morality and identification to a wider global Islamic culture.

[7] These tend to focus on the demands made by the 'new generation' of South Asians in Britain and debates on social cohesion, poverty and deprivation and how the concept of citizenship and multiculturalism is articulated within South Asian communities: see Modood (2007).

superior, monolithic and homogeneous) and instead points to a postmodern analyses of law and legal relations which highlights 'a diversity of laws' and 'inter-legality'. As a result, Muslims have reconstructed personal law systems of law within localised Muslim communities. Yilmaz (2005) identifies four key conditions which have led to the emergence of Sharia councils in Britain: first, according to Muslim tradition, family issues are purposively left to 'extra-judicial' regulation and this continues within Muslim diasporic communities today which choose to resolve disputes in the private sphere. Secondly, Muslims do not recognise the authority and legitimacy of Western secular law on a par with Muslim law. Thirdly, the familial notions of honour and shame prevent family disputes from being discussed in the 'public sphere' and subsequently religious laws are given greater legitimacy within religious communities. And finally, the failure of the state to recognise plural legal orders has led to the development of 'alternative' dispute resolution processes in the private sphere. This body of work challenges the essentialism and uniformity assumed in state law relations and celebrates difference in relation to the emerging parallel systems of law in operation within British society. More specifically, it contributes to our understanding of how contemporary societies are 'increasingly confronted within minority groups demanding recognition of their ethnicity and accommodation of their cultural and religious differences' (Hussain and Bagguley 2005: 13). However, it also adopts a legal prescriptive approach to understanding the emergence of Sharia councils in which they are viewed in their relationship to and oppositional role to state law with little substantive and empirical analysis of the internal dynamics of power.

More recently, research has explored the comparative nature of religious councils and tribunals operating in Britain. A recent study entitled, *Social Cohesion and Civil Law: Marriage, Divorce and Religious Courts in England and Wales* (2011) led by Professor Gillian Douglas (see chapter eleven of this book) looked specifically at the relationship between religion, divorce and access of law. The study focused on the work of three tribunals, the Birmingham Sharia Council, the London Beth Din of the United Synagogue and the National Tribunal for Wales of the Roman Catholic Church. It found both diversity and commonalities between these three mechanisms of dispute resolution but each sought to avoid conflict with state law in matters of family law. The authors found the process of resolving disputes to be more open and flexible rather than based on rigid religious laws. For example:

> Each religious tribunal in our study sees itself as applying a body of religious 'law' in the sense of a code regarded by adherents as binding on them. However either the autonomous position of the particular tribunal, or the breadth of the rules which might be applied to the case before it, provides a degree of flexibility to the decision-maker. None of the three tribunals we studied is constrained by a system of binding precedent.

On the question of recognition, the report concludes,

our findings show that, at present, religious annulments and divorces remain completely outside the civil legal system, and none, including Jewish divorces where the Matrimonial Causes Acts is invoked to delay the civil decree absolute, is 'recognised' by the law.

This report was therefore able to provide insights into the areas of commonality and difference between these models of religious dispute resolution and the extent to which they seek to complement and/or conflict with English civil law mechanisms.

III THE MUSLIM ARBITRATION TRIBUNAL: A CHALLENGE TO CIVIL LAW IN MATTERS OF FAMILY LAW?

The Muslim Arbitration Tribunal (MAT) was set up in June 2007 and aims to settle disputes in accordance with religious Sharia law. The authority of this tribunal rests with the Arbitration Act 1996 which permits civil matters to be resolved in accordance with Muslim law and within the ambit of state law. For many, this process of resolving disputes may provide the ideal forum that allows the arbitrating parties to resolve disputes according to English law while fulfilling any obligations under Islamic law. The advantages of arbitration, it is argued, allow the parties to achieve some level of autonomy in the decision-making process. This, coupled with the informal setting, lower costs, flexibility and time efficiency means that for some it may prove a more attractive alternative to the adversarial courts system in England and Wales. However, there remain real concerns over whether this process can restrict women's equality and over issues of fairness and justice in family law.

At present, there are five tribunals operating as part of the MAT across Britain. Apart from addressing religious divorce and other Muslim family law matters (including marriage contracts, wills and inheritance disputes) these tribunals also arbitrate on matters relating to forced marriage and domestic violence. The MAT states that all agreements are settled in accordance with:

1. Qur'anic Injunctions and Prophetic Practice as determined by the recognised Schools of Islamic Sacred Law;
2. as fairly, quickly and efficiently as possible; and
3. where appropriate, that members of the Tribunal have responsibility for ensuring this in the interests of the parties to the proceedings and in the wider public interest.

It is held that Islamic decisions can be reached quickly and cheaply, and can be used as evidence before the civil court when seeking other remedies. It does not deal with criminal offences but states that

> where there are criminal charges such as assault within the context of domestic violence, the parties will be able ask MAT to assist in reaching reconciliation which is observed and approved by MAT as an independent organisation. The terms of such

reconciliation can then be passed by MAT on to the Crown Prosecution Service (CPS) though the local Police Domestic Violence Liaison Officers with a view to reconsidering the criminal charges. Note that the final decision to prosecute always remains with the CPS.

In 2008, *The Sunday Times* reported that the Tribunal had

> divided the estate of a Muslim man between his two sons and three daughters. Keeping with Islamic religious law, the sons were awarded twice as much money as the daughters. In six domestic violence cases on which the tribunal last year, the rulings required no further punishment for the husbands than anger management classes and community mentoring. After these rulings were issued, all six women withdrew their complaints to the UK police (Taher 2008; Madeira 2010: 3).

In 2008, the MAT produced a report entitled, *Liberation from Forced Marriages*, which stated that the MAT was the most appropriate forum for the Muslim community to resolve problems such as forced marriage. It put forward proposals to combat the practice of forced marriage as a community-driven initiative with emphasis placed on protecting British citizens marrying abroad who are victims of forced marriage. These include requesting the foreign spouse to submit voluntarily 'an oral deposition to the Judges of the MAT, satisfying them that the marriage he/she entered into was neither forced nor coerced'. As a voluntary deposition by the British citizen rather than a legal requirement the judges of the MAT would then produce a written declaration that they were satisfied that the marriage entered into was without any force or coercion. The proposal further states that

> the British citizen can then use this declaration to support the application of the foreign spouse to settle in the UK. If however, the foreign spouse fails to produce such a declaration from MAT or any other appropriate evidence, then it would be open for the ECO at the entry clearance point, to draw such inferences deemed appropriate as to the status of the marriage (Muslim Arbitration Tribunal 2008: 25).

The decisions of the MAT judges are recorded on tape and hearings recorded on camera. Evidence may include speaking to family members 'to highlight the wider consequences of participating or being complicit in a coerced or forced marriage'. The use of community elders as a source of social scrutiny to embarrass perpetrators is also proposed as a source of action. So the proposal envisages a scenario where the MAT hopes to work closely with both perpetrators and victims of forced marriage. Indeed, since its establishment, the MAT has generated much hostility in the press which has focused on the assumed threat it poses to English law and the due process of law. So what is the remit of religious courts under the Arbitration Act 1996? The establishment of the MAT has been controversial for a number of reasons. First, it has been claimed that Sharia courts have been allowed through the back door; secondly, that they directly challenge the superiority of the English legal system; and finally that they undermine the principles on which English family law are based.

As Blackett (2009: 13) says,

it is important to point out that the Muslim Arbitration Tribunal does not resemble or operate as a court but is an arbitration tribunal that must have the consent of the parties to rule on an issue. MAT has no power of enforcement but decisions can be enforced by the English county or high courts. This process therefore means that the decisions made by these arbitration bodies have to be in line with principles of English law or judges will not enforce them under sovereign rule.

The authority within the law of these courts was outlined by the Parliamentary under Secretary of State, Bridget Prentice, in the House of Commons in October 2008:

If, in a family dispute dealing with money or children, the parties to a judgement in a Sharia council wish to have this recognised by English authorities, they are at liberty to draft a consent order embodying the terms of the agreement and submit it to an English court. This allows English judges to scrutinise it to ensure that it complies with English legal tenets.

She added:

Arbitration does not apply to family law and the only decisions which can be enforced are those relating to civil disputes.[8]

However John Eekelaar (2011) has recently questioned this understanding, pointing out that:

There is, however, nothing in the Arbitration Act that so restricts arbitration. It is not clear that the Children Act 1989 would necessarily prevent an arbitral award concerning children being enforced because the court's duty to apply the best interests principle under the Children Act only applies when the court makes a determination about the upbringing of the child, which is arguably not the case when an arbitral award is enforced. It is true that an arbitration agreement is unlikely to prevent a party from invoking the courts jurisdiction in family matters because courts will not permit parties to oust that jurisdiction, but that depends on a party both wishing to escape from the arbitral award and being willing to apply to the court. So it seems that at least theoretically, family arbitrations might be capable of being enforced in the civil courts.

Under English law, parties cannot agree that a court should apply Sharia law, but in arbitration the position is different. Section 46 of the Arbitration Act 1996 provides:

(1) (a) The arbitral tribunal shall decide the disputes in accordance with the law chosen by the parties as applicable to the substance of the dispute; or (b) if the parties so agree, in accordance with such other considerations as are agreed by them or determined by the tribunal.

(2) For this purpose the choice of laws of a country shall be understood to refer to the substantive laws of that country and not its conflict of laws rules.

---

[8] *Hansard* (23 October 2008) Written Answers, col 562W.

Hence the parties can agree that the arbitrators will decide their dispute according to Sharia law. The Arbitration Act 1996 contains a number of safeguards. An agreement to arbitrate is, in a sense, just like any other contract, and so it is necessary for both parties to show a genuine agreement to arbitrate. Contracts obtained by duress will not be enforced; neither will contracts with minors or the incompetent. Agreements to arbitrate must be evidenced in writing. An arbitration award is, in itself, of no effect. It is of value only to the extent that a court is prepared to enforce it. Courts may refuse to enforce awards on various grounds, including (a) that a party was under some incapacity; (b) that the agreement was not valid under the applicable law; (c) that a party did not have proper notice of the arbitrator's appointment or of the proceedings or was unable to present their case; (d) if the award deals with a matter which it was not agreed would be submitted to arbitration; (e) if the award relates to a matter which is not capable of being settled by arbitration; and (f) if it would be contrary to public policy to enforce the award.

An arbitration award which is given under some law other than English law cannot be appealed on the grounds that the arbitrators got that law wrong, but it can be challenged and set aside by an English court under section 68 of the Arbitration Act 1996 on various grounds, including failure by the tribunal to comply with its general duty to act fairly and impartially.

Furthermore, the Supreme Court has confirmed that the provisions of the European Employment Equality (Religion and Belief) Regulations 2003 do not apply to arbitration agreements, so that they do not prevent the parties specifying the religious affiliation of the arbitrators. The Supreme Court also expressed the view that the religious affiliation of an arbitrator was capable of being objectively justified as a 'genuine occupational requirement'.[9] Matthew Gearing (2011) explains the importance of this ruling:

> The Court's decision demonstrates an understanding that, besides the functional component in terms of application of a given national law to the dispute, arbitration has a very significant process-based dimension which is largely left to the discretion of the arbitrators by most national arbitration legislations, major institutional rules and other international codes (such as the UNCITRAL Model Law), subject only to certain safeguards necessary in the public interest. The exercise of this discretion and an arbitrator's approach to the resolution of the dispute are bound to be influenced by a number of characteristics linked to his/her nationality, cultural background, ethos, legal training and experience. Indeed, even if, in fact, an arbitrator is not so influenced, the objective perception of the parties would always be otherwise. This point is well illustrated by the different attitudes and practices of arbitrators from diverse legal, cultural and regional backgrounds, which might manifest themselves in a predisposition towards adversarial or inquisitorial or conciliatory approach, or attitude towards confidentiality.

---

[9] *Hashwani v Jivraj* [2011] UKSC 40.

It is clear that, as Andrea Jarman (2008) notes that arbitration is a jurisdictional hybrid of private and public law. Redfern and Hunter (2004: 3) point out that

> it begins as a private agreement between the parties. It continues by way of private proceedings, in which the wishes of the parties are of great importance. Yet it ends with an award which has binding legal force and effect and which, on appropriate conditions being met . . . the courts . . . will be prepared to recognise and enforce.

More recently, the relationship between arbitration and the Human Rights Act has been explored in three recent judgments.[10] The question in these cases involved whether it was possible during the course of the arbitration agreement to forego one of the convention rights, namely Article 6 and the right to a fair trial. It was found that the terms of the 1996 Arbitration Act did fulfil the requirements of Article 6 as long as the arbitration agreement was entered into 'freely' or was 'agreed without constraint' and the agreement itself 'did not run counter to any important public interest'. Central to all this was the need for the tribunal to be impartial and to follow procedural fairness. So how does the MAT run as an arbitration body and does it fulfil key requirements of the Arbitration Act? At present there is no body of case law to analyse its effectiveness but we can see its institutional structure is paralleled on state law mechanisms but which also emanates from social and cultural postulates. The legitimacy of various legal and social domains mixes up our understandings of law and decision making. But to what extent does this approach challenge liberal conceptions of equality, human rights, individual choice and undermine gender equality?

IV THE QUESTION OF RELIGION AND ACCESS TO JUSTICE: THE ARBITRATION AND MEDIATION SERVICES (EQUALITY) BILL 2011

In 2011 a Private Member's Bill, the Arbitration and Mediation Services (Equality) Bill was introduced by Baroness Cox in the House of Lords. This Bill generated considerable media attention as it aimed to make clear the limits of arbitration and make amendments to the Arbitration Act to ensure its compliance with the Equality Act 2010 while seeking to outlaw discrimination on the grounds of sex. Clause 7 of the Bill proposes amending the Courts and Legal Services Act 1990 so as to criminalise anyone 'falsely claiming legal jurisdiction' or who 'otherwise falsely purports to adjudicate on any matter which that person knows or ought to know is within the jurisdiction of the criminal or family courts'. Although the Bill does not specifically mention Islamic law, it was widely believed to target Muslim communities and to attempt to limit the powers of organisations such as the MAT and Sharia councils. But for many

---

[10] *Stretford v Football Association* [2007] All ER (D) 346; *Sumukan Ltd v The Commonwealth Secretariat* [2007] EWCA Civ 243 and *Shuttari v The Solicitors Indemnity Fund* [2007] APP.L.R. 03/21.

scholars it raised the question of the extent to which state law should intervene in religious councils and tribunals. The debates in Ontario have formed the backdrop to understanding this relationship between civil and religious law (see Ahmed 2010; Bowen 2011). In Ontario, the extent to which family disputes should be allowed to take part under the Ontario Arbitration Act was brought into sharp relief when the Canadian Society of Muslims sought to establish a Sharia tribunal and use the Ontario Arbitration Act to resolve family law type disputes. Canadian Muslim women's organisations challenged this proposal and the findings of the Boyd Report which called for the recognition of religious tribunals as long as some safeguards were in place. The furore led to the government rejecting that position. As Eekelaar (2012) points out:

> The result was that, while religious bodies may still carry out arbitration in family matters under the Arbitration Act they must do so according to the law of Ontario or of another Canadian jurisdiction. Furthermore, regulations require family law arbitrators to undergo training in the law of Canada, that cases are screened for 'power imbalances and domestic violence, by someone other than the arbitrator' and that a written record be kept of the proceedings.

Shachar (2008: 573) points out succinctly that 'The vision of privatised diversity in its fully-fledged "unregulated islands of jurisdiction" variant poses a challenge to the superiority of secular family law by its old adversary: religion'. This vision of privatised diversity can be applied to the new MAT if we understand privatised diversity as a model in which to achieve and possibly separate the secular from the religious in the public space, in effect encouraging individuals to contract out of state involvement and into a traditional non-state forum when resolving family disputes. This would include religious tribunals arbitrating according to a different set of principles than those enshrined in English law. This approach was recently advocated by the Archbishop of Canterbury, Dr Rowan Williams (2008: 2) who stated that 'there are ways at looking at marital disputes, for example, which provide an alternative to the divorce courts as we understand them. In some cultural and religious settings they would seem more appropriate'. He also suggested that the recognition of Sharia in Britain seems 'unavoidable' and advised that we need to find a 'constructive accommodation' of Sharia in the law. Although he was careful not to restrict his general argument to Muslims per se, but more broadly to all those belonging to religious communities, the focal point was Muslim and the recognition of Sharia in English law. Lord Phillips CJ (Phillips 2008: 4) added further weight to the argument when he stated 'there is no reason why principles of Sharia law, or any other religious code, should not be the basis for mediation or other forms of alternative dispute resolution'. Both speakers suggested that Islamic mechanisms of family disputes could perform a function not dissimilar to that of the Jewish Beth Din courts which deal with matters relating to marriage and divorce.

For Shachar (2008: 580) there are real concerns of individuals being expected to live 'as undifferentiated citizens in the public sphere, but remain free to express our distinct cultural or religious identities in the private domain of family and communal life'. For her and many other liberal scholars, the issue surrounds the contentious question of where private identity and life ends and public identity begins. She quite rightly points out that, if we are expected to express personal identities in the private, at which point in the public sphere do they cease to be so? Shachar also discusses the fact that the vision of privatised diversity will evoke different feelings for different people. For those who want to establish a pluralistic system of law that recognises claims of culture and religion, this would not be so terrifying, but those who are 'blind' to these needs will see it as challenging the superiority of universal laws that apply to all:

> [F]or others who endorse a strict separationist approach, or 'blindness' towards religious or cultural affiliation, the idea that we might find unregulated 'religious islands of binding jurisdiction' mushrooming on the terrain of state law is seen as evidence of the dangers of accommodating diversity, potentially chipping away, however slightly as the foundational, modernist citizenship formula of 'one law for all'.

Such arguments are echoed by Parkinson (1996: 24), who remarks that: 'Acceptance of cultural diversity, and recognition of cultural issues in the application of the law, are especially important in relation to family law, for families play such an important role in the development of a person's cultural identity'. Therefore, the intimate relations between the individual, family and community must to some extent be recognised by a legal system that increasingly serves plural and multicultural Western societies.

The Arbitration and Mediation Services (Equality) Bill has been criticised for promoting the idea that the practice of Muslim family law is not only based on unfair and unequal principles, but specifically targets and discriminates against Muslim women as primary users of Muslim dispute resolution bodies. Furthermore, the formalist top-down state interventionist approach as epitomised by the Bill in seeking to limit the powers of religious bodies has also been criticised as being predicated on fixed and homogenous notions of Islam and Islamic legal practice which fails to recognise the dynamism and pluralism within the communities themselves. As Eekelaar (2011) argues:

> It is a mistake to think of Shari'a as a monolithic system, impervious to change. In fact the bodies apply it in different ways, and it is subject to internal arguments and contestation. Might it be better to allow it to develop within its communities and responding to its internal critiques and influenced by the culture around it? Alongside this, its adherents could be encouraged to make more use of the civil law, including a greater readiness to enter legally recognised marriages without thereby severing their relationship with their religious norms.

But what are the experiences of Muslim women using religious mechanisms of dispute resolution in family law matters? Do religious tribunals promote patriarchy and gender inequality?

V MUSLIM WOMEN AND THE QUESTION OF PERSONAL AUTONOMY

For many scholars, the question of personal autonomy and choice underpins debates on the recognition of religious councils and tribunals in Britain (see, for example, Ahmed 2010). The debates fall largely within two spectrums of scholarly work. The first can be described broadly as orientalist discourses which accord Muslim women little if any agency and personal choice as members of Muslim families and communities (see, for example, the critiques by Razack 2008) and the second points to the fact that all debates on equality and free choice are circumscribed by 'difference' along multiple and complex factors including, context, place and time with notions of belonging, identity and being. The extent to which free choice is therefore expressed can simply be one based on personal and strategic decision-making in the face of conflicting and competing demands.

For example, the discussions referred to above on arbitration and the question of autonomy, choice and decision-making capacities for parties wishing to use arbitration have largely focused on the debates that have taken place in Ontario in 2004–06. The Boyd Report – which was commissioned in response to calls for the establishment of a civil law system to incorporate Muslim family law matters into civil law – found that religious arbitration in family law matters should be allowed to continue as long as safeguards were put into place which emphasised procedural safeguards to protect vulnerable parties who may be compelled to use these services. But the largest Muslim women's organisation in Canada (The Canadian Council of Muslim Women) was critical of such recommendations and argued that they undermined the Canadian Constitution which promotes 'equality before the law' for all its citizens. And recent work (Ahmed and Luk 2011) has focused on the question: 'if religious arbitration does have the potential to harm autonomy, what kind of legal safeguards can counteract or mitigate this potential?'; and how the autonomy of certain vulnerable persons might be affected by religious arbitration.

In matters of family law, the primary function of a Sharia council is to issue Muslim women with a Muslim divorce certificate in cases where a Muslim husband may fail to unilaterally divorce his wife.[11] Under Muslim law, and in accordance with the injunctions found in the Quran and Hadith literature, a divorce can be obtained in a number of different ways: *talaq* (unilateral repudiation by the husband); *khul* (divorce at the instance of the wife with her husband's agreement, and on condition that she will forego her right to the dower or *mahr*) and *ubara'at* (divorce by mutual consent).[12] It is against this background and in cases where a husband may refuse to grant a unilateral divorce

---

[11] There is extensive literature on the extrajudicial nature of the *talaq*. See, eg, Esposito (1988).

[12] There is of course much diversity within these approaches and huge variations in relation to the timing of the divorce and whether it can be issued verbally or it must be given in writing and the number of witnesses present. See Hamilton (1995).

that a Muslim woman may contact a Sharia council to obtain a Muslim divorce certificate. Notwithstanding the diversity of literature on Muslim divorce, legal scholars observe a number of key points of conflict with English divorce law. In England, all marriages ending in divorce must be dissolved according to English divorce laws and contained in the provisions of the Matrimonial Causes Act 1973. The recognition of religious marriages is complex depending on where the marriage took place and the domicile of the parties involved. The fact that Islam permits a unilateral divorce instigated by the husband means that if the marriage has been registered according to English law, the female applicant remains married according to the civil law although not by Islamic law. Similarly, if the woman obtains a civil divorce but her husband refuses to grant her a Muslim divorce, she is in a situation described by Pearl and Menski (1998) as a 'limping marriage'. Yilmaz (2005) points out that

> if the woman is not religiously divorced from her husband, it does not matter that she is divorced under the civil law, in the eyes of the community her remarriage will be regarded as adulterous and any possible offspring will be illegitimate since it is not allowed under the religious law.

So, in reality, until the religious divorce is obtained, the civil divorce remains ineffective because one party is unable to remarry. The second issue relates to the type of Muslim divorce granted to the women by the Sharia councils and this raises the question of fairness. For example, if a *khul* is granted, it means that the female applicant must give up her right to dower or *mahr* in return for the divorce and this can mean an unfair outcome for Muslim women.[13] There are also other important issues regarding the validity of foreign divorces in English law which has been extensively discussed in case law commentary and analysis.[14] It is, however, beyond the scope of this chapter to discuss these complex areas of law and private international law in any depth, suffice to point out that they raise important questions relating to the type of advice given by religious scholars and legal practitioners.

Interviewed in my research (Bano 2007), Sheikh Abdullah, explained:

> As Muslims, we have a duty to live according to the Qu'ran and Sunnah even though we may have chosen to live in non Muslim countries. I think it is incumbent upon us to live up to this responsibility because of the effect of western influences upon our children and ourselves. It is easy to neglect our duties in this secular environment.

Thus the language of choice, commitment and faith as described by the religious scholars fits in neatly with the discourse of belonging to a wider Muslim

---

[13] Pearl and Menski (1998: 213) describe this process: 'Usually the wife will offer to pay a certain sum, normally the amount of the dower either given to her or promised to her, in return for the agreement of the husband to release her from the marriage tie'.

[14] There are a number of key cases which address the issue of validity of foreign divorces: see *Qureshi v Qureshi* [1971] 1 All ER 325. On the issue of whether English law could recognise a *talaq*, see *R v Secretary of State for the Home Department, ex parte Ghulam Fatima* and *R v Secretary for the Home Department, ex parte Shafeena Bi* [1985] QB 190.

community (*Umma*) and the importance attached to the development and formation of a local Muslim community-identity. In this way the community space
(inhabited by Sharia councils) is deemed the obvious site on which the long
established practice of Muslim dispute resolution takes place. And in this
respect it seems clear that the religious scholars seek to establish authority with
respect to family law matters and require all participants to take the proceedings seriously. While the process of disputing itself reveals striking similarities
to the development of family mediation in English family law, most religious
scholars describe this process as distinct from the English family law approach
to settling family disputes and the process is in fact framed as in opposition to
state law mediation practices. It is also conceptualised in terms of a *duty* on all
Muslims to abide by the requirements of the Sharia and the stipulations of the
Sharia councils. This shared understanding stems from the belief that the secular space inhabited by English family law principles cannot in itself bring about
genuine resolution of matrimonial disputes for Muslims living in Britain.[15]

In my research (Bano 2007), with the exception of one interviewee, all the
women had contacted a Sharia council voluntarily, notwithstanding guidance
they may have received from family, friends and/or the local imam. In most
cases, initial contact had been made via the telephone, and this was followed up
with an application form citing the reasons for seeking a religious dissolution of
marriage. The most obvious questions concern the autonomy and independence of the women during this process of dispute resolution and their experience of mediation and reconciliation. Although not all women are marginalised
and denied equal bargaining power during official mediation processes, there
exists evidence to suggest that there is deep anxiety among many women at the
prospect of initiating both official and unofficial mediation, an anxiety that
persists throughout the process (Bottomley and Conaghan 1993). This ambivalence was reflected in the data: some women described the initial advice they
received as helpful and sympathetic, enabling them to pursue the divorce,
whereas others were critical of the initial impression given by the scholars at
these bodies. Sameena explained:

> I rang the number of this Shariah Council that our Maulvi had given to us. I told them
> what had happened to me and that I wanted to divorce my husband, but that he wasn't
> happy with it and wouldn't agree to it. They were very helpful; they explained that
> divorce was wrong, but that in Islam, in some circumstances, it was allowed . . . they
> took my address and contact details and told me they would send me some forms to
> fill in and then decide whether it would be possible (Sameena, London).

---

[15] This perception of English law being based on secular principles has been questioned by critical legal theorists (see Fitzpatrick 1992). A recent White Paper on constitutional reform reiterated
the centrality of the Church of England to state–law relations. It stated 'the Church of England is by
law established as the Church of England and the Monarch is its supreme governor. The government
remains committed to this position': see 'The Governance of Britain' (2007) presented to Parliament
by the Secretary of State for Justice and Lord Chancellor, Jack Straw MP, July 2007, para 25.

In cases where documents such as proof of marriage (ie, a copy of the *nikah* certificate or certificate of civil marriage) were unavailable, the women were required to provide an affidavit to confirm that the marriage had taken place. Notably, most women did not have a copy of their *nikah* certificate, and in these cases they provided an affidavit instead. Unsurprisingly, perhaps, what we ascertain quickly from the interview data is the desire of all the women to complete the process with minimal disruption and conflict. Despite this, a total of 23 women complained about the process as being incoherent, time-consuming and at odds with the Sharia council's own claims that it is sympathetic to the needs of women:

> I got a letter back from them saying they were looking into the case, and in the meantime I think they had met with my husband and heard his side of the story. But I'm not sure – every time I asked what was going on I never got an answer (Rabia, Birmingham).

For all the Sharia councils, the process of reconciliation and/or mediation is principally an investigation into the possibility of reconciling the parties. It is by no means an uncomplicated process, and it actually gives rise to an interesting set of cultural and religious practices which are overlapping and, at times, in conflict. What becomes clear, when the process is examined closely, is the centrality of gender relations, which frame the terms of the discussion on which the basis for reconciliation is sought. These 'common understandings' regarding the position and representation of Muslim women are in fact crucial to the outcome of the dispute. Interviews with religious scholars reveal the importance attached to reconciling the parties. In this context, reconciliation is understood both as a moral duty (to preserve the sanctity of the Muslim family) and a religious obligation (a divorce cannot be pronounced without reconciliation). My interviewee Mohammed Raza explains:

> We do not just distribute divorces on a footpath . . . we are not encouraging divorce – that's not our role. When a woman rings here to find out about divorce or to request an application form, we are initially reluctant to issue a divorce application. We ask her that you should try to rethink your position, because divorce is something that is considered a stigma in society and divorce is nothing good for you, and if they have children that will be another problem after divorce so we discourage it.

With the exception of one Sharia council, all female applicants are expected to participate in the reconciliation and/or mediation process. One important question is whether or not the characteristics and parameters of this alternative dispute resolution process can determine specific outcomes for Muslim women. Although religious scholars are associated with sources that claim divine authority, interview research also revealed that religious scholars were keen to promote the idea of the Sharia council ADR framework as a system whose authority, legitimacy and validity can mirror that of state law. To this end, each religious scholar was keen to emphasise that although they did avoid persuading female applicants to reconcile with estranged husbands this option nevertheless was always put forward to all applicants:

They wanted me to meet with my husband. In fact they said that I couldn't have a divorce unless we both met with the Imam. But it wasn't as bad as I thought. My husband took it very seriously . . . what the Imam was saying. I think he needed a religious person to explain to him where he was going wrong and why I was leaving him (Sabia, London).

I needed to explore the possibility of us getting back together from an Islamic perspective. I'm a Muslim, so it helps if you can get advice and assistance from another Muslim. I think a Muslim woman would have been able to understand where I was coming from (Humeira, London).

Feminist scholars have warned of the dangers of trying to resolve marital disputes outside the protection of formal law. This may include situations where cultural norms deny women decision-making authority or where the mediator is not neutral and yet still provides the normative framework for discussion a situation which can transform the nature of the discussion and curtail the autonomy of the disputant. Roberts (2008) raises concerns that negotiations might well occur in private 'without the presence of partisan lawyers and without access to appeal'. Numerous studies point to the fact that official mediation places women in a weak bargaining position, and encourages them to accept a settlement considerably inferior to one that they might have obtained had they gone through the adversarial process. In their study of mediation and divorce, Greatbach and Dingwall (1993: 203) found that mediators do not act in a neutral way, and they enter the mediation process and guide the participants towards particular outcomes, with the consequence that there is a strong imbalance of power – the parties are not equal and cannot respond in an equal way. Furthermore, Bottomley and Conaghan (1993: 45) remind us that conciliation 'has not arisen in a vacuum and is not practised in one', and that we need to explore the dynamics of power which underpin this process. Thus, we can say that mediation promotes a particular familial ideology that is based on social control and patriarchal norms and values, and operates through subliminal, covert forms of power and coercion. In contrast, formal law provides protection against abuse in the private sphere, and so in response to the move towards private legal ordering, critics argue that mediation fails to deliver on the key issue of 'justice'. Eekelaar (2000) describes this development of social and legal norms as one which

exists within society a network of social norms which is formally independent of the legal system, but which is in constant interaction with it. Formal law sometimes seeks to strengthen the social norms. Sometimes it allows them to serve its purposes without the necessity of direct intervention; sometimes it tries to weaken or destroy them and sometimes it withdraws from enforcement, not in an attempt to subvert them, but because countervailing values make conflicts better resolved outside the legal arena.

Feminists have extensively critiqued this tenuous relationship between family and state intervention across a wide spectrum of disciplines. For example, Thornton (1995: 120) points out that unofficial family mediation ensures that the state absolves itself of responsibility to adequately protect vulnerable women. She explains: 'In mediating interests which appear to be irreconcilable, the task of the liberal state is made easier if there are some areas conceptualised as "private" with which it does not have to grapple'. In other words, privatised family mediation allows the state to avoid intervention on the grounds of respecting cultural and religious difference. For organisations such as Southall Black Sisters, the multiculturalists treat racial-minority women in a way that they would not treat white women, that is, ignoring the violence directed against them in the interest of respecting culture.

Yet it is precisely the fact that women have such divergent experiences of family mediation that renders problematic any proposals to develop family mediation as a more formalised process to suit the specific needs of minority ethnic communities. There seems to be an inherent conflict between recognising identities as multiple and fluid and formulating social policy initiatives that are based on specific cultural practices, precisely because cultural and religious practices are open to change, contestation and interpretation. At the very least, we must ensure that mechanisms are in place so that those who choose not to participate in such processes are not compelled to do so. It is in this context that concerns have been raised about how such proposals will lead to delegating rights to communities to regulate matters of family law, which is effectively a move towards some form of cultural autonomy. Maclean (2000: 67) rightly asks: 'What are the implications for family justice of this move towards private ordering? Is this form of "privatisation" safe?' Undoubtedly, in this context formal law provides protection against abuse in the 'private' sphere – the sphere in which this legal ordering operates. Maclean goes on to ask: 'is it dangerous to remove disputes from the legal system with the advantage of due process, plus protection of those at the wrong end of the far from level playing field, and visible negotiation and settlement which takes place of not in court than in the shadow of the law?' Interview data with the sample of women in this study confirms the significance Sharia councils place on reconciling the parties in the process of issuing Muslim divorce certificates. It can be seen not only that gender relations are central to the dispute resolution process, but also and perhaps most importantly, that the process is contested and resisted by the women themselves.

VI CONCLUSION

In chapter one of this book, Eekelaar puts forward an approach he describes as 'cultural voluntarism' which would allow individuals to following group norms as long as they comply with civil law norms. He explains:

[F]amily courts could make orders based on agreements reached under religious law but only if the agreement was genuine and followed independent advice, and was consistent with overriding policy goals (for example the best interests of the child). State law would be available at all times to anyone who chose to invoke it and access to it should be safeguarded and encouraged.

However, as with all religious mechanisms of dispute resolution, Sharia councils and the MAT do not sufficiently address the issue of power and power relations within the context of family, home and community. The issue of control and powerlessness in the resolution of matrimonial disputes for many female users of religious councils and tribunals are crucial and cannot be ignored. Penny Booth (2008: 936) argues that such tribunals can create a system of coercive control for women:

> The danger is in the development of a parallel system of (any) law where the choice as to which system or principle is used is determined not by the individual or the issue but by the group bullies. In family law this danger could arise where the determination of system and approach is not made by the woman but the men; not through female but through the male dominated system.

Denis MacEoin (2009: 76) remains critical of the MAT arguing that

> it is a challenge to what we believe to be the rights and freedoms of the individual to our concept of a legal system based on what Parliament enacts, and to the right of all of us to live in a society as free as possible from ethnic-religious division or communal claims to superiority and a special status that puts them in some respects above the law to which we are all bound.

This argument is flawed in multiple ways, not least because it fails to recognise the plural nature of ADR and law and to understand how in practice law evolves, develops and seeks to accommodate the needs of all its citizens from multiple and diverse backgrounds. Therefore, instead of promoting an exclusive move back towards state law (the state as we know has never been a neutral arbiter of disputes) we need instead to better understand the experiences of Muslim women as primary users of the MAT and to understand *why* they may choose to use the MAT. As Anitha and Gill (2009: 168) point out:

> Women exercise their agency in complex and often contradictory ways, as they assess the options that are open to them, weigh the costs and benefits of their actions, and seek to balance their often competing needs with the expectations and desires. While there remains a need to recognise gendered power imbalances at the same time there also remains a need to respect women's exercise of agency . . . We need to give more support to those women who wish to express their subjectivity within the framework of the communities of which they perceive themselves to be such a fundamental part.

At present, there are little if any data documenting the experiences of Muslim women who use such religious dispute mechanisms. My empirical work with British Muslim women using Sharia councils to obtain a Muslim divorce certificate reveals that the management of the marital dispute in the sphere of privatised religious dispute resolution gives rise to a different set of responsibilities and obligations. Women who participated in the Sharia councils process viewed themselves as not only individuals, but as members of families and communities. In a situation where notions of religious identity, belonging and familial norms and values interact with the values of individual choice and consent, some women were successfully able to negotiate between the plurality of norms and values that exist within the context of family, home and Sharia councils. An important aspect of such findings, therefore, is to challenge the perceived inherent marginality of Muslim women in this process of dispute resolution. For example, it is interesting to note that several women reported that they were aware that the meanings and interpretations of some Islamic perspectives put forward by religious scholars were contested and therefore open to change. In this way they were able to disregard them and were fully aware of the need to utilise state law for their protection and entitlement of rights. For this reason they were able to challenge their weak bargaining position in the marriage within the family context, to occupying a more 'open' space at the Sharia council as a basis for entering into negotiation, dialogue and possible change. In such a situation some women participated in the reconciliation process as a strategic manoeuvre to challenge conflicting interests. Yet this shift of dispute resolution from the public to the private sphere also raises serious concerns on how power is effectively reconfigured from the state to the family and community. From such a perspective the differential treatment of women in the process of marriage and divorce can lead to a conflict between equality and autonomy and the conflicting interests of the protection of family, culture and religion as enshrined by the norms and values of Sharia Councils and the MAT.

The process of 'reform' within communities can be a long and fractured one, often contextual and dependent on state support and subsidy (see Abbas 2005). To better understand the complex ways in which Muslims live their lives in Britain and utilise Muslim family law, the focus cannot simply be on debates of cultural and religious diversity versus secular systems of civil law and the claims for legal recognition of Muslim family law. This is simply not enough. Narratives from Muslim women using religious mechanisms of dispute resolution reveal both their strategic and the complex use of these bodies. But this use does not then simply translate into calls for 'recognition' or accommodation (albeit limited in various ways) of religious norms in family disputes. Instead I caution against such moves and question whether such demands are being made. Most Sharia councils are critical of any such recognition. I also caution against the idea that Muslim women are unable to exercise their agency and personal autonomy while using religious bodies to resolve matrimonial disputes. Some are, but others are not. What existing research does reveal is the complexity of this use, but also that we simply lack sufficient knowledge about these bodies or the experience of their primary users, Muslim women. The sociologist Stuart Hall (1992) reminds us that the state is not a neutral arbiter of disputes because the state as history informs us does not at times act in a neutral, fair and objective way. However, he also reminds us that the state has the legal responsibility and obligation to protect all vulnerable individuals. Religious bodies lack this capacity and the due process of law. In order to better understand this process we need more in-depth, empirically rich, research that draws on the complexity of this issue. Until this time I caution against debates on the extent to which religious laws can be accommodated into English civil law. My research found that Muslim women are critical of such moves and if we are to seek and promote equality, fairness and justice then their narratives must be heard.

REFERENCES

Abbas, T (2005) *Muslim Communities Under Pressure* (London, Zed Books).

Abel, R (1984) 'Popular Justice, Populist Politics: Law in Community Organizing' 1 *Social and Legal Studies* 177.

Akber, S Ahmed and Donnan, H (1994) *Islam, Globalization and Postmodernity* (London, Routledge).

Ahmed, F (2010) 'Personal Autonomy and the Option of Religious Law' 24 *International Journal of Law, Policy and the Family* 222.

Ahmed, F and Luk, S (2011) 'Religious Arbitration: A Study of Legal Safeguards' 77 *Arbitration* 290.

Anitha, S and Gill, A (2009) 'Coercion, Consent and the Forced Marriage Debate' 17 *Feminist Legal Studies* 165.

An-Naim, A (1990) *Toward an Islamic Reformation: Civil Liberties, Human Rights and International Law* (New York, Syracuse University Press).

Bano, S (2007) 'Muslim Family Justice and Human Rights: The Experience of British Muslim Women' 2 *Journal of Comparative Law* 42.

Barlas, A (2006) *Believing Women in Islam: Unreading Patriarchal Interpretations of the Qu'ran* (Austin, University of Texas Press).

Blackett, R (2009) 'The Status of "Religious Courts" in English Law' *Decisions: Dispute Resolution & International Arbitration Newsletter* 11.

Booth, P (2008) 'Judging Sharia' 38 *Family Law* 935.

Bottomley, A and Conaghan, J (1993) *Feminist Legal Theory and Legal Strategy* (Oxford, Blackwell).

Bowen, J (2011) 'How Could English Courts Recognize Shariah?' 7 *St Thomas Law Review* 411.

Bunt, G (1998) 'Decision-Making Concerns in British Islamic Environments' 19 *Islam and Christian–Muslim Relations* 103.

Caplan, P (1995) *Anthropology and the Study of Disputes in Understanding Disputes: The Politics of Argument* (London, Routledge).

Centre for Social Cohesion (2009) *Beth Din: Jewish Law in the UK* (London, Centre for Social Cohesion).

Chiba, M (1986) *Asian Indigenous Law* (London, Kegan Paul).

Coulson, N (1969) *The History of Islamic Law* (Edinburgh, Edinburgh University Press).

Eekelaar, J (2000) 'Uncovering Social Obligations: Family Law and the Responsible Citizen' in M Maclean (ed), *Making Law for Families* (Oxford, Hart Publishing).

—— (2011) 'The Arbitration and Mediation Services (Equality) Bill 2011' 41 *Family Law* 1209.

—— (2012) 'Family Law – What Family Law?' in R Probert and C Barton (eds), *Fifty Years in Family Law: Essays for Stephen Cretney* (Cambridge, Intersentia).

Esposito, JL (1988) *Islam - The Straight Path* (Oxford University Press, New York).

Esposito, JL (1982) *Women in Muslim Family Law* (New York, Syracuse University Press).

Fitzpatrick, P (1992) *The Mythology of Modern Law* (London, Routledge).

Gearing, M (2011) '*Jivraj v Hashwani*: A Pro-Choice, Corrective Ruling from the Supreme Court' Kluwer Arbitration Blog: kluwerarbitrationblog.com.

Genn, H (1999) *What People Do and Think about Going to Law* (Oxford, Hart Publishing).

Douglas GF, Gilliat-Ray S, Doe N, Sandberg R and Khan A (2011) *Social Cohesion and Civil Law: Marriage, Divorce and Religious Courts in England and Wales* (Cardiff, Cardiff University).

Greatbatch, D and Dingwall, R (1993) 'Who is in Charge? Rhetoric and Evidence in the Study of Mediation' 17 *Journal of Social Welfare and Family Law* 199.

Hall, S (1992) 'The Question of Cultural Identity' in D Hall, T Held and T McGrew (eds), *Modernity and its Future* (Cambridge, Polity Press).

Hamilton, C (1995) *Family, Law and Religion* (London, Sweet & Maxwell).

Home Office (2000) 'A choice by right: The report of the working group on forced marriage' (London, Home Office Communications Directorate) available at: www.fco.gov.uk/Files/KFile/AChoiceByRightJune2000.pdf.

Hussain, Y and Bagguley, P (2005) *Riotous Citizens: Ethnic Conflict in Multicultural Britain* (Farnham, Ashgate).

Jarman, A (2008) 'The Limits of Legal Pluralism, CRONEM conference, University of Surrey' (unpublished paper).

Phillips, Lord (2008) 'Equality before the Law' speech at the East London Muslim Centre (3 July).

Lewis, P (1994) 'Being Muslim and Being British: The Dynamics of Islamic Reconstruction in Bradford' in R Ballard et al (eds), *Desh Pardesh: The South Asian Presence in Britain* (London, C Hurst & Co Ltd).

MacEoin, D (2009) *Sharia Law or 'One Law for All'?* (London, Civitas, Institute for the Study of Civil Society).

Madeira, MA (2010) 'Shari'a or the State?: Islamic Law Tribunals in Western Democracies' (International Sociological Association Conference, 12 February).

Maclean, M (2000) (ed), *Making Law for Families* Onati International Series in Law and Society (Oxford, Hart Publishing).

Menski, W (1997) 'South Asian Muslim Law Today: An Overview' 9 *Sharqiyyat* 16.

—— (2001) 'Muslim Law in Britain' 62 *Journal of Asian and African Studies* 202.

Ministry of Justice and Bano, S (forthcoming) *An Exploratory Study of Shariah Councils in England with Respect to Family Law*.

Modood, T (2007) *Multiculturalism: A Civic Idea* (Cambridge, Polity Press).

Muslim Arbitration Tribunal (2008) *Liberation from Forced Marriages* (London, MAT).

Nasir, J (1986) *The Islamic Law of Personal Status* (London, Graham and Trotman).

Parkinson, P (1996) 'Multiculturalism and the Recognition of Marital Status in Australia' in G Douglas and N Lowe (eds), *Families Across Frontiers* (London, Kluwer).

Pearl, D and Menski, W (1998) *Muslim Family Law* (London, Sweet and Maxwell).

Phillips, A and Dustin, M (2004) 'UK Initiatives on Forced Marriage: Regulation, Dialogue and Exit' 52 *Political Studies* 531.

Razack, S (2008) *Casting Out: The Eviction of Muslims from Western Law and Politics* (Toronto, University of Toronto Press).

Redfern A and Hunter M (2004) *International Commercial Arbitration* (Cambridge, Cambridge University Press).

Roberts, M (2008) *Mediation in Family Disputes, Principles of Practice* (Farnham, Ashgate).

Shachar, A (2008) 'Privatizing Diversity: A Cautionary Tale from Religious Arbitration in Family Law' 9 *Theoretical Inquiries in Law* 573.

Shah-Kazemi, NS (2001) *Untying the Knot: Muslim Women, Divorce and the Shariah* (London, The Nuffield Foundation).

Soyal, NY (2000) 'Citizenship and Identity: Living in Diasporas in Post-war Europe' 23 *Ethnic and Racial Studies* 1.

Taher, A (2008) 'Revealed: UK's first official Sharia courts' *The Sunday Times* (14 September 2008).

Taylor, C (2007) *A Secular Age* (Cambridge, MA, Harvard University Press).

Thornton, M (1995) *Public and Private: Feminist Legal Debates* (Melbourne, Oxford University Press).

Vertovec, S (1996) 'Multiculturalism, Culturalism and Public Incorporation' 19 *Ethnic and Racial Studies* 48.

Wheeler, BM (1996) *Applying the Canon in Islam: The Authorization and Maintenance of Interpretive Reasoning in Hanafi Scholarship* (Albany, GA, Albany State University Press).

Williams, R (2008) 'Civil and Religious Law in England: A Religious Perspective' 10 *Ecclesiastical Law Journal* 262.

Yilmaz, I (2002) 'The Challenge of Post-modern Legality and Muslim Legal Pluralism in England' 28 *Journal of Ethnic and Migration Studies* 343.

—— (2005) *Muslim Law, Politics and Society in Modern Nation States: Dynamic Legal Pluralisms in England, Turkey and Pakistan* (Farnham, Ashgate).

Part II

Regulating the Interaction between Religious and Secular Norms in Different Jurisdictions

5

A *'Deviant'* Solution: The Israeli Agunah *and the* Religious Sanctions Law

PASCALE FOURNIER,* PASCAL MCDOUGALL
AND MERISSA LICHTSZTRAL

I INTRODUCTION

U NDER *HALACHA* (JEWISH law), a man holds all the power to grant his wife a religious divorce (the *get*). A Jewish woman who is refused a *get* by her husband will be called an *agunah* (chained wife), a status which precludes her from marrying another man religiously or to have legitimate children in the eyes of Jewish law, notwithstanding any civil divorce. In Israel and in various Western countries, this legal situation has given rise to extortion and manipulation of Jewish women on divorce (Yefet 2009: 447; Nichols 2007: 158), a tragic outcome referred to by some scholars as the 'plight of the *agunah*' (Breitowitz 1993).

Multicultural dilemmas spawned by such unequal religious rules are often framed in terms of the relation between the neutral, secular state, one the one hand, and the 'cultural'/religious law, on the other. Thus, the question often remains framed in terms of whether and how the state can manipulate and regulate religious norms to further universal goals of gender equality.[1] In our opinion, this ideological framework is inadequate.[2] To demonstrate this, rather than

* I am grateful for funding received to support this project from the Québec Bar Foundation, the Foundation for Legal Research, Borden Ladner Gervais, the Law Foundation of Ontario and the Social Sciences and Humanities Research Council of Canada. I thank Viviane Bartlett and Ashley Shaffer for their research assistance, Leehee Goldenberg for the transcription and translation of the interviews from Hebrew to English and I acknowledge the *William & Mary Journal of Women and the Law*'s permission to reprint parts of previously published material.

[1] See, for instance, Benhabib (2002: 128); Stopler (2003); Okin (1999: 7); and Phillips (2005: 113).

[2] Indeed, the conception of the secular state as a neutral arbiter may need reconsideration. Courts and the state can and should be analysed as culturally/ideologically oriented institutions (Caughey (2009: 323); Althusser 1997: 127). Furthermore, state 'tolerance' and 'accommodation' have been exposed by many scholars to be based on euro-centric notions: see Beaman (2011) and

exposing Western state officials' ideological, contradictory and equally 'cultural' treatment of religious laws, something which was done in past work,[3] this chapter will employ the reverse strategy of presenting the context of the non-Western, non-secular state of Israel. Israel's family law regime confers jurisdiction over divorce and marriage to (religious) rabbinical courts.[4] The divorce procedures, which are the focus of this chapter, are governed by strictly religious law[5] and there is no civil marriage to speak of.[6] What is it that we can see once we have reversed the gaze inwards? Is secularisation[7] of the state or implementation of the (Western-based) corpus of human rights[8] a precondition for deviance to be controlled? What exactly can be referred to as 'deviance'? Is religious law 'patriarchal in nature' (Halperin-Kaddari, 2004: 227) and thus wholly unable to protect women against male deviant practices?

The chapter will attempt to comprehend Israeli women's condition by analysing, through socio-legal fieldwork and interviews with Israeli Jewish women, the operation of the Sanctions Law,[9] a religious legislation intended to address the plight of the *agunah*. This legislation, which grants rabbinical courts the power to accompany certain divorce compulsion orders with sanctions to ensure compliance by the husband, is considered by many Israeli *agunah* women as a helpful, albeit imperfect, legal instrument. The perspectives provided by the women will serve to demonstrate that religious subjects are not waiting for the benevolent watch of a secular state or a Declaration of Human Rights to make their own lives better.[10] Instead, they are struggling on a daily basis to shape and influence religious institutions from the inside, a strategy which, for Israel's state law as much as for 'unofficial' Jewish laws of the diaspora, can often prove more effective than labelling religious institutions as acceptably 'diverse' and

---

Brown (2006). Finally, American legal realism has long demonstrated that 'non-intervention' by the state can always be seen to be some form of indirect regulation and background rule-setting (Hale, 1923). Thus, multiculturalism's (and 'cultural voluntarism's') invocation of group autonomy obscures rather than clarifies the distributive impacts of state policies. For more on this with regards to Islamic law, see Fournier (2010a). These social realities, which should inform state policies, are too often occulted by Western law's 'methodological nationalism' (Shah 2009: 73).

[3] With regard to the legal treatment of Islamic family law, see Fournier (2010b). For the legal treatment of 'crimes of honour,' see Fournier, McDougall and Dekker (2012).

[4] s 1 The Rabbinical Courts Jurisdictions (Marriage and Divorce) Law, 5713-1953, Law Book of the State of Israel; Navot (2007: 21).

[5] That being said, certain ancillary areas of divorce law such as custody and matrimonial property are governed by civil law and adjudicated by civil courts (Shifman 1990: 538).

[6] A Bill was passed in May 2010 to allow civil marriage for partners who are both considered as 'lacking a religion'. However, it seems to apply to only a few Israelis (Lerner 2011: 214).

[7] As argued in the context of Israel by Marsha Freeman (2003: 71) and Yuval (2005). Also see positions presented by Raday (1996b: 551) and Shifman (1986).

[8] See Stopler (2004) and Shalev (1995: 93).

[9] Rabbinical Courts Law (Enforcement of Divorce Judgments) 5755-1995, Law Book of the State of Israel [*Sanctions Law*].

[10] Human rights could even be shown to be counter-productive to the cause of minority women. While falling outside the purview of this chapter, a critique of the 'complex and contradictory nature of the human rights terrain' and of its 'dark sides' is necessary (Kapur 2006: 687). Also see Mutua (2001).

others as inevitably 'deviant'. What Israeli women reveal is that diverse practices can be turned by adjudicators and parties into deviance, but that the reverse is also true: deviant practices can be manipulated from the inside and changed for the better, flying in the face of an a priori categorisation.

II SANCTIONING DIVORCE: EMPOWERMENT THROUGH RELIGION

This chapter presents a portrait of the religious sphere of family law and Israeli women's navigation through the contradictory forces which shape the patriarchal structures that they inhabit. It starts by presenting the classical Jewish law of divorce, general rules which are followed with more or less rigidity by various denominations of Judaism.[11] The authority to divorce in Jewish law is found in the Torah at verse 24:1 in the book of Deuteronomy which states that:

> When a man taketh a wife, and marrieth her, then it cometh to pass, if she find no favour in his eyes, because he hath found some unseemly thing in her, that he writeth her a bill of divorcement, and giveth it in her hand, and sendeth her out of his house.

This passage was interpreted as bestowing the exclusive privilege to divorce on the husband (Kaplan 2004: 61). Moreover, the words 'if she find no favor in his eyes' were interpreted by medieval rabbinical scholars to imply that a divorce must be offered out of the complete free will of the husband (Kaplan 2004: 61; Bitton 2009: 117–18). This requirement was repeated throughout the centuries by religious scholars and has become an undefeatable condition for a valid divorce.

A Jewish divorce is executed by the granting of a writ of divorce (the *get*) on behalf of the man to the woman. For the *get* to be valid, a rabbinical court or *Beth Din* (pl *Batei Din*) composed of three Jewish judges (*Dayanim*) must oversee the divorce process. However, the *Beth Din* cannot enact the divorce itself, as the 'man's consent [is] the *sine qua non* of the entire process' (Berger and Lipstadt 1998: 99). A wife, on the other hand, may refuse her husband's *get*, but her bargaining power is severely hampered by a set of rules relating to her marriage status which essentially do not apply to men. For instance, if a woman enters into a relationship before having obtained a *get* from her husband, she will be considered 'adulterous' and she will not be allowed, even after an eventual Jewish divorce, to marry her partner under Jewish law or remarry her ex-husband (Cohn 2004: 66). Any child she may bear with her partner is considered a *mamzer* (pl *mamzerim*, bastard children) and is 'effectively excluded from Judaism' (Nichols 2007: 155). The *mamzer* status continues on for generations down the line and *mamzerim* are only permitted to marry each other (Rayner 2001: 43). Men, on the other hand, are not subject to these consequences. Indeed, a man's marriage with another woman in the absence of a *get* is halachically valid and

---

[11] For competing religious interpretations of the *agunah* problem, see Rosenthal (2006: 521).

that man's children are legitimate. He is not considered to have committed adultery, but merely to have contravened to a rabbinical decree prescribing monogamy (Nichols, 2007: 155). He can marry his adulterous lover, have legitimate children with her and even receive a permit from an Israeli rabbinical court to remarry if his wife refuses to accept the *get*.[12]

Whether it is the husband who is withholding the *get* or the woman who is refusing it, the rabbinical court can only order the parties to divorce on very specific halachic grounds and may not enact the divorce itself. If there are no grounds for divorce, there is nothing short of an agreement of the spouses that can dissolve the marriage. Oftentimes, if the wife is subject to physical or verbal abuse by her husband, if the husband is impotent or sterile or if he fails to provide maintenance, an order to divorce may be granted (Lieber, Schereschewsky and Drori 2007: 712–13). Inversely, the husband can claim the compulsion of *get* acceptance if he proves that he has reasons to suspect his wife of being adulterous or if she leads him to transgress Jewish law (Lieber, Schereschewsky and Drori 2007: 712–13; Haut 1983). Although the rabbinical court judges do not often issue orders compelling or obligating the giving and receiving of a *get*,[13] when they do, the 1995 Sanctions Law allows them to issue sanctions and a variety of restrictive orders on a recalcitrant spouse. The power of the community to use indirect pressure to influence a 'deviant' husband to issue a bill of divorce – which in the past was done through ostracism and excommunication – is now said to be translated into legislation by allowing the courts to withhold certain benefits from the husband (Halperin-Kaddari 2004: 238–39). For instance, the law allows for the imposition of restrictions on the right to leave the country, obtain an Israeli passport, maintain a driver's licence, work in a profession regulated by law or operate a business requiring a licence or legal permit, open or maintain a bank account, etc (Kaplan 2004: 123). Section 3 of the Law even allows for imprisonment to compel compliance with a divorce order. The period of imprisonment that a rabbinical court may impose is limited to five years, a term that may be extended by the court as long as the total term does not exceed ten years.[14] A further section of the Law goes as far as to allow the rabbinical court to impose sanctions on a husband who may already be serving a jail sentence.[15]

The Israeli rabbinical courts ordered the issuing of sanctions 73 times in 2008: 20 arrest warrants were issued and private investigators were hired by the courts 36 times to locate recalcitrant husbands who had disappeared in Israel or

---

[12] Yefet (2009: 447) quotes a Supreme Court of Israel decision which held, 'in a case where the rabbinical court granted a remarriage permit to a husband over his wife's objection, that the rabbinical court enjoys a broad discretion to grant permits and that it may do so in order to compel a wife to accept the *get*'.

[13] A rabbinical court may order *kfiat get* (a compulsion decree), which means that a party is 'compelled to give or accept a get', or *chiyuv get*, where a rabbinical court declares that there is 'an obligation to realize a get' (Blecher-Prigat and Shmueli 2009: 282–83).

[14] Sanctions Law, above (n 9) s 3(b).

[15] ibid, s 2(7).

abroad.[16] Further statistics show that the Sanctions Law was used several times in 2006,[17] and that between 1995 and 1998, 106 legal procedures resulted effectively in 43 divorces.[18] Professor Einhorn argues that the Sanctions Law has 'encouraged Jewish spouses to apply for a Jewish divorce in the Israeli rabbinical courts' (2009: 214). On its face, the response of the Israeli State thus seems to bring at least some solution to the plight of the *agunah*. We sought to measure how this plays out for Israeli women in practice.

Our fieldwork in Israel is based on interviews[19] conducted with six women who were all once married according to Jewish law.[20] The women interviewed varied in their level of religious commitment, although all were practising Jews. Two women were of the Orthodox denomination. Four women were already divorced and two were struggling to obtain their *get*. Four of these women had the Sanctions Law applied against their husbands by the rabbinical court, a process whereby their husbands were either put in jail, had their driver's licences taken away, had their passports confiscated and/or were disqualified from certain honours in the synagogue.[21] Most of our participants confirmed that indeed the Sanctions Law brought some empowerment to them. They had had recourse to several of the sanctions available under the Law and found that some were ineffective, but through trial and error they found remedies that had the desired effect and successfully disciplined their husbands.

---

[16] Administration of the Rabbinical Courts: Yearly Summary 2008 (Hebrew), available at: www. rbc.gov.il/statistics/2008/2008.pdf.

[17] Nissan Ratzlav-Katz, Statistics Dispel Claims of Thousands of Israeli Agunot, Israel National News (27 June 2007), available at: www.israelnationalnews.com/News/News.aspx/122884#.

[18] Gail Lichtman, 'No Exit: Jerusalem organizations are working to ease the plight of "agunot", women denied divorce' *Jerusalem Magazine* (January 2000), available at: www.legalaid.org.il/noexit.htm.

[19] The interviews lasted about one hour each and concerned demographics, religious background, the divorce, the civil legislation and the religious Sanctions Law. Four interviews were held in Hebrew with a Hebrew-English translator who asked the questions under the supervision of Merissa Lichtsztral who understands Hebrew, and two interviews were held in English in one-on-one conversations. Four of the interviews took place at coffee shops, while two women invited us to their homes to conduct the interview.

[20] This chapter focuses on Jewish law, but we acknowledge that Israel is a multinational and culturally diverse country which comprises notable Muslim and Christian Arab populations, among others. Field research has been completed among Israeli Muslim women in early 2012 to complement the perspectives offered in this chapter. This research is funded by the Social Sciences and Humanities Research Council of Canada.

[21] We began looking for interview participants by contacting university professors and various organisations and centres established in Israel which help women, financially and otherwise, in legal matter pertaining to the process of obtaining a *get*, a method which was approved by application to the Research Ethics Committee of the University of Ottawa. We met with representatives from the following organization: Yad L'Isha, Mavoi Satum, the International Coalition for Agunah Rights and the Ruth and Emmanuel Rackman Center for Advancement of Women's Studies at Bar Ilan University. All of our interview participants were found through the help of representatives from these organisations. The assistance and kindness of these people to connect us with these women was greatly appreciated, and the project could not have been a success without them.

Participant 2:

At the beginning I asked for alimony. [. . .] We sued him and the National Insurance Institute paid because of course he has no money and it didn't bother him because he wasn't paying. And then he still didn't want to [give the *get*]. Afterwards, we applied for an exit delay from the country, but he doesn't have the money to drive into town, so what do you think he is going to do abroad? So that neither [worked]. Afterwards I realised what would really shake him up would be his driver's license. He has a handicap, because of the alcohol: it damaged his leg. It led to necrosis in his hip bone. [. . .] And after he had a very difficult surgery and it was hard for him to walk, and he needed a car, so I told my rabbinical advocate: 'I think that we should ask to take his driver's licence'. She was sceptical, and I told her: 'No, I know him'. [. . .] We sent in a request for sanctions and they actually took his licence and then he started going wild. He appealed to the high rabbinical court in Jerusalem and we went. And there the rabbis were even more determined, like 'No you won't get your licence back until you give her a *get*, you are obligated to give her a *get!*'

Participant 3:

He was in prison for four months, and every time they brought him from prison to the rabbinical court he said 'No, I'm not ready, you can arrest me forever'. [. . .] So they brought him back to prison again and then back to court again and again and again. He thought 'That's the way it is', and the last time they said 'Ok we won't give you any date for court, you'll remain arrested until you say "I want [to give the *get*]"' and it didn't take a long time (laughter). [. . .] [He agreed to give the *get*] because he had no choice, because if he didn't agree he would have continued sitting in prison. And then one day they brought him and they convinced him and he gave the *get* through much suffering. You could really see that the man was suffering, but at the end he gave it because he understood that he would stay in prison.

The Sanctions Law thus left some room for empowerment for those women who were able to play out the Israeli legal system to their advantage. Furthermore, it is instructive to compare the rabbinical courts and Israeli civil courts, which have concurrent jurisdiction over ancillary matters such as property division and custody.[22] Civil courts are sometimes said to render decisions that are more sympathetic to women than those of rabbinical courts (Halperin-Kaddari 2004: 233). However, as Daphna Hacker convincingly argues, the ability for women to litigate before the civil courts is significantly hampered by poor access to justice in the civil realm, compared to less expensive and simpler procedures before the rabbinical courts (2012: 16). Bogoch and Halperin-Kaddari (2006) likewise argue that the workings of the civil courts and legislation in Israel have occulted persisting imbalances and access to justice problems for women. Our participants confirmed that litigating ancillary claims before civil courts represents a heavy financial burden and is often ineffective.

---

[22] If the file is opened at the civil court before the actual divorce petition in the rabbinical court, the relevant ancillary claims will be heard separately from the main divorce action which remains before the rabbinical court (Cohn 2004: 62).

Participant 6:

In the civil court, the property settlement dragged on for eight years. And in the end it was just thrown out, the whole thing. I'll get to that. But [it took] eight years of litigation, thousands and thousands and thousands of dollars. My parents helped me sometimes, I helped sometimes, I took loans sometimes. I'm still paying back the loans.

Participant 4:

I opened the file with the civil court and we divided the property. Not that it has even happened yet, even today the house is still in limbo; he isn't moving anything. And that's it. Everyone went in their direction and nothing came from this division of property. It remained as is. Get a lawyer: that costs money. Bring a private investigator: that will take money from you. So I said: 'I am not letting this happen anymore. I did it once and never again'.

Participant 1:

The [civil] family court wanted me to lower [the amount I was demanding] and they raised a stink. Nothing moved!

Furthermore, it should be noted that some of our participants did not view the civil courts as inherently favourable to women. They described how they felt equally miscarried by both religious and civil courts.

Participant 6:

I can't even say that it's only the *beit din* and that the *beit hamishpat* [civil court] was wonderful. I was also felt very, very, very frustrated by the *beit hamishpat*, the secular court.

Participant 1:

It was very difficult for me in the rabbinical courts, but also in the civil courts, which is where I did the division [of property]. [. . .] Both courts tortured me quite a bit, really. Our system doesn't have a clue what is going on!

Our participants also expressed dissatisfaction with the religious judicial process, but found that the existing legal aid services specifically dedicated to litigation in rabbinical courts greatly helped. Also, the possibility of retaining the services of a rabbinical advocate, an expert of Jewish law who generally commands a lower fee than a regular lawyer but who can only appear before the rabbinical court (Mandelbaum and Koenig 1985: 13–14), no doubt renders the religious sphere more attractive than the civil sphere for *some* women.

Participant 3:

Only when I was represented by Yad L'Isha [did things move in the right direction]. First of all Yad L'Isha immediately spoke to the police and ask that he be arrested. It didn't take a long time, maybe two weeks and then the police all of a sudden found him and arrested him [. . .].

Participant 2:

I went to Yad L'Isha, and there are women there who are amazing and ready to help. It's better than any well-known attorney or lawyer!

Thus, a basic cost/benefits analysis may thus direct the woman towards a rabbinical court instead of a civil court. Furthermore, the women we interviewed gave us some fascinating insights into the personal empowerment they experienced while sanctioning their husbands. The *get* refusal and the disciplinary practices actually allowed some women to gain an autonomy they could not otherwise have enjoyed.

Participant 3:

When he was in jail [for *get* refusal] he was constantly contacting me by phone. [. . .] It went on for months and he kept on harassing me on the phone and begged and begged but I knew that it was in vain because there was no way that I would give in until I achieved what I wanted to achieve.

Participant 6:

The empowerment, the process of empowerment that I went through, from when I was emotionally abused and tolerating that, to taking responsibility for my life and leaving him, [. . .] opening up my own post office box and changing my bank account. All these little teeny things which were necessary gave me the belief that somebody's helping me, that God wanted me to do this. If I hadn't been divorced, I'd still be living in that neighbourhood and I would not be the same person. [. . .] I am absolutely a new person . . . absolutely a new person. I still have scars inside, I still have bandages. I was abused and there are still scars, but most of the time I can cover them up and I feel empowered. And I will not let anybody step on me ever again.

Our participants thus indicated that some forms of empowerment resulted from the disciplinary power of the religious sphere. This empirical finding serves to demonstrate that the solution can often come from within the religious realm. The Sanctions Law remains, however, deeply flawed, as our participants have indicated. This next section will explore the Law's insufficiencies and its impact on women.

III INDETERMINACY, RABBINICAL RELUCTANCE AND THE VAGARIES OF ADJUDICATION

The literature has abundantly described the shortcomings of the Sanctions Law. For one, the rabbinical courts have been very reluctant to issue orders to compel the *get*. Only a small number of these compulsion decrees are issued each year (Blecher-Prigat and Shmueli 2009: 282). Furthermore, '[e]ven when men are commanded to divorce, the court seldom applies the coercive measures that it was legislatively authorised to use in 1995' (Yefet 2009: 448). As a result, the Sanctions Law is quite often un-enforced (Miller 1997: 14; Clinton 2000: 306).

For our participants, the unenforceability of the sanctions resulted in part from the actions of judicial actors and the police, in charge of executing the ordinances rendered under the Sanctions Law.

Participant 3:

It is a very difficult process, a very difficult process. [. . .] Every time, it was prolonged for another reason. It went on and they threatened him with arrest and he said 'Please go ahead and arrest me'. Then the rabbinical court put out a warrant to arrest him and the police didn't do anything with it. For more than a year the police did nothing, they didn't arrest him and then the rabbinical court decided to close the case.

Participant 6:

[We got] the *chiyuv get* and once we got that, the *toen rabbani* [rabbinical advocate] said 'Ok, now it's just a matter of time'. And then they said something like 'If he doesn't give you a *get* in 30 days he'll be arrested'. Now, they had already put out a court order that he had to come at one o'clock, because he had skipped some of these hearings. [. . .] What happened? The police went and looked for him, he wasn't there. I told them to look at his sister's house, I told them to look at his brother's house, everywhere they went to look, he wasn't there. He ended up showing up anyways. What did I learn from that? I can't count on the police that they're going to find him. Court order, shmourt order! [. . .] I can sit at home and hold this nice piece of paper and have it framed on the wall, and he's still going to do whatever he wants.

The unenforceability of the sanctions were also said to result from the rabbis themselves. In fact, the participants indicated that hearings at the rabbinical courts were delayed because the rabbis were reticent and unsympathetic to the women's plight.

Participant 4:

Q: Were there other sanctions against him besides putting him in prison?

A: We started all of them but they [the rabbis] actually didn't want to do them [the sanctions]. You see I learned the rabbinical court's ways. [. . .] They start something but they don't follow it all the way through to the end. It's like they feel . . . it's not comfortable for them to hurt people. [. . .] It was a waste of time, they applied sanctions, they brought notes to his synagogue so that he won't be [allowed to be] a cantor, but they didn't hang them; they told me to hang them. Why should I go into a men's synagogue and hang the notes? The men from the synagogue would kill me! What is this logic?

Participant 5:

I don't think that the rabbis do their job the way they should. We go into a hearing and we're invited for 10:30, and we go in at like 12:30 and at one o'clock, when they have to go home, they put on their coat and their hat and they say 'Ok, we've heard enough and we'll send you a decision in the mail'. [. . .] The rabbis wait a long time until they actually go ahead and give you an arrest warrant.

These testimonies echo the views of scholars for whom the rabbinical courts' reluctance to issue orders compelling divorce stems from the fear that applying sanctions on the recalcitrant husband will render the eventual giving of the *get* invalid due to force or undue pressure (Blecher-Prigat and Shmueli 2009: 283; Einhorn 2000: 151; Shifman 1999: 245). Rabbis are said to be very careful because a *get* that is given forcibly or under pressure will be rendered invalid (a '*get* meuseh') (Yefet 2009: 446; Bitton 2009: 117–18; Kaplan 2004: 61). Robyn Shames[23] also explained that some rabbis encourage women to settle by telling them 'pay him what he wants, you see what type of person he is, just pay him what he wants'. She also described the conceptions of rabbis she encountered: for them, women will only hurt themselves by refusing the conditions men put forth in order to grant them a *get,* sometimes becoming 'get refusers' in the eyes of the court. A rabbi's ideological and personal inclinations may thus influence the adjudicative process. Accordingly, the religious composition of Israeli courts was always the object of much academic interest. Scholars have described the 'monopoly' (Raday 1996a: 214)[24] that Orthodox groups enjoy over family law in Israel. Moreover, Orthodox rabbis are considered to form the majority of rabbinical court judges in the country (Woods 2008: xvi; Halperin-Kaddari 2000– 01: 348) and are said to be partial to the arguments of the husband (Halperin-Kaddari 2004: 233; Clinton 2000: 306). Some participants have indicated that the verdicts issued by the rabbinical courts are indeed inconsistent and depend on the backgrounds, personalities and religious ideologies of the judges.

Participant 1:

I don't know what their [the rabbinical courts'] process is. I just don't understand it and I was always mad at them until the end. [. . .] It was very hard because they did not see the importance of it [getting the *get*].

Participant 2:

I would talk and the rabbis would ignore me. They would only use his arguments and what he said; they only care about what the man wants not what the woman wants. They treated me like I wasn't even there. Then I said: 'I came to ask to be free, not for money or anything, just to be free'.[. . .] When the rabbis saw that I have a rabbinical advocate and that I am determined, that I want [a divorce] and that I am doing everything to get it, then they were easier.

Joanne Zack-Pakes:[25]

Once in a while we will get a rabbinical court that has guts, that will put the pressure on the guy. But it is unpredictable, there's nothing uniform in the decision making. It's all based on whim and which three judges are sitting and half the time there aren't even three judges there so they can't make a decision. They show up late for work,

[23] Director of the International Coalition for Agunah Rights, an international affiliation of groups advocating for the empowerment of *agunah* women. See: www.icar.org.il.

[24] On the importance of Orthodox Judaism with regard to other religious denominations in Israel, see Cohen and Susser (2000: 121).

[25] Social worker at Mavoi Satum, a Jerusalem-based organisation which provides assistance and legal aid to *agunah* women. See: www.mavoisatum.org.

they leave early from work. . . . There is nothing uniform about the rabbinical courts, one rabbi is rigid, one is not rigid.

As a result of this phenomenon, lawyers and rabbinical advocates will strategise to bring their clients in front of judges they deem more lenient. Participants had often wanted a particular rabbi to adjudicate their divorce petition because of these perceived ideological, religious or personal inclinations in their favour.

Participant 1:

We needed to go to the high rabbinical court. And only there was I saved, because we had there rabbi Lazare[26] who worked with my boss, and he came to a lot of the hearings. I called him many times and asked him to help.

Participant 6:

Everybody knew, even I knew that I needed to be in [rabbi] Rav Feldman's[27] group, the panel with the three of them. [. . .] Now in the *beit hadin hagadol* (high rabbinical court), there was only one *dayan*, one of those rabbis who would understand. [. . .] So we knew that we needed to get to Rav Shmuel Feldman.[28]

Participant 4:

I have to say, in the rabbinical court it didn't go through at first. [. . .] He sued me at the high rabbinical court, because he was against this rabbinical court here. He came to Jerusalem, in front of Rabbi Nissan[29] and two others. So then I arrived with my lawyer and his lawyer came alone. He says to him: 'Where is your client?' He says 'He couldn't make it', so he says 'Ok so tell him you have to give a get and we'll be done with this story'. [. . .] And I said 'Wow we reached these guys! Wow! This is going to be something! Like finally something in my favour, they really went in my favour!'

Even though participants did experience frustration at the leniency manifested by the rabbinical court towards their husbands, the existence of a legal right to sanctions and the community-based nature of the rabbinical courts allowed some of them to personally put pressure on the rabbis.

Participant 1:

I am even crying now. It was a really sad process, because every Monday and Thursday I would go to the rabbinical court. . . . He would not come and they would treat him with forgiveness. Because of my connections I was able to get the cell number of the rabbinical court judge and every time I would nag him, call him. I told him: 'What do you want me to do? You tell me not to sin, how can I not sin?'

Likewise, and notwithstanding widespread complaints that rabbis are overly sympathetic to men, some participants were able to play out their image against that of their husband's to successfully influence the rabbis. According to Halperin-Kaddari, the religious courts, when rendering decisions, will put more

---

[26] Fictitious name.
[27] ibid.
[28] ibid.
[29] ibid.

emphasis on moral and religious questions than do the civil courts and their application of the law may be tainted by their religious perspective (2004: 250). Moreover, Ariel Rosen-Zvi indicates that the rabbinical court will likely favour the 'more religious' parent for custody purposes (1989: 352). Exploiting the perception that the rabbis had of their personal ethics and situation could constitute a fertile strategic avenue for many religious women, as evidenced by our participants' testimonies.

Participant 6:

Watching him in action yelling at the judges, [. . .] that was what convinced them that I needed a *get*. [. . .] I mean also, I'm this together lady, and when they saw him ranting and raving they didn't like him. [. . .] So then, at one point, towards the end, we finally got a *chiyuv* [order that the *get* be given].

Participant 2:

Three rabbis were sitting at the *beit din*, and I said 'When you go to sleep think that I am your daughter. Would you relate to your daughter like you are acting to me?' I don't know if it did anything to them but the next time, they changed, they decided they had to give me a *get*. They treated me like a human.

Thus, the major flaw of the Sanctions Law is its indeterminacy and its permeability to ideological manipulation.[30] However, as we have seen, in some cases this phenomenon can be exploited by the women to manipulate religious law in their favour. Focusing on 'the moment of instability, the choice available at the moment of decision' (Rittich 2000: 929) and the way it plays out for real Jewish women involved in divorce proceedings teaches us that the Sanctions Law can be empowering to women, at least as often as it serves to disempower them.

IV CONCLUSION

This chapter has depicted the concrete impacts of a *religious* solution to the 'deviant' Jewish rules which create the *agunah* problem. By assessing the experiences of Jewish women navigating divorce in Israel, we have come across instances of legal subjects exercising 'agency embedded in religion'.[31] The religious sphere has shown a potential to produce differentiated bargaining endowments for women in various situations.[32] Furthermore, despite its numerous flaws and shortcomings, the very existence of the (religious) Sanctions Law seems to indicate that Israeli women have attained some form of (long fought for) empowerment. Our fieldwork on the workings of this law in fact supports Susan Weiss's view that

[30] This is not to suggest, of course, that religious law is indeterminate whereas secular law is determinate. For the application of the indeterminacy thesis in Western systems, see Kennedy (1997: 133); Tushnet (1996).

[31] See, on the topic of Muslim women's agency, Korteweg (2008).

[32] For thorough exploration of this idea in the Canadian context, see Fournier (2012).

[h]alakhah is not a collection of harsh and uniform rules, but rather embraces various and contradictory voices [and that the] outcome of a given case depends upon the rabbinical authority consulted, the 'facts' he deems worthy of emphasis, and the voices he chooses to heed (2004: 63).[33]

Indeed, just as Islamic law cannot be considered as an inherent violation of gender equality (Fournier 2010b; Korteweg and Selby 2012), Jewish law does not seem to be a homogeneous body of oppressive rules but an open-ended toolbox which is used in various contradictory ways by different rabbis. The growing mass of feminist Jewish scholarship[34] is interesting in this regard, contradicting as it does the claim that equality is at odds with the tenets of Jewish faith.[35] Thus, rather than seeing religion as the problem and law as the solution, lawyers and policymakers must, as this chapter has done, inquire into religion's 'complex and contradictory' potential uses (Cesari 2005: 92).

Given this indeterminacy, our interview participants were right to take on their rabbis in the hope of tilting adjudication in their favour, rather than seeking disavowal of their religion from a secular institution or human rights officials. This should not be taken to suggest that the religious sphere is somehow systematically more favourable to women, or even that it should be respected as a form of 'identity'. Rather, it indicates that any approach to marriage should account for our finding that in *some* social contexts, religion can prove to be empowering. Uncovering the concrete *distributive* implications of both secular and religious norms through socio-legal fieldwork should thus inform the research agenda. Adopting this methodological posture, especially in a non-secular, non-Western context, evidences that we can do without extensive theorising on the ways in which the state should control religious practices.[36] Indeed, 'constructive interaction' (Krivenko 2009: 5) between religious/'cultural' norms and international (and national) human rights is already happening, right before our eyes. The messy interactions of 'religion-at-law' (Jukier and Van Praagh 2008: 388) which take place both in secular and religious states can help unearth creative solutions to religious/cultural 'deviance'. This kind of 'adaptation policy',[37] whereby religious law is allowed to continue to coexist with and to be influenced by (inter)national human rights is probably the best way forward, rather than a pick-and-choose approach to religion which takes for granted the state's ability to act as a 'replacement for the socio-religious legal order' (Shah 2010: 139). Such an approach is inappropriate if it presumes of state policy's impacts on the ground, which our fieldwork has shown to be ethereal, ever-changing and profoundly contradictory. This chapter has argued that rather than looking for predictable and stable answers on which practices they

---

[33] For a similar argument see Strum (1989: 496).

[34] eg, Sassoon (2011: 119); Fuchs (2009: 1); Graetz (2005: 3); Ross (2004); Joseph (2005: 3) and Hauptman (1994: 40). For a critical account of this kind of work see Fuchs (2003: 225) and Levitt (1997: 91).

[35] This echoes Fournier's findings on Islamic law and Muslim women, see Fournier (2012).

[36] See generally Nichols (2011).

[37] Pearl and Menski (1998: 83). See also Fishbayn (2008).

should deem deviant and which practices they should embrace, policymakers around the globe need to look further into law's inconsistency and unpredictability. This will allow them to start taking stock of both religious and state law's many uneven 'openings for creativity and invention in reshaping the social world' (Ewick and Silbey 1995: 222).

REFERENCES

Althusser, L (1997) 'Ideology and Ideological State Apparatuses' in L Althusser, *Lenin and Philosophy and Other Essays* (trans Ben Brewster) (New York, Monthly Review Press).

Beaman, L (2011) '"It was all Slightly Unreal": What's Wrong with Tolerance and Accommodation in the Adjudication of Religious Freedom?' 23 *Canadian Journal of Women and Law* 442.

Benhabib, S (2002) *The Claims of Culture: Equality and Diversity in the Global Era* (New Jersey, Princeton University Press).

Berger, MS and Lipstadt, DE (1998) 'Women in Judaism from the Perspective of Human Rights' in MJ Broyde and J Witte (eds), *Human Rights in Judaism: Cultural, Religious and Political Perspectives* (Jerusalem, Jason Aronson).

Bitton, Y (2009) 'Public Hierarchy and Private Harm: Tort Law as a Remedy for Gender Inequality in Israeli Family Law' in L Dresdner and LS Peterson (eds), *(Re) Interpretations: The Shapes of Justice in Women's Experience* (Newcastle upon Tyne, Cambridge Scholars Publishing).

Blecher-Prigat, A and Shmueli, B (2009) 'The Interplay between Tort Law and Religious Family Law: The Israeli Case' 26 *Arizona Journal of International & Comparative Law* 279.

Bogoch, B and Halperin-Kaddari, R (2006) 'Divorce Israeli Style: Professional Perceptions of Gender and Power in Mediated and Lawyer-Negotiated Divorces' 28 *Law & Policy* 137.

Breitowitz, IA (1993) *Between Civil and Religious Law: The Plight of the Agunah in American Society* (Westport, Greenwood Press).

Brown, W (2006) *Regulating Aversion: Tolerance in the Age of Identity and Empire* (Princeton, Princeton University Press).

Caughey, JL (2009) 'The Anthropologist as Expert Witness: The Case of a Murder in Maine' in MC Foblets and AD Renteln (eds), *Multicultural Jurisprudence: Comparative Perspectives on the Cultural Defence* (Oxford, Hart Publishing).

Cesari, J (2005) 'Religion and Politics: Interaction, Confrontation and Tensions' 16 *History and Anthropology* 85.

Clinton, E (2000) 'Chains of Marriage: Israeli Women's Fight for Freedom' 3 *Journal of Gender Race & Justice* 283.

Cohen, A and Susser, B (2000) *Israel and the Politics of Jewish Identity: The Secular-Religious Impasse* (Baltimore, MD, Johns Hopkins University Press).

Cohn, M (2004) 'Women, Religious Law and Religious Courts in Israel – The Jewish Case' 27 *Retfaerd, Scandinavian Journal of Social Sciences* 55.

Einhorn, T (2000) 'Jewish Divorce in the International Arena' in J Basedow et al (eds), *Private International Law in the International Arena* (Alphen aan den Rijn, Kluwer Law International).

—— (2009) *Private International Law in Israel* (Alphen aan den Rijn, Kluwer Law International).

Ewick, P and Silbey, SS (1995) 'Subversive Stories and Hegemonic Tales: Toward a Sociology of Narrative' 29 *Law and Society Review* 197.

Fishbayn, L (2008) 'Gender, Multiculturalism and Dialogue: The Case of Jewish Divorce' 21 *Canadian Journal of Law & Jurisprudence* 71.

Fournier, P (2010a) 'Flirting with God in Western Secular Courts: Mahr in the West' 24 *International Journal of Law, Policy and the Family* 67.

—— (2010b) *Muslim Marriage in Western Courts: Lost in Transplantation* (Farnham, Ashgate).

—— (2012) 'Calculating Claims: Jewish and Muslim Women Navigating Religion, Economics and Law in Canada' 8 *International Journal of Law in Context* 47.

Fournier, P, McDougall, P and Dekker, A (2012) 'Dishonour, Provocation and Culture: Through the Beholder's Eye?' 16 *Canadian Criminal Law Review* 161.

Freeman, M (2003) 'Women, Law, Religion, and Politics in Israel: A Human Rights Perspective' in K Misra and MS Rich (eds), *Jewish Feminism in Israel: Some Contemporary Perspectives* (London, Brandeis University Press).

Fuchs, E (2003) 'Jewish Feminist Scholarship: A Critical Perspective' in LJ Greenspoon and R Simpkins (eds), *Studies in Jewish Civilization, Women and Judaism*, vol 14 (Omaha, NE, Creighton University Press).

—— (2009) 'Jewish Feminist Approaches to the Bible' in FE Greenspahn (ed), *Women and Judaism: New Insights and Scholarship* (Omaha, NE, Creighton University Press).

Graetz, N (2005) *Unlocking the Garden: A Feminist Jewish Look at the Bible, Midrash, and God* (Piscataway, NJ, Gorgias).

Hacker, D (2012) 'Religious Tribunals in Democratic States: Lessons from the Israeli Rabbinical Court' *Journal of Law and Religion*, available online at: ssrn.com/abstract=1691671.

Hale, RL (1923) 'Coercion and Distribution in a Supposedly Non-Coercive State' 38 *Political Science Quarterly* 470.

Halperin-Kaddari, R (2000–01) 'Women, Religion and Multiculturalism in Israel' 5 *UCLA Journal of International Law and Foreign Affairs* 339.

—— (2004) *Women in Israel: A State of Their Own* (Philadelphia, University of Pennsylvania Press).

Hauptman, J (1994) 'Feminist Perspectives on Rabbinic Texts' in L Davidman and S Tenenbaum (eds), *Feminist Perspectives on Jewish Studies* (London, Yale University Press).

Haut, IH (1983) *Divorce in Jewish Law and Life, Studies in Jewish Jurisprudence*, vol 5 (New York, Sepher-Hermon Press).

Joseph, N (2005) 'Jewish Law and Gender' in R Keller and RR Reuther (eds), *Encyclopedia of Women and Religion* (Bloomington, IN, Indiana University Press).

Jukier, R and Van Praagh, S (2008) 'Civil Law and Religion in the Supreme Court of Canada: What Should We *Get* out of *Bruker v Marcovitz*?' 43 *Supreme Court Law Review* 381.

Kaplan, YS (2004) 'Enforcement of Divorce Judgements by Imprisonment: Principles of Jewish Law' 15 *Jewish Law Annual* 57.

Kapur, R (2006) 'Human Rights in the 21st Century: Take a Walk on the Dark Side' 28 *Sydney Law Review* 665.

Kennedy, D (1997) *A Critique of Adjudication: fin de siècle* (Cambridge, MA, Harvard University Press).

Korteweg, A (2008) 'The Sharia Debate in Ontario: Gender, Islam, and Representations of Muslim Women's Agency' 22 *Gender & Society* 434.

Korteweg, A and Selby, J (eds) (2012) *Debating Sharia: Islam, Politics and Family Law Arbitration* (Toronto, University of Toronto Press).

Krivenko, EY (2009) *Women, Islam and International Law: Within the Context of the Convention on the Elimination of All Forms of Discrimination Against Women* (Leiden, Martinus Nijhoff Publishers).

Lerner, H (2011) *Making Constitutions in Deeply Divided Societies* (Cambridge, Cambridge University Press).

Levitt, L (1997) *Jews and Feminism: The Ambivalent Search for Home* (London, Routledge).

Lieber, DL, Schereschewsky, BZ and Drori, M (2007) 'Divorce' in M Berenbaum and F Skolnik (eds), *Encyclopaedia Judaica*, 2nd edn (Detroit, Macmillan Reference USA).

Mandelbaum, S and Koenig, M (1985) *Divorce your Lawyer* (Jerusalem, Gefen Publishing House).

Miller, JD (1997) 'History of the Agunah in America: A Clash of Religious Law and Social Progress' 19 *Women's Rights Law Reporter* 1.

Mutua, MW (2001) 'Savages, Victims, and Saviors: The Metaphor of Human Rights' 42 *Harvard International Law Journal* 201.

Navot, S (2007) *Constitutional Law of Israel* (Alphen aan den Rijn, Netherlands, Kluwer Law International).

Nichols, JA (2007) 'Multi-Tiered Marriage: Ideas and Influences from New York and Louisiana to the International Community' 40 *Vanderbilt Journal of Transnational Law* 135.

—— (2011) (ed), *Marriage and Divorce in a Multicultural Context: Multi-Tiered Marriage and the Boundaries of Civil Law and Religion* (Cambridge, Cambridge University Press).

Okin, SM (1999) 'Is Multiculturalism Bad for Women?' in J Cohen, M Howard and M Nussbaum (eds), *Is Multiculturalism Bad for Women?* (Princeton, NJ, Princeton University Press).

Pearl, D and Menski, W (1998) *Muslim Family Law*, 3rd edn (London, Sweet & Maxwell).

Phillips, A (2005) 'Dilemmas of Gender and Culture: The Judge, the Democrat and the Political Activist' in AI Eisenberg and J Spinner-Halev (eds), *Minorities Within Minorities: Equality, Rights and Diversity* (Cambridge, Cambridge University Press).

Raday, F (1996a) 'Religion, Multiculturalism and Equality: The Israeli Case' 25 *Israel Yearbook on Human Rights* 193.

—— (1996b) 'Women in Law in Israel: A Study of the Relationship between Professional Integration and Feminism' 12 *Georgia State University Law Review* 525.

Rayner, JD (2001) 'The Gender Issue in Jewish Divorce' in W Jacob and M Zemer (eds), *Gender Issues in Jewish Law* (Oxford, Bergahn Books).

Rittich, K (2000) 'Who's Afraid of the Critique of Adjudication? Tracing the Discourse of Law in Development' 22 *Cardozo Law Review* 929.

Rosenthal, RS (2006) 'Of Pearls and Fish: An Analysis of Jewish Legal Texts on Sexuality and their Significance for Contemporary American Jewish Movements' 15 *Columbia Journal of Gender and Law* 485.

Rosen-Zvi, A (1989) 'Forum Shopping Between Religious and Secular Courts (and its Impact on the Legal System)' 9 *Tel Aviv University Studies in Law* 347.

Ross, T (2004) *Expanding the Palace of Torah: Orthodoxy and Feminism* (Waltham, MA, Brandeis University Press).

Sassoon, I (2011) *The Status of Women in Jewish Tradition* (Cambridge, Cambridge University Press).

Shah, P (2009) 'Transforming to Accommodate? Reflections on the Shari'a Debate in Britain' in R Grillo et al (eds), *Legal Practice and Cultural Diversity* (Farnham, Ashgate).

—— (2010) 'Between God and the Sultana? Legal Pluralism in the British Muslim Diaspora' in JS Nielsen and L Christoffersen (eds), *Shari'a as Discourse: Legal Traditions and the Encounter with Europe* (Farnham, Ashgate).

Shalev, C (1995) 'Women in Israel: Fighting Tradition' in J Peters and A Wolper (eds), *Women's Rights, Human Rights: International Feminist Perspectives* (New York, Routledge).

Shifman, P (1986) 'State Recognition of Religious Marriage: Symbols and Content' 21 *Israel Law Review* 501.

—— (1990) 'Family Law in Israel: The Struggle between Religious and Secular Law' 24 *Israel Law Review* 537.

—— (1999) 'The Status of Women in Israeli Family Law – the Case for Reform' in H Hausmaninger et al (eds), *Developments in Austrian and Israeli Private Law* (New York, Springer-Verlag Wien).

Stopler, G (2003) 'Countenancing the Oppression of Women: How Liberals Tolerate Religious and Cultural Practices that Discriminate Against Women' 12 *Columbia Journal of Gender & Law* 154.

—— (2004) 'The Free Exercise of Discrimination: Religious Liberty, Civic Community and Women's Equality' 10 *William & Mary Journal of Women & Law* 459.

Strum, P (1989) 'Women and the Politics of Religion in Israel' 11 *Human Rights Quarterly* 483.

Tushnet, M (1996) 'Defending the Indeterminacy Thesis' 16 *Quinnipiac Law Review* 339.

Weiss, S (2004) 'Israeli Divorce Law: The Maldistribution of Power, its Abuses, and the "Status" of Jewish Women' in R Elior (ed), *Men and Women: Gender, Judaism and Democracy* (Jerusalem, The Van Leer Jerusalem Institute).

Woods, PJ (2008) *Judicial Power and National Politics: Courts and Gender in the Religious – Secular Conflict in Israel* (Albany, NY, State University of New York Press).

Yefet, KC (2009) 'Unchaining the Agunot: Enlisting the Israeli Constitution in the Service of Women's Marital Freedom' 20 *Yale Journal of Law & Feminism* 441.

Yuval, M (2005) 'The Right to Family Life and Civil Marriage under International Law and its Implementation in the State of Israel' 28 *Boston College International and Comparative Law Review* 79.

6

The Gendered Benefits and Costs of Legal Pluralism for Muslim Family Law in South Africa

WAHEEDA AMIEN

I INTRODUCTION

UNTIL THE DEMISE of apartheid in South Africa, there was only one form of marriage that was regarded as legally worthy of protection, namely, a marriage that was *de jure* monogamous. The legal system that was regulated by colonialists and implementers of apartheid laws did not recognise any marriage that was potentially polygynous, including Muslim marriages.[1] Notwithstanding the effort by the former colonialists and apartheid government to homogenise the family law system in South Africa, an unofficial form of legal pluralism exists through the operation of Muslim, Hindu, Jewish and African family laws within the respective religious and ethnic communities.

With the introduction of a constitutional democracy in 1994, the democratically elected government adopted a constitution that encompasses the principle of tolerance of difference. This is evident in the fact that it seeks to protect among others, the rights of different religious communities and their members to practise and manifest their religion and to have religious associations.[2] In fact, through section 15(3) of the Constitution, official legal pluralism is possible because it enables the South African government to enact legislation to recognise religious marriages or personal law systems provided they do not conflict with other constitutional provisions including gender equality. A precedent has already been set for the establishment of official plural legal systems in South Africa through the enactment of the Recognition of Customary Marriages Act ('RCMA'),[3] which recognises customary practices such as polygyny and enables

---

[1] *Bronn v Frits Bronn's Executors and Others* 1860 3 Searle 313; *Seedat's Executors v The Master (Natal)* 1917 AD 302; *Estate Mehta v Acting Master, High Court* 1958 (4) SA 252 (FC); *Ismail v Ismail* 1983 (1) SA 1006 (AD); *Kalla and Another v The Master and Others* 1995 1 SA 261 (T).

[2] ss 15 and 31 of the Constitution of the Republic of South Africa, 1996.

[3] No 120 of 1998.

customary practices such as *lobola* to be claimed and enforced in a secular court.[4] This chapter does not deal with the RCMA. Instead, it focuses on the gender implications of recognising Muslim family law within a secular context.

One might justifiably ask why official recognition of Muslim family law within the South African context should even be considered. The answer is quite simple: to not afford legal recognition means the continuation of the current status quo which militates mainly against women. The current status quo involves Muslim women and men being placed on a *de jure* unequal footing compared to spouses in civil marriages.[5] At the same time, Muslim women are disparately affected because they are additionally precluded from enforcing their Islamic law benefits[6] and are unable to challenge discriminatory Muslim family law rules and practices in court.[7] Although Muslim parties have the option of entering into a civil marriage in addition to their Muslim marriage so that they can access the benefits of civil law, many do not avail themselves of this option as a result of an anti-civil marriage culture that exists within the South African Muslim community, which is reinforced by negative messages conveyed by the *ulamā* (Muslim clergy) that civil marriages are *ḥarām* (forbidden). Officiators of Muslim marriages such as *imāms* can also be designated as marriage officers[8] so that when they perform a *nikah* (Muslim marriage) it would immediately be recognised as legal. The unfortunate reality is that very few *imāms* apply to be designated as marriage officers, most likely because they would then be prohibited from performing polygynous marriages. Legal recognition is therefore necessary to change the aforementioned status quo.

By invoking section 15(3) of the Constitution, the South African government undertook to bring Muslim marriages and other religious marriages within the legal ambit of family law. In 2003, it drafted the Muslim Marriages Bill ('MMB'), which seeks to recognise and regulate Muslim marriages. In 2005, it drafted the Recognition of Religious Marriages Bill ('RRMB'), which proposes to afford legal recognition to all religious marriages including Muslim marriages in South Africa. The RRMB has not yet been approved by Cabinet. However, the MMB was approved by Cabinet in 2010 and was available for public comment until the end of May 2011.[9] At the date of writing this chapter, the Department of Justice and Constitutional Development was in the process of collating the numerous submissions. Although the MMB and RRMB are yet to enter the parliamentary process, one may arguably assume that through both pieces of draft legislation,

---

[4] ss 1 and 3(4).

[5] For instance, if a Muslim person is married by Muslim rites only and is a beneficiary of a state funded pension, her or his spouse will not have a 50 per cent claim to the benefit when their marriage dissolves, which their civil law counterparts who are married to each other in community of property currently have.

[6] eg, Islamic law recognises the right of a wife to be compensated for her labour in the home.

[7] eg, a traditional interpretation of Islamic law, which is prevalent in the South African Muslim community, does not afford equal rights of divorce to men and women.

[8] s 3 of the Marriage Act 25 1961.

[9] For an explanation of the history of the Muslim Marriages Bill ('MMB'), see Amien (2010).

the government has indicated a commitment to realising the rights of minority religious communities to enjoy legal protection of their respective marriages, albeit in whichever form that realisation occurs.[10]

While the MMB and RRMB have the potential to enable the enforcement of civil and Islamic law benefits, they purport to do it in different ways. The differences between the two pieces of draft legislation are elaborated on in this chapter when I compare them and attempt to extrapolate the benefits and costs that each offers for the incorporation of Muslim marriages into the South African legal system. I demonstrate that the way in which Muslim marriages are recognised, in other words, the way in which official legal pluralism manifests, determines whether or not women's rights are positively or negatively affected. I do this by providing a description of the two Bills and their relevant provisions in the first half of this chapter while in the second half I present a cost/benefit analysis of the Bills, specifically in so far as the implications for women are concerned.

II THE MUSLIM MARRIAGES BILL ('MMB')

The MMB recommends the integration of Muslim marriages by regulating them within an Islamic law and human rights framework.[11] It is the culmination of several years of consultations between the South African Law Reform Commission ('drafters') and various sections within the South African Muslim community, which resulted in a document that is arguably a reasonable compromise between extreme positions ranging from the views of members of the *ulamā* to women's rights advocates. For example, some sections of the *ulamā* recommended that the draft legislation provides for blanket recognition of

---

[10] South Africa's total population is 44,819,778 of which the majority is Christian-based comprising 79.8 per cent of its total population. Several minority religious communities make up the balance of the South African population consisting of Muslims (1.5 per cent), African traditional beliefs (0.3 per cent), Judaism (0.2 per cent), Hinduism (1.2 per cent) and other unidentified faiths (0.6 per cent). Statistics South Africa, *Census 2001: Primary tables South Africa. Census '96 and 2001 compared* (Pretoria, Statistics South Africa, 2004) 27–28. available at: www.statssa.gov.za/census01/html/RSAPrimary.pdf.

[11] Integration involves the recognition and protection of religious diversity within a human rights framework: Ghosh (1994: 57). The MMB is especially a conglomeration of conservative and progressive interpretations of the *Sunni* tradition, particularly encompassing the *Hanafī* and *Shāfi'ī madhāhib* (schools of thought), which are followed by the majority of South African Muslims. See N Jeenah, 'The MPL Battle in South Africa. Gender Equality vs "Shari'ah"', presented at an international workshop entitled 'Shari'ah Debates and its Perceptions by Muslims and Christians in Selected African Countries', organised by the German Institute for Middle Eastern Studies, University of Bayreuth, Germany, held in Limura, Kenya (July 2004) (on file with author) 12. On the other hand, Manjoo suggests that the MMB excludes the interpretations and practices of the *Sunni Māliki* and *Hanbali madhāhib* as well as the *Shia Ja'fari madhhab*: R Manjoo (ed), 'The Recognition of Muslim Personal Laws in South Africa: Implications for Women's Human Rights' (unpublished report for the Human Rights Programme at Harvard Law School, undated) 2. Although the aforementioned *madhāhib* do not appear to have been accommodated in the MMB, this might be justified on the basis that they comprise minority groups within the South African Muslim communities.

polygyny while some women's rights groups argued for the abolition of polygyny. Instead, the drafters recommended the recognition of polygyny in a regulated manner to ensure that polygynous wives are not left unprotected. The
MMB requires a husband to apply for court approval to enter into a polygynous
marriage and for approval of a contract that regulates the future matrimonial
property regime of that marriage.[12] The MMB obliges a court to grant the order
only 'if it is satisfied that the husband is able to maintain equality between his
spouses as is prescribed by the Holy *Qur'ān*'.[13] All interested parties, particularly existing spouses, must also be joined in the proceedings.[14] Although the
Qur'ānic concept of equality could be subject to juristic interpretation and may
depend on who provides the interpretation, and despite the fact that the MMB
does not require the consent of an existing wife to enable her husband to enter
into a polygynous marriage, the MMB's provisions could still afford more protection to polygynous wives than they currently have. At present, members of
the *ulamā* who solemnise polygynous Muslim marriages do not insist that men
comply with their Islamic law obligations, including the obligation to ensure
equality among polygynous wives. In many instances, men also get away with
contracting secret polygynous marriages without their wives knowing about
each other's existence. The effect is harmful to women because among others,
they end up contributing to the maintenance of more than one family without
having consented to doing so. Furthermore, the MMB will afford an existing
wife the opportunity to be informed about the impending marriage and to
inform the court about her views regarding that marriage. It may also encourage a culture of accountability on the part of husbands.

In addition to polygyny, the MMB proposes regulating many other features
of Muslim marriages within the parameters of Islamic law. The following paragraphs summarise the main features that the MMB seeks to regulate, which
include Islamic law practices that are currently implemented by the *ulamā* and
those that are not implemented by the *ulamā*.

Islamic law practices that are implemented by the *ulamā*, which the MMB
recognises include: the requirement that the bride and groom both consent to
the marriage and that the wife can provide her guardian with a proxy to contract the marriage on her behalf; the requirement that the marriage be observed
by two witnesses under Islamic law; recognition of the husband's unilateral
obligation to *nafaqah* (maintain) his children; inclusion of the husband's obligation to provide *mahr* (dower) to his wife and to *nafaqah* her during the marriage and *iddah* (three-month waiting period that a wife must observe after
divorce); implicitly excluding the husband from post-*iddah nafaqah* obligations
toward his former wife; recognition of Islamic law forms of dissolution of marriage including *talāq*, *tafwīd al-talāq*, *faskh* and *khul'a*; the requirement for

---

[12] cl 8(6).
[13] cl (8)(7(a). The relevant provision can be found in *Qur'ān* 4:3.
[14] cl (8)(8).

mediation preceding the institution of divorce; and the wife's entitlement to *mut'ah al-talāq* (conciliatory gift) under circumstances that are permitted by Islamic law, which includes a situation where the husband unjustifiably terminates the marriage.[15] Some of these concepts require extrapolation, which is provided in the following paragraphs.

The MMB only accepts judicial dissolution of a Muslim marriage as valid, which includes the pronouncement of *talāq*.[16] This is a step away from the traditional approach that treats *talāq* as an extra-judicial form of divorce. A husband exercising his right to an irrevocable *talāq* and a wife exercising her delegated right to an irrevocable *talāq* must have their irrevocable *talāqs* registered with a marriage officer followed by the institution of legal proceedings.[17] The MMB incorporates the recommended and non-recommended *Sunni* classical views relating to irrevocable *talāq*.[18] The recommended *Sunni* form of *talāq* (*talāq-al-sunna*) involves the husband uttering *talāq* once or twice without the parties reconciling prior to the expiration of the *iddah* period, or thrice, which renders the *talāq* irrevocable (*ba'in*).[19] Prior to the utterance of the third *talāq* and before the expiration of the *iddah* period, the *talāq* is considered revocable (*raj'i*). The significant feature of revocability is that the husband has an opportunity to reconsider his decision and reconcile with his wife. Also, prior to the third utterance of *talāq* and in the event that the wife has observed her full *iddah*, the parties may remarry without the wife first having to perform *hilala* (marriage to another man, which must be consummated and dissolved before the couple are permitted to remarry each other). In contrast, the non-recommended *Sunni* form of *talāq* namely, *talāq al-bid'a* or triple *talāq* is uttered thrice successively in one sitting and results in the dissolution of the marriage without the possibility of reconciliation.[20] In the latter instance, the wife must first perform *hilala*

---

[15] cls 1, 5(1)(a), (b) and (c), 11(2)(a)–(c), 12. The MMB frames the husband's *nafaqah* obligations within the parameters of his means and the wife's reasonable needs. The MMB defines *faskh* as a fault-based judicial dissolution of the marriage, available to women and men. Grounds listed include: whereabouts of the husband unknown; failure by the husband to maintain his wife; imprisonment of the husband for a period of three or more years; mental illness or continued unconsciousness suffered by the husband; impotence or serious illness suffered by the husband; cruelty or harm committed against the wife by the husband; unreasonable failure by the husband to perform his marital obligations; husband contracts polygynous marriage/s and fails to treat the existing wife or wives justly; discord between the spouses (*shiqaq*). The MMB defines *khul'a* as a no-fault based judicial mechanism, which is based on an agreement between spouses to dissolve the marriage at the wife's behest. It entails transfer by the wife of property or anything permissible according to Islamic law. The MMB defines *tafwid al-talāq* as a conditional or unconditional delegation of *talāq* at the date of marriage or subsequently by the husband to the wife or her representative.

[16] cl 9(2). *Talāq* is the husband's unilateral and exclusive right to repudiate his wife without having to show any grounds.

[17] cl 9(3)(a), (c), (f).

[18] cl 1.

[19] cl 1. See Esposito (1991: 78, 83); Esposito and DeLong-Bas (2001: 30); Fyzee (1949: 144–46); Ajijola (1981: 167–68); Ahmed (1978: 64–65); Pearl (1979: 89–90); Rushd (1996: 76, 96); Sabiq (undated: 51).

[20] cl 1 of the MMB. Esposito and DeLong-Bas (2001: 30); Ahmed (1978: 64); Pearl (1979: 89). The MMB also accepts the pronouncement of *talāq* as irrevocable if it is expressly uttered as irrevocable.

before the parties may remarry since the husband has utilised his maximum number of three *talāqs*.

While registration of an irrevocable *talāq* was most likely intended to encourage men to take the *talāq* mechanism more seriously, the fact that the MMB does not require a revocable *talāq* to be similarly registered may result in a negation of that objective because it could result in the current practice of perpetual *iddah* being maintained. Perpetual *iddah* refers to a practice where men utter *talāq* continuously beyond the maximum three utterances and reconcile with their wives before the expiration of their *iddah* periods. It happens because the *ulamā* do not strictly apply or monitor the Islamic law relating to *talāq* and because women and men are most likely ignorant of the Islamic laws relating to *talāq*. The result is that women are placed in a highly burdensome position because from one minute to the next, they are unsure whether they are married or under *iddah* and this could prevail for any length of time.[21]

Although the MMB stipulates that the Muslim marriage may be judicially dissolved on any ground permitted by Islamic law, a conservative interpretation could preclude grounds being required for *talāq*.[22] Presumably, the recognition of grounds applies only to dissolution on the basis of *faskh*, which can be initiated by either spouse and could result in the marriage being judicially dissolved. The MMB specifies numerous Islamic law grounds for *faskh* including discord between the spouses (*shiqaq*).[23] This is arguably similar to the civil law ground of irretrievable breakdown of the marriage, which must be proven for the dissolution of a civil marriage. Moreover, the factors that a court may accept to prove irretrievable breakdown of a civil marriage are similar to those listed for *faskh*.[24]

The third form of dissolution of a Muslim marriage that the MMB recognises is *khul'a*. While *khul'a* has been interpreted by many majority Muslim countries as a form of judicial dissolution of the marriage that is initiated by the wife in exchange for the return of her *mahr* without requiring her husband's consent, the MMB incorporates a more conservative interpretation

---

[21] *Iddah* prevents women from engaging in public life and becoming romantically involved with anyone.

[22] cl 9(2).

[23] cl 1.

[24] s 4 of the Divorce Act 70 of 1979 reads: '(1) A court may grant a decree of divorce on the ground of the irretrievable break-down of a marriage if it is satisfied that the marriage relationship between the parties to the marriage has reached such a state of disintegration that there is no reasonable prospect of the restoration of a normal marriage relationship between them. Subject to the provisions of subsection (1), and without excluding any facts or circumstances which may be indicative of the irretrievable break-down of a marriage, the court may accept evidence – that the parties have not lived together as husband and wife for a continuous period of at least one year immediately prior to the date of the institution of the divorce action; that the defendant has committed adultery and that the plaintiff finds it irreconcilable with a continued marriage relationship; or that the defendant has in terms of a sentence of a court been declared an habitual criminal and is undergoing imprisonment as a result of such sentence, as proof of the irretrievable break-down of a marriage'.

of *khul'a* that does require the husband's consent for the payment of the financial consideration.[25]

Although *faskh*, *khul'a* and *tafwid al-talāq* were probably an attempt to balance the right to *talāq*, the balance still leans in favour of the husband because
the MMB does not contain an equivalent form of divorce for the wife. She will
require her husband's and/or the court's permission to be released from the
marriage and may have to forfeit property to achieve this. The MMB therefore
does not confer equal rights to divorce on the parties.

Before the Muslim marriage is judicially dissolved, the MMB affords the parties an opportunity to refer their dispute to mediation.[26] This alternative form
of dispute resolution was included presumably in response to the *ulamās* expectation that the Islamic law requirement of arbitration preceding dissolution of
the marriage should be incorporated into the MMB. If parties choose to have
their dispute mediated, the MMB stipulates that it must be mediated by a 'prescribed accredited mediation council'.[27] If an agreement arises from the mediation, it must be judicially confirmed unless the interests of any minor children
are not sufficiently protected.[28] Only if an agreement is not reached during the
mediation process can the dispute be referred for judicial adjudication.[29]

The mediation process offered by the MMB may have negative consequences
for women. For instance, many of the *'ulamā* throughout South Africa already
conduct mediation proceedings. If they succeed in obtaining accreditation for
mediation, it is likely that women may feel coerced into having their marital
disputes mediated by those bodies. This means that agreements reached as a
result of mediation processes may not necessarily favour the wife. Although the
MMB does not preclude parties from appealing against judicial confirmation of
mediation agreements, indigent women may not be able to afford the cost of
challenging them in higher courts.

A further troubling aspect that permeates the MMB is the continuous reference to Islamic law and its primary sources namely, *Qur'ān* and *Sunnah*[30] as
guiding principles in the interpretation of various provisions.[31] Conservative
interpretations of the primary sources of Islamic law will disadvantage women.
For example, the MMB requires that on divorce, guardianship, custody and
access of children should be determined on the basis of the welfare and best

---

[25] The requirement regarding 'agreement' for *khul'a* is not settled law. Countries such as Egypt,
Nigeria, Bangladesh, Pakistan and Philippines do not require the husband's consent: Women Living
Under Muslim Laws (2003: 278–79).

[26] cl 12.

[27] cl 12(1).

[28] cl 12(3).

[29] cl 12(4).

[30] *Qur'ān* and *Sunnah* are the primary sources of Islamic law. The *Qur'ān* is regarded as the lit-
eral word of God and the *Sunnah* refers to the prophetic tradition of Prophet Muhammad (p.b.u.h.).

[31] See the following clauses of the MMB: 1, 9(4)–(5)(d), 9(8)(g) (*faskh*); 1 (definition of Muslim
marriage); 5(1)(c) (witnesses); 8(7)(a) (polygyny); 9(2) (termination of Muslim marriages); 9(8)
(claims against deceased estates); 9(8)(g) (*mut'ah al-Talāq*); 9(9) (contributions after death of
spouse); and 10(1), (4)(b) (custody and access of children).

interests of the child 'with due regard to Islamic law and the report and recommendations of the Family Advocate, which must take into account Islamic norms and values'.[32] A conservative interpretation of the latter could award those rights to the father only. Furthermore, the MMB defines Islamic law as including the primary and secondary sources with the exception of *ijtihād*.[33] The exclusion of *ijtihād* may preclude courts from accepting interpretations of Muslim family law that emanate from an exercise of independent reasoning and may increase the likelihood of conservative interpretations being adopted that negatively impact on women.

Despite the possibility that provisions of the MMB that are directed to be interpreted in accordance with Islamic law, *Qur'ān* and *Sunnah* could be open to abuse by anti-women's rights interpretations, the MMB does not purport to override the Bill of Rights.[34] Although it would be preferable for the MMB to specifically direct implementers to take cognisance of South Africa's constitutional and international law obligations, it is nevertheless expected that a secular judiciary, which the MMB recommends will be tasked with interpreting its provisions, will keep those obligations foremost in mind when interpreting the provisions of the MMB.

The MMB's expectation that its provisions will be interpreted by a secular judiciary is contested by many sections of the *ulamā*, which prefer that a specialist Islamic law court be established to interpret the MMB's provisions without being held accountable to the Constitution. This is problematic on two levels: first, a separate Islamic law court would most likely be presided over by conservative members of the *ulamā* who would only be interested in maintaining the current status quo in which women's Islamic law and human rights may be undermined; and secondly, an Islamic law court that is not subject to the Constitution will not be constitutionally acceptable since the Constitution subjugates *all law* to the provisions of the Bill of Rights. If Muslim family law is recognised as law, whoever presides over such an Islamic law court will not be able to escape constitutional oversight for their decisions. Yet, that oversight can only occur if a decision is appealed to a superior court. Given the costs that are involved in appeal litigation, indigent women (and men) could be precluded from launching constitutional challenges against discriminatory Muslim family law rules and practices. In this way, discriminatory Muslim family law rules and practices could be maintained and perpetuated with legal sanction.

Alternatively, the *ulamā* may settle for a Muslim judge within the secular judiciary adjudicating with assessors who are Islamic law experts. Although the

---

[32] cl 10(1).

[33] cl 1 defines Islamic law as 'the law as derived from the Holy Qur'ān , the Sunnah (Prophetic model), the consensus of Muslim jurists (Ijma) and analogical deductions based on the primary sources (Qiyas)'. *Ijtihād* refers to the exercise of independent juristic reasoning or the formation of individual opinions or creative reinterpretations of the law. Ali (2000: 19–22); Engineer (1992: 167); Schacht (1964: 69).

[34] Jeenah, above (n 11) 12.

Indian experience teaches us that judgments about Muslim family law that are informed by Islamic law experts are more likely to be palatable to minority Muslim communities,[35] the expectation that a Muslim judge who is assisted by Islamic law experts acting as assessors raises two challenges. First, the existing paucity of Muslim judges within the South African judiciary could result in a backlog of cases that would prejudice parties seeking redress in Muslim family law-related matters (Amien 2010: 378). Secondly, determining whether or not a judge is Muslim could be difficult because implementers of the legislation will have to decide which criteria should be used to verify that a judge is Muslim (Amien 2010: 377–78). Even when one is able to ascertain that a judge is Muslim, she or he may not have the necessary expertise in Islamic law to adjudicate the matter. Similar problems could be experienced if a judge is required to adjudicate with Islamic law experts as assessors. The judicial system may not readily have experts at hand who are available as assessors, which could also result in a backlog of cases. Furthermore, assessors do not currently play a role in the adjudicating process as it pertains to the law; they simply assist the court in its decision-making process as it relates to the facts of the case.

The option that is implicitly permitted by the MMB may be more feasible, namely, that a secular judge retains the discretion to use assessors who are Islamic law experts. In the absence of assessors, legal counsel could call on Islamic law experts to provide testimony in the case at hand. The latter option is not ideal since parties have to bear the costs of expert fees. In this regard, the state could incorporate the British model into the legislation, which enables courts to call on Islamic law experts to testify at state expense.

The courts should also ensure that they do not rely only on conservative Islamic law experts because that may result in discriminatory decisions being delivered against women. This means that progressive Islamic law experts must avail themselves to either testify as experts or act as assessors. If faced with conflicting interpretations of Islamic law, the judiciary's constitutional obligation to protect and promote women's right to equality will surely justify an application of a gender-sensitive interpretation in favour of a conservative interpretation.[36]

The drafters of the MMB also attempted to ameliorate the position of women by including more progressive features of Islamic law that are not presently implemented by the South African *ulamā*. Some have been mentioned previously such as *talāq* being confirmed judicially; others include, in the case of divorce, an extension of the husband's *nafaqah* obligation to provide a separate residence for the wife when she has custody of the child(ren) if she does not own a residence and for the period of such custody only.[37] The MMB further

---

[35] An attestation to this assertion can be gleaned from the outcry by Indian Muslims to the judgment handed down by a Hindu majority court in the case of *Mohd Ahmed Khan v Shah Bano Begum and Others* (1985) 2 SCC 556.

[36] s 9(3) of the Constitution.

[37] cl 11(2)(c)(ii).

recognises the wife's *nafaqah* right to be separately remunerated for breastfeeding purposes for two years from the birth of the child.[38]

The South African *ulamā* adopt the traditional Islamic law approach to matrimonial property regimes that the estates of spouses should be kept separate on entering the marriage, during the marriage and at dissolution of the marriage. In many instances, this approach militates against women because most of the assets acquired during marriage accrue to the husband's estate so that when the marriage terminates, the wife is usually left destitute.[39] The MMB includes this traditional Islamic law approach to matrimonial property regimes.[40] Although the MMB enables parties to contract out of this regime, women are not usually sufficiently empowered to exert their rights to negotiate and contract the terms of their marriage (Commission for Gender Equality 2000: 9). Fortunately, the MMB attempts to minimise the negative consequences mentioned above by incorporating Islamic law rights that are available to women, which are not currently practised within the community. For instance, the MMB gives a court the power to make an order for the equitable division of assets where a party assists in the conduct of a family business during the marriage or 'actually' contributes to the maintenance or increase of the other's estate.[41] The former should protect a wife who is drawn into assisting in a family business during the subsistence of the marriage while the business is not registered in her name. However, the MMB does not go far enough with the latter because its reference to 'actually contribute[s]' may preclude a wife's entitlement under Islamic law to be compensated for her unpaid labour in the home (Ali 2003: 170).

The MMB also attempts to provide protection to women who are currently married by civil and Muslim rites. If those women wish to obtain dissolution of their marriages after the enactment of the MMB, the latter precludes a court from dissolving the civil marriage without proof that the Muslim marriage is dissolved.[42] This is to prevent a husband from holding his wife hostage in the Muslim marriage even though their civil marriage is terminated. Since the husband could refuse to grant *talāq* thereby preventing the wife from being released from either the civil or Muslim marriages, the MMB enables the wife to apply for and obtain *faskh* after which the matter is dispensed with according to civil legislation governing divorce.[43]

---

[38]   ibid. The breastfeeding period of two years is a *Qur'ānic* prescription. *Qur'ān* 2:233. Sabiq (undated: 363).

[39]   W Amien, *Comments on the South African Law Commission's Discussion Paper No 101. Islamic Marriages and Related Matters* (submitted on behalf of the Gender Unit & General Practice Unit, Legal Aid Clinic, University of the Western Cape, Shura Yabafazi ('Consultation of Women'), Nadel (Western Cape), Nadel Human Rights Research and Advocacy Project, 2002) 17 (on file with author).

[40]   cl 8(1). The regime is out of community of property excluding the accrual system, which involves the parties' estates being kept separate at commencement of the marriage, during marriage and at dissolution of the marriage.

[41]   cl 9(8)(b)(i)–(ii).

[42]   cl 13(1).

[43]   cl 13(2).

It is clear from the above exposition that the MMB does not fully satisfy all the interests of the *ulamā* or women's rights advocates. Although conservative and progressive groups within the Muslim community are not happy with the MMB in its entirety, 'most feel that it is a document that they can live with'.[44] As far as the more moderate members of the *ulamā* are concerned, the MMB presents an opportunity for 'marital disputes [to] be resolved more efficiently'.[45] For progressive Muslim organisations, the MMB contains more of their demands than they had expected would be included.[46] Yet, it is particularly because the MMB does not fully promote women's right to equality that the Commission for Gender Equality ('CGE') in conjunction with the State Law Advisor's Office drafted an alternative Bill namely, the RRMB, which is discussed next.[47]

III THE RECOGNITION OF RELIGIOUS MARRIAGES BILL ('RRMB')

The RRMB is a combined CGE and government initiative, which did not undergo the same level of consultation as the MMB. In fact, one might even question whether or not there was a consultation process to begin with that involved the Muslim community (Amien 2010: 369).

The RRMB proposes accommodating religious marriages by affording legal recognition to the marriages with minimal regulation by the state. Instead, the function of regulating religious marriages is left to the religious communities. Where the RRMB recommends the recognition of features that are characteristic to a particular religion, it does not attempt to regulate those features. For example, the RRMB affords blanket recognition to polygyny.[48] In the context of Muslim marriages, this means that men may not be required to comply with the Islamic law requirement that they can only marry up to four women simultaneously if they can show that they will be able to treat or maintain their wives equally. Without state regulation of polygynous marriages, it is expected that harmful gendered practices related to polygynous marriages will continue. Minimal state regulation is also evident with regard to other Muslim family law features such as the default matrimonial property system, Muslim forms of divorce and patrimonial payments.

The RRMB provides that the matrimonial property system should be 'governed by the tenets of the religion unless the spouses enter into an ante nuptial contract to regulate otherwise'.[49] Due to religious convictions and power imbalances between Muslim men and women, it is likely that most Muslim spouses

---

[44] Jeenah, above (n 11) 14.

[45] ibid, 14–15.

[46] ibid.

[47] Manjoo, above (n 11) 2.

[48] cl 2(2): 'If a person is a spouse in more than one religious marriage all such marriages entered into which comply with this Act are recognised as marriages for all purposes'.

[49] cl 9(1), (2).

will continue to adopt the separate estates approach encouraged by the *ulamā*, particularly in a way which does not recognise the contributions by one spouse to the increase or maintenance of the other spouse's estate. Unfortunately, the RRMB does not offer the types of protections afforded by civil law or the MMB, which enable a court to order an equitable distribution of assets if one of the parties contributes to an increase in the other's estate.[50]

The RRMB also provides that when granting a decree for the dissolution of a religious marriage, the court 'may, when making an order for the payment of maintenance, take into account any provision or arrangement made in accordance with the religious tenets of the spouses'. Apart from introducing the potential for conservative interpretations that exclude the possibility of post-*iddah nafaqah*, the wording of this provision makes it possible to confuse the payment of *mahr* in settlement of *nafaqah*, as is evidenced by the Indian experience.[51]

While the RRMB purports to leave the regulation of Muslim marriages within the control of the Muslim community, it proposes assimilating the process and consequences of dissolution of the marriage into the broader secular framework. This is one of the most important interventions that the RRMB offers for the protection of women's rights because it allows men and women to have equal access to divorce. The RRMB contemplates having a valid religious marriage dissolved by a secular court on the ground of 'irretrievable breakdown of a marriage', which mimics the civil law requirement for divorce.[52] The RRMB also imports a secular requirement from the Mediation in Certain Divorce Matters Act,[53] which obliges the Family Advocate's Office to conduct an inquiry when a divorce involves minor children. A court is directed to consider the recommendations of the Family Advocate's Office and to make an order that would be in the best interests of the minor children.[54] This is certainly a better option than is provided for in the MMB since the Family Advocate's Office and the court need only concentrate on what would be in the best interests of the minor child and not what Islamic law has to say about guardianship, access and custody, which may militate against the mother.

Although the RRMB appears to try to afford women and men equal rights to divorce, it fails to regulate any of the features of a Muslim divorce. This may enable the status quo to be maintained, namely, that access to dissolution of the Muslim marriage is far easier for men than it is for women. In other words, men will be able to continue to arbitrarily repudiate their wives through the *talāq* mechanism without having to provide grounds and women will continue to experience great difficulty in accessing *faskhs* by the *ulamā* (Amien 2006: 732). While the RRMB attempts to protect a wife who is unable to remarry as a result

---

[50] s 7(3) of the Divorce Act 70 of 1979.
[51] *Bai Tahira v Ali Hussain Fidaalli Chothia and Another* (1979) 2 SCC 316 at 321–22, paras 11–12; *Fuzlunbi v K Khader Vali and Another* (1980) 4 SCC 125 at 135, paras 18–19.
[52] cl 10(1)-(2). s 3(a) of the Divorce Act 70 of 1979.
[53] s 4 of the Mediation in Certain Divorce Matters Act 24 of 1987.
[54] s 6(1) of the Divorce Act 70 of 1979.

of her husband's refusal to release her from the Muslim marriage by giving a court the power to compel the recalcitrant spouse to take the 'necessary steps to have the marriage dissolved in accordance with Islamic law', it does not explain how such an order would be implemented. In practice, the current situation could be retained where the Muslim marriage remains un-dissolved because the husband refuses to *talāq* his wife or she is unable to obtain *faskh* from the *ulamā*.

Notwithstanding the benefits anticipated by the RRMB such as equal rights to divorce and to guardianship, custody and access of minor children, it seems that they may be outweighed by the negative consequences that could arise as a result of lack of regulation of Muslim family law features. In fact, it is clear from the above exposition that both the MMB and RRMB offer pros and cons for the protection of women's rights. So should either or neither be enacted? Perhaps this question depends on which draft legislation provides the greatest benefits and which results in the greatest costs to women.

IV GENDERED BENEFITS AND COSTS OF LEGAL PLURALISM FOR SOUTH AFRICAN MUSLIM FAMILY LAW

In the South African Muslim context, unofficial legal pluralism is not working to the benefit of women. As has already been mentioned, the failure to recognise Muslim family law has a negative impact on women who are not only excluded from enjoying certain civil law benefits, but are also excluded from enjoying Islamic law benefits and are unable to legally challenge discriminatory Muslim family law rules and practices. An official form of legal pluralism for the recognition of Muslim family law therefore appears to be required to reverse this status quo. In addition, it also has the potential to enable Muslim women to access their multifaceted identities as faith adherents and citizens of a constitutional democracy (Shachar 2005: 86). In other words, official recognition of Muslim family law would allow women to give expression to their religious identity while simultaneously providing them with the opportunity to access their constitutional right to equality.

The ideal solution would be for legislation to be enacted that respects freedom of religion and protects women's right to equality. However, this is an ideal that is not easily achievable because there may be instances when the two rights come into conflict with each other without a possibility of protecting both. In those instances, one right may have to be prioritised above the other. In the legislative process, women's rights advocates would most likely argue that women's right to equality should trump freedom of religion and religious advocates would most likely suggest the opposite. Since the legislative process is also influenced by political expediency, the voices of interest groups become significant. In other words, those who shout the loudest will very likely acquire protection for their interests. This was evident in the drafting process of the MMB. Initially, the drafters of the MMB consulted mostly with members of the *ulamā* because the latter purported to represent the Muslim community. It was only at the insistence of women's rights advocates that the *ulamā* does not necessarily speak for all Muslims and that the voices of Muslim women should also be heard that the feminist agenda found its way into the MMB. In fact, through this legislative drafting process, Muslim women's organisations such as Shura Yabafazi ('Consultation of Women') and networks such as the Recognition of Muslim Marriages Forum were established to, inter alia, ensure that the legislation responds to the needs of *all* parties including women. Existing Muslim organisations such as the Muslim Youth Movement's Gender Desk also advocated for the protection of women's rights within the MMB. The process not only prompted mobilisation around the MMB, but created the opportunity for empowerment campaigns to be run within the Muslim community to educate women and men about their Islamic law and civil law rights relating to marriage.

Given the vastly differing interests that emerged during the drafting process for example, the expectation by women's rights advocates that gender equality be prioritised, versus the expectation by some religious leaders that the legislation should merely codify the status quo by vesting them with the authority to interpret the content of Muslim family law, it is not surprising that the MMB does not satisfy all the conflicting interests. Instead, it seems to reflect an effort on the part of the drafters to try and find some kind of balance among the varying interests. It achieves this by regulating the many features of Muslim marriage and divorce in a way that offers protection to marginalised women. Yet, it still succumbs to the fundamental challenge that codification of religious laws presents: namely, the MMB codifies discriminatory features of Muslim family law. However, one of its saving graces lies in the fact that through codification, the MMB purports to regulate those features in a manner that offers more protection to Muslim women than they currently have. For instance, the MMB guarantees the enforcement of Islamic law benefits that women are not presently able to access. The MMB's other saving grace is that it can be subjected to constitutional scrutiny that may result in discriminatory features being struck down and/or reformed to be consistent with gender equality (Amien 2010: 378). The latter is made possible by the fact that the MMB purports to regulate Muslim family law features thereby bringing their interpretation directly within the ambit of the judiciary.[55] This would in turn make it possible for the judiciary to develop Muslim family law in accordance with human rights norms. In this way, the true objectives of Islamic law, which include equality, justice, freedom, fairness, the protection of human welfare and the condemnation of women being subordinated to men, could find expression in a meaningful way.[56]

[55] s 39(2) of the Constitution.

[56] Sabiq notes that the *Qur'ān* promotes equality between men and women in verse 49:13, which reads: 'O mankind! We created you from a single (pair) of a male and a female, and made you into nations and tribes, that ye may know each other (not that ye may despise (each other). Verily the most honoured of you In the sight of God is (he who is) the most righteous of you'. S Sabiq (undated: 105). See also Mayer (1999: 97–98); Mir-Hosseini (2003: 13); Badran (2009: 323).

In contrast, the RRMB seeks to accommodate Muslim marriages within a secular legal framework while purporting to assimilate Muslim divorces into that same secular legal framework. This results in a hybrid form of recognition of Muslim family law. In other words, while the determination of the content of Muslim family law is left to members of the *ulamā* to work out, a legal dissolution of the Muslim marriage is expected to follow civil consequences. This means that both parties will have an equal right to initiate divorce and must prove the same ground of irretrievable breakdown of the marriage. While this arrangement promotes formal equality between the spouses, it makes the achievement of substantive equality less likely because it fails to regulate the discriminatory features of Muslim family law within a human rights framework. In this way, the RRMB could contribute to the privatised oppression of Muslim women (Amien 2010: 373). A further concern with the above type of hybrid system is that since the interpretation of Muslim family law is removed from the secular court's ambit, it makes gendered reform of Muslim family law far more difficult to achieve. Although discriminatory Muslim family law features could be struck down if found to be unconstitutional, it may not be possible to develop them in a gender consistent manner because the RMMB expects the community and not the courts to interpret Muslim family law (Amien 2010: 372).

Although there is room for a great deal of improvement in both the MMB and RRMB, the MMB appears to be more responsive to the social needs of the Muslim community than the RRMB. This is perhaps due to the fact that the drafters of the MMB engaged a public participatory process, which to a large extent informed how the MMB was ultimately shaped. While the MMB remains a contentious piece of draft legislation among secular and religious extremists who would prefer that Muslim family law not be regulated by the state, it, unlike the RRMB, seems to have gained acceptance among the more moderate members of the religious leadership and women's rights advocates.

The difference between the Bills is also an indicator that mere official recognition of Muslim family law may not be sufficient to afford adequate protection for women's rights. The manner of recognition is equally important and must be context-driven. In the South African context, state regulation of the features of Muslim marriages and divorces can better ensure protection for women than simply providing official recognition that allows the Muslim community to regulate their own religious marriages. Moreover, the extraction of religious nuances from a religious community and their transference to the public domain should not be construed as a constraint on legal pluralism. On the contrary, affording official recognition of a religious legal system pays homage to its existence as well as the community's right to religious freedom; and purporting to place it alongside another or other official legal system in a way that will provide protection to the marginalised members of that community indicates respect for their fundamental rights to equality and dignity. In short, the official recognition and/or regulation of Muslim family law features transposes one type of legal system into another type of legal system, ie, from an unofficial form into an official form. Therefore, the plurality of legal systems remains unaffected.

V CONCLUSION

This chapter demonstrates that where a discriminatory form of Muslim family law exists in an unofficial form within the private sphere of a secular society, a viable option could be to recognise it officially so that its discriminatory religious rules and practices are held accountable to human rights standards.

At the same time, the manner of official recognition is important, as recognising Muslim family law in a way that enables the Muslim community to continue regulating their own family law system in a discriminatory manner would be tantamount to officially sanctioning the discrimination. Instead, where the context requires, as is the case in South Africa, state regulation of Muslim family law within a human rights framework becomes necessary. As illustrated in this chapter, regulation of Muslim family law in South Africa promises more protection for women's rights than mere recognition of Muslim family law. Yet, if regulation of Muslim family law is not accomplished in a sufficiently gender-sensitive manner, discriminatory features of Muslim family law could be retained and codified in the public sphere. Still, regulation offers the opportunity for those discriminatory features to be constitutionally challenged, which could facilitate a gendered reform of Muslim family law. In turn, such reform might help to transform the current discriminatory manifestation of Muslim family law into a more egalitarian form of Muslim family law that Islam intended it to be.

REFERENCES

Ahmed, KN (1978) *Muslim Law of Divorce* (New Delhi, Kitab Bhavan).

Ajijola, AD (1981) *Introduction to Islamic Law* (Karachi, International Islamic Publishers).

Ali, K (2003) 'Progressive Muslims and Islamic Jurisprudence: The Necessity for Critical Engagement with Marriage and Divorce Law' in O Safi (ed), *Progressive Muslims* (Oxford, One Worlds Press).

Ali, SS (2000) *Gender and Human Rights in Islam and International Law. Equal Before Allah, Unequal Before Man?* (The Hague, Kluwer Law International).

Amien, W (2006) 'Overcoming the Conflict Between the Right to Freedom of Religion and Women's Rights to Equality: A South African Case Study of Muslim Marriages' 28 *Human Rights Quarterly* 729.

—— (2010) 'A South African Case Study for the Recognition and Regulation of Muslim Family Law in a Minority Muslim Secular Context' 24 *International Journal of Law, Policy and the Family* 361.

Badran, M (2009) *Feminism in Islam. Secular and Religious Convergences* (Oxford, Oneworld Publications).

Commission for Gender Equality (2000) *Submission on Issue Paper 15 – Islamic Marriages and Related Issues* (Cape Town, Commission for Gender Equality).

Engineer, AA (1992) *The Rights of Women in Islam* (London, C Hurst & Co (Publishers) Ltd).

Esposito, JL (1991) *Islam, the Straight Path* (New York, Oxford University Press).

Esposito, JL and DeLong-Bas, NJ (2001) *Women in Muslim Family Law*, 2nd edn (New York, Syracuse University Press).

Fyzee, AAA (1949) *Outlines of Mohammadan Law* (London, Oxford University Press).

Ghosh, R (1994) 'Multicultural Policy and Social Integration: South Asian Canadian Women' 1 *Indian Journal of Gender Studies* 49.

Mayer, AE (1999) *Islam and Human Rights: Tradition and Politics* (Colorado, Westview Press).

Mir-Hosseini, Z (2003) 'The Construction of Gender in Islamic Legal Thought and Strategies for Reform' 1 *Journal of Women in the Middle East and the Islamic World* 1.

Pearl, D (1979) *A Textbook on Muslim Law* (London, Croom Helm Ltd).

Rushd, I (1996) *The Distinguished Jurist's Primer. A Translation of Bidayat Al-Mujtahid* (trans IAK Nyazee) (UK, Centre for Muslim Contribution to Civilization, Garnett Publishing Limited).

Sabiq, S (undated) *Fiqh Us-Sunnah. Doctrine of Sunnah of the Holy Prophet*, vol II (New Delhi, Millat Book Centre).

Schacht, J (1964) *An Introduction to Islamic law* (London, Oxford University Press).

Shachar, A (2005) 'Religion, State, and the Problem of Gender: New Modes of Citizenship and Governance in Diverse Societies' 50 *McGill Law Journal* 49.

Women Living Under Muslim Laws (2003) *Knowing our Rights. Women, Family, Laws and Customs in the Muslim World* (London, Women Living Under Muslim Laws).

7

Assessing the Impact of Legislating for Diversity: The Forced Marriage (Civil Protection) Act 2007

MAVIS MACLEAN

I INTRODUCTION

IN ADDRESSING THE central question of this book of how distinct cultural or religious minority groups should be accommodated within the legal framework of the wider society, we have looked at the conflict between respect for cultural and religious beliefs and rights to equality of treatment, and personal safety and autonomy. But in the context of forced marriage where some victims have been as young as nine years old, and thereby clearly constituting a child protection issue, we are relatively free from such dilemmas. There is no religious foundation for forced marriage. Freely given consent is a prerequisite of all Christian, Jewish, Hindu, Muslim and Sikh marriages. Forced marriage is widely recognised as a human rights abuse.[1] It is totally separate from the practice of assisted marriage in which both parties give their full and free consent to the marriage, indeed, assistance from the family or community in making a match has long been a part of the process in many communities and countries. Readers of Jane Austen will be familiar with the extensive efforts of English parents at the beginning of the nineteenth century to see their daughters married, and married well.[2] As the mother of two daughters in England in the twenty-first century I readily confess to promoting the cause of their most appealing male friends, and have observed many friends with sons and daughters doing the same. The practice of arranged marriage, however, where the emphasis is placed on the compatibility of two families rather than two individuals, lies somewhere between the two, and though there is no question of force, the women may experience strong community and cultural pressure to fulfil their sociocultural obligation to agree (Proudman 2011: 5).

---

[1] Universal Declaration of Human Rights, Art 16(2).
[2] See *Pride and Prejudice*, and the complete works of Jane Austen (1775–1817).

But faced with the practice of forced marriage which is embedded within certain groups within the population, largely economic migrants from remote rural areas, what can a government do? This chapter will describe the development of a legislative response, the Forced Marriage (Civil) Protection Act 2007, and comment on how it has been working in the first year following implementation, 2009. In my capacity as academic adviser to the Ministry of Justice I worked on the Department's evaluation report, published in 2009.[3] I took part in interviews with those in the courts and the community involved in implementation and draw on this experience to discuss the difficulty of moving from identification of a problem to the smooth functioning of new legislation, and the limits of what a new law can achieve. As Petracycki described a century ago in 1913 (Petracycki 1995) the law exists through our readiness to do something which others will be obliged to accept. The ideas of individuals about how they will act often differs from what is assumed by lawyers and authorities to be the law, but the skill of lawmakers is to either bring human motivation closer to the legislative object, or bring the legal project closer to what could be achieved bearing in mind the various motivations for compliance with the law. In Petracycki's words:

> The essence of legal policy issues lies in the scientifically grounded explanations of the consequences one should expect on introducing legal regulation and in the development of such principles that, if introduced through legislation, would bring about a particular and predictable result.

In the case of forced marriage, the government in the United Kingdom was cautious in its approach to legislating, relying on civil law reform and refraining from criminalising the practice for fear of making it too difficult for those affected to access the protective measures and which could result in achieving the opposite of their intentions. A great deal has been achieved through this gradual approach, but the debate continues about whether further legislation is needed to give a stronger message about the unacceptability of the forced marriage by moving the matter into the criminal jurisdiction.[4] This chapter, however, questions whether further legislation could achieve greater protection for those in need without more attention being paid by education and welfare authorities to increasing awareness of the practice and its impact, and considering the needs of those who still need long-term support to live apart from their family and culture after the legal protection is in place. There are limits to what courts and the law can achieve.

---

[3] 'One Year On: the initial impact of the Forced Marriage (Civil Protection) Act 2001 in its first year of operation', Ministry of Justice November 2009 is available on the Ministry of Justice website: www.justice.gov.uk.

[4] See, eg, 'Forced Marriage Criminalised (Scotland)' Newsline, (2012) 42 *Family Law* 2; Gill (2011); Proudman (2011).

II THE FORCED MARRIAGE (CIVIL PROTECTION) ACT 2007 (FMPA)

The pressure to move to legislation was fuelled by increasing awareness of the extent of the practice. The number of cases being recorded by official bodies was considerable and growing. The Forced Marriage Unit, set up in 2005 jointly by the Home Office and Foreign and Commonwealth Office, dealt with 1600 reports of possible forced marriage in 2008–09. Of these, 420 became cases, and children were involved in a third of them. In some cases, victims are taken overseas to marry, but in a substantial proportion, victims are subject to marriage in the UK. There are both male and female victims. But forced marriage is not just a practice; it is also a strategy for survival, both cultural and economic.[5] There are a number of reasons why members of a community might pressurise a couple to marry. In the majority of cases involving young girls, there may be family honour and family connections to maintain, or an economic aspect comprising either reward for offering a marriage as a way to facilitate economic migration, or simply to provide for a daughter. In the case of gay young men, there is pressure to marry to 'normalise' their position and avoid stigma and dishonour. In the case of adults with special needs, as they get older their parents may seek a marriage partner for a son in order to provide care within the family. Where there are these kinds of capacity issues, the victims may be older than the usual age of marriage rather than younger.

When legislation was first under consideration, the original estimate was that about 50 orders might be made in the first year of operation. But in fact 86 Forced Marriage Protection Orders were made in the first year of operation from November 2008 to November 2009. In the early months, there was little discussion about problems associated with the order as a procedure, as it was designed to build on to the current range of measures already in operation for protecting adults from domestic abuse (non-molestation orders in particular) and the measures for child protection in the Children Act 1989. The key players seemed to be the police, who were actively bringing cases forward, as in their view the Forced Marriage Protection Order can prevent further serious offences arising from the attempt to force a marriage on an unwilling young person.

But there did seem to be difficulties surrounding implementation of the Act. For local authority social services departments in particular there are longer-term issues in that if a forced marriage matter is taken up by the authority, questions arise about how to offer ongoing assessment and support for affected children. There is also some difficulty arising from dealing with young women and men in an age group which lies on the boundary between work in child protection and with vulnerable adults. There are concerns about whether orders are

---

[5] I am grateful to Prakash Shah for pointing up the inadequacy of describing forced marriage as a practice, and suggesting the term strategy.

being sought by all those who might be in need of support. Do those who need to be aware of this protection know of its existence? Where there is intervention, how often is this followed by family reconciliation and is this safe? And if the young people are not reconciled with their families, how can those affected be supported in the long term? How are the younger siblings of those affected to be monitored and protected? There were concerns about how to reach the more closed minority ethnic communities and how to encourage them to hear the messages enshrined in the Act about respect for individual choice in making a lifetime commitment to marriage and parenting.

But before giving a detailed account of the working of the Act, we turn to a closer examination of how legislation became the strategy of choice for government, and how the scope of legislative action was determined.

III BACKGROUND TO THE ACT

Before the FMPA there had been ongoing controversy about whether legislation was an appropriate way to respond to the situation, and, if it was thought to be necessary, about how far the reform should go towards the criminalisation of forced marriage. In 2005, the Forced Marriage Unit (FMU) was set up which later in the year issued a consultation entitled *Forced Marriage – A Wrong not a Right*. This sought views on whether the creation of a specific legal offence would help to combat forced marriage. By June 2006 the government had decided against introducing legislation. But Lord Lester introduced a Private Member's Bill – the Forced Marriage (Civil Protection) Bill – to provide a remedy by way of an injunction to prevent a person forcing another person into marriage, and also to protect a person after a forced marriage. Following the favourable reception of this initiative, in April 2007 the government took up the Bill at Grand Committee stage and it was passed and came into operation in November 2008, inserting additional sections into the Family Law Act 1996. After consultation, in 2006 the government had decided against specifically identifying forced marriage as a criminal offence, fearing that it might drive forced marriage underground and make it harder to help those in need of protection. But the Lester Bill focused on civil remedies rather than creating a new criminal offence, enabling the courts to make an order prohibiting somebody from committing a number of specific acts for the purpose of forcing somebody into marriage. First, the Forced Marriage (Civil) Protection Act enables family courts to make a Forced Marriage Protection Order to prevent a forced marriage occurring. When such a marriage has taken place, the courts can make orders to help remove the parties from that situation. Orders can be made to require all birth certificates and passports to be handed over, to prevent an application being made for a new passport, to stop intimidation and violence, to reveal the whereabouts of a person, to stop someone being taken abroad and to facilitate or enable a person to return to the UK within a given period.

Orders may also be made against other people not named as respondents in the application, thus recognising the complexity of the issues and the involvement of the wider community, and the numbers of people who might be involved. A power of arrest may be added where violence is threatened or used. Breach of a Forced Marriage Protection Order is not a criminal offence, but a constable may arrest a person whom they have reasonable cause to suspect is in breach of the order. Breach is dealt with as contempt of court, with the full range of sanctions including up to two years' imprisonment. There may also be separate criminal proceedings for offences committed in the course of breaching the order.

Fifteen county courts were originally designated to deal with FMPO applications, chosen by the demographic characteristics of the local population as being, on the advice of the FMU, likely to receive applications. This remains the case. As victims are often unable to protect themselves, the Act also creates the role of the Relevant Third Party (RTP) who can make an application on behalf of the victim. Statutory Guidance is available.[6] This guidance states that it is targeted at directors and senior managers of agencies dealing in forced marriage cases, and covers, for example, training, inter-agency working and outreach work, but is not intended to be consulted by front line practitioners. In June 2009, the Ministry of Justice produced *Multi-Agency Practice Guidelines* directed at professionals working in healthcare, education and the police, children's social care, adult social care and local housing authorities, in order to encourage multi-agency partnership working. The guidance is clearly set out and helpful, intended to supplement the statutory guidance. Authorities are encouraged to liaise with the FMU, and to be cautious about organising family group conferences, or disclosing information to family members or other third parties. Authorities are encouraged to liaise with the FMU in any case with a foreign element, and to refer to a family solicitor if 'specific legal advice' is required.

The Act at section 63A provides that proceedings may be commenced by a relevant third party (RTP), without needing to obtain the leave of the court. In November 2008 a public consultation was held and asked whether there was a need for RTPs, what kinds of individuals or organisations should be considered and what kinds of safeguards would be required. Those who responded generally supported making local authorities into RTPs, to support existing child and adult protection work. The government immediately set out its plans to designate local authorities, and the provision came into effect in November 2008. Discussion about whether police or education authorities should be added to the RTP category continues.

So it can be seen that the decision to legislate was made cautiously and with careful consideration, accompanied throughout by detailed consultation on a number of points and by the drafting and circulation of considered advice and

---

[6] See *The Right to Choose*, available at: www.justice.gov.uk/guidance/forced marriage.htm.

guidance. Pressure from a number of quarters, including members of the police and judiciary, continued to look for an extension of the legislation towards criminalising forced marriage.[7] But government maintained its cautious approach and was reluctant to consider any further changes at that time before evaluating the working of the FMPA in its current form.

IV THE FMPA REVIEW

The Ministry of Justice carried out a review of the impact of the FMPA in its first year of operation, using an internal team with the support of the author acting as independent academic adviser. The review examined all available statistical data, and members of the team visited the courts where orders had been made. They interviewed court staff and members of the judiciary, inviting in for consultation members of the local police and local authority welfare teams and local legal practitioners and advice workers. At one year into operation, the numbers of orders made was higher than expected; over the first year, 86 orders had been made. This could be taken to indicate either that demand was greater than anticipated, or that the procedure was more accessible and user friendly than had been feared. But there was a new cause for concern arising from the geographical distribution of the orders, which was surprisingly skewed. Five of the 15 designated courts had not yet made an order, seven had made up to three orders, while two-thirds of the orders had been made in only three of the designated courts. Given that the courts had been selected on demographic criteria and were expected to have similar incidence of the problem, this disparity could indicate local difficulties in using the procedure which needed to be investigated.

The review team visited 11 courts in the autumn of 2009 and sought feedback on the working of the Act from judges, local authority representatives, support groups and police and specialist practitioners.

A The High Volume Courts

In the three high volume courts, where two out of three of the total orders had been made, the judges described there having been considerable work locally to develop awareness of the Act, though there had been little media interest. Outside London, concern was expressed about the presence of local 'politically correct' agendas, under which there was reluctance to cause offence within some of the local ethnic minority communities. The police were thought to have been very active and effective in promoting awareness and drawing on their experience in dealing with domestic abuse. They were thought to value the FMPO as a form of

---

[7] eg, see the discussion reported by HHJ Cryan, paper to the Centre for Child and Family Law Reform, 2001, revised with DJ Dabezies and published in (2011) 4(1) *Periodical of the Centre for Child and Family Law Reform*.

crisis intervention, using a simple procedure which can provide a defence against future pressure and possible future honour-based violence.

Local authorities, on the other hand, were thought to have been less aware of the potential benefits of the Act, partly because of the lack of information and training. The local authorities were more wary about intervening, as their approach is based on in-depth assessment and review over time. According to one judge: 'These cases rub against what a social worker would normally do in child protection work . . . they must understand they cannot mediate in these cases', but must act quickly. In one area the judge thought it appropriate to make the local authority a party to the action where a social worker had been involved.

There was also concern among the judges about the effect on other members of the family – little sisters – who might be subject to the same treatment in the future. One judge thought it important to remember that the judges can always ask the local authority for a section 37 report under the Children Act 1989 when minor children were at risk, or have residence discussed on the judge's own motion. The judges were very aware of the need for the protections offered by these orders, and saw the procedure as quick and effective, though they had had to work hard to inform themselves on how to proceed. One judge said that further judicial training – even half an hour – would have helped.

The judges were agreed that making an order on application was a quick and efficiently run procedure, akin to domestic violence applications, with special procedures to protect vulnerable parties or witnesses.[8] They regretted having no information about what happens after an order is made, but this is so in all family cases. One judge suggested it would be useful to have a record of previous family proceedings involving the parties on the face of the court file, saying: 'if there had been a string of non mols,[9] I wouldn't know about it'. Every judge expressed concern about the gravity of the step the applicants were taking: 'These girls are in a cleft stick. . . . They may be in danger . . . but if they leave home they lose everything'.

Court staff in the high volume areas felt that the procedure worked well: 'the process is straightforward, we're used to non mols'; 'it's a priority'; 'it's a success . . . there should be local coverage'. They acknowledged that fees could be a problem, but said: 'We don't send people away if they haven't got the fees sorted'. Police working in the high volume areas saw themselves as specialist, energetic and dedicated. They were working to promote awareness of the Act, but were not optimistic about levels of awareness among the general public or other agencies. They saw the work as preventive, using the FMPA at an early stage to stop forced marriages occurring, and finding the third party (RTP) provisions useful when the victims are young and unable to make applications for themselves. The police did not see local authority social services departments as

---

[8] eg, using separate entrances to the court, evidence given from behind a screen or over a video link.

[9] Non-molestation Orders.

having understood the full potential of using the orders at an early stage in a problem, nor that they should be used in addition to their existing child protection procedures as a further measure for protection. One officer said,

> they (Social Services) need to be more willing to apply for orders earlier in the process. I get the impression that this is caused by uncertainty though rather than lack of knowledge of the Act . . . there seems to be an issue about threshold[10] . . . they seem to be seen in the same light by children's services as child protection measures but the same threshold doesn't apply here.[11]

The police were primarily concerned to safeguard the victim and other younger siblings and family members to prevent future acts of force to coerce a family member into a marriage and maintain the honour of the family – known collectively as 'honour-based violence' – and were anxious because others involved in the process do not appear to realise the need for urgent action. The specialist police described dealing with kidnapping, installing fireproof letterboxes and using code words in communicating with potential victims. They kept in touch with those they had helped for long periods, aware of continuing pressure on family members to back down. One policeman told of how he and his colleagues had collected enough money to buy a laptop computer for one girl living alone and far from home, to help her complete her further education course and be able to find a job: 'We hit the ground running . . . we go into schools . . . we are the lead agency . . . we would like RTP status'.

The police made reference to local authority social services failing to return urgent calls, and appearing to regard some cases of naughty children in conflict with parents as if they were equivalent. An example was given of a doctor's teenage daughter who was tired of being made to come home early after outings with friends, who sought a FMPO to try to persuade her parents to be more liberal, but where there was no real forced marriage issue. They described social services as essentially relying on existing legislation and being reluctant to use this new technique for dealing with a form of domestic abuse.

What did the local authorities have to say? The local authority legal advisers we spoke to in one high case volume area spoke with enthusiasm about the Act, but regretted the lack of wider awareness and training in their organisation as a whole. But they reminded us of how long it takes to achieve change. They described their local difficulties, including the need for independent interpreters, but also the more general difficulties of child protection work with Asian families, who 'don't come through the normal channels on child protection issues'. They added that some cases were already known to the local authority when a forced marriage issue arises, and that there may be ongoing issues if there are younger siblings, but they did not think that the link between forced marriage and domestic violence had been well understood so far. Their com-

---

[10] This is a reference to the Children Act 1989 which requires that the child's need for protection is clearly evidenced.

[11] ie, in the context of the Forced Marriage Protection Act.

ments lacked the sense of urgency of those made by the police but did display an awareness of the long-term nature of the problem. This had led to a positive assessment in one case where a FMPO overlapped with an interim care order. The girl in this case had returned to her home, but the social worker remained anxious about the outcome. She was pleased to be told that the girl was doing well and that the girl had said that the order worked to show her parents she wouldn't let this (a forced marriage) happen to her. But a more general comment was that any 'Person to be Protected' (PTBP) would need long-term support and 'where is the money coming from'?

Finally, there were the comments from the specialist lawyers: 'Overall it seems to be working. . . . Victims are willing to come forward and talk in a civil setting . . . We knew it wouldn't work in a criminal setting'. They felt that the Act is seen to have muscle, and in many cases rehabilitation with the family is thought to follow the order, though there is a need for this to be subject to careful risk assessment. Particular difficulties associated with pressure on the victim to withdraw during proceedings were noted. The lawyers stressed the need for caution in accepting a victim's claims that all is now well, especially when they are overseas.

B Low Volume Areas

Here there was concern among the judiciary about lack of local awareness despite the efforts of the courts to publicise the Act. It was thought that police and schools could do more, and there had been little media attention. The judges suggested a need for locally developed forms and procedures to cover liaison with solicitors, dealing with fees and special measures for security in and around the court. They commented on the need to take into account the safety of those using the procedure, and of the court staff and legal representatives. They emphasised that 'there is a need to get into the communities', saying: 'remember it is a huge decision for a girl to make, fear of ultimate rejection, not able to question their families'. It was also suggested that there should be legal representation for respondents appearing without a lawyer to avoid them cross-examining the victim or vulnerable witnesses, thus providing a further opportunity for intimidation. Court staff in the low volume courts said they were ready and trained for this work, and suggested that making the police RTPs could improve access. The police in these areas suggested more links with 'Multi Agency Risk Assessments' (MARACS) together with checks on spousal visas being signed by family members and closer working with immigration agencies: 'we need to change the culture'. Local authority comments in the low volume areas also lacked the sense of urgency in the police comments, but showed a greater awareness of the long-term consequences of the procedure and the serious resource implications of taking on support for a young girl with younger siblings over the long term.

Finally, we spoke to the voluntary agencies working in the field, who emphasised the need to work with local community leaders, to overcome fear of using the courts when necessary, but also to see the matter as located within a wider family network, including members outside the country, and to be aware of immigration issues and long-term support issues in this country, including the need for re-housing.

V NEXT STEPS: WHAT HAS BEEN ACHIEVED BY LEGISLATION SO FAR?

The Act is being used more than had been expected at the outset. The process is relatively straightforward, and funding issues do not hold up a swift procedure, though access to legal aid is not yet running smoothly. One policeman described having to use petty cash in one emergency situation.

The review reveals the different perspectives of the different agencies involved in this new procedure. The police are using it creatively in emergency situations to prevent further honour-based violent crime. Local authorities have been slower to respond, partly because they take a longer-term perspective and assess the family as a whole and are keenly aware that emergency intervention on behalf of an individual will be followed by long-term work, not only with a potential victim, but with a wide family network.

It appears that there may be a need for a more proactive approach from local authorities in some areas, accompanied by continuing training, and awareness work especially within the communities. On the other hand, in the light of rapid police response, there is also a need for caution in understanding the impact of an application on a young person who may then lose family and community and may need long-term support which the police cannot offer. The comments of those interviewed provide a complex and detailed picture of the need for moving slowly and carefully in such a difficult area, where national legislation needs to be informed by detailed local knowledge of family behaviour and the social context.

The FMPA as a piece of legislation is carefully drafted, and has been implemented cautiously. But it is already clear that legislation can only effect limited change in the face of community resistance and limited public resources. So what happens next? The limited effectiveness of the FMPA has led to further calls for more effective training and more drastic legislation, to stamp out the practice of forced marriage by criminalising the practice. David Cameron, in a speech on illegal immigration on 11 October 2011,[12] despite contrary advice from the Home Office, announced plans to consult on criminalising forced marriage, which he described as 'little more than slavery'. To the cynical this might appear as an issue involving little cost, and many headlines tapping into public concerns about immigration.

---

[12] See BBC News website (11 October 2011).

The case for more specialist training, however, is strong. To quote the paper from the Centre for Child and Family Reform:

> While applications can be relatively simple they often involve layers of complexity and a need of understanding maters infrequently encountered within domestic disputes. The technicalities of dealing with undisclosed evidence or alternatively victims or family members abroad are matters of great sensitivity It must be remembered that a case which seem simple at first instance can become complicated and dangerous to the victim very quickly.[13]

In addition, since the Ministry of Justice review was carried out, there has been a report on the introduction of 'Forced Marriage Independent Domestic Violence Advisers' (IDVAS) in five of the 11 designated courts, where a worker was dedicated to work on forced marriage cases. The Centre for Child and Family Law Reform Working Group did not, at the time of the FMPA, support the call for extending the legislation to create a new freestanding offence of forcing a person to marry. They took the view that individual criminal acts committed in the course of forcing someone to marry can often already be the subject of criminal proceedings, and also that the possibility of criminal proceedings will deter persons to be protected from commencing forced marriage proceedings against a family member. Since the Act came into effect they remain of the view that the most effective way forward would not be to create a new free standing offence, but to use the legislative approach used to deal with racially aggravated offences in the Crime and Disorder Act 1998. In this instance a number of specific offences were identified which were commonly used to further racist ends, but carried relatively low sentences. The Act added satellite offences to those offences, so, for example, racially aggravated common assault was added to common assault, and section 82 of the Act requires a court to treat this motivation as a factor making the offence more serious. A similar approach might be taken with forced marriage cases. But in the meantime the Sentencing Council could, without further legislation, use the general aggravating factors of abuse of power and abuse of trust in assessing the seriousness of an offence.

This moderate and realistic approach to raising the profile and increasing the effectiveness of the legal approach to forced marriage has great merit. It is suggested here that this is to be preferred to the calls for criminalising forced marriage such as those made by Proudman (2011) and in the recommendation of the Home Affairs Select Committee Report of 17 May 2011 which stated:

> [W]e believe it would send out a very clear and positive message to communities within the UK and internationally if it becomes a criminal act to force or to participate in forcing an individual to enter into a marriage against their will.

Proudman's interviews with young Asian women describe difficult and sometimes tragic situations, and strongly question the validity of the legal distinction between arranged and forced marriage. One young woman said: 'I don't see any

---

[13] Above (n 7).

difference, to be honest. It's manipulation, because you're brought up in a certain way, and you get influenced by other people' (2011: 30). If, however, the distinction between forced and arranged marriage is not clear, this could raise problems in moving towards criminalisation of forced marriage as it would be hard to justify treating arranged marriage in this way. Indeed, Proudman also reports that the policeman and barristers who had helped her to contact young women at risk had been opposed to further legislation without increased social and financial support for the women.

From this review of the implementation of the carefully restrained Forced Marriage (Civil Protection) Act 2007 it seems that the impact of legislation as a response to this issue is limited and could easily backfire. Aisha Gill's report (Gill 2011) on an independent survey of 74 respondents conducted by Roehampton University on the question of criminalisation of forced marriage[14] showed little appetite for more legislation among the organisations which replied, and many requests for more training, more research and better use of the existing legal framework. Law cannot run too far ahead of public opinion even where that is the opinion of a minority. Minority groups are a part of the whole society. Change will come from working together in the light of current ideas of individual rights and liberties, rather than by redefining old practices as new crimes.

REFERENCES

Gill, A (2011) 'Criminalising Forced Marriage' 41 *Family Law* 1378.

Petracycki, L (1995) *Laws and Morality* (trans HW Babb) (Cambridge, MA, Harvard University Press).

Proudman, C (2011) *Forced and Arranged Marriage among South Asian Women in England and Wales: Critically Examining the Social and Legal Ramification of Criminalisation* (Saarbrucken, Lambert Academic Publishing).

---

[14] The full report can be found at: www.roehampton.ac.uk/staff/AishaGill/pdf/Forced-Marriage-Legislation-Survey_Report%20of%20Findings_Gill_14July11_printversion_FIN.pdf.

8

Religious Freedom and Protection of the Right to Life in Minors: A Case Study*

TERESA PICONTÓ-NOVALES

I INTRODUCTION

O N 15 SEPTEMBER 1994 Marcos, a minor of 13 years of age, died in hospital in Zaragoza as a result of the consistent refusal and rejection on the part of his parents of specific medical treatment – a blood transfusion – on the grounds that this was prohibited by their religious convictions. The minor himself also did all he could to reject a blood transfusion on repeated occasions for religious reasons and as a matter of conscience. It is common knowledge that the religious principles of the Jehovah's Witnesses prohibit their members from having blood transfusions as being against their convictions and beliefs. The objections of conscience to this medical treatment have resulted in serious controversies (Martín Retortillo 1984; Ruiz Miguel 1993; Pelayo González 1997:104; Pérez Triviño 2010). The death of a child caused by the refusal of the parents to authorise a blood transfusion essential in order to save the child's life on the grounds of religious and moral convictions poses a whole series of very complex questions to which there are no easy answers.

This case involves various very significant issues relating to the difficult balance between constitutional rights and freedoms, both from the point of view of their content and scope and from the point of view of individuals and their autonomy in so far as this affects the exercise of these rights and freedoms. Clearly one of the rights at stake is that of religious freedom and freedom of conscience as guaranteed in article 16.1 of the Spanish Constitution ('freedom of ideology, religion and worship of individuals and communities'). The right to life and health is another factor to be taken into consideration. The right to life is not a question of the interpretation of article 15 of the Spanish

* This work has been carried out within the project CONSOLIDER-INGENIO 2010 *El Tiempo de los Derechos* (CSD2008-00007).

Constitution alone, but a joint interpretation of this article with article 10, that is a right to life that can be renounced in the exercise of the free development of the personality. From this perspective, in accordance with the lay character of the state, the right to life must be reconciled with respect for individual autonomy and self-determination. In this context, the state must respect the right to life of its citizens, but can in any event impose the duty to live.

Rights in respect of the ideology, religion, education and culture of minors require that the principles of equality and non-discrimination be guaranteed. Eekelaar has argued that while it is true that the wellbeing of minors (article 3 of the UN Convention of the Rights of the Child) must on some occasions be considered in light of cultural values and traditions, it should fundamentally be interpreted in the context of those rights explicitly protected by the Convention. The majority of these rights are of a protective character, while others such as freedom of conscience, thought and religion (articles 25, 30) are more concerned with minors as autonomous young men and women (Eekelaar 1991: 231–32; Banda 2005: 225–27). The rights of personality development must also be taken into account. The Convention on the Rights of the Child of 1989 contains an extensive section on rights of personality development. In particular, the Convention protects the autonomy of the child that is interrelated with the possibility of taking his or her own decisions.

II A DIFFICULT CASE AND THREE JUDICIAL DECISIONS

The case examined here is a difficult, or rather fundamental, one that inevitably involves the consideration of value judgements and other moral arguments that go beyond the limits of formal jurisprudence. This is evident from the judicial decisions relating to the case. In chronological order, there was first a decision by the Provincial Court of Huesca on 20 November 1996, this being the court which heard the case in the first instance. Secondly, there was a decision of the Supreme Court settling an appeal for cassation (ruling of Court 2a of the Supreme Court, 27 June 1997). Finally, there was a decision by the Constitutional Court (STC 154/2002, 18 July) on the appeal for protection of a fundamental right.

Following the description of the facts as stated in the Provincial Court, the events can be summarised as follows.

Marcos, a 13-year-old minor, had an accident on his bicycle, which caused a light and not apparently serious injury to one leg. Three days later he was taken by his mother to a hospital in Lerida suffering from bleeding through the nose. The doctors 'detected that the minor was at serious risk of haemorrhaging and prescribed a blood transfusion to counter the risk'. The parents of the minor opposed this treatment for religious reasons, requesting treatment for their son other than a blood transfusion. The doctors informed the parents that they 'did not know of any other treatment'. The parents then asked for their son to be discharged in order to take him to another hospital. This request was refused by the hospital in Lerida on the grounds that such an action would 'put the life of the minor in danger'. The minor was of the same religious persuasion as his parents and had also 'consciously and seriously' rejected a transfusion. The hospital therefore applied (on 9 September 1994) for the appropriate authorisation from the duty magistrates' court which half an hour later authorised the transfusion 'in the event that it was essential for saving the life of the minor'.

Having received the court authorisation, the doctors were ready to give the blood transfusion 'but the minor, of 13 years, without any intervention by his parents, rejected it in a state of genuine terror'. The doctors therefore considered that the treatment could be counterproductive in the patient's excited state and decided not to proceed with the transfusion, which they thought might 'lead to a cerebral haemorrhage'. The hospital staff, after several failed attempts to persuade the child to change his mind, 'asked the parents to try to convince the child', but they, accompanied by other members of the same religious persuasion, 'did not agree to do this'.

The doctors rejected the possibility of giving the minor a transfusion against his will, considering that this could be counterproductive, and 'after consulting the duty court by telephone' (in Lerida), 'considering that there was no other alternative treatment', on the morning of 9 September agreed to a voluntary discharge so that the child could be taken to another hospital where alternative treatment might be applied. On the afternoon of 9 September the parents took their son home, arranged to find another specialist and made an appointment for 12 September at a hospital in Barcelona.

Once at the new hospital, 'it was again considered a matter of urgency that a blood transfusion be carried out to neutralise the risk of haemorrhaging and anaemia, and then to carry out the appropriate tests' to diagnose the illness and start the corresponding treatment. The parents and the child 'again stated that their religious convictions did not allow them to accept a transfusion, and the defendants signed a statement to this effect on paper' with the letterhead of the hospital in Barcelona.

Once again 'the parents of the minor, accompanied by people of the same religion' took the child to a private hospital in Cataluña. There the doctors 'stated again that there was no alternative treatment and that a blood transfusion was needed, which was again rejected by the defendants and by the child on the grounds of their religious convictions'.

The parents did not know of any other centre where they could go and 'began the return journey home with their son', arriving on 13 September. They remained there 'all that day, without any help other than that of the local doctor'. On 14 September the Court of Instruction in Fraga (Huesca), having received a written notification from the local council on the child's situation accompanied by a medical report, and after a telephone conversation with the Department of Public Prosecutions, issued that same day a court order 'authorising entry into the home of the minor' so that he could receive the medical attention he needed, that is to say a blood transfusion. The minor was found to be in a seriously deteriorating mental and physical state and was taken by ambulance, accompanied by the police and without the opposition of his parents, to a hospital in Barbastro (Huesca) where he arrived in a deep coma. Here the blood transfusion was performed in accordance with the court order, and the child was then moved to another hospital in Zaragoza. He arrived with a cerebral haemorrhage and died on 15 September 1994.

Finally, it should perhaps be added that according to expert opinion, if the minor had received the transfusion he needed in time, he would have had 'a high probability of survival'.

In its decision 196/1996 of 20 November 1996, the court of first instance, the Provincial Court of Huesca, acquitted the minor's parents of the offence of homicide by omission. The charge had been brought by the Ministerio Fiscal (the Public Prosecutions Department) on the grounds that the death of their son had resulted from not having performed a blood transfusion. A sentence of four years' imprisonment was sought. The Court justified its decision to acquit the parents on the basis of the provisions relating to ideological and religious freedom (article 16 of the Spanish Constitution). In the grounds for its decision, the Court states that:

> The truth is that the defendants, far from being passive, went as far as their understanding and culture would allow them in order to seek appropriate medical treatment for their son (. . .), simply restricting themselves, once within the health and even legal ambit, to stating politely that, as an act of faith (albeit of a minority religion), they would not give their consent to a blood transfusion as this was contrary to their own religious convictions and those of their son.

The first instance court drew attention in its arguments to the freedom of religion and beliefs, and the pluralist and democratic dimension that the constitutional and legal recognition of such law contained (article 16.1, 3 CE; Organic Law on Religious Freedom, 5 July 1980). Considered from such a viewpoint, it constitutes a central concern of the state in placing this freedom at the same level as other constitutional principles and values such as those of articles 1.1, 9, 10 and 14 of the Spanish Constitution of 1978 (equality, justice and human dignity).

Another fundamental line of argument according to the court of first instance is the legal consideration of the conduct of the parents. The court sets out the difficult controversy arising from this complex case as follows:

> The question we have to put is whether the parents are legally obliged to request a specific treatment or medical procedure to try to save their son's life even though they firmly and seriously consider in their consciences that such a procedure is sinful, and forbidden by the Law of God, inasmuch as they understand this within the exercise of their religious freedom.

This line of argument appears again:

> We do not believe that it is incumbent on the parents of the minor (. . .) that they be obliged to renounce their religious convictions against their consciences and request

or approve a blood transfusion which they consider to be morally pernicious or inappropriate, nor that they are legally obliged to try to convince their son of some-thing that, (. . .), he himself is not convinced of and that would go against all that he has been taught in the ordinary and regular exercise of his religious freedom, this having been transmitted to the son from a long time before the accident occurred and the appearance of the first symptoms of his illness.

In summary, the Provincial Court justified the conduct of the parents considering that they were not legally obliged to go against their consciences by authorising a blood transfusion for their son against their religious beliefs by virtue of the right to religious freedom as recognised by the Spanish Constitution. Beyond recognising the democratic and pluralistic dimension of the right to religious freedom, the case was settled in this first instance as a conflict of individual rights involving religious freedom and personal autonomy of individuals, without taking into account other possible considerations expressed on the basis of the religious rights of the group in question, the Jehovah's Witnesses.

The Spanish Supreme Court decision of 27 June 1997 (sentence of Court 2a of the SC 950/1997) upheld the appeal for cassation against the decision given in the first instance by the criminal court of the Huesca Provincial Court. Rejecting the thesis maintained by the court of first instance, the Supreme Court argued in its conviction that, in the conflict of rights, clear priority should be given to the right to life and physical integrity as opposed to religious freedom. The Court stated that:

According to art 14 of the Spanish Constitution all Spanish people are equal before the law, whatever their religion (. . .). protected on an equal footing in terms of belief and freedom. Within the broad range of rights and liberties stated by the Constitution to be in a preferential group, surpassed only by the right to life and to physical and moral integrity, art 16 guarantees freedom of ideology, religion and worship of individuals and communities without limitation to their manifestations other than that necessary for protecting public order under the law.

The second line of argument is that freedom of conscience and religion is not an absolute and unconditional right, so that:

In the case of conflict or a clash, [these rights] may be limited by other constitutionally protected rights, especially when those affected are the rights of other people.

In particular, the Supreme Court took the view that the conflict represented by conscientious objection to specific medical treatments (blood transfusions in this case) 'acquire special relevance when religious convictions clash with the right to life'. This problem, according to the Supreme Court, requires 'consideration of the rights in conflict within the specific situation being dealt with'. This consideration may change substantially if the life put at risk by the refusal or opposition to a blood transfusion is that of a minor. In this case, says the Supreme Court:

It is perfectly legitimate and necessary to order that the treatment be given to the minor even if the parents have expressed their opposition. . . . [The right to life and health of the minor] can not give way to the claim of freedom of conscience or the objection of the parents. If they allow their son to die because their religious convictions do not allow hospital treatment or a blood transfusion, then criminal responsibility arises.

In short, the Spanish Supreme Court considers that the right to life and health of a minor takes precedence over the freedom of conscience or the objection of the parents. If parents allow their son to die because their religious convictions prohibit hospital treatment or a blood transfusion, 'then criminal responsibility arises'. Moreover, in contrast to the criterion maintained by the court of first instance, the opinion of the Supreme Court was not affected 'by the fact that the son, a member of the same religious group, was also opposed to a blood transfusion'. This goes against the thesis of the court of first instance that, after recognising the importance of the value of life, decided that when this value comes into conflict with personal autonomy, then the latter takes precedence.

The Spanish Supreme Court, therefore, radically changed the criterion offered by the court of first instance by giving precedence in this case to the right to life of the child over the right to religious freedom, and attributing criminal responsibility to the parents for not having protected the right to life of the minor. However, after finding the parents guilty of the offence of homicide, the Supreme Court considered that the religious motivations of the parents, while not excusing them, did represent a mitigating factor justifying a reduction in the sentence (two years and six months in prison). The Court even showed a favourable disposition towards the possibility of a pardon. Consequently, it convicted the parents of the minor on the grounds that, first, life has an unconditional precedence over religious freedom and, secondly, that the parents of the minor did not fulfil their moral and legal obligations to do everything possible to save the life of their son.

The Decision of the Constitutional Court 154/2002, of 18 July, overturned the decision 950/1997 of the Supreme Court of 27 June under which the parents were convicted for the offence of homicide by omission.[1] The Constitutional Court considered that the action of the parents was protected by the fundamental right of religious freedom (article 16.1 of the Spanish Constitution). More specifically, according to the Constitutional Court, the parents of the dead child invoked their right to religious freedom and also made the guardianship of the public authorities possible without reservation in order to protect the minor. For these reasons the Court granted the appeal and quashed the decision of the Supreme Court. In a very interesting decision, after having analysed the content and limits of religious freedom, the Constitutional Court stated that:

> The requirement on the parents of an action (. . .) permissive towards the transfusion, once they allowed without reservation the possibility of the guardianship of the

---

[1] Details of this decision can be found in Bercovitz Cano 2002; Valerio Heredia 2004: 80–87; Maceiras Rodríguez 2008; Pérez Triviño 2010. From the point of view of the best interests of the minor, see Rivero Hernández 2007.

public authorities for the protection of the minor, conflicts to the very core with their right to religious freedom and goes beyond the duty required of them by virtue of special legal position with regard to their underage son. In this context, and in the present case, the parents' condition of guarantor did not extend to complying with such requirements.

The Court concluded that:

> The action of the current appellants is protected by the fundamental right to freedom of religion (art 16.1 of the Spanish Constitution). Such right must therefore be held as infringed by the decisions appealed against for constitutional protection.

Of particular interest are the reflections of the Constitutional Court on the personal autonomy of the minor and his right to decide, even if the conclusions leave the debate open given that

> there are not enough details to conclude with certainty . . . that the deceased minor . . . had sufficiently mature judgement in order to assume a vital decision such as that we are dealing with.

For this reason, the Constitutional Court did not rest its decision on the basis of personal autonomy but on the religious freedom of the parents and their lack of objection to the public authorities assuming guardianship for the protection of the minor. In any case, the Constitutional Court considered that the fact that the minor clearly expressed, in exercising his right to freedom of religion and beliefs, a wish – coinciding with that of his parents – to reject specific medical treatment is a factor that had to be taken into account and could not be ignored. Specifically, the Constitutional Court stated that:

> In opposing outsider interference to his own body, the minor was exercising a right to self-determination over his body – which is different from the right to health or life – and which is translated into the constitutional framework as a fundamental right to physical integrity (art 15 of the Spanish Constitution).

Once the right of minors to self-determination over their physical integrity has been established by the Constitutional Court, it emphasises that 'in any event, the minor's interest is prevalent, in the charge of the parents and, if appropriate, the courts'. It is clear that the Constitutional Court is striking a difficult balance between the rights of self-determination of the minor to be heard and the right to self-determination over physical integrity, the protection of life and the full development of the personality. While rejecting the thesis of the Supreme Court in this respect and tending towards the findings set out in the decision of the court of first instance, it avoids giving a clear decision and leaves the preponderance of these rights unresolved with a casuistic observation about the lack of maturity of the minor to make decisions on such a fundamental and dramatic issue.

We accordingly find ourselves before a case which is no longer 'hard' but 'fundamental' (Dworkin 1986: 265–66; 353–54), in which the rights at issue need to be weighed up given that the legal principles and moral and political values involved are difficult to unravel. The contrasting arguments in the decisions of this case clearly demonstrate this. In fact the issues are extremely complex, perhaps more so than the arguments set out in the decisions analysed. The case will therefore be considered in depth in the following section, focusing on the rights of minors in relation to this type of conflict.

III ANALYSIS OF THE CASE

Both in the decisions of the court of first instance and the Supreme Court, irrespective of the conclusions arrived at, and in that of the Constitutional Court, the case was considered as one of a conflict of rights and individual freedoms. The first point to make is that at no point was it considered in terms of cultural or legal pluralism. In the statements made by the representatives of all the parties and in the arguments given by each court that have been analysed, the case appears to be about individual freedoms and limitations to such freedoms, always within the framework established by the Spanish Constitution.[2]

However, there is always a more complex dimension in this type of case. While the right to personal autonomy and the freedom to take decisions are legally recognised for members of religious groups and communities, should an individual choose to depart from the rules of his or her religious group (by accepting a blood transfusion, for example), such an action will be interpreted by other members of the group as a rejection and they will probably react negatively to such a decision (Ahmed 2010: 227). Such individuals or the more vulnerable groups of individuals (women or minors) are often subjected to strong pressure from the religious community to which they belong not to disobey the rules of that community. If individuals resist the pressure of the group, they may be ostracised. Therefore, the right of these individuals to freedom of choice is fully protected by law (article 16 of the Spanish Constitution), but it can have adverse consequences for the individuals in question and may result in their social and community links being broken (Ahmed 2010: 229). In the case of the most vulnerable individuals (women or children), the pressure can be so strong that it is impossible for them to make decisions freely. These obstacles to the exercise of self- autonomy by members of some social and/or religious groups arise before the state, the guarantor of the right to the autonomy and freedom of individuals, can act to make such pressures less coercive. Thus, in the situation described, the recognition of the freedom of choice of the individual is frequently not enough to remove the obstacles and objections of the system of personal law to which the individual belongs, nor to sufficiently uphold the personal autonomy of the individual (Ahmed 2010: 230; Eekelaar 2010: 349, 351).

---

[2] More clearly also than in the Amish schooling case *Wisconsin v Yoder*: see Minow 1995: 356–57.

In any event, the case under analysis was contextualised within the limits of the traditional juridical model – judicialised and essentially restrictive. At the outset, a judicial authorisation was applied for from the duty magistrates' court and subsequent developments were confined within the limits of court intervention.[3] Even when the local municipal authorities intervened, they did so through the administration of justice (the court order of the Instruction Court of Fraga, 14 September 1994). After the death of Marcos, the case continued within restrictive judicial channels with the criminal prosecution of the parents brought by the Public Prosecutions Department in accordance with Spanish legislation.

This does not appear to have been the best way forward to guarantee the rights of protection for a minor in such circumstances. Perhaps, therefore, it is relevant to examine some of the issues relating to the problem of the limits of the law and to look at the deficiencies of the traditional juridical model in resolving situations such as the one under study. Above all, it is worth considering if one of the possible explanations for the lack of effectiveness of the law when settling this case could have been that the traditional mechanisms of judicial intervention and conduct did not serve to protect the rights and interests of the child.

The objective is not to consider whether the parents should be punished. In general terms, as Mumford points out, religion for many is just one part of multiculturalism. However, religion may have a significant effect on all areas of life. If, therefore, we consider religion as a question of 'being' rather than as a question of choice, then we would be wrong to penalise an individual for what that individual 'is' (Mumford 1998: 133). The result in many cases involving cultural or religious conflict is that while the courts officially apply the criminal law, in fact they end up mitigating sentences as a consequence of religious or cultural imperatives (Rentlen 2004: 51). As mentioned previously, in the case under discussion the Spanish Supreme Court, after finding the parents guilty of homicide, considered that the religious motivations of the parents, while not excusing them, certainly justified a reduction in the sentence and the Court even showed itself to be favourable to the possibility of a pardon.

In the case under study, the question is whether the fatal outcome of the death of a child of 13 could have been avoided. In this context, it must be emphasised that the various judicial authorities dealing with the problem were not simply faced with what might be called a 'possible risk of death', but a very likely outcome of death. It is hard to imagine that a child of 13 years of age could have survived more than a few days without the blood transfusion that more than one medical report insisted was absolutely essential in order to save his life. Furthermore, the fact that a minor, given his religious convictions and beliefs, accepts that he might die is not the same as 'wanting to die'.

---

[3] This continues to be common practice, even in the case of adults. See as an example, including existing discrepancies, decision of the Audiencia Provincial de Guipúzcoa (Section 2a), 22 September 2004; decision no 2053/2005 of the Audiencia Provincial de Guipúzcoa (Section 2a) of 18 March.

The interpretation of the 'best interests of the child' as understood by parents does not necessarily adequately protect the rights of the child. This may mean that medical professionals might have to consider a course of action against the wishes of the parents. Specific disagreements between such professionals and parents need to be resolved with a degree of flexibility and speed if the life of the child is in danger and where this stage is especially tricky the public authorities should be involved in order to resolve the conflict.

In general, the state should intervene to ensure the fulfilment of legal obligations which parents have failed to observe in respect of their children. Clearly, the decision to intervene must be taken on a case- by-case basis, and the consequences of intervention must be justified as must the effects of a decision by the state not to intervene (Eekelaar 2010: 348, 352, 354). In disputes arising from individuals belonging to specific cultural communities or religious groups, even operating under the principle of non-intervention of the state in family affairs (the 'purposive abstention model'), certain practices should be prohibited on the grounds of cruelty to some members of such groups, usually the most vulnerable (women and children). In this context, the rights of women and children 'have been brought within the scope of public law and are no longer relegated to the private domain' (Ballard 2009: 305). Where children are involved, the state needs to be culturally sensitive while at the same time upholding fundamental human rights standards. There is, of course, a particular need to comply with the law when children are involved given that they are vulnerable and cannot defend themselves. Intervention is justified in those cases where children may suffer 'irreparable harm' (Rentlen 2004: 72). This does not mean that state intervention is necessary in all cases where children need specific medical treatment, but it is necessary in those cases where the criterion of 'irreparable harm' applies. Without this criterion, family and cultural autonomy could be unjustifiably diminished.

In Spain, the obligation to investigate situations of lack of protection of a child as a result of neglect on the part of the parents together with taking the measures necessary to protect the child corresponds to the public authorities (article 172.1 ss of the Spanish Civil Code and articles 12 and 17 of the Organic Law 1/1996, on the Legal Protection of Minors). It should be remembered that parents are legally obliged to take decisions in the best interests of the child. This means that the public administration has subsidiary authority – and obligation – to intervene in order to protect a child. This is the situation where, as in this case, the parents interpret the interest of their child only from a subjective viewpoint – that of their religious faith.[4]

---

[4] In general terms, Spanish civil law is not particularly open to recognising the effects of 'interlegality' or validating aspects of Islamic law. However, in the specific area of child protection, Spanish courts have applied the concept of the best interests of the child in cases of Islamic custody of minors (*kafalah*). The High Court in Anadalusia in a second instance decision (14 September 2004) equated Islamic *kafalah* with Spanish family fostering in the case of two Moroccan twin brothers resident in Spain. Specifically, the application of the principle of the best interests of the child by this Court enabled the children to receive the orphans' benefit denied to them by the court of first instance; see Colom González 2011: 169–70.

The exercise of religious freedom consists not only in having certain beliefs, but in acting in a way that is consistent with such beliefs and convictions. The right to freedom of religion is linked to other important rights and extends to several areas of life such as education, worship, conscientious objection, etc (Casuscelli 2010: 136, 138). In Spain, religious freedom includes the right of parents to bring up their children in accordance with their religious convictions (article 27.3 Spanish Constitution).

The religious denomination of the Jehovah's Witnesses is a minority religious group in Spain.[5] Among its rules is a prohibition for its members to receive blood transfusions, considered to be contrary to their convictions and beliefs. However, this should not give rise to discriminatory treatment and any prejudice in the judicial treatment of minors in this context should be avoided. Perhaps the best solution would be to prohibit only the most extreme cultural or religious practices (Rentlen 2004: 49; Ballard 2009: 311). In any event, attaching 'culpability' in cases involving 'culture' or 'religion' should be avoided, as occurred in the decision of the Spanish Supreme Court discussed above in which the Court expressed its view that the parents did not fulfil their moral obligations and allowed their son to die because of their religious convictions.

According to Mumford (1998: 125–26), in some disputes involving religious freedom there is a tendency by the courts to favour some religions over others. Furthermore, in cases where parents belong to a socially accepted and majority religion – Protestant, Catholic or Jewish – the commentaries by judges are not negative even when the religion is presumably not shared by the judge in question. Thus, judges refer to such parents as 'bringing up their children in their religious faith'. In other cases where parents belong to minority religious groups – such as the Jehovah's Witnesses – the judge may refer to the father or mother in terms of being a 'fanatic' or of belonging to a religion or sect that 'indoctrinates their children' (Mumford 1998: 126). This can lead to people sharing minority beliefs as being considered in some way as disturbed, evil or merely criminal. Such attitudes rarely help to achieve an appropriate answer to the specific situation under dispute (Ballard 2009: 314–15). Although the case under discussion did not reach such extremes, the Spanish Supreme Court in its decision of 27 June 1997 considered that in moral terms the parents did not fulfil their obligations and allowed their son to die as a result of their religious convictions, and for this reason the Court ruled that the conduct of the parents gave rise to criminal responsibility.

Turning to another aspect, in the specific case described here I consider that the intervention of the public authorities was slow and unfortunate. In my opinion they should have considered other possible options, from an initial protective intervention at the time that the 'situation of risk' of the minor was declared to the point of taking the child into local authority care – considering the situation

---

[5] The number of Jehovah's Witnesses in Spain was about 125,000 in the year 2005, according to their own data.

to be one of neglect – given the serious risk not only to the health, but to the life of the child. Another possibility would have been for the Public Prosecution Service, as the competent authority in the question of child protection, to have ordered the local authority to take the child into care.

Within the framework of a social state in which the law of the protection of minors allows intervention for the purposes of prevention, there are appropriate mechanisms for protecting minors, beyond even the opinions or the authority of the parents, if considered necessary for the effective protection of the best interests of the minor (Rentlen 2004: 48). This could have been an option in this case, though it would have been a complex decision not without its difficulties and contradictions. Specifically, though, it would have enabled the minor to have been given a blood transfusion as a way of protecting his best interests and his rights.

In the first place, such a decision would have respected the religious freedom of the parents as they would not have been obliged to act against their convictions in order to save their child's life. It is the principle of religious freedom that determines that the parents were not legally required to convince their son of something which goes against the teaching that, in the exercise of their religious freedom, they had transmitted to their son long before the time of the accident. The parents complied with their duty as guarantor as they were not legally required to do anything beyond what in fact they did (STC 154/2002). It is the state, with its subsidiary responsibility of guaranteeing the higher interests of the child and his rights, which through its institutions should have decided, according with the circumstances, whether the child had the right to self-determination as a patient; or if the child should have been given a blood transfusion even if this went against his own wishes or the wishes of the parents.[6]

However, underlying questions remain such as whether it is legitimate to substitute the will of a 13-year-old minor by that of the public authorities, or that of judges; or else if public intervention in a private family situation, going against the firm decision of the parents to object to medical treatment for their son, or to ignore the will of the minor himself when this coincides with that of

[6] In the Anglo-Saxon sphere, the courts in cases where adolescents refuse medical treatment necessary for saving their lives apply a 'test of irrationality' together with the 'outcome of the decision' criterion. In the case of younger children, judges authorise emergency treatment, ignoring or leaving aside the wishes of the parents: see *(Re R (a minor) (blood transfusion)*[1993] 2 FLR 757; *(Re O (a minor) (medical treatment)* [1993] 2 FLR 149; *Re S (a minor) (medical treatment)* [1994] 2 FLR 1065. These cases refer to babies of three and ten months, respectively, and a four-year-old child with leukemia. From the age of 16 it is considered that the child has sufficient judgement to take decisions, although judges are more exacting when assessing the decision-making capacity of adolescents who refuse medical treatment necessary for their future health. In cases of adolescent Jehovah's Witnesses who refuse blood transfusions, judges consider that such adolescents do not have sufficient judgement to make such a decision and consequently their refusal is rejected and the judge makes a decision according to the 'best interests of the child'. This occurred in *Re E (a minor) (wardship: medical treatment)* [1993] 1 FLR 386. In this case, the judicial authorisation of the blood transfusion could only be applied during two years. Once the adolescent reached the age of 18, he refused blood transfusions and died as a result. For an analysis of these and other cases, see Picontó Novales 2000: 17–61.

his parents, is justified or not. Probably the most honest course is to consider that a decision to protect a 13-year-old minor is not taken because of his incapacity to decide for himself, but simply because society, the state, and the current system of protection of minors is interested in protecting minors irrespective of their age or even of the errors and prejudices they may experience before reaching their adult majority.

From certain specific points of view, however, the situation could not be clearer. In this case, for example, it must be remembered that the minor rejected the blood transfusion 'in a state of terror' when the doctors decided to carry out this treatment after receiving the authorisation of the court. It was precisely this extreme rejection by the minor and the possible negative consequences for his health – a transfusion in such a situation could have caused a cerebral haemorrhage – that led to the decision by the doctors not to perform the transfusion. Obviously the circumstances of each case need to be carefully considered under the general criteria that the right of personality or of protection of a 13-year-old minor (of life and health) must be safeguarded in the event of a conflict with the right of religious freedom and self-determination.

Going one step further, it is worth asking if this argument can apply in the case of adolescents in similar circumstances and with the same religious beliefs. It would be inappropriate to label an adolescent as incompetent or incapable on the basis that his or her decisions reflect strongly-held beliefs instilled by his or her upbringing even if socially unacceptable.[7] Nevertheless, despite all the possible contradictions that may arise, the argument that adolescent minors affected by a serious illness have the right to be protected much more than adults seems to me to be perfectly justified. Such an argument is consistent with the theory of the rights of children according to which there is room for a degree of paternalism in the protection of their rights and interests, not only currently but also in the future (Eekelaar 1994: 42, 57).

In conclusion, in my opinion the minor should have been given the blood transfusion that he needed in time, even against his own wishes, not on the basis of the arguments put forward by the Supreme Court which I believe were wrong – the priority of an abstract right to life over religious freedom – nor even those of the Constitutional Court, but with the argument that when treating a 13-year-old minor whose life is in grave danger, the protective intervention of the public authorities is justified even when the danger results from religious beliefs. The

---

[7] The current Law 41/2002, of 14 November, regulating the self-determination of patients and the rights and obligations regarding clinical information and documentation, establishes the following with respect to minors: 'Consent by representation shall be granted in the following situations: (a) when the patient who is a minor does not have the intellectual or emotional capacity to understand the scope of the intervention. In such a case, the consent will be exercised by the legal representative of the minor after having heard the opinion of the minor if the minor has reached the age of 12 years. In the case of minors who are either with or without such capacity but are autonomous and have reached the age of 16 years, consent cannot be given by representation. However, in cases of serious risk according to the factual criteria, the parents will be informed and their opinions taken into account when the corresponding decision is made' (article 9.3a).

public authorities, acting through the social services, should have exercised their subsidiary protective functions as set out in the UN Convention of the Rights of the Child and in Spanish legislation to guarantee the right of this child to the full development of his personality and finally to health and life. Now, leaving aside the above arguments, I think that one has to be very careful when trying to resolve problems resulting from the objection to medical treatment on the part of Jehovah's Witnesses. In my view, the defence of the position of respect for life if the situation affects an adult or a minor who can be considered responsible for his or her own acts can involve an unjustified degree of paternalism. Having said this, decisions taken in relation to minors – in particular if it is considered that they are not yet fully able to take decisions for themselves – do not have to be the same as those applied to adults. Allowing the right to life to predominate in all cases can lead us on to dangerous ground, where a Jehovah's Witness could be considered to suffer discrimination when accepting the risk of death resulting from the fact that his or her religion prevents him or her from undergoing a specific medical treatment. Personally, I consider it possible that these types of decisions in themselves do not make them any less competent or autonomous for following their determinations. The refusal to be subjected to blood transfusions or other types of medical treatment should be respected in such cases and accorded the protection of the right of religious freedom and personal self-determination. To disallow these adult *patients* the capacity to make up their own minds in the difficult circumstances in which they find themselves would be like taking away their right to their own personality.

REFERENCES

Ahmed, F (2010) 'Personal Autonomy and the Option of Religious Law' 24 *International Journal of Law, Policy and the Family* 222.

Ballard, R (2009) 'Human Rights in Contexts of Ethnic Plurality: Always a Vehicle for Liberation?' in R Grillo et al (eds), *Legal Practice and Cultural Diversity* (Farnham, Ashgate).

Banda, F (2005) *Women. Law and Human Rights* (Oxford, Hart Publishing).

Bercovitz CR (2002) 'Patria potestad y protección del menor: conflicto de su derecho a la vida y a la salud con el derecho a la libertad religiosa de sus progenitores' *Aranzadi Civil-Mercantil* 11: www.westlaw.es

Casuscelli, G (2010) 'State and Religion in Europe' in S Ferrari and R Cristofori (eds), *Law and Religion in the 21st Century. Relations between States and Religious Communities* (Farnham, Ashgate).

Coady, M and Coady CAJ (1991) 'There Ought to be a Law Against it: Reflections on Child Abuse, Morality and Law in P Alston, S Parker and J Seymour (eds), *Children, Rights and the Law* (Oxford, Clarendon Press).

Colom González, F (2011) 'Entre el credo y la ley. Las minorías etno-religiosas y los fenómenos del pluralism jurídico' in F Colom González and A López Sala (eds), *Hacia una sociedad post-secular? La gestión pública de la nueva diversidad religiosa* (Zaragoza, Fundación Manuel Jiménez Abad).

Dworkin, R (1986) *Law's Empire* (London, Fontana Press).

Eekelaar, J (1991) 'The Importance of Thinking that Children have Rights' in P Alston, S Parker and J Seymour (eds), *Children, Rights and the Law* (Oxford, Clarendon Press).

—— (1994) 'The Interests of the Child and the Child's Wishes: The Role of Dynamic Self-Determinism' 8 *International Journal o f Law and the Family* 42.

—— (2010) 'From Multiculturalism to Cultural Voluntarism: A Family-based Approach' 81 *The Political Quarterly* 344.

Maceiras Rodríguez, PM (2008) 'La objeción de conciencia en relación con tratamientos e intervenciones médicas *Jurídica Aranzadi* 756.

Martín Retortillo, L (1984) 'Puede el juez ordenar una tranfusión de sangre aún en contra de la voluntad del paciente?' 13 *Rev del Poder Judicial* 31.

Martínez de Pisón Cavero, J (2000) *Constitución y libertad religiosa en España,* prol. de J. I. Lacasta-Zabalza, (Madrid, Dykinson/Universidad de La Rioja).

McGoldrick, D (1991) 'The United Nations Convention on the Rights of the Child' 5 *International Journal of Law and the Family* 132.

Minow, M (1995) 'Rights and Cultural Difference' in A Sarat and TR Kearns, *Identities, Politics and Rights* (Ann Arbor, University of Michigan Press).

Mumford, SE (1998) 'The Judicial Resolution of Disputes involving Children and Religion' 47 *International and Comparative Law Quarterly* 118.

Pelayo González, A (1997) *La intervención jurídica en la actividad médica: el consentimiento informado* (Madrid, Universidad Carlos III/Dykinson).

Pérez Triviño, JL (2010) 'Testigos de Jehová: Entre la autonomía del paciente y el paternalismo justificado' *InDret* 2010–12: www.indret.com.

Picontó Novales, T (2000) *En las fronteras del derecho. Estudio de casos y reflexiones generales* (Madrid, Dykinson).

—— (2009) 'Derechos de la Infancia: Nuevo contexto, nuevos retos' 21 *Derechos y Libertades* 57.

Rentlen, AD (2004) *The Cultural Defense* (Oxford, Oxford University Press).

Rivero Hernández, F (2007) *El interés del menor*, 2nd edn (Madrid, Dykinson).

Ruiz Miguel, A (1993) 'Autonomía individual y derecho a la propia vida. Un análisis filosófico-jurídico' 14 *Revista del Centro de Estudios Constitucionales* 143.

Santos Morón, MJ (2002) 'Sobre la capacidad del menor para el ejercicio de sus derechos fundamentales. Comentario a la STC. 154/2002, de 18 de julio', *La Ley* 5675, año XXII.

Valerio Heredia, A (2004) *Constitución, libertad religiosa y minoría de edad. Un estudio a partir de la S. 154/2002, del TC* (Valencia).

Van Bueren, G (2007) *Child Rights in Europe. Convergence and Divergence* (Strasbourg, Council of Europe Publishing).

Vargas Pavez, M (2006) 'Diagnóstico de los mecanismos de protección de los derechos a la educación y salud de niños, niñas y adolescentes' 3–4 *Rev de Derechos del Niño* 11.

9

Cultural Norms, National Laws and Human Rights: How do we Balance Respect for Diversity and the Rights of the Vulnerable? The Case of Under Age Marriage of Roma Girls and Boys in Europe

JACEK KURCZEWSKI AND MAŁGORZATA FUSZARA

I INTRODUCTION

IN 2007, IN the town of Kędzierzyn-Koźle in the south of Poland, a court sentenced a man who was charged with maintaining a sexual relationship with a minor, a girl. The penalty was eight months' in prison, suspended for three years, as well as having a custodian appointed for the duration of the suspension. The ruling was below the minimum penalty stipulated by the penal code, which calls for a minimum of one year in prison, the maximum being 12 years. The court applied the principle of extraordinary leniency due to the 'lower degree of social harmfulness' of the actions of the accused. The accused himself was a Roma man, who in 2005 had introduced his 15-year-old wife to this court-appointed custodian. They had been married in a Roma ritual and in compliance with Roma traditions. Most of the court proceedings in the case were carried out behind closed doors. Expert witnesses – specialists on Roma culture – presented their opinions, which remain confidential. The court noted that neither of the spouses had been forced to engage in sexual relations, that the spouses are a harmonious couple and that they are raising a child together. 'The decision to enter into this traditional marriage was based on mutual feelings and a strong emotional connection. The two parties involved remain in a relationship, and they have a child of whom they take attentive care', stated the judge in the oral justification of the sentence during the part of the hearing that was open to the public.

Cases like this are rarely heard by Polish courts. This particular case raises a number of interesting issues. The conflict between the unofficial laws of the worldwide Roma community and the codified official law in Europe is apparent. Under the Roma law, the marriage is valid, despite the girl's young age. Under the statutory official law, not only is the marriage not valid, but the man is also guilty of paedophilia, since it is a criminal offence to engage in sexual relations with a person under the age of 15. The couple married in a manner that is traditional in their community, and they considered themselves – and were considered in the said community – to be husband and wife. The accused and his wife were so completely unaware of the criminal aspect of the matter that they inadvertently 'turned themselves in'. The authorities were notified of the situation by the accused himself, who introduced his under age wife to his court-appointed custodian. The custodian was required by the law to notify the public prosecutor's office, which in turn was obliged to instigate proceedings. The prosecutor filed for the lowest penalty provided for by the law, and for its suspension, since he found it counterproductive to incarcerate the man, particularly in light of the fact that the family life of the parties in question could be considered harmonious.

This case – as well as the few similar cases that have occurred in Poland – caused astonishment among members of the Roma community for whom even today the fact that very young people marry is the norm. 'If they wanted to charge us with this, they would have to collect all Roma folks from all over Poland and put them in jail', says Władysław Kat from Opole. He was 17 when he married a 13-year-old girl, with whom he has recently celebrated their thirty-second wedding anniversary. Jerzy Ficowski, a Polish researcher who studied Gypsy culture, claimed that the early marriages were a result of ideas about early adulthood and short childhood in the Gypsy culture. A girl who is 12 or 13 years of age is considered mature enough to work in the household, to earn money (eg, by offering palmistry readings) and also to marry. A traditional Roma marriage ceremony (*bijav*) contains elements similar to those of a church wedding, such as making a public vow, having a knot tied across the hands of the couple with a scarf and pronouncing a phrase that symbolises the irreversibility of marriage. Such a marriage is the only ceremony that is considered significant; no other ceremony is valid from the state's perspective. Thus, in light of the national law most couples whose marriages are strictly formalised in terms of the Roma law remain in an informal relationship in the eyes of the state. Cases like this make their way to official state courts very rarely, despite the fact that they often meet all the criteria of paedophilia. Interestingly, divorce, which according to Roma law is easy for men at the expense of women (those under age or adult husbands may have already more than one under age wife) does not attract the attention of the official state legal system at all. In general, marital unions and dissolutions of Roma people are an unknown figure in the shadow of the official marriage and family laws of the country. Men who are leaders of Roma associations say that occasionally they are summoned by the authorities to clarify the circumstances when a girl younger than 15 gives birth to a child. The aim is to discover the perpetrator of the paedophilic act. For example, the president of the Social and Cultural Association of Roma in the Republic of Poland mentioned that he had been summoned by the public prosecutor's office with regard to the case of a 14-year-old Roma girl who had given birth to a child. According to him, his clarification of the Roma tradition was sufficient. He claimed that he gave a detailed explanation and it was met with full understanding.

Most likely in this case, the public prosecutor's office decided to drop the charges, although it would be difficult to find the legal grounds for such a decision. It is disputable whether the 'customary law' of any social group may constitute sufficient grounds to discontinue an investigation into a case of paedophilia. While normally impossible, in this case 'being Roma' resulted in an exception in the implementation of the official state law. Such cases are relatively rare in Poland, since the Roma community is rather small (although quite heterogeneous, since there are four different ethnic subgroups of Roma living in the country). In other countries they are more common. Romania is a good example: in one district alone, 35 men have been sentenced for having sexual relations with minors and other acts connected with marriages to minors. However, all the sentences, spanning from 5 to 12 months' imprisonment, were suspended (Bit Bitu and Morteanu 2010: 102).

II ROMA MARRIAGE

The last detailed description of a Roma wedding ceremony in Poland comes from Długosz (1978) whose research was conducted among relatively assimilated Mountain Roma (Roma Bergitka) in the southern Tatry (Spisz) region. 'According to the Gypsy rules, marriage may be conducted by very young people. The matrimonial age is somewhat within 16–18 years limits but in the past marriages between 13–14 year old girls and slightly older 15–16 year old boys occurred' (Długosz 1978: 155). Though the Roma studied by Długosz were settled in two villages, in most of the cases exogamy was preferred due to high mobility that made it possible to meet new potential partners. 'This is not the conscious legal norm', stresses Długosz (1978: 156) and results from the tradition that when 'due to patrilocality of numerically small Gypsy communities, the whole settlement was composed of members of the close family and village exogamy was necessary rule'.

According to Długosz, the courtship period was short and sometimes reduced to reconnaissance by the relatives of the families of the young people. A bad reputation of the other party prevented agreement:

> The young people cannot then count on marriage, so if their feelings are strong they may decide to escape. If, however, both sides are certain that nobody will put forward essential obstacles to the wedding, the parents of the prospective bride or bridegroom

at first make an allusion or a joke, or even directly tell them, that they should marry (. . .) It can happen that the choice of partner is made by parents against the will of their child, especially if they consider that the son or daughter is strongly interested in the opposite gender . . . Parents advise them to marry, often against their will or at least in the face of their lack of interest (Długosz 1978: 156).

The boy's parents visit the home of the girl and talk to her parents. If the parents are inclined to accept, then 'the girl's father says that his daughter is coming home late and that this should be changed. The idea is caught by boy's father who suggests that *mangavipen* for both should be arranged' (Długosz 1978: 157). *Mangavipen* is a secular ceremony of joint consumption of food (meat with bread) and drinks (vodka and beer) by the close relatives of both parties. The *papus*, a respectable older relative, improvises a speech in which he admonishes the bride and bridegroom that marriage is not a one-night event but for one's whole life, and asks the bride, *Kames les?* (Do you want him?), and if she says *hi* (yes) he approaches the bride groom: *Kames la?* (Do you want her) and after that the prospective marriage partners ask the parents if they agree to the marriage. When the parents agree, the *papus* asks the bridegroom's parents: *kamen la borakhe?* (do you want her as the daughter-in-law)? After the affirmative response, he asks the bride's parents: *Kamen les dziamuntreskhe?* (do you want him as son-in-law)? After expressing agreement, both families make a verbal contract and the fathers, by a handshake, make the *zakład* (pledge) that they will guard the permanence of the union. If the wife deserts the husband, his family has the right to cut her hair or to request back the money spent on the *Mangavipen*. If the husband deserts the wife, her family has the right to beat him and also to request the money back. There is further ritual as one of the *papus* binds the hands of the young couple with a red scarf and proclaims: *Zaphandav tumenge o vast ape calo d ivipen* (I am binding your hand for your whole life), while the second gives the couple a glass of vodka to share. From that moment Gypsies consider the young couple as legally married with all due privileges – to cohabit, to have offspring considered as legal. *Mangavipen* is the fully socially sanctioned form of marrying among the Gypsies in Spisz. Church marriages were sporadically started in the interwar period. Długosz notes cases of a collective church marriage ceremony for several *Mangavipen* couples by the local priest several years after the Second World War. Later, in the communist period, civil marriages (the only ones then considered legal) were sometimes concluded before the state authorities to obtain official recognition of the children in order to qualify for family benefits etc:

> The strong commitment of Gypsies to this form of marriage means that even the adult partners conclude *mangavipen* before a church or civil wedding. It is also the custom that perfectly fulfills its role in the case of unions between the partners who are minors in light of the state or church's law (Długosz 1978: 160).

Examples from Romania, Bulgaria and Macedonia indicate that early marriages in the Roma community are common and occur in small towns and in big cities (eg, in the Gypsy neighbourhood of Bucharest) as well as across denominations. Members of the Roma community tend to be Roman Catholics in Poland, Muslims in Macedonia and Orthodox in Bulgaria, whereas in Romania some are Orthodox and others are Protestants, often Pentecostal and Neoprotestant. The preponderance of religious law over the Roma law may seem dubious if, as Ficowski claims, the grandfather in the three-generational line of the dynasty of Roman Catholic Polish Roma kings living around the period of the First World War was supposed to have had five wives.

Among the Roma, the fundamental qualification of a woman to become a wife is her virginity. Early marriages, as well as the interpretation of actual sexual relations as marriage, are designed to prevent women from changing partners. The most drastic case reported in the literature occurred in Romania. A girl aged five was betrothed to a boy aged 16. A betrothal like this results in the girl being transferred into the husband's family, since under Roma law the wife transfers into the household of the husband's family and is subordinated to this household. The husband's family claimed that it would try to ensure that the couple refrain from sexual activity until the girl was sufficiently mature. Nonetheless, the actual relationship was deemed valid. Here the reasoning overlaps with yet another reason why the Roma community considers early marriages beneficial: the early transfer and submission of the girl. If this occurs relatively early in her life, the girl is believed to adapt more easily. Moreover, it reinforces the belief that her family of origin no longer has influence on her life. In light of the official statutory law, this is a criminal offence too: the child is handed over by its parents to another family, despite the statutory obligation to care for their children. This obligation is contained in legislative provisions in Romania just as in other European countries. In Romania, the national law also specifically requires that the child reside with its parents.

III ELOPEMENT, KIDNAPPING AND COHABITATION

Apart from the age problem, there is another Roma ritual with potential for generating conflict between Roma law and national law: a different form of entering into a marriage, namely, elopement. Many members of the Roma community emphasise that 'true' kidnappings are rare today. Much more frequently what is referred to as kidnapping is in fact a form of elopement by young people who have feelings towards each other. Roma culture equates the commencement of sexual relations between them with entering into a marriage. It is a way for young people to avoid marriages arranged for them by their parents and by the elders, which in the opinion of Romanian researchers is particularly common in large cities, such as Bucharest. After the elopement/kidnapping, there is a public ceremony (*brandy*) to celebrate the girl's virginity and the commencement of a new relationship. Ficowski (1985: 302–10), when writing of the old Roma marriage practices in Poland, mentions bridewealth – *doro* – as the

standard rule (like African *lobolo*) among some Roma tribes and stresses elopement among the Lopari and Kalderes as the way young couples escape both the
financial burden involved as well as unwelcome marital arrangements. The
bridewealth element seems least often mentioned in the literature though it
deserves detailed analysis referring to the wealth of knowledge accumulated on
that subject in the anthropological, especially Africanist, literature.

In cases like this, despite the traditional classification of these events as 'kidnapping', none of the parties are in fact being forced into the marriage. However,
actual kidnappings remain a possibility. Adolescent girls who wish to continue
their education and who prefer not to get married early often speak of their fear
of kidnapping. Their narrations tend to feature men who are interested in them
and who could force a marriage by means of kidnapping. In order to prevent
such a kidnapping, the girls have to be constantly guarded by their fathers or
brothers. Naturally, statutory law heavily penalises unlawfully depriving a person of their freedom. However, no charges have ever been filed in Poland in this
type of case. This is likely to stem from the fact that members of the Roma community are forbidden by their own rules to take problems regarding the actions
of another member of this community to the national courts, which are considered to be outside the legal domain of the Roma themselves. Recently, for the
first time, a Roma activist sued his Roma fellows in a Polish court, and that
created the turmoil in the community.

In Roma communities, power in general, and the authority to settle disputes
in particular, lies either with the 'kings' (in the 'Polska Roma' – Polish Roma –
subgroup, for example) or with the council of elders (*kris*). These are the only
authorities to which a member of the Roma community whose rights are
infringed by another member of this community may turn to for help. If under
such circumstances this person sought assistance from a state court or from
another non-Roma institution, he or she would be permanently and irrevocably
polluted. This is why families try to protect girls from kidnappings. Once a kidnapping occurs, however, the marriage is generally considered valid, even if the
girl protests against it. Other solutions are pursued only on very infrequent
occasions. Research reports one case of a girl kidnapped by an admirer to whom
the family did not wish to give the girl. He managed to carry out the kidnapping. However, the girl's mother, who had been opposed to the marriage, took
the girl to a gynaecologist, who pronounced her a virgin. Consequently, the
marriage was not considered valid. According to ethnographers, marriage by
elopement or kidnapping seems to be the recognised alternative practice to the
official (unofficial) Roma marriage by arrangement and consent of two families.
Loss of virginity is in the Roma legal system the normatively relevant fact that
leads to the recognition of such 'customary' marriage, not the elopement or
kidnapping as such.

As we have pointed out, the marriage practices of the Roma are not only custom but are partly also covered by the experience of normative binding of the
customary rules. The practices, often described in an internally contradictory

way, need to be divided into what belongs to the binding Roma law and what was or is the social practice but had not and does not have such obligatory character. This is necessary above all in regard to the escapes and elopements. In the ethnographic literature, the traditional description of elopements includes them with the customary law. However, custom, *mos* and counter-*mores*, counter-customs are different things. Malinowski has already described institutional ways of escaping the law, and elopement belongs in that dark zone between the law and crime. It is a complex set of practices. Długosz (1978) lists elopement as the third form of concluding marriage after those comprising the proper *Mangavipen* ceremony and factual cohabitation. Kowarska (2005: 101–24) on the other hand distinguished between categories of elopement: (1) if the girl is only apparently kidnapped while the parents 'often' agreed and hired the hotel apartment for the young couple. Here the girl escapes willingly and the escape is not real but agreed; (2) if the parents disagree but the couple escapes on their own 'often' with support of their other relatives; and (3) the real kidnapping of the girl. The confusion of the circumstances is already present in the ethnographic sources, but evidently there are three types of *chwytel*: (1) staged elopement that supports the theory of the preservation of the old-fashioned macho ideal of the young male; (2) escape of the couple in love, often with the help of other relatives and friends, when the parents of both or one do not agree to the marriage; (3) kidnapping the girl by the suitor (Godlewska-Goska and Kopańska 2011: 342). In the third case, seemingly it is not the kidnapping that legalises the union, but the suspected loss of virginity that necessitates the acceptance of the union with the kidnapper as binding. This appears from one of the cases described earlier that once the defloration can be disclaimed the kidnapping does not result in marriage but remains a transgression of Roma law.

Cohabitation as such with passage of time leads – as in all communities – to recognition of the couple as a union but does not seem to be a form of marriage. Our claim that neither cohabitation as such nor 'elopement' is marriage in the Gypsy law sense is substantiated by several details which one finds in the related literature but which seems to have escaped the attention of the ethnographers. Even the already cited case of the kidnapping in which the gynecologist confirmed the virginity of the recovered girl proves that kidnapping is perhaps a traditional pattern of conduct by the young man but not the traditional legal way of entering into marriage. As to cohabitation as such, in Gypsy as in many other societies it leads through *usus* (similar to *usucapio*) from the factual union to a union recognised as legal and creating several rights and obligations, though the relationship is complex and subject to conflicting interpretations. (Lind 2008). 'Sometimes as among the *Kelderashi* the young ones could have been *stigmatised as unclean due to the breach of the rules* (our emphasis) and the wishes of the parents. Despite that, the marriage had been recognised and could not have been broken while 'actual or pretended kidnapping was sanctioned by the group due to the consummation of marriage that had to

happen in the group's belief' (Mirga and Mróz 1994: 259–60). In order to interpret it properly we must refer to the Hindu concept of pollution as an objective
event independent of the intention of actors. The illicit sexual union is polluting
in itself, and legality is the *conditio sine qua non* of the recognition of cleanli-
ness of the partners. Such legality is assumed in order to help not only the couple, but their relatives who could otherwise be polluted. Sexual union is thus the
way to enter the legal union for unmarried people, while marital union is the
way to enter unpolluted sexual cohabitation. The Romans used to treat continuous cohabitation for one year as the *usus* leading to legal recognition of the
union but the cohabitation as such was not the way to make the union valid.
Neither is it so in the case of Gypsies. As Godlewska-Goska and Kopańska
write: 'it is unthinkable for a man to abuse the woman, that is to kidnap her and
to cohabit with her sexually while not be willing to be her husband' (2011: 358).
The kidnapping does not make the marriage, as legitimisation by the parents is
necessary. The kidnapping does not make the marriage if the defloration did not
happen. Even defloration does not make the marriage as the marriage will not
be recognised if the kidnapper is already married. Conditions other than the
cohabitation as such must be fulfilled.

IV CONFLICTS BETWEEN ROMA LAW AND OTHER LAWS

Fundamental differences between national law and Roma law have existed in
some countries (including Poland) ever since the first appearance of the Roma. In
the multicultural Poland of old, many legal systems coexisted, and minority
groups like German burghers, Jews, Tartars, Armenians or even the Wallachian
shepherds were allowed to live by their own laws and use their own judicial systems. With the arrival of Roma people in the fifteenth century, Polish kings established the institution of 'Gypsy kings' whom they appointed, and who held power
in their communities and acted as go-betweens, connecting the two worlds. In
modern times national law was unified, and the status of laws of minority groups
fell to that of unofficial law. It was unofficial in the sense of not being recognised
by the state, though most of Roma law is based on the authority of kings and
councils recognised by the Roma themselves and thus it is official *Roma* law, with
its own 'customary' codes, administration of justice and even legislation.

As always, family law is an important part of the law of any social group, and
even more so among Roma who have almost no communal institutions other
than family and kin to link them. A family law which is based on the principle
of inter-family arranged marriage and family corporationism excluding individual free will is a strong element of the ethnic identity of Roma people. But it
can be subject to change. For example, Roma law and culture in general is based
on the notion of pollution, like many other traditional ethnic cultures, which
helps to separate the two genders. The polluting agency of women is dependent
not on 'age' but on menstruation, and the menarche determines the achieve-

ment of full female status. But Ficowski mentions how one of the Polish Roma kings, the last of the above mentioned dynasty, when dying, promulgated a series of the new 'customs', one of which exempted female artists from the ban on wearing trousers by women. These authorities, who are 'unofficial' from the perspective of the state are, of course, strategic partners with whom ways of eliminating conflict between Roma law and official state (and EU) law should be discussed. It is also important to realise that by no means the whole 'living law' of Roma is their official Roma law.

The Roma of today, and especially the most educated, often live in two worlds simultaneously. This is well illustrated by a quote from an interview with a PhD student, a Roma woman, a mother and a wife. She answered the question on how she copes with the fact that at work she runs a project and manages men who work under her supervision, while at the same time living among the Roma, where she holds a subordinate position merely by virtue of being a woman:

> It is often like this, we are in the office or at an event, something goes on, and so on . . . I am in charge, I run it all, I organise, and then later there is a reception and all I do is I serve the food . . . (she laughs) I just put a different hat on. And I also wear a different hat when there is a celebration. Then I am not a person who is educated and who works for the benefit of the community, because nobody cares about that (. . .) then I sit with women at one table, because men sit at another table, or even in a different part of the room completely. And I don't have a problem with that . . . OK, well, I will admit that now after so many years I don't feel like a fish in the water (. . .) But I learned to function like that.

The conclusion is that in Poland, in the European Union, in Europe and in the whole world, wherever Roma and kin groups are living, we are dealing with communities that have their own law, unwritten, though recorded by ethnographers, a law that is socially sanctioned inside the group, a law that includes marriage and family law. We also deal here with some non-normative customs (escape or cohabitation) that are in conflict with Roma law. Some of these customs – as are some of the norms of the Roma official customary law (age of marital capacity, extent of the parental authority) – are also potentially in conflict with the state, and more importantly with international humanitarian standards prohibiting gender discrimination, protection of minors and freedom of marital choice.

One possible solution to this problem – although by no means guaranteeing one hundred per cent success (but is that ever possible?) – would be to officially acknowledge the Roma customary law. The European continental legal culture of a unitary legal order in the monopoly of the state may demand this course because, without such recognition, the Roma are officially lawless, though that is contrary to the facts. But one cannot negotiate the transformation of unrecognised institutions, before recognising them at least in a conditional way. In the civil law culture prevailing in the European Union, this is above all in the hands of the executive power, though cooperation with the legislature and judiciary is also necessary.

A positive effect of such recognition is that it respects another important human right to collective identity and cultural tradition. In the Old Polish-Lithuanian Respublica, the legal autonomy of estates was recognised and that included self-government by Jews, Armenians, Tartars and also Gypsies. Each of these communities was allowed to live according to their own laws. The 'rational centralisation' of the 'Age of Enlightenment' brought an end to legal pluralism of that kind, to which we are slowly returning. Non-recognition of Roma law coincided with distrust by Gypsies of the official state law. This was justified in terms of anti-Gypsy discrimination characteristic of nineteenth and twentieth century state administration, but it also helped to perpetuate practices that were benefiting the dominant group within the Gypsy society, that is the patriarchal elderly and aristocratic clans. This led to securing a monopoly of power in their hands. 'Rejected, despised by *Gajis* (non-Roma people) Gypsies reciprocate with similar despising and rejection of *Gaji*'s customs, rules, language, legislation and state as the form of organisation alien to their world outlook' (Bartosz 1994: 148). Bartosz (2008) – in a polemical exchange with Wisłocki (2007) – who praised the 'old customs', pointed out that these customs are by no means practised completely by educated Roma families. But contemporary pluralism assumes that self-governing communities implement their autonomy in a democratic way and with respect to the human rights. One should here quote Article 4 2 of the Declaration on the Rights of Persons Belonging to National or Ethnic, Religious and Linguistic Minorities:

> States shall take measures to create favourable conditions to enable persons belonging to minorities to express their characteristics and to develop their culture, language, religion, traditions and customs, except where specific practices are in violation of national law and contrary to international standards.

European states were not inclined to accept the collective subject as a minority, and as we shall see, the relevant claims are phrased in reference to Article 14 of the European Convention on Human Rights forbidding discrimination based on ethnic and similar differences. More specifically, the 2003 UNESCO Convention on Protection of Intangible Cultural Heritage defined such heritage as

> practices, representations, expressions, knowledge, skills – as well as the instruments, objects, artifacts and cultural spaces associated therewith – that communities, groups and, in some cases, individuals recognise as part of their cultural heritage. This intangible cultural heritage, transmitted from generation to generation, is constantly recreated by communities and groups in response to their environment, their interaction with nature and their history, and provides them with a sense of identity and continuity, thus promoting respect for cultural diversity and human creativity.

As the *Wayuu* normative system was included on the Representative List of Intangible Cultural Heritage, the Roma customary law could also have been included (Kurczewski 2012). However, the crucial controversy concerning Roma marriage and family law should have been settled as the Convention adds that: 'For the purposes of this Convention, consideration will be given solely to such intangible cultural heritage as is compatible with existing international human rights instruments, as well as with the requirements of mutual respect among communities, groups and individuals, and of sustainable development'.

If a representative of Roma public opinion demanded the recognition of the Roma marriage rite as equivalent to the Jewish or Canon Law rite, such a claim is legitimate as following from the right of every community to preserve its cultural identity. Such a rite, under the name *Mangavipen*, was exampled above as used by the Roma Bergitka. One should differentiate the performance of the rite composed of certain prescribed locutory acts and performative gestures that results in certain duties and obligations for the new couple from the wedding feast in the form of the common meal shared by close relatives of the newly married couple.

V RECOGNITION OF ROMA MARRIAGES

We see no reason why an oral contract made during the wedding ceremony should not be written down and signed by the young couple and their parents. The simplest way to achieve such a goal would be to recognise the marriage performed according to the Roma rite on the same principles that led to the recognition of church marriages. The marriage is then celebrated in accordance with the rules of the given denomination but is recognised only if it satisfies the conditions set by the official law of the given state. Of these conditions, some may be controversial for the Roma people, especially the consent principle at the conclusion the marriage agreement. But with regard to age, one should point out that in some instances in the Roma community it is difficult to differentiate between betrothal and marriage. Betrothal − to which the state official law remains blind − may be concluded much earlier than the marriage. In one of the controversial cases described above, the parents of the little girl from Romania explained that the union concluded by the children was not the marriage as such but just the promise of marriage, and that they would not begin the sexual cohabitation until adulthood (though that is early as defined by the Roma law) (Bitu Bit and Morteanu 2010: 103–04). The betrothal in this case could have been judged as meaningless from the state official perspective if the girl had not been transferred to the home of the future husband. In the literature other cases are mentioned that assume the legal form of adoption but which cover the transfer of the girl to the parents of her prospective husband (Bitu Bit and Morteanu 2010: 103–04). This is why the betrothal would have to be separated from the 'transfer'. The children would have education guaranteed and the marriage according to the Roma rite should be allowed only after achieving the state official legal age limit.

At present Roma in Spain, Romania and Germany are demanding that marriages according to their law and rite should be recognised (Courthiade 2008: 28–29, Marushiakova and Popow 2008). In Colombia, Roma drafted a law granting them cultural autonomy including recognition of their law referring to the ILO Convention 169 of 1989 on rights of native people (Gómez 2008:128). Nowhere has Roma law been recognised as part of the state official law and any such project that undermines the principle of treating every citizen as equal before the law is controversial. But this does not mean that some harmonisation and mutual recognition of legal orders and adjudication is impossible. There is no reason why Roma should not marry according to their rite after meeting the same conditions required for officially recognised religious marriages. This would fulfill the conditions set by the family law and satisfy the duty to inform the relevant body (in Poland the civil status office) that a marriage had been concluded. Such a solution would necessitate a readiness on the part of the government to accept the new forms of marriage and on the part of the Roma to accept the formalities involved in exchange for recognition of their marriage rites.

Such a procedure would be sufficient – and only possible – in the case of the Roma tribes that do not have an internal political structure like the Polish highland Roma (Roma *Bergitka*). The Roma tribe living in Poland for several centuries ('Polska Roma' – Polish Roma) has a complex structure that even today vests authority in one person (Great Head – '*Baro Shero*') (Ficowski 1985; Mirga and Mróz 1994). The Headman of the Polish Roma has the supreme legislative, judicial and executive power. The office is inherited in one lineage, though the successor must be accepted by the *kris* meeting of the whole tribe and – as oral history shows – can be suspended if a grave infraction of the law is committed. To govern the tribe, the *Baro Shero* has deputies at his disposal all over the territory where Polish Roma live. In contrast to that centralised structure, another tribe that came to Polish territories in the nineteenth century from the Balkans (the *Kelderashi*) is organised into self-governing communities operating through the *kris*, a meeting of adult Roma men of good standing. Observers confirm that in practice these bodies are far from the ideal of equality, with influential and rich actors, mostly men. Recognition of such self-governing bodies, nevertheless, would provide an occasion to demand the introduction of equality (age, gender and social status) into their functioning.

Courthiade (2008: 28–29, fn 12) observes that authorities in Berlin-Brandenburg recognise marriages by Roma rite recorded on a special form prepared by the civil marriages register office. This seems a reasonable approach. He also quotes favourably a decision by Labour Tribunal 12 in Madrid (SCC 217/2002) recognising the right of a Roma woman to receive her widow's benefit although she was married only by the *gitano* rite:

> In our country the Roma minority (etnia gitana) has been present since time immemorial and it is known that this minority solemnises marriage according to rites and traditions that are legally binding on the parties. These marriages are not regarded as being contrary to morality or public order and are recognised socially.

The case, however, developed in the much more complex way after his publication. The lower tribunal's verdict was annulled by the Madrid Higher Court of Justice (637/2002):

In accordance with the foregoing, if a civil marriage is to be solemnised through regulated formalities, that must also be the case for a religious marriage, whose formalities will be those of the religious denomination – such formalities being laid down by the State, or otherwise accepted by its legislation. [It will be in such circumstances] that the marriage produces civil effects. A marriage solemnised solely and exclusively according to Roma rites is not covered by any of the above-mentioned cases, as even though an ethnic group is concerned, the norms or formalities of that group do no produce any legal effect outside its own environment and are not enshrined in the law that provides for the impugned pension.

This decision was confirmed by the Spanish Constitutional Court on 24 May 2007, holding that the possibility of marrying in a civil form was 'neutral from a racial or ethnic point of view', and as such no discrimination had taken place. With the help of the Spanish Roma Association, the case was brought before the European Court of Human Rights. In *Muñoz Díaz v Spain*[1] the Court held that Spain had violated Article 14 (prohibition of discrimination) of the European Convention on Human Rights in conjunction with Article 1 of Protocol 1 to the Convention (right to peaceful enjoyment of possessions). The Court 'concluded that the applicant's good faith, confirmed by the actions of the State in recognising her marriage in other contexts, gave her a legitimate expectation of entitlement to a survivor's pension' but also explicitly rejected the claim that the marriage in question was valid, saying that

> the Court finds that the fact that Roma marriage has no civil effects as desired by the applicant does not constitute discrimination prohibited by Article 14. It follows that this complaint is manifestly ill-founded and must be rejected under Article 35 §§ 3 and 4 of the Convention.

The Court observed that whereas in 1971 – when the applicant married – only religious marriages were recognised in Spain and that civil marriage was only permissible in cases of apostasy, the law had subsequently been amended. It observed that, since 1981, civil marriages had been available without distinction and that no requirement existed to declare one's religious beliefs or to belong to a cultural, linguistic, ethnic or other group. Finally, it observed that, while certain religious forms of marriage are recognised by virtue of agreements with the state, this distinction 'does not prohibit or impede civil marriage for those of other beliefs or ethnicities'. The enthusiasm with which this verdict had been greeted by the Roma activists (eg, Gimenez and Rey 2009) therefore seems to be ill-founded. The Court did not acknowledge the widow's claim because her marriage was valid but because, while the fact of belonging to a minority does not create an exemption from complying with marriage laws, it may have an effect on the manner in which those laws are applied. The Court had already had occasion to point out (albeit in a different context) that the vulnerable position of the Roma means that some special consideration should be given to their needs and their different lifestyle, both in the relevant regulatory framework

---

[1] *Muñoz Díaz v Spain*, App no 49151/07, 8 December 2009.

and in reaching decisions in particular cases.[2] The following argument by the Court seems to be crucial:

> It is true that certain religious forms of expression of consent are accepted under Spanish law, but those religious forms (Catholic, Protestant, Muslim and Jewish) are recognised by virtue of agreements with the State and thus produce the same effects as civil marriage, whereas other forms (religious or traditional) are not recognised. The Court observes, however, that this is a distinction derived from religious affiliation, which is not pertinent in the case of the Roma community. But that distinction does not impede or prohibit civil marriage, which is open to the Roma under the same conditions of equality as to persons not belonging to their community, and is a response to considerations that have to be taken into account by the legislature within its margin of appreciation, as the Government have argued (*Munoz Diaz v Spain*, 80: 23).

By referring to the fact that the Roma community is not a community identified by a different faith, the Court leaves a way open to seeking recognition of the fact that a community with a long-established normative system has the right to have its laws treated in the same (non-discriminatory) way as religious communities. In Poland, 11 such communities – from the Roman Catholic Church to Armenian and Jewish religious communities – have, as a result of specific agreement with Polish State, the right to marry believers but are obliged, within seven days of the marriage, to send the documents to the register office to check if the marriage fulfills the Polish legal criteria (lack of certain conditions such as proper age, etc). One could imagine a similar agreement between the state and Roma official representation if the Roma themselves could establish such representation.

Apart from such a procedure, it seems relatively easy to recognise agreements made before the Roma *kris* as settlements through mediation. The basic method used by the *kris* is ideally an elaboration of a settlement acceptable to both parties. We see no obstacle to recognising such agreements by the official state courts that could enforce such an agreement after checking whether its contents are consistent with state official law. That would demand acceptance of the appropriateness and positive value of such agreements, and from the Roma themselves the usefulness of official recognition of their agreements. Though the Roma themselves consider the decisions as binding, some dissatisfied Roma have brought this to a state court. One may safely assume that all Roma know that there is possibility of 'appeal', so the present situation could be made more official if transformed into formalised mediation which includes *Shero Rom* and *kris* members in the list of mediators recognised by courts and social security agencies and treating their adjudications as voluntary arbitration and conciliatory justice which also has its place within the civil law European systems. It has been observed that first registrations of civil (state) marriages between Roma

---

[2] See *Buckley v the United Kingdom*, App no 20348/92, §§ 76, 80 and 84, Reports 1996-IV, 25 September 1996, *Chapman v the United Kingdom* ([GC], App no 27238/95 § 96, , 2001-I and *Connors v the United Kingdom*, App no 66746/01, § 84, 27 May 2004.

started when social benefits were related to the registration. Such practical inducements might be useful to the Roma people themselves. The need is much greater, however, in the case of children as (a matter ignored by many policy-makers) the births of Roma children are sometimes not registered at all, so the extent of the Roma population remains unknown, to the detriment of educational and social assistance administration.

VI CONCLUSION

Recognition of ethnic self-government is difficult in European countries, though in Scandinavia there are examples of institutionalised parliaments of the *Saami* people. This assumes earlier registration of the *Saami* people under a list of criteria that had been negotiated with organisations considered as representative of *Saami* public opinion (Kurczewski 2007: 255–80). In communist Poland, the practice was to institutionalise ethnic representation by the officially registered Cultural-Social Associations of Jews, Ukrainians, Byelorussians, etc. This practice still continues in democratic Poland. Since 1989, the German minority is recognised and is organised into several associations of that kind, able to take part in local, regional and national elections. At national level, Germans have one or two of their own representatives in the Polish Parliament elected in a general vote from the list of the German Cultural-Social Association. In Poland, as on the international level, the process of the sometimes turbulent ethnic mobilisation of the Roma started a few decades ago and still continues (Godlewska-Goska and Kopańska 2011: chapter 2). The fact that Roma in Poland are divided in terms of associations of that kind is not surprising and the plurality of Roma organisations does not mean that negotiating with them is impossible. Let us take as the example the Polish trade union movement that is extremely pluralistic and despite this able to take part in negotiations at tripartite forums (government – employers – employees) so it should be possible to open negotiations concerning Roma marriage law. The starting position would be that if the Roma wish to have the Roma marriage rite recognised, they must somehow document the marriage either as a marriage contract between consenting parties authorised by *papus*, or in a register held by the *kris* or the *Baro Shero*. It could also take the form of a marriage contract registered by a notary.

In the rite as such, the controversial element concerns the consent of parents to the marriage of their offspring. To officially recognise Roma marriage would require ascertaining whether the couple has freely consented to it. A statement of consent by parents – or lack of it – is from this perspective legally irrelevant. The earlier betrothal promise between the parents of the minors is also irrelevant; what is legally important is the consent of the parties at the marriage ceremony proper. Roma marriage completed according the Roma rite would divide into those recognised by official law and those not so recognised. One may say this is a small gain, but in fact it would introduce some protection of the rights of minors inside the Roma communities and would enforce the modernisation of Roma law. The last argument claims that it is better to modernise Roma practices through recognising Roma cultural identity and selective recognition of their law being an important resource for their identity, than by strengthening the confrontation between the *Gajio* (English, Polish or European) law and Roma law.

REFERENCES

Bartosz, A (1994) *Nie bój się Cygana (Don't Be Afraid of Gypsy)* (Sejny, Pogranicze).
—— (2008) 'O nieromskiej tradycji "Łupania panieneczek na sianku"' '(Non-Roma Tradition of "Screwing the Girls in the Hay"') *Studia Romologica* 1/2008 Tarnów.
Bitu Bit, N and Morteanu, C (2010) *Are the Rights of the Child Negotiable? The Case of Early Marriages within Roma Communities in Romania* (Bucharest, Romani CRISS, UNICEF).
Courthiade, M (2008) 'O rromskim sądzie obyczajowy' (Roma Customary Court) *Studia Romologica* 1/2008 Tarnów.
Długosz, M (1978) 'Mangavipen – zaślubiny cygańskie' (Mangavipen – Gipsy Wedding) *Etnografia Polska* (2) 22.
Ficowski, J (1985) *Cyganie na polskich drogach (Gipsies on Polish Roads)* (Kraków, WL).
Gimenez, S and Rey, F (2009) 'La discriminación de una mujer gitana ante el Tribunal Europeo de Derechos Humanos' *Gitanos* 51–52.
Godlewska-Goska, M and Kopańska, J (2011) *Życie w dwóch światach. Tożsamość współczesnych Romów (Living in Two Worlds. Identity of Contemporary Roma)* (Warszawa, DiF).
Gómez, AD (2008) 'Rromani Kris w Kolumbii' (Rromani Kris in Columbia) *Studia Romologica* 1/2008 Tarnów.
Kowarska, AJ (2005) *Polska Roma. Tradycja i nowoczesność (Polish Roma. Tradition and Modernity)* (Warszawa. DiG).
Kurczewski, J (2007) 'Tubylcy Europy' (European Natives) in A Bartkiewicz (ed), *Ludy tubylcze* (Warszawa, Comandor).
—— (2012) *Prawo do prawa (Right to Law)* forthcoming.
Lind, G (2008) *Common Law Marriage. A Legal Institution for Cohabitation* (Oxford, Oxford University Press).
Marushiakova, E and Popow, V (2008) 'Sąd cygański w Europie Wschodniej' (Gipsy Court in Eastern Europe) *Studia Romologica* 1/2008 Tarnów.
Mirga, A and Mróz, L (1994) *Cyganie. Odmiennośći nietolerancja (Gypsies. Difference and Tolerance)* (Warszawa, PWN).
Wisłocki, SA (2007) 'Szacunek i tradycja' ('Respect and Tradition') *Dialog/Pheniben*.

10

Child Access Services in France: A Universal Service serving Diverse Clients

YASMINE DEBARGE AND BENOIT BASTARD

I INTRODUCTION

T HE FRENCH CONSTITUTION declares that 'the French Republic is indivisible, secular, democratic and social: it ensures equality before the law for every citizen without any distinction of origin, race or religion'.[1] France does not recognise any cultural or religious specificity that would distinguish its citizens. This principle can also be found in its family law. This is one element of French republicanism: indifference to difference (Amiraux and Simon 2006). It goes so far that, when ratifying the UN Convention on the Rights of the Child, France entered a reservation with respect to article 30, the right for the child 'to enjoy his or her culture, to profess and practice his or her own religion, or to use his or her own language', arguing that, 'in the light of article 2 of the Constitution of the French Republic, article 30 is not applicable so far as the Republic is concerned'.[2]

As well as this position towards cultural and religious distinctions within the republican space (public schools, public administrations) France also provides a specific context in terms of research on cultural diversity: statistics on religious adherence, on ethnicity or on political affiliation are illegal.[3] In 1978, the

---

[1] Art 1 of the French Constitution of 4 October 1958.

[2] Art 2. The language of the Republic is French. Its national emblem is the three colours flag, blue, white, red. The national anthem is la Marseillaise. The Republic motto is 'Freedom, Equality, Fraternity'. Its principle is: government of the people, by the people and for the people (translation by YD).

[3] 'The law of 6 January 1978 outlaws the keeping in digital memory, without the agreement of the concerned person, data specified with a name which would reveal "racial origins, or political, philosophical or religious opinions or union affiliations of persons"; the national commission of information technology and freedoms is the guarantee of regulations of data qualified as "sensitive" which includes all variables likely to describe the individual's origins, even, for example, the place of birth of the person' (Meron 2009) (translation by YD).

legislators were motivated by the memory of the Second World War and, more specifically, how the Vichy government used administrative records. Their intention in passing this law on 'delicate data' was to avoid the possibility of administrations classifying citizens on the basis of their origins, religion or political affiliation and therefore to establish distinctive practices according to this affiliation. However, to look at French society with today's intellectual and political perspectives and understand its dynamics often necessitates the acknowledgement of a history of populations coming from the former French colonies. If such analysis has to be more detailed, social scientists face difficulty in being able to describe a reality in which cultural background and skin colour do have an impact on social interactions. How can a sociologist investigate discrimination without proper words or data to do so? For more than ten years now, this debate has been raging in the amphitheatres of universities and research institutes (see Tripier (2004) for a historical review of the evolution of migration studies in French sociology). Furthermore, a certain political climate yields additional difficulties in producing such research. Xenophobia has permeated immigration and security policies. Immigration has been criminalised while discourses on public safety stigmatise the younger generations born from previous migrations (Tsoukala 2002; Rea 2003). There is a tension between the state practices of population management which are covered by discourses on republicanism and how these specific populations are living. Scientific research seeks to describe this tension, its expressions and its origins.

This tension affects family policies. This is a sector in which can be observed 'the values politically promoted as constituents of society' (Commaille 1986). Throughout history, alongside the law, the state provided itself with tools to modify the forms that family takes: genealogy and demography are examples (Lenoir 2003). It is still a common conception that family disorders, especially those of the 'popular' family, lead to social disorder. This idea is a motivation for state intervention within the private sphere. This chapter focuses on a certain type of social intervention which is recent but also revealing of the state's position on family issues: Child Access Services. Such services illustrate the rising interest in upholding relations between parents and children in spite of conflicting family situations. Those are places where a guardian parent can leave the child so that the other parent can practice his or her visitation right for a certain time. The visitation is supervised by a third person not related to the couple. The use of a child access service is sometimes an initiative of the parents, but in 95 per cent of cases, the parents are sent by judges.

In 2010, we conducted research on the place of parents within Child Access Services in two centres located in the suburbs of Paris. We collected 70 hours' of observations, 22 interviews with parents and 11 with professionals. Observations are currently being carried out in a third centre in Paris. The research was not designed to collect data on cultural diversity. This question arose from observations: at least within the Parisian area, a great number of attenders at Child Access Services are migrants or children of migrants. Could it be said that the over-representation of families with migrant origins simply reflects the demographic composition of the areas concerned? Such an effect is difficult to confirm. Or rather, does it show how specific difficulties encountered by populations of different cultures are the object of special support – and control? If so, would it lead to an understanding of their presence in greater numbers in such services? If not, how does one explain their greater numbers?

In the first part of this chapter, we will present the characteristics of Child Access Services as a form of social intervention. In the second part, we will observe how cultures can be treated as a specific aspect of the intervention as an element of negotiation and also how they can be voluntarily dismissed.

II CHILD ACCESS SERVICES: ISSUES OF KINSHIP

Several aspects of Child Access Services must be underlined before going further. First, we will briefly introduce the legal setting. Then we will articulate anthropological issues regarding the law linked to such a service. Finally, we will explain the characteristics of the Child Access Service as a tool for regulating behaviours.

A The Legal Setting

Just as any legal apparatus addressing conflicting family situations, Child Access Services subscribe to a peculiar perspective regarding parental relations. It mirrors a key idea of the 2002 law on parental authority: the notion of 'co-parenting', which implies that parents must cooperate in all decisions related to their children and organise themselves so as to jointly direct their education. If Child Access Services were not included in the 2002 law, they have been legally instituted by an article in the 2007 Child Protection Law. This states that 'when it is required for the continuity and the effectiveness of the bonds with the child, the family judge can organise child visitation rights in a child access service designated for that purpose'.[4] This is almost literally translated into reality: the vast majority of parents attending the Child Access Services could not reach an agreement in court and were referred by a judge.

Ever since 2004, the mission of family courts has been to pacify the parties while protecting the children. Marc Juston, himself a family judge, explains:

> In fact, today, the legislator expects from the family judge, who got to orchestrate the family, not only to apply the law, but also to be the craftsman of family peace, by prompting the parties towards dialogue and negotiated solutions which, then, would have a chance of being applied. The family judge (it is also the case for the lawyer) has the mission to work in a different state of mind than they did before; more consensual

---

[4] Loi 2007-293 art 22 II alinéa 1 et 2.

and less and less conflictual, in order to protect the child from damaging conflicts (2008: 93–98) (translation by YD).

Set in the perspective of the necessity to maintain contact between the child and both parents, including the parents' family lines, a conception they share with the judges who send the parents to them, Child Access Services seek to limit their actions strictly to this one aim: to ensure that children using the facilities keep in touch with the parent, and through him or her the whole family line from whom they are separated because of the marital or family conflict. It should be underlined that *parents* are sent, not mothers and fathers: within the judgment and the rules, gender is erased. When assessing how to reach this final aim, the Child Access Service professionals consider that the specificities of the parents, such as gender or social or cultural origins are not significant.

i Issues of Descent: Anthropology as a Reminder

By applying the precept of maintaining a contact with the other family line, Child Access Services comprehend, at least implicitly, what is described by anthropologists as the European system of kinship, which belongs to the group of 'cognatic descent' (Godelier 2005). A descent is a group of people with a common ancestry. Cognatic descent is a mode of descent in which relations are traced through both the father and the mother. In such cases, the child refers himself the same way to both sides. To quote Maurice Godelier (2005: 441):

> [I]in Western societies with a cognatic kinship, in the absence of clans and lineages, whereas monogamous marital families can be found, rules organizing possible alliances are exclusively negative and apply to direct descent, to the close collaterals, members of the marital family and kin from very close alliances.[5]

This equality between sides differentiates this system from other configurations of kinship. The other forms would be 'unilinear' from either the father's side or the mother's side, or 'bilateral', which requires specific duties from each side. Child Access Services comply with this system of equal attachment to both sides. For instance, a guidebook delivered by one of the services studied in this research starts with this sentence: 'A child suffers by not being in contact with each of his parents or grandparents' (Guidebook, Centre B, September 2010).

Child Access Services are built on a clinical knowledge which grew extensively over the years and which argues that cutting a child from some of its origins can only be damaging to his development. Their operation is conceived expressly so that children avoid an over-exposure to the conflict of their parents when they move from one side of the family to the other. The goal is to affix both lines which constitute them. While families are now viewed as elective and step-parents are voicing their demands for recognition, the commitment of these services to attach children to their biological ties may seem astonishing. This tenacity can be attrib-

---

[5] Translation by YD. In French there is a distinction between descent which precedes Ego and descent which comes from Ego. Godelier uses both words. The English word 'descent' includes both.

uted to their dedication to the model described earlier. Our intention is not to engage in any anthropological debate, a discipline which is not our specialty, but to use this initial statement to attempt an analysis of how cultural diversity is perceived and treated by the Child Access Services professionals.

We saw that Child Access Services serve as a tool for judges facing situations in which they cannot solve a conflict or overcome a difficulty only through court hearings and procedures. Sending the parents to the service is seen as a temporary move towards conciliation. It is not a punishment. The intention is to 'normalise', not to correct, which raises the question: what is the norm related to parenthood?

Like the law and the practice of family courts when it comes to children, Child Access Services assume that they evade the gender issue. An illustration is the general use of the neutral word 'parent' rather than 'mother' or 'father'. This language erases, at least in the vocabulary, the fact that visiting parents are usually men, and that residential parents, with whom the children live, are more often than not women. This linguistic convention could also be understood as being concerned to conceal the specialisation of marital roles and to avoid the under-investment of men into parenting – which the separation renders discernible. On that account, the strategy is to pretend that all parents come with the same intention of building up a relationship with the child even if within the public there must be some differences related to what it means to be a parent. What about issues of culture and social origins? Could attendance to such specificities be similar to the treatment of gender?

ii A Dispositif

Child Access Services is a certain type of organisation which is called in French *dispositif*. The common English translations 'device' or 'apparatus' do not fully grasp the whole significance of this notion. Therefore, it seems appropriate to briefly define it and describe its use in French social sciences.

The notion of *dispositif* was introduced by Michel Foucault in the 1960s. His approach demonstrated how some *dispositifs* drew the limits of what is normal and what is not. Even if Foucault did not set forth a definition of the *dispositif*, he did offer some clarification of his use of the notion in an interview in 1977 (194–228):

> What I'm trying to pick out with this term is, firstly, a thoroughly heterogeneous ensemble consisting of discourses, institutions, architectural forms, regulatory decisions, laws, administrative measures, scientific statements, philosophical, moral and philanthropic propositions – in short, the said as much as the unsaid. Such are the elements of the apparatus. The apparatus itself is the system of relations that can be established between these elements.[6]

---

[6] In this English edition of the interview in 1977, translation of *dispositif* is 'apparatus'; we respect this choice and did not modify the text.

French administrations – especially in the social policies area – started to use the term widely in the 1980s to designate a type of politico-administrative intervention (Ion and Ravon 2005). Since then, it has become ubiquitous in public policies. The *dispositif* is thought to continue over a short period; its purpose is to be a transition between a situation A – equivalent to the initial problem – to a situation B – in which the problem is solved. It addresses one specific question and its purpose is to answer it. What seduced policymakers is the ability of the *dispositif* to adapt to heterogeneity. It includes a form of flexibility allowing the action to be fitted to the subject of the intervention.

iii Accepting the Heterogeneity of Parents

The mission of Child Access Services is to ensure that the visiting parent sees the child. In accordance with this goal, the services accept all cases regardless of the specificities of the parents. This impression of uniformity around the quality of parent sets the *dispositif* in a posture of receptiveness towards the potential heterogeneity of its public and situations.

The first illustration of this heterogeneity is the appropriateness of Child Access Services to receive people who are in conflict, some of them having gone through episodes of violence. Those parents might have had a lot in common, but they are still standing on opposite sides. Child Access Services present themselves as neutral places able to reduce the hostility by limiting the interactions of the parents with each other and intervening if it proves necessary. They work from one principle: acting on the norm which requires the child to remain close to the other lineage. The service does not consider any other dimension other than the relation between the child and the parent with whom he or she does not live. In an interview, one professional said:

> I believe that in order to work in a Child Access Service, one must be convinced that the one thing which matters the most is that the child is in contact with his real parent so that he can do something with that and so that he is not subjected to the discourse of the other parent. If you do not believe in that, then sometimes it is unbearable (interview with a worker, Centre B, June 2010).

Whether such a conception of certain family relations as most valuable is an ideology, this idea is propounded in the law and shared with other actors, especially judges. The systematic approach, equal to all, adopted by Child Access Services follows the French 'Republican' principles, in a similar way to an educational school applying an 'institutional programme', to borrow the expression of François Dubet (2002). Officially, what is attributed to a culture is not considered relevant in the Child Access Services. The analysis of practices will show how cultural specificities are worked with in spite of a legal setting which requires total neutrality. They can be the object of a specific individual treatment, but can also be ignored notwithstanding the requests of the parents.

III HOW DO CHILD ACCESS SERVICES TREAT CULTURAL SPECIFICITIES?

If Child Access Services cannot officially treat cultural specificities as such on the grounds of French republicanism, the presence in great numbers of parents of migrant origin, or who are themselves migrants, is left unexplained.

One possible answer to this question could be that considering the current social tension around cultural issues – which today are a matter of debate in France – institutions might be sensitive to threats based on culture and might seek to conceal such conflicts by sending parents to Child Access Services, which as a *dispositif* can address the specificities of each case without treating culture as an essential feature of parenthood, which would be against French republican principles. The model used by the services is applied to everyone – through an apparatus capable of reflecting differences and normalising relations – by forcing some of the population to forget a part of its specificities. This leads us to another explanation. It could be that some of the parental behaviours are those of a different culture and do not match what is considered 'appropriate parental behaviour'. Here we think more specifically of some fathers who do not know how to behave with children without a female presence. Since this can be observed in the case of men from within the cultural majority, the over-representation of minorities could be explained on the basis that cultural differences are interpreted as a discrediting factor in the evaluation of parental abilities (Kruse 2009: 47–49). Those hypotheses are left as such since testing them requires statistics. Instead, we offer our observations on how Child Access Services respond to cultural specificities. Given that the law is neutral, is there differential treatment?

Child Access Services workers have to face very conflictual situations. The core of their activity is to create a context so that different actors, parents and children, interact with each other in a peaceful manner. In some circumstances, professionals do take into account cultures. At a certain level, they even 'work with them'. A cultural practice can be so obvious that it cannot be ignored and therefore professionals treat is as it is: a cultural specificity. From the observations within the centres, a range of answers could be drawn out to describe how the workers 'work with' culture-related issues. It does not reflect a scheme that workers refer to in order to adapt to a specific behaviour. This range has been conceived with a sociological perspective on responses to parents who present a cultural behaviour interpreted as such by the worker. The following examples will illustrate this range of reactions. They have been compiled under four categories: approving, acknowledging, ignoring and refusing.

A The Negotiation of Cultures?

i Approving

A cultural specificity can appear to professionals as an opportunity to reinforce a relationship between parent and child. It then becomes a tool or a positive element in the evaluation of the relationship:

> In this discussion between two professionals, one tells the other that she thought the last contact between father and child was really good because the father brought musical instruments typical of his culture and initiated the child: 'it's good because he shared an activity with the child who showed some interest and at the same time he also transmitted something of his culture (staff meeting, Centre A, June 2010).

This example shows that a cultural specificity can be a medium for establishing communication between parent and child. The professionals base their judgment on a leading component of the interaction. It is the transmission of a knowledge with which the child will be able to identify, since it came from one of his lineage but also, and most of all, even if it is left unsaid in this extract, this transmission does not seem to lead to a conflict with the mother.

ii Acknowledging

Acknowledging is the recognition that there is a cultural specificity and that it must be worked with. It can take different forms. In this first case, there is an assumption about what is the difference linked to an origin:

> This couple got married in Algeria. They have three daughters. It seems to be a forced marriage . . . What leads me to suspect is that both of their families know each other in Algeria. Well, they arrived in France 10 years ago. After some time, probably Madame realised that life for women can be different. She used the legal system here and she asked for divorce. She says that there was domestic violence. Actually, there was a protection order from the judge.[7] When I talk with her, she seems to have fully integrated the French law. The father on the other hand says that she is a bad wife because she left. He only talks about her. When he mentions the children, he talks about them as 'my children', never pronouncing their first name. I think he is in the Algerian legal system in his head *(implying that it sides for men)*. We will have to make him understand the French system: she has a right to divorce and he has a right to see his children. We also have to make him see his children 'as subjects', each of them, instead of a property (one professional presenting a new case in a staff meeting, Centre C, October 2011).

---

[7] The 'protection order' refers to an emergency order from the family judge using the law of 9 July 2010 punishing violence towards women, within couples and its impact on children. Usually, the judge issues an order for the man to stay away from the woman and children for at least four months, or else he can be imprisoned.

The following Saturday, the father arrived late and a professional told him that the rule is that he should be on time. There was no mention of a legal system. The strategy there is to use the frame in order to impose the model, and the model refers to the law.

In all situations, it is expected that parents should compromise with each other. In such a professional framework, culture-based conflicts are only one form, among others, that conflicts take. They should be resisted. In the following situation, the child sees his father for the first time in two years:

> The father speaks French with a very strong accent. The child is crying loudly, even screaming. The father himself is almost crying. The professional tries to quieten down the child. She starts a dialogue with him.
>
> What is your name?
>
> Ahmed Abdelkhafir.[8]
>
> What is the name of your father?
>
> The child suddenly stops crying before he answers.
>
> Mohammed Abdelkhafir.
>
> And what is the name of your mother?
>
> Anne-Marie Dupont.
>
> It means you are a mix of two countries (Observation, Centre B, 26 June 2010).

The professional – in this case a psychologist – is using the names to suggest the origins of the parents. Through the foreign-sounding family name, she reminds the child that he belongs to two different family groups, to two different lines from two different national entities. The family name plays a key role in placing the child in the position of the next generation to his father. However, with subtlety, the professional states the equality of attachment to the child.

B The Negation of Cultures

As described in the previous examples, this *dispositif* is a place which practices a form of control over the parental behaviour. Someone is watching the visitations. Substantially, the professionals are expected to intervene in case they observe something inappropriate. It should not be forgotten that Child Access Services deal with parents in a serious conflict. This implies that these parents would use any means to hurt one another: culture difference then becomes a resource in their conflict.

---

[8] All names have been changed.

i Ignoring

One option is to ignore the source of the conflict, and it may be cultural. This seems to be a common behaviour for professionals:

> A visiting parent complains that the child eats pork at home while the mother knows that the father respects Muslim food practices: he tells me 'there is nothing I can do about it'. When I relate this situation to the professionals, they answer: 'she is the one who feeds the kid everyday: she'll do whatever she wants for that matter, so he must accept it. Plus, as long as the kid doesn't eat pork in front of him' (observation, Centre B, 20 November 2010).

Two things appear in this short story. The first is that transmission from one generation to another sometimes requires full dedication on the part of the child. For instance, dietary practices are often involved in such a commitment. In this case, the professionals considered the matter settled as long as there was no provocation. They also admitted that the parent with whom the child lives, because she cooks and therefore works for this child every day, has the right to decide what should be eaten and therefore to the cultural transmission through diet. It is an indirect recognition of the inequality between the parents in terms of transmission of the culture. Presence on an everyday basis and the work associated with it confer the power of decision in terms of transferring values from one generation to the next, from one parent to the child. This leads to the second aspect of this story. By stating that 'he must accept it', the professionals even insist that the visiting parent should be aware of and assimilate this fact. However, another example nuances this first interpretation:

> 'I remember a Jewish mother. Everything had to be kosher, even candies . . . That's pushing it too far!' (interview, June 2010).

According to this professional, this diet restricted the visiting parent in their abilities to interact with the child. She did not require the mother to abandon her dietary prescription. She told the mother that information about what happened during the visits was not given to the other parent (which is true) and relied on the fact that the child would not tell his mother about the secular sweets. This was not provocation since the child gladly ate the candies.

In a further case, the child lived with his mother:

> The mother explains that she is scared of the father because he threatened to bewitch the child or herself. The professional only answers that 'everything will be fine and there is nothing to worry about' (observation, Centre A, 5 June 2010).

Later we arranged to have an interview with this mother. After describing the type of physical threat she underwent, she mentions the magic:

> 'He even threatened to call his mother in his country so she would go see a sorcerer who would kill me within six months. Since I am *(she doesn't finish her sentence)*, since I believe in those things, I know they exist, when someone tells you that, fear tends to take over' (interview, September 2010).

This type of request is usually denied any possibility of discussion: the contingency of magic cannot be argued against. The mother expressed a belief that the professional could not demonstrate as true or false: she simply reassured her with the statement that she should not worry.[9]

In another case, a mother is the visiting parent:

> She is a practising Muslim. The child lives with her Christian father who has a new partner living with them. As she comes to the Child Access Centre, the child wears a necklace with a picture of the Virgin Mary. The mother is very upset. She throws away the necklace. It must be said that when the mother gives presents to the daughter, the father takes them away from the child. After this necklace event, the father complains by mail to the director that it was a present of his new partner to the child and that the mother should be blamed for destruction of private property. The director writes a different letter to each parent. To the mother, she explains that the use of the facilities is conditional on respect for its rules, which include that the child should leave with the same outfit as she came in. She also requests her to return the necklace. The letter to the father is an answer to his doubts on the ability of the professionals to supervise the visits. After insisting on the professional qualities of the employees, the director tells him that he shouldn't put the child in the heart of the conflict and that it is damaging to the child (staff meeting, Centre A, 2 October 2010).

Here, we can observe how the director refers to the rules in order to ignore a conflict relevant to cultures. She does not address the parents directly on the question of culture, but addresses them on their provocative behaviours. If some culturally framed interactions are at best considered positive for the child, or at least acknowledged, the professionals can also ignore them or even refuse them because they are defined as unbearable within the Child Access Service.

ii Refusing

The most typical example of refusing to acknowledge a cultural specificity is the common requirement to speak in French in the child access facilities. This reflects the 'republican' principle, and the law, which established French as the sole language of public administrations. Strictly applying this rule in the case of Child Access Services is questionable: a parent visiting a child is not an administrative interaction. Considering that professionals have to understand the contents of the interaction between child and parent, it is clearly more comfortable

---

[9] A wide range of literature has been produced on the psychological interpretation of the impact of 'sorcery' on individuals, especially on migrants and children of migrants. These works also introduced and established methodological approaches which take into account the cultural surrounding for treating patients, assuming that psychological pathologies are being ground in a culture through symbols (myth) and social processes (migration). In France, one of the most renowned groups of researchers is at the 'Centre d'ethnopsychiatrie' named after Georges Devereux. This literature was a subject of controversy. The child access professionals do not apply such references, probably because they are not typical in the discipline, but mainly because they do not consider their activity to be a therapy and therefore will not conceptualise their interactions with the parents within a therapeutic frame.

for them if this interaction happens in French. In fact this rule has not been contested in any observed centres. This is a source of difficulties, even humiliation, for the parents. The children, whose everyday language at school and with friends is French, can speak it fluently, while the visiting parent is put in an inferior situation by looking for words, obviously limited in the interaction, waiting for the professional to be away in order to speak in their native language. Language being a crucial factor of culture transmission, not allowing anyone to speak in any language other than French is a form of control over minorities, no matter the motivations.

Another example of refusal to acknowledge a cultural specificity is drawn from the understanding of the word 'parent'. In the law, parents are understood as mother and father. Grandparents are associated with 'other persons', who can also bring legal proceedings, but in a slightly different procedure from that available to a parent. If the parents bring proceedings to gain access to the child, the judge can prescribe visitation at the Child Access Service. However, unless the judge specifies that the parent can be accompanied by someone from his or her family, this matter is left open. This gives the Child Access Services scope for interpretation:

> I introduce myself to a father who tells me he won't be able to answer my questions because he is leaving the Child Access Service. When I ask him why, he explains to me that there was no point in continuing the visitations there because his son didn't have the opportunity to get to know his cousins. When I come back two weeks later, the workers inform me that he sent a letter stating that he will no longer come (observation, Centre B, 29 May 2010).

Usually, Child Access Services do not accept anyone other than the visiting parent: the right is individualised. If the parent wants to walk in with someone else, the professionals refuse them entrance. They might tolerate a half-brother or half-sister of the child, sometimes a grandmother. They either refuse or ask the authorisation of the parent with whom the child lives. Cousins are not accepted. In most cultures, other members of the family are important in the definition of parenthood: the parent has a role in inscribing the child in the family by making sure that the child meets his relatives and maintains a close relationship with them. By not hearing the request of these parents, Child Access Services impose a model of parenting as an individualised practice. This model belongs to Western societies, and cannot be presented as a general practice since different practices have been and are still being observed. The fact that such a model should be promoted, through the law and its implementation in a service, raises many questions. The professionals consider it inappropriate to have debates on culture within the service. The role of the service is 'only to take care of' the question of bonding. Such a posture could be considered a paradox, since ignoring the requests of cultural transmission is denying that the parental bond refers to the kinship group which necessarily has cultural specificities.

Child Access Services do address diversity. Even though, as a *dispositif*, they have the ability to take charge of it, the services will not recognise explicitly that culture could be a specific aspect of its work. The professionals consider that the only activity that makes sense is individualised work on the parent–child relationship. When asked why, it is in the cause of the bonding with the separated line.

IV CONCLUSION

So, the aim of Child Access Services is to maintain or sometimes establish or re-establish a relationship between two individuals: a parent and a child. The activity of 'working on a relationship', because of the subjective implication it requires, cannot be neutral. By itself, the aim is already culturally determined: at least two cultural aspects which are imposed on other cultures have been identified. The first is a structure of parenthood passed through the apparatus. It refers to a cognatic descent system in which both lineages are equal. The second is the promotion of an individualised relationship with the child. A parent can only come on their own to see the child, even if he or she situates his or her parenthood within a group.

Throughout the analysis of different situations, we can conclude that culture, alongside gender, is mostly left unsaid, even though it is present in terms of interactions. From the observations within the Child Access Services, culture is considered to be one element of the individual's identity. Then two positions can be taken: these positions were observed with respect to other sources of conflict between the parents, so culture can be seen as equivalent to any other factor crystallising the conflict. In the first, culture can be an object of negotiation. In the second, culture is negated. Those two positions are not opposed to each other, but rather stretched within a range with four markers: approving, acknowledging, ignoring and refusing.

These reactions could also be understood from the perspective of an ideal of parenthood: being a good parent is to be able to discuss with the other parent, to recognise the individuality of the child, to listen to professional advice. Child Access Services are ready to accept cultural specificities as long as they fit this model, or at least do not contest it. If not, the limits of their approval are reached and they at best ignore the specificity, and at worst dismiss its expression. Therefore, the '*dispositif*' and its capacity to recognise individuals as subjects reaches a level of nuances which can 'treat' cultural specificities which do not adhere to the French model of parenting, and at the same time remain 'republican', in its French meaning.

REFERENCES

Amiraux, V and Simon, P (2006) 'There Are no Minorities Here: Cultures of Scholarship and Public Debate on Immigrants and Integration in France' 47 *International Journal of Comparative Sociology* 191.

Ballmer-Cao, ThH, Mottier, V et Sgier, L (2000) *Genre et Politique; Débats et perspective* (Paris, Gallimard, 'folio essais').

Bastard, B (2001) 'La séparation mais le lien' 36 *Terrain* 5.

—— (ed) (2001) *L'enfant séparé, les voies de l'attachement, coll Autrement* (Paris, Seuil).

Cardia-Vonèche, L and Bastard, B (2005) 'Vers un nouvel encadrement de la parentalité?' 122 *Informations sociales* 110.

Commaille, J (1986) 'D'une sociologie de la famille à une sociologie du droit. D'une sociologie du droit à une sociologie des régulations sociales' 18 *Sociologie et sociétés* 113.

Commaille, J, Strobel, P and Villac, M (2002) *La politique de la famille* (Paris, La découverte).

De Singly, F (2000) *Libres ensemble. L'individualisme dans la vie commune* (Nathan, collection Essais et recherches).

Dubet, F (2002) Le déclin de l'institution (Paris, Le Seuil).

Erhenberg, A (1991) La fatigue d'être soi (Paris, Odile Jacob).

Foucault, M (1975) Surveiller et punir. Naissance de la prison (Paris, Gallimard).

—— (1976) Histoire de la sexualité, 1: La volonté de savoir (Paris, Gallimard).

—— (1977) 'The Confession of the Flesh' interview in C Gordon (ed), *Power/Knowledge: Selected Interviews and Other Writings*

Godelier, M (2005) *Métamorphoses de la parenté* CV (Paris, Fayard).

Ion, J, and Ravon, B (2005) 'Insitutions et dipositifs' in J Ion (ed), *Le travail social en débat(s)* (Paris, La découverte).

Kruse, C (2009) 'La diversité culturelle dans les espaces de rencontre. Entre déni et idéologie' 58 *Le Furet*. 47.

Juston, M (2008) 'Se séparer en parents responsables' 4 *Empan* 72.

Lenoir, R (2003) *Généalogie de la morale familiale* (Paris, Seuil).

Meron, M (2009) 'Statistiques ethniques: tabous et boutades' 21 *Travail, genre et sociétés* 55.

Neyrand, G (2007) 'La parentalité comme dispositif: mise en perspective des rapports familiaux et de la filiation' 4 *Recherches familiales* 71.

Prioux, F et Mazuy, M (2009) 'L'évolution démographique récente en France: dix ans pour le pacs, plus d'un million de contractants' 64 *Population* 445.

Rea, A (2003) 'Politiques d'immigration: criminalisation ou tolérance?' 10 *La pensée de midi* 111.

Tripier, M (2004) 'L'immigré, analyseur de la société (note critique)' 7 *Terrains & travaux* 173.

Tsoukala, A (2002) 'Le traitement médiatique de la criminalité étrangère en Europe' 26 *Déviance et Société* 61.

Part III

Non-state Responses to the Interpenetration of Social Norms between Communities

11

Accommodating Religious Divorce in the Secular State: A Case Study Analysis

GILLIAN DOUGLAS WITH NORMAN DOE, RUSSELL SANDBERG,
SOPHIE GILLIAT-RAY AND ASMA KHAN

I INTRODUCTION

T HIS CHAPTER PRESENTS findings from a multidisciplinary research project[1] which sought to collect information on the role and practice of religious tribunals in England and Wales in providing annulments and divorces. The aim was to contribute to debate concerning how the democratic state can approach the place of religion in people's lives and in particular, how far English law should accommodate religious legal systems. By 'accommodation' we adopt the meaning used by Jeremy Waldron (2010: 103) as follows:

[A]ccommodation within a modern legal system of the norms and requirements of [a minority's] culture or religion or of the law associated with their culture or religion . . . [occurring] within a framework of a comprehensive system of law in a modern democratic state.

Our focus is on what Ayelet Shachar, in discussing a failed attempt in Canada to establish a 'Private Islamic Court of Justice', has termed 'public accommodation' – the recognition and inclusion of minority norms and processes within the public sphere – in contrast to her argument that minorities may make claims for a 'privatised diversity' which she defines as '*opting out of*, or seceding from, the effects of the polity's public laws and norms'. While this might have been the goal of the proponents of the Islamic Court in Canada,[2] it does not seem to be the

[1] The study was funded by the UK's Arts and Humanities Research Council, and was conducted in Cardiff Law School and the Centre for the Study of Islam in the UK at Cardiff University. For the full report see Douglas et al (2011).
[2] Their attempt failed, and resulted in the banning of all binding religious arbitration in the field of family law. For an attempt to produce a similar ban, see the Arbitration and Mediation Services (Equality) Bill (HL Bill 72), introduced into the House of Lords in 2011 by Baroness Cox, which

objective of mainstream religious groupings in the United Kingdom where, at most, calls have been for the introduction of separate personal laws for different religious adherents which, as Shachar points out, is a 'state-accommodationist' approach which 'publically and officially recognize[s] and facilitate[s] a degree of diversity in the regulation of the family' (2008: 580–81). We discuss this approach further below.

We examined three particular religious tribunals, the Shariah Council of the Birmingham Central Mosque, the London Beth Din of the United Synagogue and the National Tribunal for Wales of the Roman Catholic Church. We do not claim that these tribunals are typical or representative (indeed, the Shariah Council, in particular, appears to be quite unusual in the 'liberal' approach that it takes to its work, not least by including a woman member). The study's focus was on gaining an understanding of how they work, what their place is within their religious community and how those working within them regard their role, but we do not suggest that the findings would necessarily apply to all such institutions. We are also aware that the bulk of our information derives from interviews with officials and those working in the tribunals, and not from litigants themselves. It is quite likely that they sought to present us with a positive and 'official' picture of their workings. Nonetheless, we consider that the study does give us an insight into the world of religious tribunals, and adds to the picture provided in previous empirical studies (see in particular, in relation to Shariah councils, the work of Shah-Kazemi 2001 and Bano 2008).

The rationale for conducting a comparative study of religious tribunals across different faiths (rather than within a single faith) was threefold. First, insofar as *religions* may make distinctive claims to recognition and respect from society and state, it was important to examine more than one religion to draw out any common themes and messages which are distinct from claims based on culture or ethnicity. Secondly, and again focusing on religion as the defining feature under investigation, while much recent debate has been focused on Islam, it is important to be aware of the experiences – often, of course, gained over a much longer timespan – of other religious groups who have regulated their adherents' status and behaviour within the wider British community. Thirdly, there is a high degree of ignorance as to how and how far different religious laws have been 'accommodated' by the state in English law, resulting in the kind of moral panic that followed the speech by the Archbishop of Canterbury in 2008 (Williams 2008) which appeared to advocate some greater recognition of Shariah law, and misleading claims as to how far different faiths, particularly Judaism, have been 'privileged' over others, especially in the field of divorce law. It is important to have an accurate comparative study to correct such misconceptions.

---

would, inter alia, prohibit the arbitration or adjudication of any matter pertaining to the criminal or family courts.

This chapter focuses on three key aspects of the findings from the study which are relevant to considering how (far) in practical terms the state could or should accommodate the operation of religious tribunals in regulating aspects of family life:

1. The degree of flexibility which operates, both in relation to the choice by adherents whether to use particular religious tribunals and to how those tribunals approach the religious rules they then apply to them.
2. The centrality of status and the importance of the 'licence to remarry' as the essence of the divorce or dissolution process being conducted by these tribunals.
3. The relationship between the civil law of divorce and the religious determination

II MODELLING RELIGIOUS ACCOMMODATION

In exploring and analysing these findings, the chapter identifies three empirical models of legal approaches to religious diversity. In so doing, we are following what seems to be something of a tradition in this field of study, in that models always appear to come in threes. For example, John Eekelaar, in chapter one, discusses the 'authorisation' model, 'wherein the state expressly or tacitly gives the force of state law to norms and decisions made within families'; the 'delegation' model, 'wherein the state prescribes and gives legal force to the norms to be followed within families so that families can be seen as delegates through which state law and policy is applied'; and the 'purposive abstention' model, 'wherein moral or social obligations within families are not normally given the force of law, unless their failure threatens community interests, or to achieve justice when families fall apart. However, the general law of the state, including human rights norms, remains always applicable, and states are free to influence family behaviour in other ways'. He subsequently applies these models to possible approaches to multiculturalism.

Similarly, Pascale Fournier, in her study of the approaches by civil courts to arguments over the enforceability of *mahr* (Islamic dower), describes 'the liberal-legal pluralist' approach – a multiculturalist approach which focuses on the identity of the group as a form of recognition politics; the 'liberal-formal equality' approach under which a secular understanding strips out the religious dimension and is focused on the position of the individual; and the 'liberal-substantive equality' approach which is concerned with the position of the person (in her context, the Muslim wife) in an attempt to provide a substantively fair outcome (2010).

Here, we describe the three empirical models that we draw on as the 'personal law', 'cohabitation' and 'integration' models.

A Personal law

The personal law model is the classic legal pluralist system, such as the 'millet' system in the Ottoman Empire, and the personal laws in modern India, Malaysia, Singapore and Israel. Under such systems, each of the religious groups that have been given recognition is regarded as of equal standing by the state to provide and enforce laws regulating aspects of the lives of their adherents.[3] People are governed by laws according to their professed religion. This is a clear form of legal pluralism under which there are civilly-recognised rules of equal, rather than hierarchical, standing. It equates to Fournier's liberal legal pluralism approach or Shachar's 'public accommodation'. It recognises and preserves the individual's religious identity without expecting them to 'abandon' any aspects of this, subject to rules which might require the religious bodies themselves, eg, to register, provide certain procedural safeguards, etc, as has happened in those jurisdictions which do have personal law systems (Gaudreault-DesBiens 2010 and Ahmed 2010). Gaudreault-DesBiens (2010: 163) comments, however, that

> while intellectually appealing from an abstract perspective and possibly conducive to social peace in certain circumstances, such models remain largely rooted in non-Western societies and constitute solutions to the particular ethno-religious configuration of such societies, in addition to relying on religious and political conceptions that are themselves rooted in intellectual traditions that were never dominant in modern Western states.

A variant, as Fournier shows, are European states that apply a conflict of laws approach based on nationality to determine which law applies in family matters. Where a person is a citizen of a state itself applying a religious law, as in the Middle East, they will be subject to that law rather than the municipal law, subject to considerations of public order (public policy).

B The Cohabitation Model

The cohabitation model is similar to Fournier's liberal formal equality approach whereby state law ignores the religious meaning of the activity for the adherent and simply applies the civil law equivalent to their situation. The legal systems run in parallel, but without state recognition of the religious code. This is the position with private Muslim wedding (*nikah*) ceremonies in England and Wales currently. People may go through the religious process and may believe that they are married in the eyes of the state, but they are not.[4] Thus, not only

---

[3] But Gaudreault-DesBiens (2010: 164) notes that this was not necessarily historically true.

[4] The position is similar to that found in England and Wales in relation to people's views of their legal position as unmarried cohabitants, referred to by Barlow et al (2005: 28) as the 'common law marriage myth'.

do the systems 'cohabit' in the sense of occupying parallel spaces with each other, but religious systems are also in the position of non-recognised cohabitants (and indeed, literally, those who undertake religious marriages are simply treated as cohabitants by the civil law).

C The Integration Model

The integration model draws on the dictionary definition of integration: 'the act of amalgamating a racial or religious group within an existing community'/ 'combining or adding parts to make a unified whole'. Integration, as distinct from assimilation, is usually seen as providing an appropriate balance between the indigenous or majority population and the minority group seeking recognition. By contrast, despite its benign dictionary definition – 'to become absorbed, incorporated or learned and understood; to bring or come into harmony, adjust or become adjusted; to become or cause to become similar' – assimilation is usually regarded by religious or minority ethnic groups as producing a loss of their identity, because their distinctiveness is 'absorbed' within the wider society. Prakash Shah, for example, defines assimilation as 'the abandonment of one's inherited cultural traditions, and conformism to a dominant British legal culture' (2005: 31) and Rex Ahdar and Nicholas Aroney (2010: 25) view the state's treatment of minorities and their religious and cultural needs as spread along a continuum from assimilation which '[In] its pure form, . . . allows no exceptions at all for minorities'.

In our analysis, the integration model is that which is provided by English marriage law in its acceptance of religious *rites* as giving rise to a legally recognised marriage (so long as certain prescribed preliminary requirements are fulfilled, such as the presence of witnesses and an authorised celebrant).[5] The reason for classifying this as 'integration' is that, while enabling religious groups to bring about a marriage which is recognised both by state and religious authorities, as far as the civil law is concerned, what is being created and *recognised* is an English legal marriage – not a Jewish, Catholic or Muslim one. So far as English law is concerned, then, Jews cannot divorce each other by mutual consent; Catholics cannot exclude each other from divorcing at all; and Muslim husbands domiciled in England and Wales cannot form actually polygamous marriages. All that has been done is that their rites are regarded as equivalent to those applying in civil law.

The English approach preserves the primacy of the state law in determining the consequences of the religious marriage, and thus it is arguable that this mechanism should be seen as closer to the more suspect 'assimilation' end of Adhar and Aroney's continuum, but its concern to provide some recognition of religious sensibilities, within the parameters of state views on justice and

---

[5] Compare Eekelaar (ch 1) who considers this an example of his 'authorisation' model.

fairness (eg, as regards human rights and non-discrimination) suggests that it should rather be seen as equivalent to Fournier's liberal substantive equality approach.

Drawing on findings from our study, we show that religious divorces or annulments currently fall within the 'cohabitation' model in England and Wales. We also suggest that the empirical evidence shows no particular desire by the religious bodies granting or recognising these determinations which we studied, to move away from this towards the 'personal law' model; indeed, rather the reverse. We conclude by suggesting, however, that, just as it enables religious marriage to give rise to civil marital status in England and Wales, the 'integration' model could accommodate religious divorce in ways that would be compatible with and promote the objectives of a tolerant, human rights compliant legal regime in a multicultural and largely secular society.

III THE CIVIL LAW ON TERMINATION OF MARRIAGE

The reason for examining the work of these tribunals in relation to the termination of marriage was because most debate on the extent to which law might recognise religious rulings has focused on family issues (on which Shachar has written extensively: 2001, 2008, 2010). It is therefore useful to set out very briefly the current civil law on the termination of marriage, to provide a comparator and context for the discussion on the religious dimension.

Under English law,[6] a divorce may only be obtained on the basis of the irretrievable breakdown of the marriage, to be established by proof of one or more of five specified 'facts', including marital fault (such as adultery) or periods of separation. Nearly all divorces are undefended, and are handled by the courts without an oral hearing.[7] The applicant submits their application to the court and the respondent is given the opportunity to file an 'answer' in response. If there are children of the marriage, the applicant must set out the proposed arrangements for their upbringing which the court must consider before granting the divorce (but in respect of which no order need be made). Financial arrangements do not have to be the subject of an application, but if they are, the parties are encouraged to settle these by negotiation or methods of dispute resolution outside the adversarial court process. The divorce is pronounced in two stages, a decree *nisi* followed not less than six weeks later by a decree absolute which is the final step legally dissolving the marriage. Parties may also seek an annulment of their marriage, by establishing that it is void or voidable on various grounds related primarily to capacity (eg, consanguinity, age, bigamy or same sex in the case of void marriages; or lack of consent, mental capacity or incapacity/wilful refusal to consummate, in the case of voidable marriages).

---

[6] Matrimonial Causes Act 1973 s 1.
[7] Defended divorces are subject to a hearing.

IV FLEXIBILITY IN THE RESORT TO, AND APPROACH OF, RELIGIOUS TRIBUNALS

It is important to appreciate that there is no monolithic community representing the entire body in any of the three faiths we studied. Even the much greater homogeneity of the Roman Catholic Church is influenced by its local cultural and social contexts – the Catholic Church in Africa may well approach the practice of the religion differently from the church in the United States or in Wales, and within both Islam and Judaism, there are several degrees of orthodoxy and versions of interpretation. Similarly, there is a multiplicity of religious tribunals within the Jewish and Muslim communities in terms of the basis of their authority and adherence by those using them. Different communities within these faiths have their own religious tribunals ruling on matters relevant to their particular adherents, and, in the same way that Fournier et al (in chapter five) have discerned an element of 'forum shopping' among applicants to *batei din* in Israel, so too in England and Wales, Jewish and Muslim litigants can, to some extent, choose which tribunal they go to according to the way in which (they think) the law will be applied to them:

> Because there are different schools of thought and there are different views . . . they'd say well if somebody doesn't agree with a decision they'll say 'well what does he know?' . . . When you have different mosques I suppose people go to different places don't they? Where they feel comfortable with, where they feel they would accept the decision from and where they think they've been understood (member of the Shariah Council).

This does not apply to the Roman Catholic tribunal which operates clear jurisdictional rules determined by the nature of the issue, or by geography. However, it remains, of course, the choice of the individual whether to invoke the jurisdiction of the Tribunal and they are likely to be advised and guided by their parish priest in so deciding.

Moreover, there is no 'hierarchy' of courts within the Jewish and Muslim communities, and no appeal structure. This may partly explain the resort to forum shopping – while a party cannot appeal against an adverse decision, it is apparently open to a Jewish or Muslim person to make use of a different religious tribunal if they could not get 'satisfaction' from the first one approached. This is more likely in the Muslim community, by virtue of the lack of any structural linkages between mosques according to the religious school of thought that they follow (for discussion of the background to the development of Shariah councils, see Bano in chapter four). For Jewish people, the positions adopted by the more liberal wings of Judaism would not be recognised in the orthodox communities, so those who belong to such wings might choose to make use of a more orthodox Beth Din in order to secure broader recognition:

> We often find that the non-Orthodox communities will refer to us even though, say for example, the Reform won't necessarily say that they believe it is necessary for a *get* to

be given, they do recognise and they will often tell their members that 'if you were married in an Orthodox way you must realise that if you want your marriage to be ended from an Orthodox point of view this is what you need to do' and we will have referrals from members of say the Reform and other communities who will seek a *get* (member of the Beth Din).

The Roman Catholic Church is different. All cases are reviewed by a tribunal of second instance, before a decision (known as a 'sentence') by the first instance tribunal is confirmed or over-turned. There is then a right of appeal to the Rota in Rome.

In the absence of some overarching structure for each religion's tribunals, this multiplicity of bodies could make it difficult for the state to 'recognise' the rulings of individual tribunals, particularly if these did not recognise each other's. Why – and how – should the civil law, for example, recognise the decision of a reform Beth Din, when a more orthodox Beth Din would decline to do so? (See also Saeed 2010: 236; Bowen 2011: 422.)

Each religious tribunal in our study sees itself as applying a body of religious 'law' regarded by adherents as binding on them. However, either the autonomous position of the particular tribunal, or the breadth of the rules which might be applied to the case before it, provides a degree of flexibility to the decision-maker. None of the three tribunals we studied is constrained by a system of binding precedent. For example, the particular Shariah Council in this project draws on different schools of thought to arrive at what it regards as just and fair decisions and does not regard its own previous decisions as binding on it. The National Tribunal, too, draws on commentaries as well as the Code of Canon Law, and regards rulings from Rome as persuasive but not strictly binding (Doe 1994).

The Beth Din will look to a range of opinions and rulings from other *batei din* in reaching its judgments but is not *bound* by any prior ruling. However, it should be noted that the particular role that the Beth Din plays in relation to divorce limits the scope for variation anyway since Jewish law as interpreted by this Beth Din is focused squarely on *witnessing* the parties' consent to divorce each other rather than pronouncing a dissolution, and is not governed by 'grounds' (for a discussion and critique of this approach, see Jackson 2011). As Fournier et al (chapter five) discuss, the problem of the 'chained wife' or *agunah*, whose husband will not agree to a divorce, and who therefore cannot remarry under Jewish law, has been a major difficulty for Jewish courts both in Israel and the diaspora to handle. In England and Wales, it resulted in an amendment to civil divorce law to enable the divorce court to hold up the grant of a civil divorce until the *get* has been granted.[8] This provision works where the husband, as well as the wife, wishes to have a civil divorce, but cannot help the situation where he does not.

---

[8] Divorce (Religious Marriages) Act 2002, inserting s 10A into the Matrimonial Causes Act 1973. For Scotland, see Divorce (Scotland) Act 1976 s 3A inserted by the Family Law (Scotland) Act 2006 s 15.

Leaving the Jewish system aside, the other two systems provide degrees of flexibility within their codes which enable the religious tribunals – if they so choose – to find a ground which will enable them to terminate the marriage or pronounce it void. In the case of the Shariah Council that we studied, given that the husband may unilaterally divorce his wife under Islamic law, it is not surprising that applicants are almost always wives.[9] The focus for the Council is on determining whether the marriage is no longer workable, and there is a mandatory mediation – or rather reconciliation – stage prior to a ruling being given to see if the marriage can be saved. If not, then the Council looks to see if the marriage can be terminated by means of a *talaq* or *khul* (ie, by persuading the husband to divorce the wife, or to agree to her divorcing him) and finally, if this is not possible, it will then look for grounds to fit the circumstances of the case:

> In some cases when a man comes and he agrees that he has divorced her, then we just act as witnesses, so then he basically tells us that he has given her a divorce. Or if he is willing to give a divorce as well, we say 'just give her talaq in front of us' because that makes, in a sense, if a man gives a talaq he has no right to anything financial from her so that makes it easier and if he is willing there is no issue with him, so he says it and then that's fine. In the cases of *khul* where men think that she must return a certain amount of *mahr* or money to him then we speak to her . . . because we say, basically we ask a husband 'has he agreed that the marriage has been broken down and irretrievably broken down?' then, if he agrees then basically we say 'ok'.

There is a clear parallel with Jewish divorce here, with the tribunal acting as witnesses to the parties' divorce rather than giving a ruling themselves.

If that is not possible, the Shariah Council takes a stance very similar to that adopted in the English civil courts when dealing with defended divorce petitions – if one party insists the marriage is over, there is no point in telling him or her that it is not:

> if . . . any woman doesn't want to live with her partner we are not here to force the women to live with their husbands, we have to look at the situation and then come to a decision.

It could thus be said that this Shariah Council has a view of the ending of a marriage quite close to that in current English divorce law, as both focus on whether the marriage has 'irretrievably broken down' (and the facts establishing this may also be fault-based). Where a civil divorce has been obtained, this in itself will be taken as proof that the marriage cannot be saved and an Islamic divorce should be granted. Indeed, this Shariah Council will regard a civil divorce as equivalent to an Islamic divorce which obviates the need to obtain a ruling from the Council. In such a situation, it is the litigant's own desire to obtain sanction from the Shariah Council for their actions which determines whether they feel a need to take proceedings.

---

[9] Of 27 hearings that we observed in our study, only two involved male applicants.

The position in the Roman Catholic National Tribunal reflects a similar scope for discretion, albeit within the constraints of the Code of Canon Law and a mandatory review by the tribunal of second instance, for once again, there is a degree of flexibility in the selection of grounds on which a marriage could be said to be void. As one interviewee said:

> [W]hat we are particularly interested in is what went on before the exchange of consent and at the time of the exchange of consent and the first few years afterwards because it's the quality of the consent, you know, which is at the essence of the nullity process.

This may be established by evidence relating to incapacity (eg, consanguinity, age, prior marriage, lack of mental capacity) and several other grounds, including evidence that the person suffers 'from a grave lack of discretionary judgement concerning the essential matrimonial rights and obligations to be mutually given and accepted' (Canon 1095.1.2), or 'who, because of causes of a psychological nature, [is] unable to assume the essential obligations of marriage' (Canon 1095.1.3).

As the interview quotation shows, the evidence could be drawn from events during the marriage itself. In this regard, some of the grounds come closer to what English law would see as voidable, rather than void, marriages, or even facts which would establish irretrievable breakdown for the purposes of divorce, demonstrating some alignment of approach with the civil law in the attitude taken to whether a marriage should or should not be 'upheld'.

V THE LICENCE TO REMARRY

None of the courts studied has a 'legal status' in the sense of 'recognition' by the state. They derive their authority from their religious affiliation, not from the state, and that authority extends only to those who choose to submit to them. However, as far as annulment or divorce is concerned, their authority to rule on the validity/termination of a marriage does not derive from the parties' agreement to submit their 'dispute' to them in quite the same way as an arbitration clause in a contract (for which the Beth Din and some Shariah councils would also qualify to rule on civil disputes) (see Douglas et al 2011: 16–22). *Indeed, there may be no dispute*. Rather, adherents to the particular faith must make use of the religious court if they are to obtain sanction to remarry within their faith. Resort to the tribunal is therefore not 'voluntary' in the standard dispute resolution sense:

> There have been cases where a woman was pregnant by a man she wasn't married to, so we have to resolve the case in times of divorce and people are put ahead because that cannot be left to carry on like that because that would be living in sin. Islamically, it's far better to be divorced than committing adultery and so we have to make an effort to deal with it as soon as possible so that she can marry him (member of Shariah Council).

Farrah Ahmed (chapter two) characterises the work of religious tribunals as 'RADR' or religious alternative dispute resolution. However, we argue that, for the religious tribunals in our study at least, since marital *status* is their main focus, they should not be primarily regarded as conducting a form of dispute resolution akin to arbitration or mediation. This is not just a situation where the parties are being helped to reach an agreement over their future arrangements; it is a more profound and significant function, both for the parties and for the tribunals themselves. As Shachar has noted, this has both an internal and external dimension, with family law 'demarcating' the group's 'membership boundaries' in relation to the wider society (2001: 51–54).

The fundamental rationale for the grant of the religious annulment/divorce is to enable the parties to remarry within the faith. The focus is on the marriage itself, not the ancillaries (children, money and property) and this is a useful reminder that ultimately, a dissolution (or annulment or divorce) is a licence to remarry. In this regard, our view of the possible functions of family law (whatever its source) is broader than that presented by Jordi Ribot, who sees these as limited to a private law determination of mutual rights and obligations and for whom 'family law cannot be seen . . . as part of public law' (chapter sixteen). We have discussed above that state law can utilise religious rites to bring about civil marital status which must have a public law dimension. Our study showed that, in the context of annulment and divorce similarly, being able to remarry within the faith serves both to enable adherents to retain their standing within their faith community and to regularise their position with the religious authorities. This is particularly crucial in the Jewish religion, because the failure to obtain a *get* will jeopardise the legitimate status of the wife's future children and descendants.

Inevitably, process and procedure vary as between the three courts, reflecting the different approach to the role that each takes. For the Beth Din, there is no investigation by the court into the parties' grounds for seeking a *get*. If there appears to be a possibility that the parties are not sure that they wish for the divorce, they will be encouraged to seek counselling, but this is not part of the court's function itself. Rather, the function is to *supervise* and witness the parties' mutual agreement that the marriage should end:

> [T]he actual formation of a marriage and the dissolution of a marriage . . . the Beth Din will preside over it but they are the referees, they're not the players, they are not creating or dissolving the marriage.

For the Shariah Council, as already noted, there is a mandatory attempt at reconciliation as a first step in the procedure. If the applicant still wishes to proceed after such an attempt, the role of the Council is to ensure the marriage is unworkable and it will listen to the parties' evidence, and hear their witnesses, to arrive at its decision. However, it is not inquisitorial in the sense of proactively investigating the circumstances. The process is primarily adversarial in that the Shariah Council is in the hands of the parties as to what information is put forward to it and how arguments are presented. But the parties do not have the opportunity to hear or cross-examine each other's evidence at the final hearing and may not even be told what the other has said.

The National Tribunal adopts a more proactive and inquisitorial approach with different individuals appointed within the system to investigate the marriage from different perspectives – in particular, the 'Defender of the Bond' explores the potential for upholding the validity of the marriage and the Tribunal may seek evidence from its own witnesses, including independent experts. However, although the parties are interviewed, this is done separately and there is no 'hearing' of the case, the evidence being compiled on paper and then discussed by the members of the Tribunal in private. Although the Tribunal will agree with a petitioner the ground(s) on which he or she wishes the case to be dealt with, it then exercises its own judgement as to whether the ground is proved, and the second instance tribunal may substitute its own findings on other grounds if it chooses. For the National Tribunal, the whole focus is on whether the marriage is valid or not, but this is tied to resolving the question of whether it is flawed, rather than on whether it can be 'saved'; thus, it is quite likely that the Tribunal may refuse an annulment because no grounds are made out, even though it knows the parties have divorced – thus maintaining a limping marriage. By contrast, for the Beth Din and the Shariah Council, there is an acceptance (even if, in the case of the latter, this must be tested by an attempt at reconciling the spouses) that there is little point keeping a marriage in existence when there is no longer mutual agreement:

> [B]y very definition the fact that one person has written to us wanting a *get* means that at least one of the two want the divorce; usually both want the divorce (interviewee at the Beth Din).

VI THE RELATIONSHIP WITH CIVIL LAW

Given the controversy surrounding the question of accommodating religious tribunal rulings under civil law, the sensitivity of the tribunals in the study to their relationship with the state was particularly noteworthy. All three religious tribunals, being acutely aware of their position vis-à-vis the state, strongly encourage the parties to obtain a civil divorce, if applicable, before seeking a religious termination.[10] Indeed, the National Tribunal does not deal with an application for annulment until the parties have divorced – even though it may uphold the marriage as valid and subsisting in Catholic law:

> '[I]in Britain we cannot start, we cannot give an annulment without the people being divorced otherwise we're in trouble with the state, people sometimes forget that we, if

---

[10] eg, see the Code of Canon Law, Canon 22: 'Civil laws to which the law of the Church yields are to be observed in canon law with the same effects, insofar as they are not contrary to divine law and unless canon law provides otherwise'.

we try to dissolve something that the state hadn't dissolved then we would be in trouble (member of the National Tribunal).

The Beth Din will not provide the certificate that a *get* has been given until it has proof of the civil divorce (although the *get* itself may be obtained before that stage is completed if this is required because a spouse has invoked the provisions of Matrimonial Causes Act 1973 section 10A under which the grant of decree absolute may otherwise be delayed). Both the Beth Din and the Shariah Council regard the obtaining of a civil divorce as clear evidence of the parties' view that the marriage is over, and for the Shariah Council, this is conclusive:

> In cases where women are already going through the civil courts and they are sort of in the middle of that, if they come to the Shariah Council and they say that they want to have the divorce we usually say to them that, 'once that's gone ahead'. Because if we go ahead and say 'you're divorced' they're still married under the legal system, which will create a conflict and Islam doesn't want you to have that conflict of status, you know, what are you going to write? Are you 'married' or 'divorced'? So in order to not cause any conflict in the person's own mind and also in terms of the state system it's best for us to say to them 'once that's resolved then come back to us' (member of the Shariah Council).

Similarly, the extent to which the three tribunals become involved in relation to the consequences of the termination of the marriage in relation to money and property and arrangements for the children, is limited. The National Tribunal has no role in relation to dealing with the consequences of an annulment (although, from a pastoral dimension, it might wish to be informed of the arrangements the parties have made). Under Jewish law, it is possible for the parties to agree at the time of the marriage (a) that they will not withhold agreement to a *get* and (b) that they will ask the Beth Din to resolve any ancillary disputes between them. Such agreements would not amount to binding arbitration, since the jurisdiction of the civil courts on family matters may not be ousted by the parties' agreement,[11] and this is made clear to the parties by the Beth Din, which advises the parties to obtain a consent order from the divorce court. However, litigants are not obliged to use the civil courts for such matters and indeed are strongly encouraged to make private arrangements,[12] so this is a potentially important function of the Beth Din (and worth further study).

The Shariah Council similarly advises parties to make use of the civil courts to resolve disputes, in recognition that it too cannot give legally binding rulings (although for an account suggesting a more active role by another Shariah Council, at least in relation to arrangements for children, see Bowen, 2011: 420). Nonetheless, it may advise parties on what should be done with *mahr*, often in strong terms. Moreover, it is important to note that, in line with other empirical research (Bano 2008; Shah-Kazemi 2001), over half of the cases dealt with by the Shariah Council we studied involved couples who were not married under

---

[11]   Matrimonial Causes Act 1973, s 34; Children Act 1989 s 10.
[12]   Family Procedure Rules 2010, SI 2010/2955 Pt 3.

English civil law.[13] As we have pointed out above, such couples are treated in the civil law as cohabitants, with limited financial and property rights against each other. For these couples, the Tribunal could play an important role in helping them to resolve their post-separation arrangements in ways which would not impinge on the financial remedies jurisdiction exercised by the divorce courts, since this jurisdiction would not be open to them in the first place. However, the restrictive rules in Shariah on support and allocation of finances after divorce may leave women worse off, at least in relation to ongoing maintenance and where the couple had a child together, than a claim made to the family court.[14] The implications of the Cox Bill[15] for the operation of such a role are unclear.

Finally, it is important to note that none of the three tribunals in our study sought greater 'recognition' by the state and all clearly recognised the boundaries between what they do, and the sphere of the civil courts. As a member of the Beth Din stated:

> We are British citizens and we abide by British law and anything that's done from a Jewish perspective is in addition to civil law . . . a Beth Din is not comparable [to the civil courts] in any way because we are not trying to overrule or override or supplant the civil system.

VII CONCLUSION

Our findings help to show that, at present, religious annulments and divorces remain completely outside the civil legal system, and none, including Jewish divorces where the Matrimonial Causes Act is invoked to delay the civil decree absolute, is 'recognised' by the law. They thus fall within our 'cohabitation' model of accommodation of religion, which really amounts to no more than a passive tolerance of religious practice undertaken without expectation of state recognition. Given the fundamental differences between the substantive law of the three religious codes, and English divorce law, it would not currently be possible to devise a recognition process in any event. All three systems would appear to fall short of the respect and pre-eminence which, as Ribot (chapter sixteen) argues, must be accorded to human rights norms. In respect of their substantive law, the Jewish requirement that the husband deliver the *get* to the wife and the wife's inability to require him to do so, mean the law is fundamentally unequal as between the genders. Shariah provides different grounds, of differential difficulty, for husbands and wives to rely on. Moreover, arguably, none of the procedures operated in the three religions is human rights compliant, since there

---

[13] Of the 27 observed cases in our study, 14 involved only a private *nikah* ceremony, and of the remaining 13, 6 couples had married abroad and the civil status in five of these was unclear.

[14] The Children Act 1989 Sch 1 provides for both married and unmarried parents to seek support *for the child* which would extend beyond that which is apparently available under Islamic law, and which could include an element for the child-care function exercised by the applicant parent.

[15] Above (n 2).

appear to be inadequate safeguards to enable the parties to know each other's 'case' and respond to it. These shortfalls may in fact help explain the tribunals' ready acceptance that they operate 'outside' the state with no claim to have the state enforce their determinations. Any attempt to gain greater recognition would bring with it the need to satisfy such norms, in line with Shachar's suggestion for 'ex ante regulatory control' and compliance with a '"floor" of protection' for litigants (Shachar 2008: 598–602), which would require a compromise and submission to state/secular values which might be difficult for them to contemplate.

However, as noted above, it is possible under English law (and has been since 1836), for couples to choose to be married under civil law by means of different religious or civil rites, which we describe as falling within our 'integration' model, and it would be possible to treat annulment and divorce in the same way. It has already been suggested by an independent review into the family justice system that English divorce law should move to an administrative process akin to marriage registration, for all undefended cases (around 99 per cent of the current total) rather than have a judge determine the case (Norgrove 2011: para 4.166). This proposal does not envisage that the ground for divorce would be altered and it is open to doubt whether an administrator (still less a computer system) could, constitutionally, find that the ground was satisfied. But legal reform could go further, and abolish the ground of irretrievable breakdown entirely and simply permit divorce by registered repudiation (for a possible model proposed for a common European approach, see Boele-Woelki 2004). In such a case, the substantive and procedural objections noted above would be diminished. One could then envisage the introduction of a similar system as that which applies to the entry into marriage, for the grant of divorce/annulment, particularly if it operated alongside the increasing policy drive towards the private ordering of the consequences of a divorce. Couples – or one spouse – could opt to end the marriage via the religious rather than the civil route. The parties would be encouraged to settle the ancillary arrangements by private ordering, but would not be able to oust the jurisdiction of the courts to determine these, so that the state would retain its ultimate control over the consequences, in the same way that it does at the point of marriage formation.[16] Such an approach would fit our integration model, and also meet Shachar's proposal (2010: 130) for 'regulated interaction' between religious and state authorities, under which determination of the various 'sub-matters' which make up family regulation could be divided between them, leaving the option to the parties, but particularly the weaker party – and always recognising the need for that party to be properly able to exercise a genuine choice (van Bijsterveld 2010: 208) – to make use of either system as they prefer.

---

[16] This would not address the financial problems of Muslim wives who have not gone through a legally recognised marriage. It is submitted that the answer to this lies in educating them about the importance of civil marital status, and by revising the laws governing the formalities for entry into marriage to make a civil marriage more attractive to Muslims.

The religious tribunals that we studied were satisfied with their current position and were not seeking greater recognition or incorporation along these lines. But the point is that English law does have an exemplar, in its law governing entry into marriage, which suggests it could be workable. The trend toward the greater secularisation and privatisation of the civil law of marriage and divorce in Western jurisdictions like England and Wales may, paradoxically, turn out to provide the best means of accommodating the demands and desires of religious groups seeking recognition of their identity by the liberal state.

REFERENCES

Ahdar, R and Aroney, N (2010) 'The Topography of Shari'a in the Western Political Landscape' in R Ahdar and N Aroney (eds), *Shari'a in the West* (Oxford, Oxford University Press).

Ahmed, F (2010) 'Personal Autonomy and the Option of Religious Law' 24 *International Journal of Law, Policy and the Family* 222.

Bano, S (2008) 'In Pursuit of Religious and Legal Diversity: A Reply to the Archbishop of Canterbury and the "Sharia Debate" in Britain' 10 *Ecclesiastical Law Journal* 283.

Barlow, A, Duncan, S, James G and Park, A (2005) *Cohabitation, Marriage and the Law: Social Change and Legal Reform in the 21st Century* (Oxford, Hart Publishing).

Boele-Woelki, K (2004) *Principles of European Family Law regarding Divorce and Maintenance between Former Spouses* (Cambridge, Intersentia).

Bowen, J (201) 'How Could English Courts Recognize Shariah?' 7 *St Thomas Law Review* 411.

Doe, N (1994) 'Canonical Doctrines of Judicial Precedent: A Comparative Study' 54 *The Jurist* 205.

Douglas, G, Doe, N, Gilliat-Ray, S, Sandberg R and Khan, A (2011) *Social Cohesion and Civil Law: Marriage, Divorce and Religious Courts* (Cardiff, Cardiff Law School): www.law.cf.ac.uk/clr/research/cohesion.html.

Fournier, P (2010) *Muslim Marriage in Western Courts: Lost in Transplantation* (Farnham, Ashgate).

Gaudreault-DesBiens, J-F (2010) 'Religious Courts, Personal Federalism, and Legal Transplants' in R Ahdar and N Aroney (eds), *Shari'a in the West* (Oxford, Oxford University Press).

Jackson, B (2011) *Agunah: The Manchester Analysis* (Liverpool, Deborah Charles Publishing).

Norgrove D (Chair) (2011)) *Family Justice Review: Final Report* (London, Ministry of Justice, Department for Education and Welsh Government).

Saeed, A (2010) 'Reflections on the Establishment of Shari'a Courts in Australia' in R Ahdar and N Aroney (eds), *Shari'a in the West* (Oxford, Oxford University Press).

Shachar, A (2001) *Multicultural Jurisdictions: Cultural Differences and Women's Rights* (Cambridge, Cambridge University Press).

—— (2008) 'Privatizing Diversity: A Cautionary Tale from Religious Arbitration in Family Law' 9 *Theoretical Inquiries in Law* 573.

—— (2010) 'State, Religion and the Family: The New Dilemmas of Multicultural Accommodation' in R Ahdar and N Aroney (eds), *Shari'a in the West* (Oxford, Oxford University Press).

Shah, P (2005) *Legal Pluralism in Conflict: Coping with Cultural Diversity in Law* (London, Glasshouse Press).

Shah-Kazemi, S (2001) *Untying the Knot: Muslim Women, Divorce and the Shariah* (London, The Nuffield Foundation).

van Bijsterveld, S (2010) 'Negotiating the Unfamiliar: Reflections from the Netherlands on the Archbishop of Canterbury's Lecture' in R Ahdar and N Aroney (eds), *Shari'a in the West* (Oxford, Oxford University Press).

Waldron, J (2010) 'Questions about the Reasonable Accommodation of Minorities' in R Ahdar and N Aroney (eds), *Shari'a in the West* (Oxford, Oxford University Press).

Williams, R (2008) 'Civil and Religious Law in England: A Religious Perspective' 7 February 2008: www.archbishopofcanterbury.org/1575 reprinted in 10 *Ecclesiastical Law Journal* 262.

12

How Parties to Sikh Marriages use and are Influenced by the Norms of their Religion and Culture when engaging with Mediation

JAGBIR JHUTTI-JOHAL

I INTRODUCTION

IN THE SIKH tradition marriage is predetermined by God and is entered into for life. Marriage is not just a physical and legal/civil contract which can be dissolved, but is a sacred contract recognised and ordained by God. It is for this reason that the eternal Guru of the Sikhs, the Guru Granth Sahib (GGS – Sikh Holy book) contains verses, such as the *Lavan* (marriage verses sung during the *Anand Karaj*) which describe and discuss marriage (773–74).[1]

Whilst marriage is discussed and described in the Guru Granth Sahib,[2] divorce is not. However, there are some indirect references to broken marriages, but these references refer to the relationship between the worshipper and the divine (GGS: 426, 428 and 430). For example, regarding divorced (separated) women:

---

[1] In the *Anand Karaj* – ceremony of bliss, the couple sit in the presence of Guru Granth Sahib. Four verses/hymns (*lavan*) are read to solemnise the wedding. Each hymn is first read from the Guru Granth Sahib and then sung. When the hymns are sung the couple circumbulate the Guru Granth Sahib. These four verses give the couple eight opportunities to accept or reject these vows. First, when it is read from Guru Granth Sahib, and, secondly, when the hymns are sung. If they do not object they show their acceptance by bowing to Guru Granth Sahib (Jhutti 1998: Appendix II: 430). The message contained in the hymns (*lavan*) is that the bride and the groom are to unite in marriage like the human soul seeks to unite with the Divine:

> They are not said to be husband and wife, who merely sit together. They alone are called husband and wife, who have one soul in two bodies (Guru Granth Sahib: 788).

[2] The Guru Granth Sahib (GGS) is widely available and accessible through English translations. There are various translations of the GGS and for this research I have used the translation from Dr Gopal Singh (1978).

What is the value of a divorced woman's make-up and ornaments, when her husband has deserted her! She misses her children, her spouse, and the comforts of her husband's household. She lives in an emotional imbalance in a disturbed state (GGS: 363)

Regarding infidelity of men:

I say to you, O my body: listen to my advice! You slander, and then praise others; you indulge in lies and gossip. You gaze upon the wives of others, O my soul; you steal and commit evil deeds. But when the swan soul departs, you shall remain behind, like a divorced/disgraced man (abandoned woman) (GGS: 155).

Sikhs are today turning to such verses in the Guru Granth Sahib for guidance when marriages breakdown since there is no religious law. They are interpreting *shabads* (verses) in the Guru Granth Sahib to decide whether divorce is permissible or not. Interpretations vary, and depend on an individual's particular circumstances, but also on what solutions the individual is seeking. For example, the above-mentioned verses have been interpreted by some to argue that a notion of separation and unfaithfulness existed during the time of the Gurus, and that therefore it is acceptable to separate and divorce.

While there is no religious provision for divorce, neither is there a separate legal provision for divorce in India for the Sikh community. The Anand Marriage Act 1909[3] does not provide any information on divorce since the aim of the Act was not to codify the whole law relating to Sikh marriages. As a result, unlike 'Islamic' law, there is no defined Sikh law. Instead, Sikhs live by the law of the land, and are governed by a cultural system or 'customs' which can be defined as 'personal laws' rather than a civil law. These 'personal laws' function alongside the civil law in the arena of marriage and divorce, and are enforced by family, community and religious leaders. Variations exist in these 'personal laws' because even though Sikhs share many attributes, such as a common physical and geographic homeland and history, the community is not a homogenous or monolithic entity, but is instead highly diverse due to caste, regional and socio-economic differences. As a consequence of these differences between Sikhs there is no one comprehensive Sikh cultural system (Griffiths 1986; Menski 2006).

In the past, divorce used to be avoided: couples used to resolve their problems within the framework of marriage, ie, remain married but lead separate lives. In the last four decades there has been a rise in marital breakdowns. Despite this, there is a scarcity of research dealing with divorce, especially 'personal laws' and attitudes to and processes employed by Sikhs to dissolve marriages, and whether Sikhs, especially those who have migrated and assimilated or acculturated into their new host communities have created new ways of getting divorced, eg, an *Angrezi* (British) way of getting divorced (Menski 1994). This chapter will look at how a marriage is arranged and then the process employed before a decision to divorce is arrived at since there is no provision for it in the Guru

---

[3] The Anand Karaj ceremony only received legal recognition in 1909 in India, when the Anand Marriage Act was passed to remove doubts as to the validity of the Anand marriage ceremony.

Granth Sahib or the Anand Marriage Act 1909. It will consider the process of mediation – the initial process undertaken by parents, the middleman (*vachola*) or in extreme cases religious leaders – which the majority of Sikhs go through today to obtain a divorce. It will highlight the role of religion and culture in terms of the values and beliefs, but also the 'personal laws' that shape the mediation process in the UK.[4] Attitudes towards this process will also be discussed to highlight how Sikhs have negotiated the cultures and laws of the land they are in to meet their religious and cultural needs.

This chapter will also highlight the experiences and views of Sikh men and women who have either facilitated mediation or gone through the process of family/community mediation, but also Western professional mediation. It will consider how religious and cultural expectations of honour and shame have affected the negotiation process, and how mediation has been negotiated by members of the community today, particularly young women. Finally, it will briefly consider whether traditional 'neutral' community or family mediation can exist as a result of assimilation and acculturation, or whether professional Western mediation will be utilised. By focusing on the Sikh diaspora in Britain and the changes that have occurred since migration in the field of mediation, this chapter aims to add to the previous work and contribute to the slender critical corpus concerning the Sikh diaspora, marriage and divorce.

II METHODOLOGY

To understand the process and the contemporary Sikh views on mediation, an anthropological and ethnographical approach was employed to explore how Sikhs today negotiate the cultural/religious divide when interpersonal tensions arise, and the notions of patriarchy and cultural and social taboos and notions of honour (*izzat*) and shame (*behzti*) that are utilised (Ballard 1982; Jhutti 1998: 373–74; Jhutti-Johal 2011: 67–69; Singh, G and D Tatla 2006: 29–30).

Sikh men and women from two cities in the United Kingdom (London and Birmingham) were interviewed over a six-month period (2010–11). The sample consisted of 25 women and 25 men. Eleven women were between the ages of 50 and 80. Fourteen were between the ages of 18 and 50. The older women (between 50 and 80) had received little or no formal education when they were growing up. The women between the ages of 18 and 50 had received some form of education. Most of the young women had gone to university or had plans to attend. Two of the older women (aged 63 and 70) were baptised; none of the young women were baptised.[5] Twenty-five men were interviewed between the ages of 21 and 75. Three men were baptised: one was in his twenties, one in his late

---

[4] According to Singh and Tatla (2006: 2) there are 336,000 Sikhs living in Britain who have become a part of pluralist British identity (Jhutti-Johal 2011: xi).

[5] This refers to the Sikh baptism/initiation ceremony, *Amrit Sanchar*. This was introduced by the tenth Guru, Guru Gobind Singh.

fifties, and one in his late sixties. The approach taken was in the form of a semi-structured, interview-based questionnaire; however, some questions were open-ended. Face-to face interviews were conducted among 15 married couples in the UK in Punjabi and English. Nearly all the couples were happily married apart from seven who were going through a separation. All couples participated in detailed interviews, describing their attitudes to the use of formal and informal support counselling services available in times of marital crisis.[6]

All interviews were one-to-one and lasted a minimum of one to two hours. Notes were taken for all interviews, and only 12 interviews were recorded and then transcribed. All 12 of these respondents were young Sikhs. Although the issue of confidentiality and anonymity was stressed, some refused to be interviewed and expressed concern that if interviews were recorded then other people might get to hear them and that their problems or opinions – which may go against the norm – would become public knowledge.[7]

Prior to the interviews respondents were given a brief about the study, together with a sample of the questions. The ten interview questions were not made too academic or lengthy. Respondents were promised absolute confidentiality which was essential if respondents were to offer an accurate assessment of the situation, as they understood it.

III ARRANGING A MARRIAGE

Before the mediation process is examined, it is important to discuss how marriages are arranged so that we can put into context the role of mediation in marital breakdowns for Sikhs. Ever since the beginning of the Sikh religion, marriages have been arranged by parents, and this strong family involvement is carried through to what happens after one is married. Traditional 'arranged marriages' were negotiated and organised by parents, who were dependent on friends and relatives to suggest suitable partners (Ballard 1972 and 1982; Jhutti 1998). Once a candidate had been suggested, parents would make enquiries, and if the other side agreed to meet, the child was informed. In the last 40 years or so Sikh marriage practices have been modified quite substantially due to migration, westernisation and modernisation. These processes have offered young Sikhs an element of 'choice', which focuses on Western factors such as companionship, compatibility of temperament, personality, interests and ideals.[8] There are also new types of

---

[6] The principal shortcoming of this research is the sample size. There is a risk that, with such a small sample, the results are not representative of the Sikh community as a whole. It is also important to note that most of the interviewees were men, meaning that most of the qualitative data gives an exclusively male perspective.

[7] This methodology has been employed by me in other ethnographic studies I have done on the Sikh community, eg, Jhutti-Johal (2010) and Jhutti-Johal (2012).

[8] It is important to note that I am not suggesting that Sikhs are going out and marrying non-Sikhs, although there have been a few isolated incidences of this. This may become more common in the next 30 or 40 years (Jhutti-Johal 2011: 67–69).

marriage arrangements resembling the 'Coming out Balls' of the eighteenth and nineteenth centuries (Jhutti 1998: 64). For example, it is common today for parents to discreetly point out possible candidates during religious events, weddings and birthday parties, and vice versa. If the child or parents agree, the other side is approached.

Another new arrangement has come about from parents telling their children before they go away to university that if they meet someone at university, who is 'suitable', that is, same religion and caste, then they can suggest that person to them and if everything is fine, that is, caste affiliation and surname, they will organise the marriage like an arranged marriage. These changes do not go against the tradition of arranged marriage because once the couple say 'yes' and parents approve the marriage it is organised in a traditional way, namely, a friend or relative acts as the middleman because parents and the young Sikhs themselves recognise the importance of the status and approval they gain from the community if things are arranged according to custom/tradition. This family involvement is also essential for Sikhs in their attempt to ensure the sanctity and longevity of marriage.

These traditional practices of arranging a marriage have also been replaced/ substituted by less family-involved processes. While parents have turned to matrimonial columns such as *Des Pardes Weekly* because currently people are not willing to suggest possible partners due to the increasing number of marital breakdowns and the negative impact this has on their reputation, in terms of honour (*izzat*) and shame (*behzti*) (Ballard 1982), younger Sikhs – who have acculturated and assimilated – have aligned themselves to more progressive methods of arranging marriages, such as Sikh or Asian social networking sites, dating agencies, all of which are dependent on 'choice', and this choice focuses on factors which are common in Western countries, such as companionship, compatibility of temperament, personality, interests and ideals.

IV DIVORCE

While the way marriages are arranged has changed, so has what happens afterwards. Since migration there has been a steady rise in marital breakdown and divorce, but whereas the Sikh community has devised elaborate new processes for arranging marriages, the process of breaking up remains unstructured because there is no civil or religious Sikh law on divorce. Divorce is attained through the civil law of the land, but to get to this stage Sikhs have, up to now, gone through a complex process of mediation, which is governed by a patriarchal order, which enforces a system of power relations, but also a system of meaning which controls the family unit. All this operated through the operation of customary 'personal laws', which have been guided and legitimised through a discourse of '*izzat*' or family honour (Ballard 1982; Jhutti 1998; Jhutti-Johal 2011: 67–69). *Izzat* has been able to dictate acceptable standards of behaviour, and discourage, censure and prevent individuals from divorcing their partners. This has been particularly true for women because Sikh women ensure the continuation of the Sikh faith and community, but also the 'honour of the "community" and family' (Ballard 1982; Singh, G and D Tatla 2006: 29–30). As one Sikh father said:

> Until recently women's role was central within the family, and the position of our daughters has been defined in relation to marriage and divorce. If a daughter is married you have honour. If a daughter is divorced you are dishonoured.

As a result, as preservers of *izzat*, Sikh women have complied obediently with what has been said and done, because not to do so would bring shame and dishonour to the family (Ballard 1982). Parents, understanding the consequences of a deviation from the norm (namely, a divorce) have always made their children, particularly daughters, aware from an early age of the consequences of divorce for themselves and their family. For example, most women are conscious of the fact that if they do separate from their partner, speculation immediately begins as to why the marriage broke down. Culturally, the failure of a marriage is always assumed to be the woman's fault, and leads to a blemish on her reputation, even if the husband was to blame for the failure of the marriage (Jhutti 1998; Jhutti-Johal 2011: 68). They are also aware that it would tarnish their parents' reputation because they – the parents – will be criticised for not bringing up their daughter properly (Ballard 1994a: 1–34; Phillips 2003: 534; Singh and Tatla 2006: 29–30).

V PREVENTING THE DISSOLUTION OF A MARRIAGE

Mediation offered by parents, the middleman (*vachola*) or in extreme cases religious leaders, has played an important role among the South Asian communities in India and Britain for many years. Sikhs have always used family intervention and mediation to resolve problems and to prevent the termination of a religious marriage, which Sikhs recognise can only be done through civil law (Jhutti 1998: 349–52). Sikh parents and religious leaders today are aware that their authority only works if the individual concerned chooses to submit to it; that they cannot make binding rulings; that they can only make suggestions and if things cannot be resolved, they will advise the couple to seek redress from the civil courts, which is always the last resort. Mediation for Sikhs has no religious legitimation, and is grounded in culture rather than religion.[9]

---

[9] As a consequence most Sikh couples encountering marital problems, go through formal mediation as well as family mediation. It can be argued that any legal requirement for mediation may diminish family mediation amongst the Sikh community (Jhutti 1998: 349–50). This is unlikely due to the importance of family involvement in a child's marriage. This will remain strong due to the Sikh preference for abiding by the norms of their tradition and religion. Instead, what will change is the extent to which children will heed their parents' advice.

Nevertheless, the cultural authority is indirectly assigned to it via the religion due to the sanctity of marriage.

In the Western context, ideally, mediation is non-coercive and non-binding – something entered into freely. It requires the involvement of someone who is skilled, impartial and neutral, external to the couple, but most importantly someone who has an understanding and knowledge of the parties and the issues that divide them. The mediator works to facilitate and assist the couple to ana- lyse and constructively deal with issues so that they can arrive at a settlement which is mutually acceptable. From this brief description, it is clear that this does not happen within the Sikh context because Sikh mediators are known – namely, family members. If a couple cannot resolve problems on their own, then parents and the middleman (*vachola*) should intervene to mediate (whether asked or not). All the parents in my sample said that if their child's marriage was in difficulty, they would step in to help. It is nearly always the wife's parents who instigate mediation to prevent the dissolution of a marriage because they fear the consequences of a divorce, that is, it will ruin the family's reputation, and in turn injure the chances of unmarried daughters and sons finding suitable partners. A marriage that has been organised by the couple themselves or through a matrimonial column and has had no parental involvement means the couple has little protection and support from their extended family and are more dependent on their own resources.[10]

Parents arrange meetings, which are attended by them, the couple, the mid- dleman (*vachola*) and any other close relative who might be able to help, and in most instances, these relatives are male. There are three places where mediation can take place: the home of the wife's or husband's parents; the home of the middleman; or a religious venue, ie, *gurdwara*. What is clear is that the setting is rarely neutral. The parents and the middleman try to learn the issues in dispute, and then tell the couple what they should do; they are not impartial like a pro- fessional mediator whose job is not to tell a couple what to do, but to help them arrive at a solution with the least amount of hostility. In Sikh mediation an agenda and bias is always apparent, as for Sikh parents, the overriding objective of mediation is to save the marriage.

One father, an accountant, described the mediation process:

All marriages run into trouble, and most of the time the couple can work things out for themselves, but if they can't then they should ask their parents for help. If my daughter and her husband were to have a serious fight which they couldn't solve them- selves, then I, with my son-in-law's parents, the middleman and other elders would sit them down to offer guidance and support. A parent's job is to calm the couple and help them sort out their problems rationally. If a couple does not want their parents involved, which has happened, they should ask someone else, preferably an elder from the community to help. No matter who is involved, the main aim of the meetings

---

[10] It is because of the help that is offered by the middleman and other relatives when their children encounter marital problems that parents want their children's marriage to be arranged by a friend or relative.

should be to prevent the break-up of a marriage, and in turn preserve the family *izzat*. If a marriage can be saved then this should be thoroughly explored, but if it is clear that the marriage is dead then I employ the saying 'it should be buried quickly and quietly'.

Another father explained the process he used when his daughter's marriage was in trouble:

A meeting was arranged at my house. We, my wife and me, the boy's parents and the middleman, sat my daughter and her husband down and asked what the problem was. My daughter said the problem was compatibility. I couldn't understand this because she had dated her husband for a year before they got married, every day they were on the phone and most weeks they would meet at least once for dinner or lunch. How come she didn't know then that he was not compatible? She was the one who said 'yes' not us. It was so embarrassing when she said this in front of her husband's family and me. Nobody would have said this in my generation. You just got on with things and stuck together. Marriage then was for life. Nowadays there is no emphasis on making a marriage work. Children don't understand the religious and cultural significance of marriage and are very quick to take the easy option. It also doesn't help when the law of the land makes it easy for couples to divorce.

The problem has also been made worse because our daughters are educated now. Until recently we have been able to tell our daughters how to behave within the community but also outside the community. However, now that they are educated and financially independent we can't do this in the context of family and community.

A man, a lawyer by profession, who claimed to be a successful *vachola* (middleman), who had arranged over 200 marriages in the last 30 years said:

In the past I was happy to arrange a marriage because I knew it would last. However, now I am too scared. You can't trust children or parents. In the past if things went wrong I was called in to speak to the couple, and we would tease out problems and things would be ok. However, today if there is a problem, children are not prepared to listen or talk.

Today, there is a conflict between the social expectations of British society and the parents' Sikh cultural and religious values. While in the past children would focus on the cultural expectations of their community, they are now more focused on western expectations and goals. Our youngsters are losing their faith and culture, and are more interested in themselves. All they talk about today is 'it's my life' or 'I know my rights'. When I hear this I know that I cannot do anything to save the marriage.

The reasons for divorce and conflict have also changed. Today, conflict is about child rearing and responsibility to the extended family, but also working too much. There was none of this pressure that children are under today in the past. In the past if both couples were working they would do it so that at least one parent was at home when the children were at home, ie, men would do the night shift and women would work during the day. Things got done and there was not much conflict, or you just didn't hear about it. Today, both husband and wife are working long hours and spending less time with their families because living costs are high and everyone is competing with one and another. This pressure is causing breakdowns. This is made complicated today because more and more of our girls are going into highly qualified jobs, and as a result in some relationships women are more successful than their husbands who feel they have lost their identity and authority. This education and career success has empowered women with the knowledge and means (financial independence) to divorce.

The Sikh process today, however, is not as directive as it was in the past when parents and the middleman were able to impose/enforce a solution. Middlemen and parents have learnt that they have no real authority and need to play the role of a facilitator – helping couples to arrive at amicable solutions rather than enforcing solutions because this will ensure that individuals will listen and take into account their parents' feelings and views, while making their own decisions, rather than turning to outside agencies or bypassing the cultural process completely.

A 55-year-old father, whose daughter had separated from her husband noted:

Marriage isn't what it used to be, and nor is our role. We no longer have the right to tell our children what to do after they are married. If they don't want to listen to our advice that is their right, and they know that.

An elderly grandmother in her late sixties told me:

How can you tell your children to do something now? You can't! When my son was going through divorce we tried to sit him and his wife down to talk things through. That was our job. Do you know what he said to me? He said 'you can't tell me what to do? You don't understand I have to do things according to the country I live in'. He kept going on about the law. I know all this, but what he did not understand was that before he got to the stage of law there was another process that he should consider.

While many older respondents expressed the view that young Sikhs were quick to bypass their parents and family mediation because divorce was not seen as a problem, it was clear from analysing transcripts from the open-ended, semi-structured interviews with young Sikhs that they all have different ways of thinking and perceiving the value of and need for mediation and divorce.

A teacher, aged 35, described what she would do if her marriage ever broke down:

I've been married for eight years and have two children. We have our problems, but to date we have managed to resolve them amongst ourselves. If things ever got to the stage that we could not resolve our problems I am sure we would go our separate ways. Whether I would consult my parents and seek their help is another issue. I'm not sure that I would. The family's agenda will be to keep us together, no matter what. This is clear to me because of what my family did to my aunt who is in her late 60s. She was married to an alcoholic and they led very separate lives. They never divorced due to family pressure. My aunt leads a very miserable life. I am not sure whether I could make such a sacrifice. I don't think many young Sikhs could.

A young man described how his sister was prevented from divorcing her husband:

A meeting was called by the elders. We called them the 'committee', it was solely comprised of men. The only woman was my sister. The men involved included me, my father, my paternal uncle and my paternal granddad. The middleman, the husband, his father, his two older brothers, 1 maternal uncle and two paternal uncles. The men did all the talking. The husband was asked all the questions first and then my sister. She felt very intimidated, and it was clear that at times she was too scared to say anything. They had 4 meetings, each one was male dominated. The final one had a female elder; she was my mum's aunt, because we felt that my sister wasn't being heard. My aunt didn't help much though, the men continued to tell my sister what to do. They didn't make suggestions, nor did they consult her. In the end they wore her down and persuaded her to stay in the marriage for the sake of the family. I initially thought she would leave and not go through the family. She's an educated girl, in a well paid job – she could have started a new life, but instead she put her family first rather than herself, her reason for this is that she didn't want to cause our parents any shame. She's unhappy but she is just getting on with her life – she is doing what women used to do in the past.

It was clear from the interviews that the decision to divorce and the procedure to follow depends on a variety of factors, such as age, caste, religious background and education. Couples who may bypass their parents and use outside counselling services will more likely be from higher educational, occupational and socio-economic backgrounds. When young Sikhs take such action it is because they are questioning and discarding traditional expectations due to their education and financial independence. They are questioning the process, especially with reference to the hierarchy present in the mediation process which is based around age and gender. For example, in most instances the mediators are men over the age of 50. One young woman who was in the process of divorcing her husband who is an alcoholic described this:

My parents called a meeting with my husband and his family. They also invited the middleman and some other elders from the family, like my dad's eldest brother, my husband's *mama* (mother's brother). Altogether, there were seven men in the room and only two women, my mum and me. Apart from my husband and me everyone was over the age of 40. Throughout the meeting mum said nothing. I only got the opportunity to speak when I was asked a question, and there wasn't many. I did try to interrupt on several occasions because I felt something needed to be said, but I was always told to be quiet. The men didn't understand where I was coming from. They just kept telling me what I needed to do to be a good wife, like let him go out with his friends and not nag him, and if he did come home drunk to protect my children from him by keeping them in their room so that they do not witness anything bad. They didn't tell my husband to change or get help. I eventually started divorce proceedings, because the suggestions and recommendations that were made were not appropriate, and put my and my children at risk.

A young couple, both doctors – who stressed that they were happily married – described what procedure they would follow:

If we are not happy, and were ever to separate I think we would first talk amongst ourselves and see if we can resolve things. If it is clear that we cannot I think we would both start proceedings and just inform our parents. I don't think we would take up mediation because I don't think the parents would be able to offer us anything new, so why delay the process (wife agreed). This has nothing to do with being westernised, but more to do with what is the best for the individuals concerned. This is what should be important.

While the belief that divorce is not a problem is held by many graduate members of the second and third generation, there are some Sikhs, irrespective of education or immigration status, who still believe that in all circumstances parents should be involved and that divorce without the parents' involvement is only justified when the situation is clearly intolerable, ie, when it involves domestic violence. For example, young Sikhs who are educated to GCSE or A Level, while believing that divorce is an acceptable option to take if a marriage fails, are more likely to do as they are told out of concern for their family's honour, and fear of being ostracised socially and financially by their family.

One young couple, who both left school at 16 and got married at 18 described how:

> We live our extended family. If anything was to go wrong I (husband) would go first to my parents (wife agreed). This is the done thing.

One young bride from India said:

> If I was having problems I would tell my parents. I know that they are in India, but they will then contact my uncle, who also lives in the UK to intervene. I would do whatever I was told because I am new to the country, but also I don't want to be disowned by my family, because If I was I would have no one.

Despite understanding the need to involve family or the community, it is also clear that most young Sikhs, irrespective of age and education, are conscious of the fact that their elders may not understand the issues involved when a marriage breaks down, and nor how to deal with certain issues. For example, one young lady told me:

> The reasons for divorce and separation today are different from the past and parents ' don't understand this. More and more separations are due to domestic violence, drug or alcohol addiction, or criminal activity. However, some of my older female relatives say that these were present in the past, and that we should just put up with it.

It was also clear that young women did not like the way that Sikh men (elders and middlemen – always men) spoke or dealt with them. Many described how men tend to use an unemotional and reserved style, and tend to be more authoritarian in their decisions and arguments, which are firmly based on customary cultural values. Female mediators, on the other hand use religious and relational arguments based on one's personal responsibility in a relationship to one another, and family to make their case. This was evident to one young man, who was in the final stages of a divorce process:

> Mothers, when they sit you down are very gentle in the way they deal with you. The men on the other hand are very direct and stern in how they question you and when

they make suggestions, this is particularly so when they are dealing with women. They interrogate women and make them feel guilty and bad.

A young woman explained:

My meetings with the elders were useless. They, especially the men didn't understand where I was coming from. My husband had two affairs. After the first I was going to leave but my parents and the elders persuaded me to stay. They said he would change. He didn't, he had another affair. In the mediation after his second affair the men kept telling me that they had spoken to my husband and that he wouldn't do this again, but I wasn't having it. I had made up my mind that I was not going to put up with it. I had dreams and aspirations of what married life would be like – he wasn't fulfilling those so I choose to leave. When I told them this they all got very angry and told me that I was being selfish and not thinking about the family. After the meeting some of the men phoned me and tried to persuade me to change my mind – they kept going on about *izzat*. I didn't listen.

What hurt most was that my mother did tell me that in the past women would turn a blind eye to such indiscretions and that maybe I should do the same for the sake of my reputation. I refused. My mum did then try to make me feel guilty by saying that my younger sister's reputation would be tarnished by my reputation, and that she may find it difficult to find a suitable partner. She was thinking about everyone else, but me.

We do whatever our parents tell us all of our life, and if this one thing doesn't work out then in my opinion you have to do what is right for you.

VI RELIGIOUS MEDIATION

While in the majority of cases where a marriage has broken down family members will attempt to resolve the problems in-house, in the extreme and very rare case where one side simply refuses to reconcile, parents may approach community members[11] or religious leaders, such as a religious elder of a *gurdwara* or a group of five religious leaders called the *Panj Pyare* to mediate. These men will hear the facts of the situation and render a decision as to either allow or disallow the divorce from a faith perspective, as well as a cultural perspective. Despite the existence of this form of mediation there is no one religious leader or religious body in Britain who can define how mediation should be conducted.

It is because Sikhs in the United Kingdom do not have such a body which the community recognises that Sikhs do not use arbitration in religious tribunals like the London Beth Din, or the Shariah Council of the Birmingham Central mosque (Douglas et al 2011 and chapter eleven of this book). One religious leader highlighted:

We do not have official counselling bodies, or such institutions like the Sharia Councils to discuss family issues and mediate between couples. Instead, what we have are religious individuals, affiliated to religious places of worship who may offer counselling and advice. They are able to do this due to their religious authority, which ultimately

---

[11] In India mediation was also carried out by the *Panchat* (village elders).

derives from their reputation. A good mediator is impartial and takes into account the family structure, the family power structures, but also listens to all the parties. It is such religious people who will be turned to, not those who are stuck in the past. To make sure that all religious leaders know how to mediate we need to control this kind of mediation, and we as a community should set up and develop a counselling body.

Sikhs who do use religious leaders are most likely to be from baptised Sikh families, but even then although they may feel obliged to use community or religious forms of dispute resolution in the first instance they are aware that a religious decision is not legislated within Sikhism and has no legal/religious bearing, and that they can go against it. In these instances individuals will just go through the process to tick a box within the family's and the community's mind so that they can then proceed to a divorce without feeling that they have dishonoured anybody. This is evident from the response of one of my respondents who was a *granthi* (religious priest):

We are living in a society where Sikh religious values have been replaced by consumerism and individualism – we see alcohol abuse (both male and female), job related stress and financial insecurity as new causes of divorce. But we also see trivial causes such as incompatibility. I only consent to separation if domestic violence is involved.

In the past you could say something to a woman and she would listen. This is because in the past marriage gave women access to mainstream life. They had to stay within a relationship because to become divorced/separated was viewed as unacceptable and women would be shunned by the community. Also, women stayed because they were dependent on men. Today things have changed. Women are independent and are looking for something different in a partner as to what their mothers were looking for, and they know that if they are not happy then they can divorce. Today, most divorces are instigated by women because they are dissatisfied with their marriages.

One religious leader explained:

I have mediated both for baptised and non-baptised families. I have got the most compliance from the baptised families – they listen to me and take on board the Sikh values that I cite from the Guru Granth Sahib. Non-baptised Sikh families are more sceptical of what I say, especially the youngsters.

Another religious leader highlighted what the change in expectations has lead to:

Whilst we would intervene in the past, today we intervene selectively in marital disputes. Religious leaders are reluctant to intervene in cases of domestic violence, because we didn't know what to do, and we would often send women back to a dangerous situation because we felt that was our religious duty – to uphold the sanctity of marriage. When we have done this sometimes things have gone wrong and we are blamed. Today, most religious leaders do not intervene in matters which we define as belonging to the private domain. If I had to I would only do it if the individuals concerned were baptised Sikhs.

VII CONCLUSION

This chapter has looked at the Sikh cultural processes involved in mediation when marriages break down. While discussing the processes involved it has become clear that, whereas in the past the initial use of mediation was successful and outcomes were favourable, this is not the case today. It is also evident from the interviews that the strong cultural belief in family mediation means Sikhs have not fully utilised professional mediation, or, as the Sikhs call it, 'outside counselling', due to the belief that if you require outside intervention to solve marital problems, then the marriage is not worth saving, but most importantly the use of professional mediation will give other members of the community the impression that one has lost one's cultural and religious values and become too westernised.

This however, does not mean that the religious and cultural understandings of marriage and divorce, or of the mediation process brought by Sikh parents when they migrated to the UK, have remained static. Cultural norms, values, beliefs and practices of the Sikhs have been 'adapted' and 'altered', particularly by young Sikhs who have adopted a perception and acceptance of divorce and mediation which is similar to that of their British peers (Jhutti 1998; Ballard 1994a and 1994b).

Sikhs have become 'skilled cultural navigators' (Ballard 1994a: 31) who have identified to varying degrees with Western practices without forgoing their own ethnic group allegiance. By engaging and negotiating both Western and Sikh cultural and traditional practices in the realm of marriage and marital breakdown, to achieve outcomes that meet their needs, young Sikhs have developed an '*Angrezi*' way of divorcing with reference to mediation (Menski 1994). However, what happens, and the processes employed when a marriage breaks down, varies. This is because the Sikh community is not a homogenous or monolithic entity, but is highly diverse due to caste, regional and socio-economic differences. This variation is further compounded by the process of acculturation and assimilation, which is dependent on age, occupation and economic position. Individuals integrate to varying degrees, and their understanding and interpretation of religious and cultural law will differ from one Sikh to the next.

For example, one group of young Sikhs, university educated, professionals and financially independent, are integrating, assimilating, separating and marginalising themselves from their community, and as a result are not complying with Sikh mediation. They are most likely to view Western mediation positively and are reluctant to use traditional mediation because they feel that the religious leaders or parents are not equipped to deal with complex matters that arise today when a couple separate. However, most will go through some form of family mediation to preserve their status. Or, they may use Sikh mediation together with the secular divorce processes so as not to be ostracised by their family or community. On the other hand, there are young Sikhs who are pursuing a moderate approach to assimilation, and are less acculturated into British society. These Sikhs have held on to traditional values and beliefs and are far more likely to use family mediation due to the negative cultural pressure and cultural taboos against separation.

Whatever the social or educational background, all young Sikhs are also conscious of the fact that, while the community and family provide protection, they can also be very rigid in their beliefs, behaviour and recommendations, and may fail to recognise that individual and group understandings might vary and diverge, particularly with reference to community and marriage. Although acculturation and education have meant that young Sikhs view mediation and divorce in a different way from their parents and grandparents (they no longer readily accept the religious or cultural mode of mediation), the extent to which young Sikhs will entirely replace the cultural and traditional mediation system with the secular divorce processes is questionable, for while some Sikhs will approach changes with eagerness, others will be cautious due to notions of honour (*izzat*) and shame (*behzti*), which still ensure that most third and fourth generation British Sikhs use family or community-based mediation in the first instance to save a failing marriage.

Sikh parents, aware of their children's changing needs and expectations, have tried to accommodate changes, although rather reluctantly. They have realised that it is better to make these changes, rather than have their children turn to Western mediators, who are using mediation which is focused on principles of individual choice and personal freedom, grounded in the notion of individual rights which are in conflict with Sikh principles. Parents argue that the assumption that the individual is independent from family and community, fails to capture the reality of Sikh experience. Sikhs are socially interdependent through family and the arranged marriage process, and as a result Sikh identity develops because of community and family. Thus, the identity of a young Diaspora Sikh is a combination of traditional Sikh and modern Western culture, because, despite Western influences, the Sikh cultural heritage remains the major source of influence in all aspects of life, but particularly marriage. Western divorce processes fail to encompass the concept of 'community' and family adequately, and would cut young Sikhs off from a support system that is available when marriages break down.

As a consequence of this negotiation, Sikhs have developed two parallel systems which work alongside each other: religious and family mediation first and secular divorce processes (sometimes including mediation) if required. What is clear though is that Sikhs will not ask for a separate legal system to deal with divorce. Instead, what they are doing is employing/tying their practice of mediation and marital dispute resolution into the secular legal system of the land. It is also clear that without creating a 'plural jurisdiction' (Williams 2008) both systems can work alongside each other as long as there is a constructive accommodation by all mediators of the legal, but also the cultural and religious, context that the couple has grown up in.

GLOSSARY

anand karaj	Sikh marriage ceremony
angrezi	Asian/British
Behzti	Shame
granthi/giani	A Sikh priest
gurdwara	A Sikh temple
guru granth sahib (GG)	The sacred text that contains the compositions of the Sikh Gurus, as well as those of Hindu and Muslim saints. It is at the centre of all Sikh ceremonies and rituals
Izzat	Honour
lavan	The four verses read as the couple circumambulate the GG
khalsa	Literally, 'pure ones', the fellowship of Sikhs founded by Gobind Singh, the tenth Guru, in 1699
Panchat	Village elders
panj pyare	Literally, the 'five beloved'. The name given to the five men who were prepared to give up their faith. They were the first five members of the *khalsa*
shabad	Verse or hymn
vachola	Male matchmaker or middleman: the arranger of the marriage.

REFERENCES

Ballard, R (1972) 'Family Organisation among the Sikhs in Britain' 2 *New Community* 12–24.

—— (1982) 'South Asian families' in RN Rapport (ed), *Families in Britain* (London, Routledge, British Family Research Committee).

—— (1994) *Desh Pardesh. The South Asian Presence in Britain* (London, Hurst & Co Publishers Ltd).

—— (1994a) 'The Emergence of Desh Pardesh' in R Ballard (ed), *Desh Pardesh. The South Asian Presence in Britain* (London, Hurst & Co Publishers Ltd)1–34.

—— (1994b) 'Differentiation and Disjunction' in R Ballard (ed), *Desh Pardesh. The South Asian Presence in Britain* (London, Hurst & Co Publishers Ltd) 88–116.

Douglas, G, Doe, N, Gilliat-Ray, S, Sandberg R and Khan, A (2011) 'Marriage and Divorce in Religious Courts: A Case Study' 41 *Family Law* 961.

Dustin, M and Phillips, A (2008) 'Whose Agenda is it? Abuses of Women and Abuses of "Culture" in Britain' 8 *Ethnicities* 405.

Griffiths, J (1986) 'What is legal pluralism?' 24 *Journal of Legal Pluralism* 1–55.

Jhutti, J (1998) DPhil Thesis 'A Study of Changes in Marriage Practices Among the Sikhs of Britain' (Oxford, University of Oxford).

Jhutti-Johal, J (2010) 'The Role of Women in their Religious Institutions: A Contemporary Account' in D Jakobsch (ed), *Sikhism and Women: History, Texts and Experience* (India, Oxford University Press).

—— (2011) *Sikhism Today* (London, Continuum).

—— (2012) 'Sikhism and Mental Illness: Negotiating Competing Cultures' in D Cave and R Sachs Norris (eds), *The Body and Religion, Modern Science and the Construction of Religious Meaning* (Netherlands, Brill).

Menski, W (1994) 'Angrezi Shari'a: Plural Arrangements in Family Law by Muslims in Britain', unpublished paper (SOAS, University of London).

—— (2006) 'Rethinking Legal Theory in the Light of South-North Migration' in W Menski and P Shah (eds), *Migration, Diasporas and Legal Systems in Europe*. (London, Routledge Cavendish) 13–28.

Montgomery, M (1992) 'Legislating for a Multi-Faith Society' in B Hepple and EM Sczyrack (eds), *Discrimination: The Limits of Law* (London, Mansell).

Parekh, B (1990) 'Britain and the Social Logic of Pluralism' in *Britain: A Plural Society*. (London, Commission for Racial Equality).

—— (1995) 'British Citizenship and Cultural Difference' in W Kymlicka (ed), *The Rights of Minority Cultures* (Oxford, Oxford University Press).

Pearl, A (1987) 'South Asian Immigrant Communities and English Family Law 1971–1987' XIV *New Community* 84.

Phillips, A (2003) 'When Culture means Gender: Issues of Cultural Defence in the English Courts' 66 *Modern Law Review* 510–31.

Phillips, A and Dustin, M (2004) 'UK Initiatives on Forced Marriage: Regulation, Dialogue and Exit' 52(3) *Political Studies* 531–51.

Singh, G (1978) *Sri Guru Granth Sahib: English Version* 4 vols (Chandigarh, India, World Sikh University Press).

Singh, G and Tatla DS (2006) *Sikhs in Britain: The Making of a Community* (London, Zed Books Ltd).

Williams, R (2008) 'Civil and Religious Law in England: A Religious Perspective' 10 *Ecclesiastical Law Journal* 262.

13

Managing Expectations: Negotiating Succession under Plural Legal Orders in Botswana

ANNE GRIFFITHS

I INTRODUCTION

THE OVERARCHING THEME of this volume is an investigation of the ways in which law responds or ought to respond to different family practices. It explores the extent to which these practices are to be viewed merely as an aspect of diversity that is to be accommodated by a legal system, or as representing an aspect of deviance that a legal system needs to redress. Such a focus raises questions about how law is to be perceived and identified. For the application of different models of recognition may radically transform our perceptions about how to view family relations and practices within their own social constellations, as well as within the broader polities to which they belong. Put another way, it raises questions about legal pluralism and the power of different frameworks that shape legal analysis (Hellum et al 2010) that may range from the recognition of differing legal orders within the nation-state, to a more far reaching and open-ended concept of law that does not necessarily depend on state recognition for its validity (von Benda-Beckmann et al 2009).

In tackling the place of legal norms and practices of minority groups, viewed from the perspective of ethnic or religious minorities within a secular state system, or a secular minority within a religious state, the chapters in this collection range from adopting a liberal, ethical framework through which to view the dilemmas of accommodating minority laws within a legal system (Eekelaar, chapter one) and a critique of this approach (Shah, chapter three), to an approach that rejects a dichotomy between state and non-state laws on the basis that minority legal orders should not be viewed as in opposition to or resistant to state laws but should be seen as part of the community that constitutes the state (Bano, chapter four). This chapter investigates the role that gender plays in creating a 'minority' status for women in relation to succession in Botswana, despite the fact that demographically women were[1] and continue to form the majority of the population (van Klaveren et al 2009: 31–32). For despite their numerical superiority, the power of gender derived from the social roles attributed to men and women within families and households has had an adverse impact on women's capacities to negotiate access to resources and claims to property in succession. This was the case under both common law (that was based on Western style law)[2] and customary law (associated with Africans)[3] that existed within the Bechuanaland Proctectorate (1885–1966) under British indirect rule, and that continued to exist within the plural legal system of the newly independent Botswana that came into being in 1966.

Based on ethnographic research carried out in Botswana in the 1980s[4] and on more recent research funded by the Leverhulme Trust in 2009–2010,[5] my chapter investigates the shifting norms that have brought about women having greater access to resources and property, including land. It highlights what is taking place on the ground as an everyday part of the life course, focusing on uncontested and general transmissions of property through land certificates rather than on disputes.[6] It adopts this approach because it has long been acknowledged that taking disputes as a starting point for studying law is problematic and that there is a need to study trouble-less as well as 'trouble' cases (Llewellyn and Hoebel 1941; Holleman 1973). This approach provides a perspective on order in everyday life that is a dimension often missing from legal analysis. Such a perspective is important because it highlights what is often invisible in legal research, namely the context in which ordinary negotiations among family members can lead to voluntary agreements being reached over property that may differ from those reached according to formal legal norms and the projected legal standards that may have very little to do with reality.

Taking account of the varying dimensions forms part of an ethnographic approach to legal analysis – one that provides a context for studying law (Griffiths 2009: 164–86). It supplies specific data on the concrete, lived experiences that informs people's lives that not only documents individual's experiences, but traces the connections of these persons to the broader social polity to which they belong.

---

[1] See Household Income and Expenditure Surveys for 1993–94 and 2002–03 (Government of Botswana, Central Statistics Office).

[2] This is defined as 'any law, whether written or unwritten, in force in Botswana, other than customary law' (Customary Law [Application and Ascertainment Act] No 51 (1969) s 2).

[3] This is defined as 'the customary law of [a] tribe or tribal community [within Botswana] so far as it is not incompatible with the provision of any written law or contrary to morality, humanity, or natural justice' (Customary Law [Application and Ascertainment Act] No 51 (1969) s 2).

[4] For details see Griffiths (1997).

[5] This focused on the Gendered Dynamics of Land Tenure in southern Africa and involved a variety of methods including archival research, examination of court records, participant observation, interviews and extended oral life histories (over five generations) of family groups that built on my earlier research.

[6] The research covered disputes in both informal and formal legal settings including the Kweneng Land Board, the Customary Court of Appeal, the Land Tribunal, the High Court and the Court of Appeal but these will not be covered here.

A number of chapters in this volume have stressed the need 'for law to engage with the experienced normative order or living law of social groups and communities' (Ribot, chapter sixteen) and the 'need for good empirical research' that may lead to 'a greater understanding of how ethnic minorities use official systems' that enables us to 'understand how norms are embedded' (Shah, chapter three). My research seeks to provide this perspective by highlighting the social processes that are central to people's lives and which frame their approaches to law. By taking account of the ways in which individuals form part of networks which shape their world and channel their access to resources a grounded perspective is acquired that in this chapter deals with the conditions under which land is transmitted from one generation to another on succession. It has the advantage of providing more than a snapshot of a situation at a particular moment, as it is based on a longitudinal perspective that allows for a more in-depth and nuanced analysis of continuities and differences over time. This creates space for shifts in people's and institutional perceptions to surface that my chapter traces through an analysis of how communal and individual rights may be negotiated within the contexts of succession and the transmission of property. In particular, it examines the transmission of land which is a key component in providing for the alleviation of poverty and wellbeing of individuals, families and households. For as the government of Botswana notes, 'studies worldwide have shown that the impact of population growth on poverty is strongest at the micro-level, that is, at the level of households and communities acknowledging that female-headed households are among the poorest in the country'[7] and that 'poverty remains one of the major development challenges for Botswana'.[8] In tackling poverty, how land – a key resource for their livelihoods – is acquired and transferred, is an important consideration, especially for women and children whom it is generally recognised feature disproportionately among the poor (Ruzvidzo and Tiagha 2005).

II BACKGROUND TO THE RESEARCH

Before turning to constraints on women's access to property through succession, I would like to give some background to the research. Botswana is a large country, comparable in size to France or Texas in the United States. It has a relatively small population that currently stand at around 1.8 million.[9] One-third of this population, however, is clustered around the capital city of Gaborone and its ever expanding peri-urban area stretching into Kweneng district where I carried out

---

[7] *National Development Plan 6 (NDP 6) 1981–1991*: 21 (Gaberone, Ministry of Finance and Development Planning) 21.

[8] *National Development Plan 9 (NDP9) 2003-04-2008-09*: 18 (Gaberone, Ministry of Finance and Development Planning) 24.

[9] In 2006, the total population of Botswana was estimated at 1,773,249 in the *Republic of Botswana, Botswana Demographic Survey* 2006 (Gaborone, Central Statistics Office, 2006).

my research from 1981–89 and from 2009–2010. My most recent study focused on the Land Board of Kweneng district, because in its 5000 km jurisdiction, the board administers the entire spectrum of land allocation in Botswana, from rural cattle posts to peri-urban and urban residential and industrial areas. It has also been the subject of extensive litigation in the courts. Furthermore, this Land Board is based in the village of Molepolole (population around 80,000),[10] which is the capital and regional centre of Kweneng, where I carried out fieldwork between 1982 and 1989 and so was an appropriate site for my ongoing research. Part of this earlier research involved life histories of family groups from Mosotho *kgotla* (a *kgotla* is a designated space, a ward, associated with land, buildings, people and a court) covering three generations, including the Makokwe and Radipati families. The recent research has extended this so that I now have data for five generations documenting continuities and differences in intergenerational access to land.

At the centre of the Kwena polity ('tribe') its customary jurisdiction is exercised through *Dikgosi* ('chiefs') who operate through a *kgotla* system. It is the area within a town or village, or a small rural hamlet, assigned by the *Kgosi* (chief) to a group of people for their residential area. Houses and other buildings are set around an inner courtyard. A *kgotla* takes its name from the headman appointed at the time of its organisation by the chief. Traditionally, all *kgotla* members were related, and the headman was the senior male in the kinship group. For several decades – especially after the establishment of Land Boards – *kgotla* residents need no longer be related, but they are still subject to the authority of the headman in matters covered by traditional law. In the second sense, a *kgotla* is the tribal chief's or ward headman's court where disputes are adjudicated.

III PAST CONSTRAINTS ON WOMEN'S ACCESS TO PROPERTY AND LAND THROUGH SUCCESSION

From my earlier research, it is clear that transmission of property among families is focused on maintaining future generations, with emphasis on preserving assets for children. Given the patrilineal nature of Tswana society – through the man's father where the parents are married, through the woman's father where they are not – it is not surprising that male offspring are privileged over female offspring when it comes to inheritance under customary law, with the eldest son receiving the greatest share of all the property in recognition of the responsibilities that he adopts as head of the family. For this reason, he not only had the role of custodian with regard to his children, but had responsibility for representing and maintaining extended kin (beyond his immediate nuclear family)

---

[10] As projected in the Kweneng District Development Plan 6 (KDDP6), 2003–09 at 9. It is said to retain 'its position as the biggest urban village in Botswana' 9KDDP6, Foreword (i) (Gaborone, Kweneng District Council, Kweneng District Development Committee and the Ministry of Local Government).

where he was the senior male among the network of family members. Thus, family groups such as the Makokwe family group that featured in my Molepolole research were linked into cooperative networks extending across several households that contributed to the livelihoods of individuals and kin through pooling of resources among and between generations.

Among children, daughters inherited less than their brothers because it was envisaged that they would marry and go to live among their husband's relatives where their husbands would establish their own *lolwapas* (residential yards). Through marriage, these women's children would be affiliated with their husband's family group where property devolves from father to son. What daughters tended to inherit was their mother's personal property, such as clothes and domestic utensils. They might also inherit fields where these had been worked by their mothers. In contrast, brothers inherited ploughs, cattle, guns and other family property, including land, their father may have had. Among siblings, property was not shared equally but depended on birth order, as underlined in discussions below.

Among Bakwena, as with other Tswana polities (or *merafe*), it was common for parents to link brothers and sisters creating a special relationship between these individuals and their offspring in successive generations, forming a set of supportive relations. In the past, this was particularly relevant for the circulation of property because where *bogadi* (bridewealth) was paid for a daughter, the cattle received for her would go towards fulfilling her linked brother's requirement when he married and so reciprocity and obligations were constituted through ongoing generations. While linking is not referred to today, nonetheless sibling relationships continue to have an important role in maintaining family relationships and in handling inheritance. Ever since the 1930s, outmigration by significant numbers of men disrupted labour patterns, marriage has featured less prominently and large numbers of women have children but remain unmarried (Schapera 1948: 173). In these cases, where they are unable to acquire land and build their own households, they remain in the natal family compound sharing the space with other siblings and members of the household who reside there. This may create overcrowding often leading to disputes, but it may also result in their own sibling cohort making over control of the residence to them, which is contrary to customary norms of inheritance discussed below.

Conversations with customary officials, such as ward headmen in Molepolole in 2010, had much in common with earlier discussions on inheritance in the 1980s, although there were marked changes. What emerged from these dialogues was that where inheritance is concerned, sex, birth order and status continue to occupy an important role. With regard to land, headmen from Dikoloing ward explained that 'in our culture there were two ploughing fields, one allocated to the mother [wife] and one for the husband'. All agreed that the mother's field would be inherited by a daughter and that a father's field would be inherited by a son. They went on to note that 'usually the field allocated to the mother is allocated to the youngest daughter provided she is not married' and that 'the father's field goes to the eldest son' who 'will also be given the borehole and a gun'. However, they were careful to stress 'that even if it is done like this [according to tradition/culture] the children have to meet and agree even although they know that according to our tradition it has to go to the eldest son'.

When asked what happens to the residential yard, with its front and back house, the headmen from Mokgalo state that the 'front house is given to the eldest son and the back house goes to the eldest daughter'. Recognition of the eldest son is important because he represents the family in public matters, but this view was challenged by headmen from other wards who stated that it was the youngest son who inherited the residential yard. In interviews outside Molepolole, among government officials, civil servants and professionals such as lawyers, the view was expressed that it was the youngest son who got the residential yard, although some claimed that there was a difference between the north and the south of the country, with the north giving this property to the eldest son, and the south – where Molepolole is situated – going to the youngest. Given the fact that the distribution of assets is unequal, members of Mokgalo ward observed that in terms of the general distribution of the estate (excluding the residential yard) 'young children complain a lot about most of the possessions going to the eldest son. It [property division] is a very difficult issue'.

In some cases, following traditional practices, property was earmarked for certain individuals during the parents' lifetime. This was especially the case with cattle and sometimes daughters as well as sons were beneficiaries. The senior men of Dikoloing ward acknowledge that it happens 'especially with regard to livestock. Children are given cattle while their parents are still alive'. They explain, however, that while cattle may be earmarked for individuals 'that does not mean that you have complete control of that animal'. If the family is in need 'that animal can be taken and slaughtered [or sold]'. While some daughters may acquire livestock through earmarking or inheritance (particularly where a mother had beasts acquired through the sale of produce from her fields and therefore viewed as part of her estate) the general view was that 'in our society boys usually look after livestock and women do domestic activities. Boys inherit livestock and women will inherit household equipment'.

My earlier research documented how women generally found themselves at a disadvantage with regard to acquiring resources because of their position within the hierarchy of a family network constructed around patrilineal norms that subordinated their claims to property.

IV SHIFTING PARAMETERS ALLOWING FOR CHANGE

What is clear from my recent research is that, while there is continuity in the upholding of some customary norms, there has also been a shift in others. For example, in cases of divorce, especially those recorded in the High Court, women now feature as custodians of the family residence for their children.

This means that the customary land certificate will bear their name, instead of that of their ex-husband. It is important to note that this recognition only exists to enable them to hold the property until their children come of age. Changes in the law have made it possible for married women to hold property in their own right. Under the Abolition of Marital Power Act 2004, women married under community of property laws are no longer subject to their husband's exercise of marital power over matrimonial property. This means that married women can now acquire land certificates in their own right as amendments have also been made to the Deeds Registry Act.[11]

Similarly, the position of widows seems to have acquired a different status. This is evident from headmen in Molepolole acknowledging that today 'when the husband dies everything is transferred to the wife including the brand of cattle' whereas in my discussion in the 1980s, it was the deceased's brothers and uncles who were said to oversee the estate and determine transfers to beneficiaries. What is clear is that norms for both written and unwritten law prove to be mutually constitutive in their shift towards a more inclusive approach to women that removes barriers underpinning their minority status, regardless of whether they are located within the formally designated systems of 'common' or 'customary' law. Within this shifting milieu of institutional and legal change, there is also the situation of family members reaching their own voluntary agreements about distribution of land on succession that may differ in practice from the established norms of customary law with regard to birth order, sex and status of the beneficiary. This is recognised by the headmen themselves who stressed that what is central to the process of inheritance is the consultation and consensus reached between family members – especially the deceased's children – as to how the property should be distributed.

V ADMINISTRATION OF LAND UNDER CUSTOMARY TENURE

To obtain a sense of the extent to which families substituted their own decisions in place of recognised customary norms with regard to beneficiaries – especially women – I examined land certificates at Kweneng Sub-Land Board dealing with transfers of both residential and arable land. This is because – while there are three types of land tenure in Botswana: state land (used to develop cities, commercial urban activities); freehold (a miniscule segment, recognising nineteenth-century grants to South Africans); and customary land tenure, the latter represents 70 per cent of land tenure in the country and forms the basis of tenure in Kweneng district. Today, land under customary tenure is administered by Land Boards under the Tribal Land Act 1968, passed barely two years after the country acquired its independence. It promoted substantial changes to the dominant Tswana tribal systems of land tenure which had been left intact during the colonial era. The Act handed over powers previously vested under

[11] See s 18 of the Deeds Registry Act [Cap 33:02].

customary law in chiefs and their representatives to newly-established Land Boards. There are currently 12 Land Boards throughout the country.

A What Rights Land Boards Can Grant: Customary and Common Law

In dealing with tribal land, Land Boards could issue customary land certificates for residence (*motse*), arable agriculture (*tshimo*) and grazing (*moraka*) but not hunting. These certificates cannot be given for non-customary uses such as trading, manufacturing, business or commerce.

To deal with these latter, Land Boards were given powers to allocate common law rights under leases. The introduction of common law leases on tribal land was designed to commercialise land rights in rural areas. This was in the expectation that lessees would 'develop commercial ranches and reduce pressure on communal land'. One of the most important reasons for pursuing common-law title and leases is that it can be used as a security for loans that are granted to develop businesses or property. Ordinary customary grants cannot because they are not regarded as marketable securities by formal lending institutions.

To acquire a sense of women's access to land (beyond life histories) my recent research involved examining land certificates at Kweneng Sub-Land Board. This involved examining records for both residential and arable land over ten years (from 1999 to 2009); 4041 certificates were examined. These dealt with residential plot allocations, transfers and extensions, as well as field allocations/registrations, transfers and extensions. In addition, I examined 1200 leases of which 600 were residential and 600 were commercial. The limitations of written records are well known but it was important to examine these data because there is very little empirical evidence on the extent to which women are featuring when it comes to applying for land. As Ng'on'ola, professor of law at Botswana University, observed to me:

> Land Boards claim to follow a gender neutral policy on allocations. But it would be interesting to apply your type of analysis to the actual situation on the ground. There is not much information on how women have been faring in their dealings with Land Boards (personal communication, 2003).

B Persons who may Claim Land under these Conditions from Land Boards

Initially the Act sought to retain tribal affiliation as the prerequisite for occupation and use of land in tribal areas. This was amended in 1993 to provide that

> all rights and title to land in each tribal area . . . vest in the Land Board . . . in trust for the benefit and advantage of citizens of Botswana and for the purpose of promoting the economic and social development of all the peoples of Botswana.[12]

---

[12] Under s 10(1).

This means that any citizen of Botswana can apply to any Land Board in the country for land. The importance here is that land is no longer linked to tribal affiliation. This has been the subject of strong contestation.

Membership of Land Boards is derived from a number of sources including those elected by people living within the jurisdiction of the Land Board, those appointed by the minister, plus appointees from the Ministries of Agriculture and of Commerce and Industry. Chiefs were initially included as ex-officio members of the Board then removed, and I gather that the latest amendment to proposed legislation is considering writing them in again. When my research was carried out, Kweneng Sub-Land Board was operating under par with only nine instead of twelve members. Of these members, elected at the chief's *kgotla* or appointed by the ministry, four were women. In 1973, subordinate Land Boards were created and empowered to allocate land under customary law for residential purposes, ploughing, grazing cattle and other stock and of other 'communal' uses. There are seven such Land Boards in Kweneng.[13]

i Dealing with Land in Relation to Inheritance

While Land Boards are responsible for the allocation and transfer of all tribal land, when it comes to questions of inheritance, they refer the matter to the tribal authorities under the jurisdiction of the chief and the chief's representatives. Once these have made a determination, the matter is remitted back to the Land Board to reject or implement the transfer by amending the land certificate. In this process the norms of customary law are applied, unless there is a written will that supersedes its application, or some other factor operates to remove it from the operation of the customary system.

ii Findings from Customary Land Certificates

To obtain a sense of the extent to which families substituted their own decisions as to beneficiaries, especially with regard to women, I examined land certificates at Kweneng Sub-Land Board dealing with transfers of both residential and arable land from 1999 to 2009. Inheritance involves the transfer of land that must be approved and certified by the Land Board through an alteration to the land certificate. And now we get to the problem of written records! It is important to note that it was not possible to conduct a random sample of certificates for each year because of the state of Sub-Land Board records. Relevant information specifying the sex, age and marital status of both transferor and transferee, and whether or not they are related, is not always available given the failure to keep adequate records in the past. Inadequate record keeping has been a complaint ever since Land Boards were established and surfaces time and again in appeals

---

[13] These are Lephephe, Thamaga, Mogoditshane, Letlhakeng, Lentsweletau, Molepolole (Sub-Land Board) and Motokwe.

taken to the Land Tribunal. This meant that my research assistant, Phidelia Dintwe,[14] and I were limited to examining those records that we could actually get our hands on. Of the 4041 certificates that we studied, 629 involved residential transfers and 367 dealt with fields. In addition, 259 appointments recorded in the chief's *kgotla* for 2009, dealing with the administration of deceased persons' estates, were scrutinised to find out the sex of those appointed to administer the estate and the degree to which there was a family relationship between the appointee and the deceased. Given concerns over property grabbing – especially by brothers and uncles of the deceased in the past – seeing who acquires authority to administrate an estate is important with regard to who has legal control over it, although it may not prevent de facto seizing of assets.

iii Residential Transfers

Not all transfers involve cases of inheritance. While customary land cannot be sold, developments on such land can be sold subject to approval by the Land Board. Out of the 629 residential transfers, 327 were to women, 297 were to men and five whose gender was unclear.[15] Thus women, with 52 per cent of transfers, slightly outnumbered men with 47 per cent. Of these transfers, 189 (on the information available) were to parties that were related, that is 30 per cent, although the actual numbers may be higher. This is because application forms that should have been lodged with the certificates, recording gender, relationship of transferor to transferee, marital status, etc were often missing so that data were lacking. This was particularly the case for the years from 1999 to 2004.

For the years from 2005 to 2009 we have a total of 436 transfers with full information. These break down in terms of transferees as follows (Tables 1 and 2):

Table 1: All residential transfers to women and men

Year	Wt-re	Wt-no	Ta-wom	Mt-re	Mt-no	Ta-men	Tt-W+M
2009	41	62	103	26	61	87	190
2008	15	23	38	10	20	30	68
2007	17	14	31	13	15	28	59
2006	12	7	19	15	8	23	42
2005	20	18	38	20	19	39	77
Total	105	124	229	84	123	207	436

[14] I am indebted to Phidelia, Kawina Power and Boineelo Baakile for all their support and assistance with the research.

[15] In Botswana citizens have an identity card, an Omang, whose fifth number reveals the sex of the holder. If it is a 1 it is male and if it is a 2 it is female. Where this information was not available or clearly incorrect the name was used, but it should be noted that there are many names in Botswana where the sex of the person is ambiguous and therefore cannot be verified without further information.

Key to Table 1

Wt-re = total number of transfers to women where parties related
Wt-no = total number of transfers to women where no information on relationship
Ta-wom = total number of all transfers to women for the year
Mt-re = total number of transfers to men where parties related
Mt-no = total number of transfers to men where no information on relationship
Ta-men = total number of all transfers to men for the year
Tt-W+M = total number of all transfers to women and men *for the year.*

Table 2: Residential transfers according to relationship data

Year	Wt-re	Mt-re	Tr-W+M	Wt-no	Mt-no	Tn-W+M	Tt-W+M
2009	41	26	67	62	61	123	190
2008	15	10	25	23	20	43	68
2007	17	13	30	14	15	29	59
2006	12	15	27	7	8	15	42
2005	20	20	40	18	19	37	77
Total	105	84	189	124	123	247	436

Key

Wt-re = total number of transfers to women where parties related
Mt-re = total number of transfers to men where parties related
Tr-W+M = total number of transfers to women and men for the year where parties related
Wt-no = total number of transfers to women where no information on relationship
Mt-no = total number of transfers to men where no information on relationship
Tn-W+M= total number of transfers to women and men for the year where no information on relationship
Tt-W+M = total number of all transfers to women and men for the year.

From these records, we find women featuring as transferees along with men. It appears that there are more transfers where parties are not related, but as I said earlier, some of these may simply not have documented an existing relationship. On the other hand, I am not surprised by this finding because people do transfer residential plots for money, especially in the catchment area for the capital city, Gaborone, where there is huge pressure on land. The number of transfers to women and men appear to be more or less equal, with slightly more to women.

Table 3: Residential transfers – relationships between transferee and transferor 2005–09

Relation	2009	2008	2007	2006	2005	Women	Men	Total
Daughter	21	10	10	8	10	59		59
Son	16	4	7	8	13		48	48
Wife	5		2	2	5	13	1	14
Sister	5	2	2	1	2	12		12
Brother	1	4	2	3	2		12	12
Nephew	3	2	1	3	2		11	11
Niece	2		2		2	6		6
Cousin	4		1		1	4	2	6
Gson	4				1		5	5
Gdaughter	1	2	1			4		4
Uncle	1		1		1		3	3
Uns relative	2			1		2	1	3
Mother	1			1		2		2
Father			1				1	1
Aunt		1				1		1
Dau-in-Law	1					1		1
Other					1	1		1
Husband								0
Son-in-Law								0
Total	67	25	30	27	40	105	84	189

Where parties were related, the majority of transfers involved direct descendants of the nuclear family, that is, daughters and sons – 57 per cent of the transfers. Among this group, there were more transfers to daughters than to sons. These results suggest that property is being circulated and transmitted among a smaller, more nuclear family rather than among more extended kin.

It is clear from examining these certificates that in 189 cases where parties are recorded as related transfers are a form of inheritance (Table 3). This is because the transfer is supported by a written agreement made by family members and witnessed by their local headman. In most of these cases – 129 out of 189 – the transfer is recorded as being post-mortem. This may be contrasted with those cases for which there is no relationship information, where the overwhelming majority of transfers, 211 of 247, are inter-vivos.

iv Field Transfers

Out of the 246 transfers compiled for the years from 2005 to 2009, a higher proportion went to men: 59 per cent compared with 41 per cent of women (Tables 4 and 5). However, it must be noted that it was particularly hard to get access to data on fields as many of the records appear to have been misplaced in the move to the sub-land board's new premises. Finding women less represented than men was somewhat surprising given my earlier findings from the life histories where this was one type of property that women did appear to inherit and pass on.

Table 4: All field transfers to women and men

Year	Wt-re	Wt-no	Ta-wom	Mt-re	Mt-no	Ta-men	Tt-W+M
2009	21	21	42	20	45	64	106
2008	17	6	23	18	17	35	58
2007	10	6	16	4	7	11	27
2006	0	8	8	7	12	19	27
2005	3	8	11	4	13	17	28
Total	51	49	100	53	94	146	246

Key

Wt-re	=	total number of transfers to women where parties related
Wt-no	=	total number of transfers to women where no information on relationship
Ta-wom	=	total number of all transfers to women for the year
Mt-re	=	total number of transfers to men where parties related
Mt-no	=	total number of transfers to men where no information on relationship
Ta-men	=	total number of all transfers to men for the year
Tt-W+M	=	total number of all transfers to women and men for the year.

Table 5: Field transfers according to relationship data

Year	Wt-re	Mt-re	Tr-W+M	Wt-no	Mt-no	Tn-W+M	Tt-W+M
2009	22	19	41	20	45	65	106
2008	17	18	35	6	17	23	58
2007	11	3	14	5	8	13	27
2006	0	7	7	8	12	20	27
2005	3	4	7	8	13	21	28
Total	53	51	104	47	95	142	246

Key to Table 5

Wt-re	=	total number of transfers to women where parties related
Mt-re	=	total number of transfers to men where parties related
Tr-W+M	=	total number of transfers to women and men for the year where parties related
Wt-no	=	total number of transfers to women where no information on relationship
Mt-no	=	total number of transfers to men where no information on relationship
Tn-W+M	=	total number of transfers to women and men for the year where no information on relationship
Tt-W+M	=	total number of all transfers to women and men for the year.

Where parties were related the majority of field transfers, as with residential plots, were to sons and daughters (70 per cent of cases) with overall numbers of women and men almost equally split between 51 women and 53 men, most transfers were post-mortem (Table 6).

Table 6: Field transfers – relationships between transferee and transferor 2005–09

Rel	2009	2008	2007	2006	2005	Women	Men	Total
Daughter	17	11	9		2	39		39
Son	14	12	1	4	3		34	34
Nephew	3	3	1	2			9	9
Wife		4	1			5		5
Other	1	1	1	1			4	4
Brother	2	1					3	3
Gson		1	1		1		3	3
Niece	1	1				2		2
Cousin		1			1	2		2
Dau-in-Law	2					2		2
Sister	1					1		1
Husband								0
Mother								0
Father								0
Aunt								0
Uncle								0
Gdaughter								0
Son-in-Law								0
Uns relative								0
Total	41	35	14	7	7	51	53	104

When it comes to status, 51 per cent of the residential transfers involve women and men who are single compared with 31 per cent who are married. Out of those who are single, the majority are to be found clustered in the 21–50 age group, whereas among those that are married, the majority are to be found in the 26–45 age group. The picture emerging from field transfers is somewhat different (although it must be viewed with caution given the problems with acquiring data were outlined earlier). Out of the certificates that were located, 46 per cent represented transferees who were married and of these around one-third were women and two-thirds men. The majority of these were located in the 31–55 age group. The single transferees amounted to 34 per cent of the total number of transfers and the majority of these were in the 21–50 age group (Tables 7 and 8).

Table 7: Residential transfers – total breakdown by age, status and sex

Age	Single		Married		Widowed		Divorced		Unclear		Total
	Wom	Men	Wom	Men	Wom	Men	Wom	Men	Wom	Men	
13	2										2
16–20	4	6	1								11
21–25	14	17	1								32
26–30	23	30	8	2	1				1		65
31–35	23	12	8	15	3		1		1	1	64
36–40	13	9	7	20		1	1		1	1	53
41–45	14	11	5	19	3		2	1	1		56
46–50	20	2	7	8	4		1		2	1	45
51–55	6	4	2	7	6			2	2	1	30
56–60	3	1	6	4	1					1	16
61–65	2		2	2					1		7
66–70	3		3	1	5				1		13
71–75		1		3					1		5
76–80		1		2		1					4
81–85					1						1
unclear	1	1							11	19	32
Total	128	95	50	83	24	2	5	3	22	24	436

Table 8: Field transfers – total breakdown by age, status and sex

Age	Single		Married		Widowed		Divorced		Unclear		Total
	Wom	Men	Wom	Men	Wom	Men	Wom	Men	Wom	Men	
13											0
16–20		1		1							2
21–25	6	3									9
26–30	4	8	1								13
31–35	4	11	8	9						1	33
36–40	3	7	4	12							26
41–45	6	3	6	15	1		1				32
46–50	6	3	9	18	1			2		3	42
51–55	4		3	10	1	1		1	1		21
56–60	4	1	2	5	1	1	1	1			16
61–65	1	1	1	2	2						7
66–70		2	2	4							8
71–75	1						1			1	3
76–80				1	1						2
81–85											0
unclear	3	1			1				11	16	32
Total	42	41	36	77	8	3	2	4	12	21	246

What is clear from the records is that women are inheriting residential plots and, to a lesser extent, fields. This is in line with more general findings, including the records from Kweneng Sub-Land Board. Out of the 4041 certificates referred to earlier, over half (2063) were registered in women's names. Women also featured with regard to leases. Out of the 600 that were residential, there were 292 women and out of the 600 commercial leases there were 196 women.

In transfers, women are not only featuring as transferees, but are engaged in transferring property as transferors. Out of the 439 residential transfers from 2005 to 2009, 191 were by women compared with 195 by men. Out of the 246 field transfers, 130 transferors were women compared with 86 men.

C Customary Land Tenure and Records: Compliance and Change

While there are examples of customary norms being adhered to in the records, with the youngest son inheriting the residential family homestead, the records clearly show that families are also agreeing among themselves to depart from the norms of customary law outlined earlier with its emphasis on male inheritance. Thus, women are inheriting land although they are neither male nor the eldest or the youngest child in the family.[16] What is happening is that siblings are agreeing to a different form of distribution in terms of affidavits that are submitted as part of the transfer process. Thus, families are clearly negotiating their own forms of distribution and departing from normative expectations outlined earlier in the chapter. This is an important finding because it marks what is happening on the ground that may go unnoticed where too much emphasis is placed on the study of conflict or disputes or, alternatively, on statements about customary law that are generalisations, in the sense of using them as a foundational point from which to assess what is going on in a community at large. It is also important to note, however, that the norms of customary law also stress the significance of reaching consensus among family members so that choosing a daughter as a beneficiary can be seen to be accommodated within the customary system. What is crucial is that family discussions are central to reaching a decision on how the property is to be dealt with and this was something that was stressed in our public meetings in 2010 in *dikgotla* as well as among the family groups.

So, for example, in Ntlooengwae ward the headman explained that the reason why women are appearing on certificates today is because 'sometimes when one of the siblings looks after the other siblings or parents the plot will be transferred to the person who was looking after other family members' and women often take on the caring role. Or, he explains that 'maybe the yard was developed by that particular person and having invested a lot in that plot the certificate will be transferred to the person who developed the plot'.

Much emphasis was made of how much it cost to develop a residential plot today in ward meetings where people observed that buildings need no longer be huts made of mud but may represent substantial investments. Among the Radipati family that featured in my research, Radipati's daughter Goitsemang found herself in this position in the 1980s, having rebuilt the family homestead, incurring costs for breeze bricks to make a house where a hut once stood, window frames, glass and a tin roof. Although she never had a formal land certificate in her name, Mosotho *kgotla* members supported her over her brother David's attempt to take control over the family household for this reason, as well as on the basis that as a married man, David should not have been seeking to chase away his unmarried sister. In an interview in 2010 with Bongi, Goitsemang's nephew, I asked what will happen to the homestead and he noted that while David has not been permitted to take over the homestead he has been allowed to build on the premises but the family have agreed that 'all six children have an equal and undivided share and it will remain like that. We all gather here at Christmas and at the other long holidays and we call it our home. It will never pass into private hands'.

---

[16] Findings elsewhere in Botswana also support these results: see Kalabamu (2005: 67–90).

In reaching agreement as to distribution, Ntlooengwae ward members note that decisions may be influenced by the wealth and status of the siblings, in other words, 'the poorest sibling who may be unemployed will be given the yard because the other siblings are in work and have already acquired other plots'. These practices were confirmed in other interviews. One Molepolole Sub-Land Board member, for example, explained that he is one of eight children which includes six girls and two boys and that he is the eldest child. He notes that he and his siblings 'have given our mother's house in Tshosa ward to our younger sister. This is because she is still young and doesn't have a lot of money. Most of us are old enough to look after ourselves'. It turns out that this sister is not the youngest in the family. Of the four sisters who come after him, one is a nurse, one is an engineer who studied in the UK, one is a civil engineer in Gaborone in the roads department and his fourth sister is working for the Land Board. They are all married. Following them is the sister who is not married and who is working in Jwaneng 'in a very simple job in one of the shops'. His brother has graduated from university and is now working for CEDA (Citizen Entrepenurial Development Agency). The youngest child, a sister, set to graduate in 2010, was studying information technology at the University of Botswana. He explains that the siblings did not give the plot to their youngest sister 'because she will be able to pursue a good living [while] my poor sister is not married and not getting a lot of money'. In the family's view 'my youngest sister will be able to look after herself'.

Such arrangements may also be found among Makokwe's descendants. His only daughter, Olebeng, who was the youngest child in the family, was given control over the natal household in Mosotho *kgotla* in the 1980s because her five older brothers had all married and established their own households. In these processes it is not only women who benefit from these distributions. In Makokwe's family, his son Nkgakikang's daughter, Kgomotso, inherited the family ploughfield but since she is married and had another field that she acquired from a *rakgadiaagwe* (patrilineal aunt) she has given the field to her elder brother, Ranko. In another case, taken from the records, a 43-year-old single man was the beneficiary of his deceased brother's residential plot because his siblings, including sisters, and his mother already had their own plots. The family decided that as he did not have a homestead he was 'fitted to have the plot'. Having sufficient resources that individuals and families can draw on provides more scope for negotiation and consensual decision-making with regard to distribution of property.

That there has been a shift in attitudes is marked by appointments to the estates of deceased persons in 2009 in the chief's *kgotla*.

D 2009 Records from the Chief's Kgotla

Table 9: Relationship of appointee to deceased where sex of appointee known

	Women	%	Men	%	Total
Wife	54	23			54
Daughter	45	20			45
Son			29	13	29
Mother	25	11			25
Sister	18	8			18
Brother			16	7	16
Uns relative	16	7	9	4	16
Husband			6	3	6
Father			3	1	3
Gdaughter	3	1			3
Niece	2	1			2
Other			2	1	2
Nephew			1	1	1
Aunt	1				1
Gson					0
Uncle					0
Total	164	71	66	30	230

Out of the 230 cases where the sex of appointee is known, 71 per cent were women and 29 per cent men. The majority of appointees were wives (54) and these women featured as an appointee in 111 deceased men's estates. Overall wives accounted for 21 per cent of the total appointments, and for 49 per cent of appointments out of the 111 deceased men's estates (Table 9). This is an interesting development as my past research found that wives were not regarded as being the appropriate persons for dealing with a deceased person's estate whereas today they are featuring and headmen are acknowledging that where their husbands die they are to take over the property.

What is interesting here, is that in 28 cases the wives' appointments were approved by a male relative, and of these over half (15) involved approval by the deceased's brother, that is a wife's brother-in-law, who was the person designated in my past research for dealing with the estate. In the other 26 cases where wives' appointments were approved by women, the appointments were spread between the appointees' and a deceased's daughters (8), the appointees' sisters–in-law (9) and the appointee's mother-in-law (6).

After wives, the largest category of relatives to be appointed were the deceased's daughters who accounted for 45 appointments, and then the deceased's sons who were appointed in 29 cases, so that overall appointments of children to the deceased amounted to 33 per cent. Of the daughters, over half the approval of appointments by a family member were made by males (26 of 45 cases), of these over half were appointments approved by male siblings, that is brothers (18 of 26 cases: 69 per cent). Where daughters' appointments were approved by female relatives (17 of 45 cases: 38 per cent) appointments were principally spread among female siblings, that is sisters (6), and the sisters of the deceased, that is their aunts (6). Out of the sons, just over half were appointed by siblings (14 of 29 cases), and then by uncles and aunts (5 cases) and mothers (3 cases).

VI   CURRENT SITUATION OF WOMEN NOT JUST DUE TO DEMOGRAPHY

Today in Botswana there are more women than men and this has been the case for a number of years. In Kweneng district, the female population like that of the rest of the country is just above that of males at slightly over 52 per cent.[17] Women in the district generally outlive men. Many of these women remain unmarried but have children. The 2006 Demographic Survey records that 65 per cent of the population has never married and that 47 per cent of the households in the country are headed by women. The public are well aware of this, as one female Sub-Land Board member observed 'most women are not married so they go ahead in applying for land [because they have no husband to depend on]'. Her observation is borne out by the records which make it clear that where women feature on land board certificates the vast majority of them are unmarried, featuring at all ages, so that their status is not simply due to where they are located in their lifecycle. The same is true for men, although when it comes to field transfers two-thirds of the men are married (see tables 6 and 7). This member also commented that 'Batswana women have children before marriage. Then they think of having their own place. They don't want to stay in the family home [because this may cause quarrels]'. Indeed, the acting deputy Land Board secretary notes that 'even if women are married, we recognize that divorce rates are high and that a woman might [apply for land because] she might be chased away and obliged to return to her family home'.

Women featuring in transfers cannot just be accounted for on the basis of demography. As the records discussed above – including those from the chief's *kgotla* and interviews show – women still continue to feature even where there are males who could substitute for them in the family. So, for example, out of 21 cases involving residential transfers to daughters in 2009, 10 had data on the siblings involved beyond simply stating that the siblings consented to the transfer and this was as follows:

---

[17] *Kweneng District Development Plan* (KDDP6) 2003–2009 (Kweneng District Council, Kweneng District Development Committee, Ministry of Local Government) 7.

- Five involved consents of both male and females siblings.
- Three involved all male siblings agreeing transfer to their sister and in two of these cases their sister was the youngest child in the family.
- Only two involved cases where the siblings were all female.

What emerges from all these sources is a blend of compliance and change that is underpinned by family consensus allowing for customary norms on inheritance to be followed in some cases, as in the case of Ngkadigang's youngest son Rammulta, who has taken over his family's residential household, while at the same time allowing for divergent approaches to be implemented featuring women as beneficiaries.

VII THE BROADER DIMENSIONS OF CONTEXTS FOR ACTION

My chapter has not dealt with disputes because it seeks to make visible what is happening in everyday life that does not necessarily involve courts when dealing with the question posed by the editors of this book at the workshop in Onati as to what response the law has or should have to different family practices and the extent to which there can be voluntarism in family law. This is in order to explore how different norms and approaches can be accommodated within a social group.

Much has been written on customary law in relation to gender and its impact on women. For Botswana this was highlighted by the case of *Unity Dow v the Attorney General*.[18] This resulted in a formal legal ruling by the High Court, reaffirmed by the Court of Appeal, that an argument to the effect that section 15 of the Constitution dealing with discrimination declined to cover sex because customary law is based on patrilineal norms which are discriminatory by their very nature, could not be upheld. As a result the government amended the Citizenship Act to allow the children of Batswana women married to foreigners to acquire citizenship and ratified the Convention on Elimination of All Forms of Discrimination against Women (CEDAW), thereby acknowledging the importance of human rights. Other formal legal changes that have been implemented to remove discrimination against women include the Abolition of Marital Power Act 2004 (referred to earlier) and amendments made to the Deeds Registry Act enabling married women to hold land in their own right. In addition there is a statute on Succession (Rights of the surviving Spouse and Inheritance Provisions)[19] that allows the surviving spouse to inherit an intestate deceased's estate under certain conditions, where the parties were married in or out of community of property under statutory law. This Act does not, however, apply to estates dealt with under customary law.[20]

---

[18] *Unity Dow v The Attorney General*, High Court Misca. No 124/90, or [1991] LRC (Const) 623 and *The Attorney General v Unity Dow*, Court of Appeal, Civil Appeal No 4/91 or 1992 LRC (Const) 574. For discussion of different perceptions of culture and rights see Griffiths (2001: 102–26).

[19] Cap 31:03.

[20] See s 3.

However, changes to formal laws in a national context do not necessarily take root on the ground. What is interesting is the way in which attitudes towards women's access to resources, including land, have shifted at a number of levels. This involves recognition of norms that circulate from the top down and from the bottom up so that they find common ground in the communities in which they operate. In this process the role of NGOs requires recognition for they have consistently raised public awareness and entered into dialogues with government in promoting gender issues and human rights. Unity Dow, a lawyer, for example, was a founder member of an NGO Emang Basadi (Stand Up Women) that supported her during her court case, interacting with other international organisations, for example, the Urban Morgan Institute for Human Rights, University of Cincinnati College of Law, that lodged an amicus brief in support of Dow with the High Court during the trial. Similar pressure was successfully exerted on challenging an educational policy that required pregnant female students to leave college for a year that was also held to discriminatory by the High Court.[21] Since the Dow case, the Botswana Centre for Human Rights, Ditshwanelo, was established in 1993 with a regional office now operating out of Kasane in the north of the country. These developments have been accompanied by regional initiatives such as the SADC Declaration on Gender and Development in 1997, the Optional Protocol to CEDAW[22] and the Protocol to the African Charter on Human and People's Rights on the Rights of Women in Africa.[23] While Botswana has upgraded the Women's Affairs Unit to a Department of Women's Affairs that is seeking to make every ministry engage in gender mainstreaming, it has not yet ratified the Protocol to the African Charter on Human Rights and funding for the department is limited compared with other areas such as youth justice.[24]

The role that NGOs – such as Emang Basadi and Ditshwanelo – have played in raising public awareness about gender issues and human rights cannot be ignored.[25] Thus, the acting deputy Land Board secretary recognises that these organisations have played an important role in educating the public. They 'have promoted women's empowerment and the government seems to be supporting them'. As one main Land Board member, a woman, stated in her interview, Ditshwanelo have made a contribution to women featuring in land certificates and leases because 'they run workshops. One of their recommendations was

---

[21] *Student Representative Council of Molepolole College of Education v Attorney General* Civil Appeal No 13 of 1994 [1995] (3)LRC 447.

[22] Botswana acceded to the Optional Protocol in 2007.

[23] For further details see Griffiths (2010: 737–76).

[24] This was revealed in interviews with the director of the department and her staff and in interviews with Emang Basadi, Ditshwanelo and the Women's Finance House in 2010. It is, however, important to note that 35.4 per cent of the population is under the age of 15 according to the Demographic Survey 2006, see above (n 16) 7.

[25] Sadly, funding for these organisations is under threat as new contracts have to be negotiated with donors who are reluctant to provide further funding because of Botswana's elevation to a middle ranking country and the effect of the recent global recession on their finances.

that having a spouse should not be a hindrance for women to acquire land. The Land Board adopted that recommendation'. How people view what is appropriate derives from a range of factors that come into play. In earlier ward discussions headmen acknowledged that when a man dies the property goes to the surviving spouse before being distributed to the children. While there are statutory provisions to this effect under the Succession Act referred to above, these do not apply to customary law. Although the same kind of legal arguments applied by *Dow* to citizenship could be applied on a human rights basis to questions of succession, this has not been necessary because it would appear that this norm regarding the surviving spouse has been absorbed by local communities within Molepolole. Similarly, in discussions in Mokgalo ward, while outlining customary norms of inheritance, the headman acknowledged that what he had observed related to the past and that 'nowadays it is different' because they now divide possessions equally among the boys and girls. When questioned further about whether this was really the case and if so why this is happening he replied: 'nowadays women can speak for themselves but in the past they couldn't (that is why they didn't get an equal share)'. My interpreter, Kawina Power, expanded on this response saying that 'it is because of the Beijing Conference on Women'. He went on to elaborate that 'the government [of Botswana] has listened and made appropriate policies'. What this demonstrates is that there is some awareness of human rights that has percolated local domains.

Underpinning these perceptions is a view expressed by the director of housing who notes that 'there has been a move to women being more proactive and taking advantage of situations that exist because women have to fend for their families'. The deputy director of social services endorses this view commenting 'that more and more women are applying for land now'. She attributes this to 'women becoming more independent. In the past women held marriage as an ideal but now over time women have seen other single women who have made it in life without a man'. She also observes that 'there are many independent women who are now doing well on their own, even those with low literacy levels. Perhaps they are doing well with small businesses and their success can motivate other women'. Education has had a role to play here. The deputy director of social services notes that in the last decades 'more women have gone to school' and that 'more and more women have become empowered in management positions'. However, she also observes that 'there is still a problem for uneducated and poor women'. The Education Statistics Brief for the country as a whole in 2009 records that primary school enrolment for girls in 2009 accounted for 49 per cent of enrolments for that year. With regard to enrolment for secondary schools, 52 per cent were female students. However, at the level of tertiary education, there were more men than women obtaining degrees and certificates. According to van Klaveren et al (2009) 'in 2006, 22,100 men in the total population turned out to have a university degree or to be a postgraduate' representing 15 per cent of all males, compared with '15,600 women' representing 11 per cent of all females.

Nonetheless, the director of housing commented that today there are 'more women entering the employment sector so they can take up more opportunities than previously'. The Women's Finance House, an NGO, also points to changes in women's formal employment 'where previously women only engaged in unpaid work or producing food in fields where women's access to resources was bogged down by perishables so that they accumulated nothing'. While the 2006 Demographic Survey found that unemployment is higher for women at 20 per cent compared with 15 per cent for men, overall women in formal employment accounted for 48 per cent of those employed, which indicates a marked improvement from the past. The informal sector has always been important for women who account for 68 per cent of those operating in this domain according to the 2007 Informal Sector Survey. In commenting on the results, the Ministry of Trade and Industry deputy permanent secretary, Kedibonye Laletsang, observed that 'the [informal] sector represents an important part of the economy and the labour market as it plays a major role in creating employment, production and income generation, with an increase in growth of 72 per cent since 1999'. In part this is due to government programmes that support these developments. The deputy director of social services sees women 'empowering themselves through trade encouraged by government, for example, baking bread and selling it to schools and during the harvesting season selling home grown watermelons to schools' as well as schemes that exist to enable 'women to access credit for small businesses'. Other activities women engage in include sewing, textiles, providing food at lunch, trade kiosks (tuck shops), hair salons, poultry, selling airtime, coffee, jam, that exist to enable 'women to access credit for small businesses'.

As the deputy permanent secretary at the Ministry of Labour and Home Affairs acknowledges, 'the lifestyle has changed in Botswana'. He attributes this to the number of programmes that provide assistance so that 'when you look at women and economic empowerment, there are so many packages [available] that you see many women coming up'.[26] While these represent positive developments, problems exist. Thus, the deputy director of social services observes that 'there is still a problem for uneducated and poor women'. Emang Basadi also cautioned that while 'things have changed men resist this'. They acknowledge that men are very frustrated because 'their voices are now faint' and that this leads to gender based violence. One of the reasons for this, they argue, is because as women become more proactive 'men may feel displaced from their roles and responsibilities' including their role as breadwinner. They maintain one reason why this has come about is 'because women never used to work formally'.

What emerges from this research are the dynamic processes that underpin family approaches to succession. These provide scope for the recognition of a diverse set of beneficiaries to inherit land – from the youngest son to the eldest daughter and siblings in between – through consensus reached among family members by negotiation. While disputes may arise, for many families this

---

[26] For a more detailed account see Griffiths (forthcoming).

reflects a voluntary exercise that is not dependent on legal intervention, except with regard to the formal processes of land transfer. With regard to customary land tenure, it is clear that the norms in operation reflect the interrelationship between social norms in the wider society and those of the families themselves and the communities of which they form part. These underpin the operation of law, both common and customary, in ways that reveal their mutually permeable character and that negates any view of a Hooker (1975) type of legal pluralism that promotes separate and autonomous or parallel systems of law. In this process it is clear that social networks continue to play an important role in facilitating access to and control over land, for they embody a constellation of factors that contribute to the accumulation of human/social as well as economic capital. These include education, employment (formal and informal), capacity to enhance one's self-development and proactively pursue opportunities, all of which may be linked to familial networks and their genealogical histories. What is crucial are the factors that contribute to these networks and individuals' upward or downward mobility and that have an impact on their capacity to negotiate poverty and access to justice in both formal and informal domains.

In the context of this book, dealing with how to characterise 'diversity' and 'deviance' in relation to family practices – with implicit judgements about whether such practices are acceptable or unacceptable – I would argue for the application of a more enthnographic or socio-legally grounded approach to law. This would have the advantage of making explicit the standpoints from which approaches to classification of practices as constituting diversity or deviance are addressed. It would also reveal the framework on which constructions of 'minority' or 'ethnic' or other types of status are based. For these statuses cannot be taken as self-evident, but must be fleshed out through articulating the features on which they are based. Indeed, they always exist in relation to other social constellations (Wilmsen 1996) so it is essential to spell out what these relations entail and from whose perspective these labels are being applied and to what ends. This enables a better understanding to be acquired about how these forms of classification are used for ideological or strategic purposes in ongoing social/legal processes that may be subject to transformations. In these processes a key element for discussion is the role of the state and the extent to which it should or should not regulate various practices in negotiating communal and individual rights and aspirations. Yet what is meant by 'the state' also needs to be carefully addressed for it is not a homogenous entity and its actions through personnel and institutions in one sphere may run contrary to what takes place in another. Such tensions have led Woodman (1998) to critique a tendency to treat the state as a uniform entity and to argue for a more informed and differentiated account of what state legal pluralism entails so that a more complex account of convergence and divergence is acquired. This raises the question of power in all its varying configurations, not least in the formulation of group or community dynamics that have an impact on individuals' capacity to negotiate terms of membership. Understanding what these dynamics involve is essential if legal policies dealing with minority and ethnic groups are to be constructed, for example, around options for entry or exit, a point raised by Shah (chapter three). What is clear is that normative approaches to law in the legal treatment of groups and individuals in relation to family practices need to be tempered by an understanding of socio-legal reality.

REFERENCES

Griffiths, A (1997) *In the Shadow of Marriage: Gender and Justice in an African Community* (Chicago, IL, University of Chicago Press).

—— (2001) 'Gendering Culture: Towards a Plural Perspective on Kwena Women's Rights' in J Cowan, MB Dembour and R Wilson (eds), *Culture and Rights: Anthropological Perspectives* (Cambridge, Cambridge University Press).

—— (2009) 'Anthropological Perspectives on Legal Pluralism and Governance in a Transnational World' in M Freeman and D Napier (eds), *Law and Anthropology* (Oxford, Oxford University Press).

—— (2010) 'International Human Rights, Women, Gender and Culture: Perspectives from Africa' in MC Foblets, JF Gaudreault-Desbiens and A Dundes Renteln (eds), *Cultural Diversity and the Law: State Responses from Around the World* (Brussels, Bruylant).

—— (forthcoming) 'Families, Networks and Life Cycles: Legal Pluralism and Women's Access to Land in Botswana' *Acta Juridica*.

Hellum, A, Ali, SS and Griffiths A (eds), (2010) *From Transnational Relations to Transnational Laws: Northern European Law at the Crossroads* (London, Ashgate).

Holleman, JF (1973) 'Trouble-cases and Trouble-less Cases in the Study of Customary Law and Legal Reform' 7 *Law & Society Review* 585.

Hooker, M (1975) *Legal Pluralism: An Introduction to Colonial and Neo-Colonial Laws* (Oxford, Oxford University Press).

Kalabamu, FT (2005) 'Perceptions on Renegotiated Customary Inheritance in Tlokweng, Botswana' in FT Kalabamu, MM Mapetla and A Sayer (eds), *Gender, Generation and Urban Living Conditions in Southern Africa* (Lesotho, Institute of Southern African Studies).

Llewellyn, KN and Hoebel, EA (1941) *The Cheyenne Way: Conflict and Case Law in Primitive Jurisprudence* (Norman, University of Oklahoma Press).

Ruzvidzo, T and Tiagha, HN (2005) 'The African Gender Development Index' in C van der Westhuizen (ed), *Gender Instruments in Africa* (Pretoria, South Africa, Institute for Global Dialogue).

Schapera, IN (1948) *Migrant Labour and Tribal Life: A Study of the Condition of the Bechuanaland Protectorate* (London, Oxford University Press).

van Klaveren, M, Tijdens, T, Hughie-Williams, M and Martin NR (2009) 'An Overview of Women's Work and Employment in Botswana' Working Paper 09-81 (Amsterdam, Amsterdam Institute for Advanced Labour Studies, University of Amsterdam).

von Benda-Beckmann F, von Benda-Beckmann K and Griffiths A (eds), (2009) *The Power of Law in a Transnational World: Anthropological Enquiries* (Oxford, Berghahn Press).

Wilmsen, EN (1996) *The Politics of Difference: Ethnic Premises in a World of Power* (Chicago, University of Chicago Press).

Woodman, G (1998) 'Ideological Combat and Social Observations: Recent Debate about Legal Pluralism' 42 *Journal of Legal Pluralism and Unofficial Law* 21.

14

Rights, Women and Human Rights Change in Iran

NAZILA GHANEA

I INTRODUCTION: THE CONTEXT

A NUMBER OF key areas of contention in Iranian family law have been widely identified since the Iranian revolution of 1979 as sites of women's resistance. There have been notable changes in family law and policy in these five key areas and we will consider the main rationales that have been given for these changes. When considering this against theories of human rights change, we see that, despite the environment in Iran not being hospitable to human rights, nevertheless some accommodation of demands with respect to family law has been possible. However, since such accommodation has resulted from a strategic and reluctant response to advocacy, its successes have proven fragile and there remains the constant risk of reversal.

The role of the law in Iran regarding family practice has been very narrow and controlling for decades. This control and intervention is evident through a profound lack of recognition of diversity in law in general. The law in Iran has long provided no evidence of embracing multiculturalism or acknowledging its population's rich diversity (Ghanea and Hass 2011). This has had numerous consequences, not least in the field of family law. The impact on the family has been profound, particularly after the revolution of 1979 where the 'complete amalgamation of political and religious power has had considerable implications for gender equality' (Hoodfar and Sadr 2010: 890).

Even here, though, there has been a very limited acknowledgement of the existence of some recognised religious minorities in the law, namely the controlled and highly limited recognition granted to three religious minorities in Iran: Zoroastrians, Christians and Jews. The Constitution states that they are granted recognised religious minority status, representation in the Parliament, and their own laws (Sanasarian 2000). This recognition eventually also led to the equalisation of the blood money penalty or '*diyeh*' payment offered on the killing of a Zoroastrian, Christian or Jewish man. Until 2004, the penalty for killing a Zoroastrian, Christian or Jewish man was half that for killing a Muslim man, but this was equalised in that year.[1] The penalty for killing a Zoroastrian, Christian, Jewish or Muslim woman is half, and no payment for men or women belonging to other religions (such as Bahá'ís) or beliefs is required. The Constitution also mentions ethnic minorities, which constitute around half of the country's population if one uses the international human rights understanding of 'minority'(see Ghanea and Hass 2011) though it grants them only limited rights. A highly problematic category in Iranian law is that of Iranian women married to non-Iranians. Citizenship cannot be conveyed through the mother and this has jeopardised the status of thousands, for example, the families of Iranian women married to Afghans, who at one point numbered over three million in Iran. Legal developments in recent years have begun to address this lacuna. Another area of severe persecution has concerned the largest religious minority community, whose existence the Iranian Constitution and Iranian laws and policies have refused even to acknowledge: the Bahá'ís.[2]

Having noted this broader context, the challenges to women in Iranian family law nevertheless merit special consideration. Laws in Iran regarding women are, of course, not limited to family law matters. There are gender-related laws enforcing strict dress codes for women and men (though they are clearly much more severe for women) and the style of hair and beards for men. There is insistence that males are heads of the family, and discriminatory provisions against women regarding the seeking of divorce, custody of children, polygamy, guardianship and inheritance, giving testimony, education and employment, criminal punishments and leadership. A whole range of laws discriminate against women and girls.

The Islamic revolution of 1979 was a turning point in gender relations in Iran. In many respects, women's legal position within society regressed and their situation within the family structure was downgraded: consider the husband's right to repudiate women, to take charge of the children after divorce, to contract multiple marriages (polygamy), the weakening of the legal claims of women against the man, the requirement for women to show the written consent of the husband for any trip to a foreign country, the degradation of the standing of women in testimony before the court (half the weight of a man) and the inability of women to hold specific jobs (such as a judge, or the President of the Republic) (Khosrokhavar and Ghaneirad 2010).

This is the context in which we examine women's activism as a site of resistance regarding family law. Key dates in considering Iranian family laws are the years 1967, 1975, 1979 and 2007. The Family Protection Act was brought into force under Muhammad Reza Shah in 1967[3] and 1973. These had

---

[1] *Payvand Iran News*, 'Iran's minorities hail approval of law on equal blood money' (29 December 2003) available at: www.payvand.com/news/03/dec/1211.html.

[2] For further discussion, see Ghanea (2003) and Brookshaw and Fazel (2008).

[3] Iran Human Rights Documentation Centre: www.iranhrdc.org/english/human-rights-documents/iranian-codes/3199-family-protection-act.html.

modestly improved the position of women within marriage: the right to divorce, previously a husband's prerogative, became subject to a family court decision; and polygamous marriages became conditional on the permission of the first wife or the court. The act also slightly expanded women's custody rights, based on the 'child's best interests' (Hoodfar and Sadr 2010: 888).

The 1967 Act had abolished extra-judicial divorce, limited polygamy and established Family Courts. The 1975 Act extended the grounds of divorce.[4] It also increased the age of marriage to 18 for girls and 20 for boys. These changes were vehemently opposed by Ayatollah Khomeini while in opposition and exile and then annulled within two weeks of his accession to power in 1979 (Hoodfar and Sadr 2010: 891). In the new Constitution drafted by the Islamic revolutionary government, women have been recognised as 'the corner-stone of the home and the hearth' (Afshar 2000: 188). The 1989 Constitution states that the family is

> the fundamental unit of society and the central kernel for growth and development of humanity which must be nurtured and protected . . . this is central to our creed and it is the duty of the Islamic Republic to achieve this end . . . such a position on the family removes women from being objects of pleasure or tools of production and frees them from the burdens of exploitation and imperialism and enables them to find once more their critical duties of motherhood and raising of humanity.[5]

In order to advance such a 'central creed', women were now to be separated from boys in schooling, early marriage was reintroduced, female judges were removed, women needed their husband's permission to work or leave the country and a strict dress code was introduced.

II THE EBB AND FLOW OF FAMILY LAW[6]

Many areas of family law pertaining to the majority Muslim population have been subject to repeated criticism and advocacy by women's groups in Iran. Statistics alone indicate the resistance of Iranian women and girls to the constitutional and ideological role which has been assigned to them. The effort to restrict them to the domestic sphere has been defied by the numbers in higher education[7]

---

[4] S McGlinn, 'Family Law in Iran', an essay prepared at the University of Leiden in 2000–01, 22–23, available at: www.sonjavank.com/sen/pdfs/iranlaw.pdf.

[5] Constitution of Iran, as quoted by Afshar 2000: 188–89.

[6] Parvin Ardalan refers to this as 'a Game of 'Snakes and Ladders'. Parvin Ardalan, 'The Women's Movement in a Game of 'Snakes and Ladders' 12 January 2008, see: www.payvand.com/news/08/dec/1001.html.

[7] With the encouragement of large family size during the Iran–Iraq war (1980–88) 'Iran's population grew by 70% to 60 million in the 1980s, with half of the population being under 20 years of age': see Künkler (2004: 377). In educational accomplishment it should be noted that 'In 1965–66 female students were 23.7 percent of the total in Iranian institutions of higher education. Just before the Islamic Revolution of 1979, in the academic year 1977–78, their participation rose to 30.9 percent. In 2004–05, it rose to 53.9 percent of the total, with more women being enrolled in the universities than men. The yearly statistics show a continuous rise between 1965 and 2007' Khosrokhavar and Ghaneirad (2010: 224). As confirmed by a 2003 UN study, and quoted by Bahramitash and

and employment;[8] and the effort to bring about early marriage is defied by the increased average age of marriage Bahramitash and Kazemipour (2006). This mobilisation has resulted in the modification of a number of laws relating to women and the family since 1979.

A Early Marriage

With the annulment of the former Family Protection Law in 1979, the age of marriage was reduced for girls from 18 to nine and for boys from 20 to 14 (Hoodfar and Sadr 2010: 891). Activism, however, brought about an increase in the age of marriage for girls to puberty. Moreover, statistical evidence suggests that the average age of first marriage for women has risen to 23 and the number of single women has increased (Bahramitash and Kazemipour 2006: 127).

B Temporary Marriage

Temporary marriage was encouraged, particularly during the Iran–Iraq war. Criticised as 'legal prostitution',[9] it allows for legitimate relationships from two hours to 99 years.

C Divorce and Polygamy

'Men regained the unilateral right to divorce and to polygamy' (Hoodfar and Sadr 2010: 891). A Bill of 2007 required women to pay tax on the *mehrieh* (*mahr* or dowry) at a very high rate. Reportedly this was removed at the second reading, which instead introduced an unclear distinction between conventional and unconventional gift money.[10] The possibility of women seeking divorce on a very limited number of grounds was introduced in 1992.[11]

Kazemipour (2006: 119), women constituted more than 60 per cent of Iran's 1.6 million university students in that year. 'Not only are more women in higher education but they also have a higher propensity than men to finish their education'.

  [8] '[W]omen social actors who aspire to form and assert their social identity have been able to realize change in their status through work and the rejection of women's strict function as biological reproduces and houseworkers': (Kian 1995: 407).

  [9] Shahla Forouzanfar in the *Financial Times*: 9 September 2008, available at www.ft.com/cms/s/0/4f97b8d6-7e7c-11dd-b1af-000077b07658.html#axzz1LKAvdcK5.

  [10] Campaign for Equality, Stop the Anti-Family Law ratified by Iran's Parliament, 17 February 2010, available at: planet-iran.com/index.php/news/10097.

  [11] The 1992 amendments extend the wife's access to divorce by the addition of the following grounds: husband's non-maintenance for up to six months for any reason, husband's bad behaviour, keeping bad company, etc making continuation of married life impossible for wife, husband's incurable disease constituting danger to wife, husband's madness in cases where annulment would not be possible according to *shari'a*, husband's non-compliance with court order to avoid demeaning or dishonourable employment, husband's conviction to sentence of five or more years, husband's

D The Custody of Children

This went to the ex-husband when a girl reaches age seven and the boy age two. In all instances, if the ex-wife remarries, she loses custody, but no such stipulation attaches to a remarried man. As a result of women's advocacy, the mother may be granted custody in exceptional circumstances if the father is proven unfit to care for the child.

E Polygamy

This was particularly encouraged during the Iran–Iraq war. Statistical evidence available in 2004 showing an increasing number of single women indicates that polygny is not a widely accepted practice (Bahramitash and Kazemipour 2006: 127). However, the 2007 Family Law Bill, whose fate is in limbo, removed the conditions required for a husband to show he has adequate financial means before entering into subsequent marriages, as well as the consent of the first wife unless she has a terminal illness.[12] Even knowledge of the first wife is not required.[13]

III REASONS FOR CHANGE

A number of reasons have been suggested for the modest successes – or at least the reinstatement of the modest achievements that had been attained by the 1960s after 70 years of lobbying by women.[14]

A Women's Rights Advocacy

There have been a number of campaigns targeting specific aspects of discrimination against women. These include activism to allow women access to a wider

---

addiction constituting a danger to family and marriage (determined by the court), husband's desertion or leaving marital home for six months without legitimate cause (determined by the court), husband's conviction for crime bringing dishonour to family (determined by the court), husband's infertility for five years of marriage or his contracting sexually transmitted disease, husband's disappearance for six months and husband's polygamous marriage without first wife's consent if the court considers co-wives are not being treated equally. For a further discussion, see Mir-Hosseini (2000).

[12] Najmeh Bozorgmehr, 'Iran Family Law Bill stirs controversy' *Financial Times* (9 September 2008) available at: www.ft.com/cms/s/0/4f97b8d6-7e7c-11dd-b1af-000077b07658.html#axzz1LKAvdcK5.

[13] Campaign for Equality above (n 10).

[14] Since the first Iranian Constitution of 1906. Hoodfar and Sadr (2010: 890) argue that 'The new regime's ideologues envisioned an Islamic society based on gender apartheid, effectively eradicating the gains that women's rights activists had made over seven decades'.

range of university courses,[15] to allow women to study abroad without being accompanied by a male relative, to allow women to participate in and watch sports and so on. In the area of family law, such campaigns have targeted all five issues outlined above and impacted all of them to some extent. Such campaigns need much initiative and persistence, due to the fact that 'in Iran, women have to fight against the combined effects of two predicaments: social and cultural prejudice against them and a juridical system that does not give them the opportunity to compete fairly for higher status' (Khosrokhavar and Ghaneirad 2010: 238). They have also proved challenging because of infighting and factionalism between women's rights activists.

B Educational Expansion

Some rationalise these modifications as being primarily due to the large educational expansion in the country since the revolution:

> The modernization of women and their awakening through an educational system that intended to promote the 'Islamic women' changed the gender situation in Iran. The new awareness is particularly strong among the new generation of women who are much better educated than before and very conscious of the unfair legal system that hinders their social promotion within society. This new self-awareness has given rise to new standards, of which women's positioning within the educational system and higher education is only one major aspect. A new social dynamics has set in, due to the changes introduced in the cultural system by the new generations that have been the very product of the cultural and educational system in Iran' (Khosrokhavar and Ghaneirad 2010: 224).

To appreciate this claim, it should be noted that the statistics suggest that the 'noticeable headway' made by Iranian women in terms of access to education relates to both the developed and underdeveloped parts of the country; leading to the interesting observation that their presence is 'far larger than during the last years of the Pahlavi era when their juridical status was closer to modern norms of justice than now' (Khosrokhavar and Ghaneirad 2010: 229).

From 1990 to 2000, women's tertiary enrolment ratio – the number of female students in higher education as a percentage of all women aged from 19 to 24 – rose from seven per cent to 21 per cent. In 1996, female high-school graduates come to outnumber male graduates. In 1999, girls started to outnumber boys in early childhood education. From 2001, more women were pursuing bachelor's degrees than men (Kurzman 2008: 298).

---

[15] 'Among the many measures that women Parliamentarians [in 1991] fought for and lost was one to amend the 1985 Bill for State funded scholarships for men and married women to study abroad. They failed to amend the law to benefit single women, even those over 28 years of age (who would be considered unmarriageable)': Afshar (2000: 200).

C Socio-economic Factors

Overall, the trend in Iran has been one of continuity rather than change in terms of the status of women, sidelining arguments which rely on an 'overemphasis on the role of culture at the expense of socio-economic factors' (Bahramitash and Kazemipour 2006: 112) and the assumption that 'rising support for political Islam has been categorically negative for women (Bahramitash and Kazemipour 2006: 111). Since 1979 for example

> the overall social trends have been toward a rising age of first marriage, a declining age gap between spouses, a declining role of the bride's family in the selection of the spouse (arranged marriages), a declining number of married women as a percentage of all women over the age of 15, rising divorce rates, the declining numbers of children per family (fertility reduction). It is true that these trends were interrupted briefly when Islamic laws pertaining to marriage were applied in the early 1980s. By the late 1980s, however, the trends resumed and have continued along the same path that had emerged by the mid-1970s' (Bahramitash and Kazemipour 2006: 112).

As Kurzman (2008: 298–99) argues:

> If, despite the government's best efforts, this widening cohort of women educated in the Islamic Republic aspires to equality with men in important ways, then perhaps educational and generational change are more susceptible to global trends than to government doctrines.

D A Pragmatic Regime Susceptible to Political Pressure?

Addressing the moderation of family law policies in order to introduce mandatory birth control and the modification of child custody, Künkler (2004: 378) reveals that

> Scholars writing on behalf of the women's movement admit today that despite the women's demands, these advances mostly resulted from a dramatically deteriorating social situation rather than a moderation of the government's take on women's issues caused by gender-egalitarian advocacy.

Many of the above changes came in the late 1990s. The political climate had changed:

> Khatami's unexpected success in 1997 shifted the categorisation of political parties and factions from being based on economic policies to their social and political perspectives. Women (and youth) had changed the political landscape. . . . In many ways 1997 also signalled to conservatives that they could no longer assume that the religiosity of women would automatically translate into votes for them (Hoodfar and Sadr 2010: 895).

However, this relatively conducive environment (for example, the more relaxed enforcement of the dress code, and the largest number of female parliamentarians during the sixth Majlis: 13 out of a total of 290 members) did not last and did not deliver on expectations. Many efforts towards women's rights were blocked by the conservative-dominated Guardian Council and judiciary. These included the proposed ratification of CEDAW (Convention on the Elimination of All Forms of Discrimination against Women) the attempt to allow single women to study abroad and advocacy to allow women into sports grounds. The 'reformists' were defeated in the 2005 elections and this propelled women to combine forces:

> Faced with the lack of advancement and a threat of even more regressive gender policies, both reformist and Islamist activist women concluded they could not count on their male counterparts for the realisation of gender justice. In order to reach out to the public and use every possible political space, they revived or formed their own women-only organisations and coalitions around particular political parties' (Hoodfar and Sadr 2010: 896).

Women's rights, and relevant provisions of the family law, are also increasingly susceptible to political manoeuvring and posturing. Since the recent Presidencies (one so-called 'reformist' and the other 'conservative') have made a mark on this issue and become a focal point for advocacy, a pro-women's rights stance has come to mean being pro-President Khatami and anti-President Ahmadinejad:

> The heavy handedness of Ahmadinejad's government has brought women of all tendencies together to form pragmatic coalitions to challenge the government, particularly in response to the imposition of a more restrictive dress code, greater control over public spaces using a larger and better-pail 'moral police force', the quiet implementation of a quota system to limit women's access to universities, and especially the proposed family code, which in practice would nullify almost all the reforms women have managed to push through over the previous decades' (Hoodfar and Sadr 2010: 900).

The fact that the 2007 Family Protection Bill was debated in Parliament in 2008 (and then introduced again in 2010)[16] was considered by some to have merely been anti-President Ahmadinejad showcasing:

> Analysts believe the debate was partly motivated by a fight for women's votes and that government opponents seized on the bill as an opportunity to turn women against Mr Ahmadi-Nejad ahead of next June's presidential election.[17]

The ability to make a political impact is, of course, as a result of successful campaigning and coalition-building by women's rights activists, who note the absence in the Bill of any consideration of wives: 'the Bill doesn't address what would happen to the family if the husband were to develop an addiction, become sterile, or leave the home':[18]

---

[16] R Mostaghim and A Sandels, 'Iran: Hardliners push for family-law bill that activists say further erodes women's rights' *Los Angeles Times* (26 August 2010) available at: latimesblogs.latimes.com/babylonbeyond/2010/08/iran-women-elections-feminism-rights-human-ahmadinejad-divorce.html.

[17] Bozorgmehr, above (n 12).

[18] Questions raised by Asieh Amini. See: Golnaz Esfandiari, 'Controversial "Family Bill" Returns to Iranian Parliament's Agenda' *Radio Free Europe Radio Liberty* (24 August 2010) available at:

In 2008 an alliance was formed with the participation of women activists and equal rights advocates who organised mass protests against the introduction of the Bill, which they called the 'Anti-Family Bill'. They distributed brochures and leaflets, released statements and wrote widely about the dire implications of the amendments for the already discriminatory family law. The formation of the 'No to the Anti-Family Bill Great Alliance' attracted the largest number of women from among women's activists inside and outside the country. They campaigned vigorously; collected signatures, sent text messages on mobiles, sent postcards 'no to the Bill', and assembled in the parliament's corridors en-masse until articles 23 and 25 were removed from the Bill.[19]

E Capturing the Discourse: Cooperation between Secular and Muslim Activists

Afshar (2000: 189) suggests that the longstanding division[20] between secularists and Islamist groups found a degree of rapprochement by the late 1990s, but this provides only part of the explanation for these modest successes. Khosrakhavar and Ghaneirad (2010: 238) explain this tendency to act individually as being in part due to 'the choice of individual agency, rather than collective'. The high price paid for such activism – along with the social, cultural, political, legal and other obstacles facing such activism – goes some way towards providing further explanation. The opportunities provided by the above sites of resistance and other emerging networks provide optimism for enhanced possibilities for organising on such matters.

It can be seen that in resisting gender biased family law provisions there has been a combination of strategies used utilising both secular and Islamist argumentation.[21] The strategy used by Islamist women, whether in Iran or elsewhere, draws its strength from the imposition of laws and policies by government authorities in the name of Islam. This means that, in turn

> Islamist women have had to counter these views by resorting to the Islamic discourse and reconstructing new interpretations that would meet their demands . . . The defence of rights here is not articulated in the language of liberty or even equality. What the Islamist women demand is entitlements that are balanced by duties. The demands are located firmly within the framework of responsibilities, mutual obligations and complementary roles' (Afshar 2000: 196).

According to Künkler (2004), some two decades after Iran's Islamic revolution there had been a shift towards 'secular and religious women in Iran' combining

www.rferl.org/content/Controversial_Family_Bill_Returns_To_Iranian_Parliaments_Agenda/
2136632.html.

[19] Campaign for Equality, above (n 10).
[20] Kian (1995: 408) sees that '[t]here types of women social actors with distinct social and cultural identities and class backgrounds can be distinguished in post-revolutionary Iran: traditionalist-Islamists, and modernist-Islamists, and modernist-seculars'.
[21] For a broader discussion, see Ghanea (2004).

forces 'to frame arguments in favour of women's rights in Islamic terms rather than with reference to liberal human rights discourses':

> As women are excluded from reaching clerical positions that would endow them with the authority to engage in theologically recognized reinterpretation of the Islamic sacred texts, this encounter has hinged . . . on a collaboration with male reform-minded clerics, whose arguments the women's movement has learned to appropriate and advance for its own purposes and interests. The campaign for women's rights in Iran has thus necessitated a rare symbiosis not only between secular and religious women, but also between women and male reformist clerics (2004: 375).

Künkler primarily examines these arguments as advocated through publications, especially *Zane-Ruz*, *Payame-Hajar*, *Zanan*, *Jens-e Dovvom*, *Farzaneh* and *Hoquqe Zanan*. 'The predominant medium in this endeavour has been the women's press, providing the forum for the publication, distribution and advocacy of such arguments' (2004: 376). She goes so far as to state that 'the women's movement in Iran has achieved reconciling feminism with Islam' (2004: 385). It may, more modestly, be referred to as the adoption of 'women-friendly readings of Islamic texts, challenging the conservative male interpretation of women's rights in Islam' (Hoodfar and Sadr 2010: 892). It is perhaps this experience that has led others too to find that 'at least in the case of Iran and Shi'ism, the larger obstacle to gender (and minorities') equality has more to do with the undemocratic state–society relations that persist in Iran and less to do with the actual or potential compatibility (or lack thereof) of religious traditions or practices with democratic principles' (Hoodfar and Sadr: 885).

Afshar (2000: 197) has described this effort of advancing women's rights through Islamist thinking as a 'long and industrious process of de-construction and reinterpretation'; and also one which if fraught with risks:

> The difficulty that Islamist women have is that by embracing the concepts of difference and complementarity they, of necessity, accept some notions of essentialism. For the male hierarchy this essentialism includes the belief that women are 'naturally irrational' and their campaigns are conducted in a hysterical and feminine manner (2000: 200).

In other countries, the articulation of women's rights through a Muslim framework has raised other challenges. However, these have not surfaced in Iran because of the very elementary nature of the demands at present, and where the arguments 'for gender equality from within an Islamic framework . . . has minimised the gap between "Islamic" and secularist/modernist/human rights perspectives' (Hoofar and Sadr 2010: 886). As more pronounced demands surface it is doubtful whether this cooperation can continue to stand the test of time.

The collaboration of secular and Muslim voices on women's rights in Iran, however, seems to be reactive, strategic and partial. Since the family policies and gender policies were brought about in the name of Islam, over time women's rights advocacy has adopted the only language accommodated within the regime for protest:

[I]nadvertently these policies have prompted the flourishing of a diverse and increasingly cohesive women's movement that is in practice questioning the secular-religious divide (which both modernists and Islamists have tried so hard to erect) by crossing that boundary and coming together around concrete issues to demand gender equality. This state of affairs has led to lively, if contradictory, intellectual and political developments which continue to test the capacity of the Islamic regime to accommodate democracy, pluralism and gender equality (Hoodfar and Sadr 2010: 886).

IV GLOBAL COMMITMENTS, LOCAL CHANGE?

There has been a growing body of literature over the past decade or so which addresses theories of human rights change. These mainly political science and international relations theories, address human rights change through various models such as the spiral model, the boomerang model (Risse and Sikkink 1999: 17–35), socialisation and others.

Present day Iran does *not* offer a very amenable context for the examination of theories of human rights change. As Helfer (2002: 1843) has observed:

A key concept shared by . . . scholars is a focus on the state as a transparent entity composed of disaggregated governmental and nongovernmental actors, each with its own distinct functions and interests. The diverse and often divergent preferences of these actors allow for a rich series of domestic and transnational interactions. But the very fact that these parties act with at least nominal independence says much about the political structures in which they are embedded. For if a state is controlled by a totalitarian or other nondemocratic political authority, these actors (to the extent they exist at all) will have little or no ability to oppose the forces exercising political power.

Many states do not offer a transparent model of the state with vibrant and independent non-governmental actors. They are, in fact, much closer to the model of a controlling state within which non-governmental actors are not given the space to oppose political power. Nevertheless, and as this example of Iran illustrates, such amenable conditions are not absolutely required for the application of these theories. What many states do have are some independent voices who continue to express their concern with human rights both from within that country and independent actors that do so abroad. Indeed the 'boomerang' model of influence precisely addresses a context where

domestic groups in a repressive state bypass their state and directly search out international allies to try to bring pressure on their states from outside. National opposition groups, NGOs, and social movements link up with transnational networks and INGOs [international nongovernmental organizations] who then convince international human rights organizations, donor institutions, and/or great powers to pressure norm-violating states (Risse and Sikkink 1999: 18).

Furthermore, Grugel and Peruzzotti (2010: 56) have observed that

global rights instruments and domestic activist frameworks influence each other in manifold ways. The global level does not simply provide an alternative arena for local activists when domestic channels are closed, but can also redefine the very landscape of domestic advocacy, even in those areas where there might be little initial norm salience.

It is clear, therefore, that where domestic political processes are thwarted, where government is not transparent and an independent civil society is not tolerated, then human rights pressure has to be channelled from outside and the global level has to provide the arena for advocacy focused on the domestic scene. The push-back against Iranian Family Law offers precisely such a context.

V. NEGOTIATING WITH A RELUCTANT STATE

Goodman and Jinks (2004) have put forward three processes by which international law seeks to impress human rights on recalcitrant states. They suggest that, in addition to the processes of coercion and persuasion, international law should recognise a supplementary process: 'acculturation'. Let's consider each of these processes and their application to Iran:

1. 'Coercion' is 'coercing states (and individuals) to comply with regime rules'.
- The Iranian human rights context has attracted a number of such 'benefits of conformity or . . . costs of nonconformity through material rewards and punishments' (2004: 633) – one example being economic sanctions.

2. 'Persuasion' is 'persuading states (and individuals) of the validity and legitimacy of human rights law' (2004: 625) through 'the active, often strategic, inculcation of norms' (2004: 635).
- The Iranian human rights context illustrates a number of such efforts, one being that of the EU human right dialogue.

3. 'Acculturation' is 'the general process by which actors adopt the beliefs and behavioural patterns of the surrounding culture' (2004: 726). It is reliant on 'pressures to assimilate . . . mimicry, identification, and status maximisation' (2004: 626), therefore relying on pressures imposed by both other actors and the state itself.
- The study of Iran would therefore consider the social pressures felt by the Iranian state to identify with the international community of states and its 'cultural and associational aspects' (2004: 696). This process requires monitoring, reporting, social rewards and sanctions and especially 'external surveillance and reporting – especially by third-party states and organizations' (2004: 626). In the Iranian context, this would emphasise the importance of visibility of its human rights record.

Goodman and Jinks (2008) also emphasise domestic openings for the advancement of human rights in terms of offering a 'political opportunity structure [POS]' for the mobilisation of social actors (2008: 734). They suggest that this political opportunity structure is composed of four principal elements, each of which can 'independently inspire social groups to mobilise' (2008: 734). What are these four elements and what do they tell us about the opportunities for the advancement of women's rights in Iran?

A 'The Relative Openness of the Institutionalised Political System'

The first element is quite self-evident: the more open the political system then the more likely it is for social movements to mobilise for human rights:

> Even the formal commitment to a rights-based norm, or its rhetorical endorsement by governmental leaders, can create the perceived political opening that mobilizes social movements . . . [by] signalling the legitimacy of particular grievances or potential state receptivity and willingness to address related claims. . . . [and due to the fact that it] disproportionately empowers groups and individuals dedicated to the cause of human rights by imbuing them and their causes with social legitimacy and by emboldening private citizens to seek formal redress and human rights reforms (2008: 734).

Simmons (2009) focuses on the pressure brought about by what she refers to as 'rights' stakeholders'. When a government ratifies a human rights treaty, this increases 'the value that individuals place on the associated right (by legitimating the right) and increasing the perceived likelihood for successfully protecting the right. . . . these effects lead to political change because they increase the "expected value of mobilizing"' (Goodman and Jinks 2008: 735).

B 'The Stability of Elite Alignments Supporting the Polity' and

C 'The Presence of Elite Allies for a given Movement or Issue'

The second and third elements relate to domestic and international human rights elite alignments and allies respectively. In describing political opportunity structures, the presence of international allies is considered 'a significant spur to social [domestic] mobilization for greater policy reform' (2008: 736). In fact:

> The leading qualitative studies of successful human rights campaigns highlight complementary ties and interactions between international and domestic groups – what those researchers call a 'boomerang' pattern – in progressively producing effective domestic policy change (2008: 737–38).

D 'The State's Capacity and Propensity for Repression'

The fourth element observes that mobilisation increases when state repression decreases. We have already discussed this in the Iranian context. Goodman and

Jinks note that 'a reduction in the propensity of the state to resort to repressive measures will often encourage social movements to mobilize', though they also observe that 'international linkages may indirectly reduce the exposure of local advocates to state violence' (2008: 737). They go on to note that the

> international facilitation of domestic social movements may involve the diminution of the established regime's repressive capacity. The emergence of 'new allies' and the collapse of previously stable elite alliances often have significant effects on the will or ability of the target regime to repress opposition movements (2008: 737).

VI CONGRUITIES AND INCONGRUITIES

We have observed that there is some correlation between the Goodman–Jinks theory and the opening for mobilisation for human rights change for women in the family in Iran. Periods of *relative* openness of the institutionalised political system allowed for some modifications to laws and policies to be introduced. Opportunities were taken to drive a wedge between pro-regime elites to advance such changes, and elite allies were used to maximum effect. The state's recent increased capacity and propensity for repression has, regretfully, forcibly driven many of the actors behind such changes either abroad, underground or into prison.

These theories of domestic human rights change encouraged us to focus on the impact of both universal human rights norms and advocacy pressures for the advancement of rights. We observed that since the receptivity of domestic political structures to human rights norms has been highly constrained, and despite the 'political opportunity structure [POS]' for the mobilisation of social actors (Goodman and Jinks 2008: 734) being highly inhospitable in Iran, an impressive human rights mobilisation for women's rights can be observed. Despite the crackdowns in Iran, recent years have not managed to silence such activism but have shifted it. Domestic voices have been supplemented by an increasing number of international allies. Risse and Sikkink's observation seems to concur exactly with Iranian women's rights in the family situation: 'domestic groups in a repressive state bypass their state and directly search out international allies to try to bring pressure on their states from outside' (1999: 18). As more and more human rights actors are forced into exile, the international linkages they establish augment the international allies and broaden the international network. As this happens, perhaps we will see more evidence for the observation that 'The global level does not simply provide an alternative arena for local activists when domestic channels are closed, but can also redefine the very little initial norm salience' (Grugel and Peruzzotti 2010: 56).

REFERENCES

Afshar, H (2000) 'Women and Politics in Iran' 12 *The European Journal of Development Research* 188.

Bahramitash, R and Kazemipour, S (2006) 'Myths and Realities of the Impact of Islam on Women: Changing Marital Status in Iran' 15 *Middle East Critique* 111.

Brookshaw, DP and Fazel, S (2008) *The Baha'is in Iran: Socio-historical Studies* (London, Routledge).

Ghanea, N (2003) *The UN, Human Rights and the Baha'is in Iran* (The Hague, Kluwer/ Martinus Nijhoff).

—— (2004) 'Convergences and Disparities between the Human Rights of Religious Minorities and of Women in the Middle East' 26 *Human Rights Quarterly* 705.

Ghanea, N and Hass, B (2011) *Seeking Justice and an End to Neglect: Iran's Minorities Today* (London, Minority Rights Group International) available at: www.minorityrights. org/download.php?id=939.

Goodman, R and Jinks, D (2004) 'How to Influence States: Socialization and International Human Rights Law' 54 *Duke Law Journal* 621.

—— (2008) 'Incomplete Internationalization and Compliance with Human Rights Law' 19 *European Journal of International Law* 725.

Grugel, J and Peruzzotti, E (2010) 'Grounding Global Norms in Domestic Politics: Advocacy Coalitions and the Convention on the Rights of the Child in Argentina' 42 *Journal of Latin American Studies* 29.

Helfer, LA (2002) 'Overlegalizing Human Rights: International Relations Theory and the Commonwealth Caribbean Backlash Against Human Rights Regimes' 102 *Columbia Law Review* 1832.

Hoodfar, H and Sadr, S (2010) 'Islamic Politics and Women's Quest for Gender Equality in Iran' 31 *Third World Quarterly* 885.

Khosrokhavar, F and Ghaneirad, A (2010) 'Iranian Women's Participation in the Academic World' 43 *Iranian Studies* 223.

Kian, A (1995) 'Gendered Occupation and Women's Status in Post-revolutionary Iran' 31 *Middle Eastern Studies* 421.

Künkler, M (2004) 'In the Language of the Islamic Sacred Texts: The Tripartite Struggle for Advocating Women's Rights in the Iran of the 1990s' 24 *Journal of Muslim Minority Affairs* 375.

Kurzman, C (2008) 'A Feminist Generation in Iran?' 41 *Iranian Studies* 297.

Mir-Hosseini, Z (2000) *Marriage on Trial: A Study of Islamic Family Law*, revised edn (London, IB Tauris).

Risse, T and Sikkink, K (1999) 'The Socialization of International Human Rights Norms into Domestic Practices: Introduction' in T Risse et al (eds), *The Power of Human Rights: International Norms and Domestic Change* (Cambridge, Cambridge University Press).

Sanasarian, E (2000) *Religious Minorities in Iran* (Cambridge, Cambridge University Press).

Simmons, BA (2009) *Mobilizing for Human Rights: International Law in Domestic Politics* (Cambridge, Cambridge University Press).

15

Muslim Family Law in Bangladesh: Resistance to Secularisation

FARAH DEEBA CHOWDHURY

I INTRODUCTION

BANGLADESH (the former East Pakistan) achieved independence in 1971 from Pakistan. The legislation enacted by Pakistan remained the basis of Bangladeshi personal status laws. The *Hanafi* School is the predominant *madhhab* (Muslim school of Law) in Bangladesh. The legal status of Muslim women in Bangladesh is defined by the Muslim personal law along with the general law which is secular in nature. The Muslim personal law covers the areas of marriage, divorce, maintenance, guardianship of children and inheritance. The general law deals with the rights under the Constitution, penal codes, the civil and criminal procedure codes, evidence and such matters.[1] In the areas of marriage, divorce, maintenance, guardianship of children and inheritance in Bangladesh, Muslim family law is mostly based on the substantive equality approach, which also recognises differences (Wentholt 1999: 55).

Monsoor argues that existing law in Bangladesh does not need any major reform and has the potential to protect women from economic deprivation and violence (1999: 258–59). She also advocates reform within an Islamic framework, arguing that as patriarchal society did not grant women rights under Islamic law, radical change outside the Islamic framework will give rise to more conservatism. Women's organisations have been active in promoting the introduction of a Uniform Family Code following a secular approach. Monsoor (1999: 134) doubts whether this will be possible. She points out that family law in Bangladesh is based on religion and does not operate on the basis of absolute equality between men and women (1999: 4). She argues that gender equity rather than full-fledged gender equality can be meaningfully developed in Bangladeshi family law through implementation of the existing law (1999: 3). Al Hibri (1997) argues that a secular approach will not work for the advancement of Muslim women. Esposito and DeLong-Bas (2001: 127) point out:

---

[1] Sultana Kamal, Law for Muslim Women in Bangladesh, www.wluml.org/english/pubs/pdf/dossier4/D4-Bangladesh.pdf.

The true effectiveness of existing reforms is dependent upon their acceptance not simply by those who legislate but by the entire Muslim community. Thus, reforms must be rooted in a consistent Islamic rationale, one that would demonstrate a link of continuity between change and past tradition.

In this chapter I argue that existing law in Bangladesh does not need any major reform and has the potential to protect women's rights. The effectiveness of family law reform in Bangladesh depends on its acceptance by the people of Bangladesh. Although the Islamic revival movement in Bangladesh is not so strong, Bangladeshis have strong attachments to Islam, which is the religion of almost 90 per cent of the population. Most Bangladeshi people display their devotion to Islam in public. If reform is carried out within an Islamic framework, people will accept it. A secular approach will not work in Bangladesh.

II ISLAM AND POLITICS IN BANGLADESH

It is important to understand the role of Islam in Bangladeshi politics in order to analyse its family law. The Awami League that led Bangladesh to independence first ruled the country on the basis of the 1970 election in which it won a landslide victory in East Pakistan, receiving all but two of the 162 seats. On 16 December 1972, Bangladesh entrenched a fully-fledged constitution. Secularism was adopted as the state ideology, and at first this meant that religious symbols would not be used in state activities. Secular slogans such as *joi Bangla* (Victory of Bengal) were used in public meetings, and on radio and television rather than religious slogans such as *Allah 'hu' Akbar* (God is Great). However, people considered the non-use of religious symbols as an anti-Muslim and pro-Indian ideology. Under popular pressure, the government began defining secularism as giving equal status to all religions in public life (Jahan 1987: 115–16). In 1975, General Ziaur Rahman (popularly called Zia) came to power through coup and countercoup. Zia included *'Bismillaher Rahmaner Rahim'* (In the name of Allah, the Beneficent the Merciful) at the beginning of the Constitution and substituted 'secularism' with 'absolute trust and faith in the Almighty Allah'. Zia reintroduced the multiparty system and also allowed and legitimised Islamic politics which was banned under the previous government on the ground of promoting communalism (Haider 1999). The Zia government amended the Constitution through proclamation orders issued at different times between August 1975 and April 1979. The amendments were ratified by the Fifth Amendment to the Constitution of Bangladesh (Hakim and Haque 1995). After the overthrow of the Zia government, the Ershad government emphasised Islamic values. He made 'Islam' the state religion of Bangladesh to gain popularity.

In the 1991 election, the issue of secularism versus 'absolute trust and faith in the Almighty Allah' was a widely debated issue. The Awami League declared that it would re-establish secularism as in the original 1972 Constitution. The

Bangladesh Nationalist Party (BNP), founded by Ziaur Rahman declared that it would not return to the 1972 Constitution. Khaleda Zia, who led the BNP to victory and became the first female prime minister said: 'We do not want to establish impiousness in the name of secularism. We want to ensure the equal rights of people of all religions'.[2] An eight-party alliance led by the Awami League declared that it did not oppose keeping *Bismillaher Rahmaner Rahim* in the Constitution.[3] In the 1991 parliamentary election, the BNP secured 46.7 per cent of seats, while the Awami League received 29.3 per cent of seats. Following the election, the BNP headed by Khaleda Zia formed the government with the support of the Jamaat-e-Islami, Bangladesh (JIB) which secured six per cent of seats.

Islam plays a very important role in society and politics. People want to see the use of religious symbols at the state level. Sheikh Hasina (the current Prime Minister) and Khaleda Zia frequently perform *Hajj* (pilgrimage) and attend religious functions, which make the people understand that they are practising Muslims. They follow the Islamic dress code by covering their heads with *sari*. Sheikh Hasina and Khaleda Zia also ensured their participation and visibility in the politics of Bangladesh by showing that they follow the Islamic dress code (Chowdhury 2009: 557).

Despite claiming to be a secular party, the Awami League always uses religion to get mass support. Before the ninth parliamentary elections scheduled to be held on 22 January 2007, it signed a memorandum of understanding with the Bangladesh Khelafat Majlish, an Islamic fundamentalist party.[4] The accord stated that, if voted to power, the alliance would not enact any law which contradicted the values of the Qur'an, Sunnah and Sharia. The accord also stipulated that the alliance would 'reserve the right' of certain categories of Islamic clerics 'to issue fatwa', and that criticism of the prophets and their associates would be considered a criminal offence and that steps would be taken to ensure government recognition of certificates awarded by the *Qaumi* madrasa which are private and not regulated by the Bangladesh Madrasa Education Board.[5] Sheikh Hasina defended the agreement with the Khelafat on a 'tactical ground' to ensure its victory in the parliamentary elections against the BNP-led four-party alliance.[6] The elections scheduled for 22 January were cancelled and the President declared the state of emergency in the wake of the Awami League-led grand alliance's boycott of the parliamentary elections and its series of mass strikes and demonstrations to resist the polls.[7] Again both the Awami League and the BNP used Islam to get mass support in the ninth parliamentary elections held on 29 December 2008. Khaleda Zia and Sheikh Hasina both launched

---

[2] *The Daily Ittefaq* (4 January 1991).
[3] *The Daily Ittefaq* (8 January 1991).
[4] *New Age* (26 December 2006).
[5] ibid.
[6] ibid. The three coalition partners of the BNP were the Jamaat-i-Islami, Bangladesh, the Bangladesh Jatiya Party led by Naziur Rahman and the Islami Oikya Jote.
[7] *The Daily Star* (12 January 2007).

their election campaigns with a visit to the holy shrine of Shah Jalal at Sylhet. Khaleda Zia urged people, 'Save the country and Islam by voting for BNP and its alliance, and don't cast your vote for those who defamed the religion'.[8] Sheikh Hasina pledged not to enact any laws or formulate any regulations which went against the Qur'an and the Sunnah.[9] The Awami League election manifesto of the ninth parliamentary elections 2008 said: 'Laws repugnant to Quran and Sunnah shall not be made'.[10] John L Esposito and Dalia Mogahed found in a Gallup research study of 35 Muslim majority nations between 2001 and 2007 that most people in Muslim majority countries want to see Sharia as a source of legislation (2007: 6). They found that most of the people in Bangladesh want Sharia as the only source of legislation (2007:48). They do not want any legislation which is inconsistent with Islamic law.

III INHERITANCE LAW: A CASE STUDY

In my view, if reform of family law is carried out within an Islamic framework, then people will accept it. A secular approach will not work in Bangladesh. This can be illustrated by the example of the attempt to change inheritance laws.

In 2008, the caretaker government announced the National Women Development policy which made some radical recommendations to ensure equality in personal rights, as well as to property, land and at work. Some religious political parties started staging demonstrations against it. The *ulemas* (Muslim scholars) protested because they thought that the government would change the inheritance law on the basis of this policy. Although the Awami League election manifesto of the ninth parliamentary elections 2008 said: 'Laws repugnant to the Quran and Sunnah shall not be made',[11] Sheikh Hasina announced that women should have equal rights to property and her government would repeal the laws that discriminated against women.[12]

In 2011, the Cabinet approved the National Women Development Policy 2011. Section 23.5 of the National Women Development Policy 2011 stipulates that women should have equal opportunities and shares in property, employment, market and trading. The concept of property has a number of dimensions: movable property, fixed property, earned property or inherited property.[13] The *ulemas* of Bangladesh considered that the government had tactfully avoided referring to inherited property.[14] The law minister and state minister for women declared that there was nothing contradictory between the policy and Muslim

---

[8] *The Daily Star* (23 December 2008).

[9] *New Age* (16 December 2008).

[10] The Election Manifesto, Ninth Parliamentary Elections 2008, Bangladesh Awami League.

[11] The Election Manifesto, Ninth Parliamentary Elections 2008, Bangladesh Awami League.

[12] *The Daily Star* (9 March 2010).

[13] Farhana Urmee, 'Women Development Policy Forward Looking But Not Flawless' *The Star – A Weekly Publication of the Daily Star* vol. 10, issue 12 (25 March 2011).

[14] *Amardesh* (4 April 2011).

inheritance law. In this policy, equal shares in inherited property are not mentioned.[15] However, the majority of Muslims in Bangladesh are not convinced by their arguments. The Islamic Law Implementation Committee, a platform of some Islamist parties, a group linked to a faction of the Islami Oikya Jote (IOJ) and led by Fazlul Huq Aminee, called a dawn-to-dusk nationwide general strike on 4 April 2011 to protest against the newly-introduced Women Development Policy 2011. On 2 April 2011, a *madrasa* student was shot dead and 30 others, including 10 policemen, were injured when they clashed in the city of Jessore after police had intercepted a procession in support of a general strike.[16] The general strike enforced by Islamic activists ended in violence leaving over 250 people, including 16 policemen, injured and 200 detained. The protesters wore white clothes symbolising shrouds and carried copies of the holy Qur'an. The activists of Islamist groups carried the Qur'an during the general strike. This was the first time the holy book was used during a demonstration.[17]

In my view, any change in the inheritance law following the secular approach could not be implemented. Under the existing inheritance legislation, a daughter's share is half that of a son. This is because under Islamic law women have no financial obligation to support their husbands and children, but they do have the right to independent control over their personal assets. In fact, although the Constitution of Bangladesh allows every citizen to 'have the right to acquire, hold, transfer or dispose of property', in most cases women are deprived of their current entitlement to inherited property.[18] Indeed, most Bangladeshi women do not claim the property they inherit from their parents. They wish to maintain good relations with their brothers, because sometimes they return to their natal home after widowhood or divorce. Adnan (1989) points out that if a married woman claims her inherited property it is usually operated and controlled by her husband. Practically it is men (brothers or husbands) who 'take over *de facto* control' of property inherited by women'. A study of two villages in Bangladesh found that 77 per cent of women whose families owned land did not wish to claim their legal share in their parents' property so that they could continue the relationship with their natal families (Monsoor 2008: 112).

Since women are not presently receiving the half share of their brothers as granted by Islamic law, how will women obtain a share equal to that of their brothers? I have observed that even many devout Muslims in Bangladesh deprive women of their due share in the parental property. Most married women in Bangladesh cannot control their income although they have every right to control it. Husbands and in some cases fathers-in-law and mothers-in-law control wives' money directly or indirectly (Chowdhury 2010; Rashid 2006). The ability

---

[15] ibid

[16] *The Daily Star* (3 April 2011).

[17] *The Daily Star* (5 April 2011).

[18] Art 42(1) of the Constitution of Bangladesh says: 'Subject to any restrictions imposed by laws, every citizen shall have the right to acquire, hold, transfer or otherwise dispose of property, and no property shall be compulsorily acquired, nationalised or requisitioned save by authority of law' (Constitution of the People's Republic of Bangladesh).

to control resources is important for the empowerment of women and Bangladeshi women can achieve it through the use of Islamic law.

IV CONCLUSION

Islamic law recognises the physical and biological differences between men and women and it gives importance to the 'complementary but equally important roles of men and women' in the family (Venratraman 1995). Considering these differences, Islamic law places the financial responsibility for wives and children on men to ensure women's economic security within marriage. To ensure women's economic security divorce law should be changed and framed in such a way that divorce should not be effective unless the payments of dower and maintenance are made. The marriage contract or *kabinnama* should automatically provide for delegated divorce. There can be a legal provision for compensation for a divorced wife if she is not at fault. This legal reform would not be contrary to Islam, because 'divorce is a last resort, permissible but not encouraged' in Islam. Under the Dissolution of Muslim Marriages Act 1939[19] a woman is entitled to obtain a decree for the dissolution of her marriage on the ground that her husband has taken an additional wife violating the provisions of the Muslim Family Laws Ordinance 1961. A woman who does not want to stay within a polygamous marriage can divorce her husband. Although women in Bangladesh are not happy with their husbands' remarriage, and even if they know their legal rights, they often accept the remarriage of their husbands. Many women in Bangladesh prefer to live with abusive husbands or co-wives due to the financial, social and sexual vulnerabilities. In view of these realities, it is reasonable to place restrictions on polygamy, but prohibiting polygamy is unrealistic for Bangladeshi society. It will create 'the problem of successive monogamy instead of simultaneous polygamy'. If maintenance and dower laws are implemented properly then polygamy will decrease and will only happen in special circumstances.

Bangladesh can make a law stating that the best interests of a child will be the determining factor regarding child custody and guardianship, as rules about child custody are not found in the Qur'an and Sunnah. In most cases women are deprived of their legal share of their inherited property. Married women's property is usually operated and controlled by men (brothers or husbands). If equal rights are introduced in inheritance law, how would women obtain this equal share when they are not getting the half share of their brothers as granted by Islamic law?

---

[19] The Dissolution of Muslim Marriage Act 1939: bdlaws.minlaw.gov.bd/print_sections.php?id= 180&vol=&sections_id=4813.

REFERENCES

Adnan, S (1989) 'Birds in a Cage: Institutional Change and Women's Position in Bangladesh' 46 *The Journal of Social Studies* 5.

al-Hibri, A (1997) 'Islam, Law and Custom: Redefining Muslim Women's Rights' *American University Journal of International Law and Policy* 1.

Chowdhury, FD (2009) 'Problems of Women's Participation in Bangladesh Politics' 98 *The Round Table* 404, 557.

—— (2010) 'Middle Class Married Women's Income in Bangladesh: Who Controls it and How?' 9 *African and Asian Studies* 1.

Esposito, JL and DeLong-Bas, NJ (2001) *Women in Muslim Family Law*, 2nd edition (New York, Syracuse University Press).

Esposito, JL and Mogahed, D (2007) *Who Speaks for Islam/What a Billion Muslims Really Think* (New York, Gallup Press).

Haider, Z (1999) 'Role of Military in the Politics of Bangladesh: Mujib, Zia, and Ershad Regimes (1972–1990)' XXII *Journal of South Asian and Middle Eastern Studies* 73.

Hakim, MA and Haque, AS (1995) 'Governmental Change and Constitutional Amendments in Bangladesh' 2 *South Asian Survey* 262.

Jahan, R (1987) *Bangladesh Politics: Problems and Issues* (Dhaka, University Press Limited).

Monsoor, T (1999) *From Patriarchy to Gender Equity: Family Law and its Impact on Women in Bangladesh* (Dhaka, The University Press Limited).

—— (2008) *Gender Equity and Economic Empowerment: Family law and Women in Bangladesh* (Dhaka, British Council EWLR).

Rashid, SF (2006) 'Emerging Changes in Reproductive Behaviour Among Married Adolescent Girls in an Urban Slum in Dhaka, Bangladesh' 14 *Reproductive Health Matters* 156.

Venratraman, BA (1995) 'Islamic States and the United Nations Convention of All Forms of Discrimination Against Women: Are the Sharia and the Convention Compatible?' 44 *The American University Law Review* 1949.

Wentholt, K (1999) 'Formal and Substantive Equal Treatment: The Limitations and the Potential of the Legal Concept of Equality' in T Loenen and PR Rodrigues (eds), *Non-Discrimination Law: Comparative Perspectives* (London, Kluwer Law International).

Part IV

Reflections

16

How much Family Conduct do we need to Regulate through Family Law?

Can a man excuse his practices to the contrary because of his religious belief? To permit this would be to make the professed doctrines of religious belief superior to the law of the land, and in effect to permit every citizen to become a law unto himself. Government could exist only in name under such circumstances.

Chief Justice Waite in Reynolds v United States, 98 U.S. 145 (1878).

Within limits the law – our family law – will tolerate things which society as a whole may find undesirable. Where precisely those limits are to be drawn is often a matter of controversy. There is no 'bright-line' test that the law can set. The infinite variety of the human condition precludes arbitrary definition.

Singh v Entry Clearance Officer, New Delhi [2004] EWCA Civ 1075, [2005] QB
608, [2005] 1 FLR 308, [2004] 3 FCR 72 per Munby, J.

I INTRODUCTION

THIS CHAPTER IS about how much family conduct we need to regulate through family law. First of all, let's clarify that by 'family law' we mean the set of rules providing remedies to private individuals concerning the personal as well as the financial consequences of their mutual interaction with other individuals acting as members of the same family.

[1] This research is supported by the Consolidated Research Groups Programme of the Catalan Government (Ref. 2009 SGR 614). I'd like to thank Mavis Maclean and John Eekelaar for their invitation to take part in the Oñati seminar on *Families: Deviance, Diversity and the Law*, as well as the participants in the Seminar for their constructive comments. I am also grateful to Ann Estin, Josep Ferrer Riba, José Ramón García Vicente and Antoni Vaquer, who read a previous draft, suggested changes and provided very useful insights. The usual contention applies that mistakes that remain are only mine.

We are therefore dealing with the *private law* for the family, which must be kept apart from other branches of the law, although these may take the family and family relationships into account as a point of departure, for instance, when granting rights or imposing obligations on individuals. We not dealing either with criminal law linked to family status, although punishment of individuals on this basis may be seen as a way to bolster family law.[2]

On the other hand, for our present purposes, the private law rules for the family are to be understood in a broader way than usual and matters of personal law and inheritance rules are to be included. These questions are often intertwined with family law rules, as in the case of survivorship rights or status-related matters linked to affiliation or to adoption. In addition, this larger field of law is the ambit wherein ethnic, cultural and religious groups are claiming to have some standing.[3]

My understanding of the suggested topic is that we should try to envisage the ideal scope for family law, assuming that other branches of the law have a (perhaps more important) role to play; but also that non-official sources such as religious norms or customary rules may also help in achieving goals assigned so far to family law. In fact, this approach is prompted by the assertion that the state's abstention in family matters could make it easier to provide ethnic, cultural or religious groups with more room to apply their own rules.[4] Indeed, these groups have much to say about the factual grounds of the individual's motivations to comply (or not) with the demands that state family law may be advancing. When conflicting demands arise from state law and from cultural practices, this may easily result in a refusal to act according the requirements of the law. It has thus been contended that one must 'speak to people's beliefs and attitudes' to minimise the likelihood of these types of disputes (Malik 2000: 147–49). This should aid in the recognition of people's sense of belonging while strengthening the law's authority.[5]

The scope of family law could thus be sensibly limited. In particular, individuals belonging to minority groups who are willing to settle conflicts arising in family matters according to their non-state ethnic, cultural or religious norms could be provided with a higher degree of freedom for individual family choices (Shachar 2010: 130). The critical issue is, however, the feasibility and the limits of a family law model that surrenders essential elements of the organisation of social life to arrangements conforming to normative codes or patterns of conduct of ethnic, cultural or religious groups. Regardless of how effective the

---

[2] See Collins et al (2008: 1351–52).

[3] International Council on Human Rights Policy (2009: 66); Shachar (2010: 121) terms it the *demarcating function* of family law: when political autonomy is lacking 'religious personal laws that define marriage, divorce, and lineage have come to serve an important role in regulating membership boundaries'.

[4] See Eekelaar (ch 1 in this book); see also Eekelaar (2010: 351).

[5] Cotterrell (2006: 35) (quoting Ehrlich's contentions): 'If the law is to strengthen its authority with social roots it must, in its own practice, engage with the experienced normative order or living law of social groups and communities'.

latter are in controlling the member's behaviour, the overlapping of both sources inevitably brings about the vexing question of where to draw the line for the abstention of the state. This point is inescapable insofar as we assume universal value for human rights, including individual self-determination and gender equality (Estin 2004a: 525). As Jeremy Waldron has put it, 'those concerns ought to inform our laws anyway. And they ought equally to inform our receptiveness to other customs, particularly if these customs are going to be upheld and enforced in our name' (2010: 113).

II SOCIAL NORMS AND FAMILY LAW

Any exploration of the reach of family law must start by asking whether and how its rules interact with social norms. Family law may be conceived as a network of personal rights and obligations, including social as well as legal ones.[6] Most non-state legal orders are based upon normative social uses conveying duties and conferring rights, and have credited their capacity to guide the conduct of the persons concerned. One possible family law model could limit legal rules to a minimum under the assumption that strong social norms do most of the work that would be expected of state law (Maclean 2000: 2).

The relationship between state law and social norms is nevertheless complex and the resulting picture is neither totally coherent nor conclusive. As already stressed, when social norms are very strong their legal articulation appears to be unnecessary. In this case, absence of legal articulation of social norms does not imply the absence of any obligation. A family practice may even be so widespread that alternative arrangements are marginalised and social mores push to get them prohibited by state law. On the other hand, legal intervention may also indicate that social norms are waning (Eekelaar 2000: 22). Historical experience offers a number of examples of social norms that became legally compulsory only at a later stage, in response to perceived threats to their normative force.[7] On occasion, state law turns out to be oppressive if it keeps trying to enforce patterns of behaviour that have become obsolete. If social norms have fallen into disuse, the likely outcome is that their legal parallel norms are sooner or later also repealed.

The law may withdraw the enforcement of prevailing social norms. The rationale of the law's withdrawal is in this case that countervailing values make conflicts better resolved outside the legal arena (Eekelaar 2000: 16). The examples provided by the legal regulation of parental authority or spousal infidelity

---

[6] Eekelaar (2000: 27) 'It is a body of law that operates in a sphere rich with non-legal obligations that people take seriously'; Ellman (2003: 700).

[7] For instance, see Zimmermann (2007: 34–35) on the origins of the *querela inofficiosi testamenti* in the breaking down of moral consensus as to the acceptable contents of a will. See also Van Houtte and Breda (2005: 246) on the demise of moral obligations vis-à-vis adult relatives in need that prompted the establishment of legal maintenance obligations.

are revealing, as well as the trend to give up considering spouses' fault when dealing with claims after divorce (Agell 1998: 128). The state's abstention in family matters is justified on the basis that even if a certain outcome is seen as socially undesirable (ie, marriage breakdown) and most people think it should be avoided, tools other than legal remedies seem to be better for trying to deal with the issue.

Finally, widespread practices and implicit social norms that support them may at some point be challenged by the law. Ineffectiveness is, however, too often, the result of underlying social practices not being aligned with the law. This fact is likely to trigger frustration, especially if the unsuccessful provisions are aimed at protecting the legitimate interests of vulnerable parts of the society.[8] Conceding that extralegal supplementary tools are most needed here is the first response when facing the limits of the law in curbing hateful practices such as violence against women or child chastisement.

In summary: the position of state law with regard to social norms governing individuals' private lives is not uniform. Accordingly, how much family law is needed is not linked with the actual reach of social norms. Abstention of the state is not based on one and the same rationale: legal remedies are withheld either on the grounds of sufficiency of social norms, because they have fallen into disuse or when legalising the claim is seen to be counterproductive and against other values that family law wishes to recognise.

III WHAT IS FAMILY LAW FOR?

Once we admit that the alternatives are manifold and that family law can either rely on social practices, provide them or not with enforcement measures, or reject giving them any normative value, the scope of family law is to be linked to its very purpose. If we know what family law is for, we will be better prepared to answer the question as to how much of it we need.

As Ira Ellman explained some years ago in his famous inaugural speech, making family law is hard because many people count on it for achieving fundamental societal goals. As he pointed out, since so much family law is statutory, 'citizens engage the political system to obtain family law rules that reflect their views' (Ellman 2003: 701). For decades, and still to a great extent, Western legal orders have been infused with Christian ideals or morals. Unsurprisingly, the so-called 'culture wars' have often found their battlefields in the family law arena. This is so because family law is conceived as a powerful symbolic tool whose main goal is accordingly to encapsulate values and principles to unite the members of the community around certain uncontested truths. Finding the path to law books would reinforce this truth, thereby strengthening the values

---

[8] Contemporary legal challenges to domestic violence or physical chastisement of children have had at best only moderate success, probably due to this gap between law and social norms.

shared by the community against the hesitant or the sceptical. Significantly, claims aiming to increase pluralism in legal orders may also be seen as a route through which the prevailing elites in minority groups are seeking to gain the status of law in order to support their own assumptions about ethnic, cultural or religious norms, challenging thereby possible alternative practices or interpretations.[9]

In the same vein, but focusing on less transcendental aims, the justificatory enterprise of family law can also be built on some general welfare goals, like the removal of gender inequality, the stabilisation of society or the improvement of children's education and behaviour. Bearing in mind that most human societies, if not all, are based on networks of family units, many people tend to handle family law rules as tools able to control the functioning of these complex social mechanisms.[10] Any legal design is thus justified by its capacity to conduct families and society towards certain desired goals.

To my mind these points of view are based on a fundamental misconception about the actual ability of family law rules to influence social behaviour. As Ellman also recalled, 'whether one sees nature or culture at work, what seems clear is that law is a less important causal agent in family relations than one might think from the heated debates over its content' (2003: 702). It is instead the surrounding social and economic conditions that prompt legal changes, rather than the other way round.[11] Furthermore, if the goals to which family law should surrender were to be seriously pursued, unbearable intrusive measures would be required that no democratic legislator can afford.[12] The rejection of such measures 'show[s] clearly that fairness concerns set boundaries around our choice of family law rules' (2003: 707).

Ellman's comments convey some deep truths about the very foundations of family law.[13] Once we give up the idea of finding some 'instrumental rationale for family law', it becomes clearer that the gist of family law must emerge from its function as a tool for seeking an answer to the individual's request for justice

---

[9] See International Council on Human Rights Policy (2009: 18): 'the significance and power of law cannot be dismissed. The power of law as well as its attraction and danger lie in its ability to create and impose social reality, meanings and values, and eventually to make them appear natural and self-evident and thus uncontested [. . .] This power is what lies behind demands for the recognition of diverse kinds of norms as *law*' (emphasis in original; internal references omitted). See also pages 61 and 81 of the report.

[10] For instance, rules on prohibited degrees for marriage are often justified on the view that lacking such rules, sexual requirements among relatives would unsettle basic social units. See a critical appraisal of such a view, in Harding (2008: 174ff) (contending that these rules cannot claim any deterrent effect under current social conditions).

[11] Ellman (2003: 706). See also Eekelaar and Maclean (1994: 18) ('it is often very difficult to know whether the "law" [. . .] is attempting to impose behavioural patterns or mainly reacting to community norms and assumptions'). With regard to marriage, see Roca (2010: 56ff).

[12] See Ellman (2003: 706). The author comments on the ineffectiveness of Swedish law, which backs with numerous substantive rules the explicit goal of sharing of family responsibilities to remove gender roles in marriage. See also Agell (1998: 136) (criticising the Swedish legal programme as imposing 'a forced pattern of living').

[13] See also Carrasco Perera (2006: 34).

within family relationships. It is this endeavour for justice, which lies at the heart of any branch of private law, which makes family law plausible and necessary, regardless of how important the symbolic messages conveyed by legal provisions are or how beneficial the ultimate goals sought by them might be.[14]

The goal of any private law rule may be described in such a way as 'to define our mutual legitimate claims and expectations in our daily interactions under some internal values that find expression on the individual relationship of bipolarity that distinguishes private legal relationships' (Dagan 2008: 395). Family law is thus a set of rules devised to provide individuals with tools to pursue their legitimate claims in family matters and that seeks to render them a fair outcome by defining the parties' mutual entitlements.[15] Any measure of the reasonable reach of contemporary family law must thus focus on those internal social values that justify the parties' mutual entitlements.

This task is fulfilled in two complementary settings, both of which can be referred as the *cogency* of family law: some family law rules *must* exist and some of them are never to be *set aside* by individuals or groups when making their own family arrangements. The pursuit of fairness by reconciling the rights (or interests) of individuals involved in family relationships is in both settings the driving force of enacting private law rules for families (Eekelaar and Maclean 1994: 19–20). But it is also its intrinsic limitation. We need as many family law rules as required to ensure that certain individual interests of any party are given due consideration in a family relationship. But family law must stop where private law remedies are deemed too intrusive into family life and other tools are available to efficiently protect the relevant interests of the parties.[16] To this end, currently family law cannot be seen − if ever it has − as part of public law.

IV HOW INACTIVE CAN THE STATE BE?

A Diverse versus Deviant Practices

Two points seem clear from departure. First, that states are entitled to reject traditions seen as causing harm or inequality.[17] Accordingly, arrangements or

---

[14] Parallel considerations underlie the distinction held by Waldron between *exemptions* related with policy oriented preventive goals and *exceptions* concerning right-based rules. See Waldron (2010: 106).

[15] On the internal social values expressed in individual relationships, Dagan (2008: 395).

[16] See now art 235-50 Civil Code of Catalonia, introduced by Act 25/2010, of 29 of July, which states that adoptive parents have the duty to disclose the fact of the adoption to the child as early as he or she is mature enough, or when he or she is 12 years old at the latest. This provision has given rise to critical claims of disproportionate interference in family life. The rule rests, however, on the criterion that parents must exercise their responsibilities according to the best interests of the child, and that adoptive children have a legally protected interest to gain knowledge about their origins (see art 235-49). The burden posed on parents is thus instrumental, although the lack of legal remedies attached to it makes it a clear candidate to be called 'symbolic legislation'.

[17] Hamilton (1995: 81). See also Waldron (2010: 109) and more references therein.

practices impairing individual human rights are to be considered deviant practices, which in principle cannot be enforced and that may also be punished by criminal law. The second point is that even with regard to alternative arrangements that are to be seen as diverse rather than as deviant, state law is not always compelled to provide enforcement measures or merely recognise them. Tolerance requires that no legal action is taken against such practices but all cultural, ethnic or religious practices are not necessarily to be recognised.[18] The margin of appreciation in any policy decision is to be applied here. Ensuring fairness might well be, however, a driving force for new legal developments or for judicial creative responses to individuals' demands.

Deviant practices are therefore defined on the basis of their harming of individual human rights, including practices and arrangements based exclusively on discrimination against women. However, in order not to impose 'decontextualised overriding values' (Freeman 1998: 297) even here an effort should be made to put the conflicting primary values in a wider cultural context. As Freeman has stressed, any practice must be subject 'to an internal critique . . . deconstructing the arguments that are used to support it' (1998: 302) with 'a deeper understanding of [its] cultural context' (1998: 303).

From this process it may result that differences exist between cultures and legal orders, but also that most of them are not intractable. Some practices, however, will not stand this sort of assessment. The example that immediately comes to mind is the so-called 'female circumcision',[19] which amounts to so much physical and psychological harm that outweighs any supposed social or cultural benefits. Even if the price of preservation of physical and psychological integrity is that of becoming a social outcast in one's community, this argument shall have no bearing vis-à-vis state law because no ethnic, cultural or religious community can be allowed to require its would-be members to yield their basic human goods to be accepted.[20] In addition, as regards the global stance against them, these practices must be confronted forthrightly as they are performed usually on young or very young girls, whose consent is not to be presumed in any case (Freeman 1998: 301–02).

In the area of family private law parallel concerns arise in the case of forced marriages allowed in some areas, either in connection with child brides or even with regard to older woman in different settings. Like female circumcision, forced marriages entail a degree of coercion that is untenable and that prevents this act from being called a legal act. Apart from the infringement of the internationally protected 'right to marry' with the free and full consent of the intending spouses, the very basis of the act is coercion and abuse. Two problems may arise, however, from not enforcing or recognising these 'marriages'. First, it may be doubtful when marriage can be considered forced or is simply imposed by the

---

[18] Hamilton (1995: 80). See also Estin (2004a: 518).

[19] Moreno Antón (2007: 122ff). But see also La Barbera (2010) and more references therein.

[20] On the very different prevailing view on male circumcision see also Moreno Antón (2007: 210). See also Freeman (1998: 303). More recently see the critical account of Askola (2011: 100–19).

circumstances of any of the spouses or of both. Age and maturity of the intending spouse could be legally relevant and indeed it is, but thoughtful attention to the relevant facts is required to avoid overstating the case for void marriages. The difference between forced and arranged marriages seems of particular importance here.[21] Besides that, one may also wonder whether nullity, or even non-existence of the legal act, could provide reasonable protection to the victims of these practices. As in other cases of deviant practices in direct conflict with individual human rights, a pragmatic approach would leave open at least the possibility of basing the protection of the victim on marriage remedies.

Another common area of conflict between non-Western religious norms and state law is polygamy: in fact polygyny. As is well-known, polygyny is allowed and practised in a substantial part of the globe but is directly opposed by state law in most if not all Western jurisdictions. Indeed, bigamy amounts usually to criminal liability and second and successive simultaneous marriages are void. Currently, however, such a legal stance can no longer be based on the sole fact that such practices are *contra bonos mores* since in democratic societies no community can claim to hold a true moral right. The prevailing doctrine focuses instead on the fact that the equal treatment of men and women would be irrevocably compromised if polygyny is accepted. As the argument goes, as long as the wife is not entitled to take more than one husband, these practices are based on essential discrimination in the exercise of the right to marry and within marriage (Hamilton 1995: 72–73). But does this mean that the answer could be different if such a possibility were open to both husband and wife?[22] Less theoretically, second marriages entered into in countries that allow such a practice have been at least partially recognised in many Western countries. As Hamilton also pointed out, American courts found that 'the refusal of any [matrimonial relief] to [second] wives was seen to operate extremely harshly'.[23] A parallel process has taken place in other jurisdictions. International private lawyers term 'attenuated public order' the pragmatic approach held by courts and administrative bodies that grant some if not all the legal effects to (second) marriages to offer protection regarded as fair to the wife.[24]

Concerning issues related to minor children, deviant practices would be those that do not comply with the minimum standards of upbringing for all children. A balance must be struck here between accepting diversity and ensuring these

---

[21] See Maclean, ch 7 in this book.

[22] The answer is probably yes, but material conditions regarding communities such as the fundamentalists Mormons, make a legal reform regulating polygamous marriages along liberal, egalitarian lines, a rather idealistic image. See in this sense D'Onofrio (2005: 391). As Judith Stacey and Tey Meadow (2009: 193) put it 'legalizing plural marriages could lead to fewer rather than more of them. Were age of consent laws strictly enforced and women genuinely free to consent to enter polygynous marriages, we doubt that hordes would clamor to do so'.

[23] Hamilton (1995: 70–71). In fact, attempts to change laws permitting polygamy in some African states have been socially unacceptable because they provide too little protection for second wives (ibid 73, at fn 42).

[24] Adroher Biosca (2003: 331). On the attempt to regulate polygyny through secular regulations of Muslim marriages, see Waheeda Amien, ch 6 in this book.

minimum standards (Bainham 1995: 244). Proceeding from cultural voluntarism here would mean, first, to see families other than the nuclear family based on marriage as diverse and not necessarily a kind of deviance; but also that cultural practices or religious norms that deny children any voice or impose religious or cultural considerations entirely alien to the child's welfare should be overridden.[25] This is the case of practices, for example, which consist of automatically granting custody rights to fathers against the interests of mothers or relying exclusively on the basis of the religion or ethnic origin of the parents.

The religious norms or cultural practices that provide for different family arrangements without directly impairing the individual human rights of the parties involved may be not only tolerated, but cultural voluntarism would seek to justify their recognition and find the ways for them to be legally enforced. This outcome derives from the fact that, although different from the law of the land, they accord the internal social values that the legal adjudication process pursues. Accordingly, instead of giving too much weight to the accidental differences of cultural practices or religious norms with the law of the land, a functional assessment of these rules is required that focuses on the substantive consequences of its application and protection of the parties' relevant interests.

This analysis is to be applied to different family law scenarios where accommodation of diverse practices is at stake.

B Access to Legally Valid Marriage

From a pluralist standpoint, recognition of religious marriages or of other non-official marriages should not be difficult. In fact, in many Western countries state law overtly admits the legal validity of marriage solemnised by clerical acts. The historical process that led to this result is well known and the varieties of arrangements of the relationship between states and church(es) are manifold. The integration of diverse practices at this level requires, however, some thought about the aims of state law when recognising certain relationships of couples as 'marriage', as well as the justification of both the formal and the substantive requirements laid down in state law. To my mind, states have a wide margin of appreciation when conferring the condition of marriage on a certain couple, but they cannot introduce obstacles that are overwhelming or that directly or indirectly cause unjustified discrimination, especially on the grounds of ethnic, cultural or religious origin. Besides this, the formal requirements that are common to all legal systems must be connected with the privileged standing that marriage currently enjoys, and the need of the state to control who is married and to whom.[26]

---

[25] As regards life-threatening parental decisions based on religious considerations, see Teresa Picontó-Novales, ch 8 in this book.

[26] See on this point the illuminating approach of Estin (2009: 477ff).

Apart from the requirement of heterosexuality – which does not seem to be one of the battlefields of non-official legal orders[27] – recognition and enforcement of ethnic or religious marriages poses the question of how to deal with 'underage marriages'. Against the background of international human rights standards, the problem arises due to the fact that in many cultures social norms start from the assumption that once puberty has been reached marriage is already appropriate and even needed, bearing in mind the widespread dislike of extramarital sexual relationships in traditional communities. These concerns also partly underline the permission given for underage marriage when entered into with parental consent or judicial dispensation.[28] The international human rights standards seem to be justified to obtain the goal of preventing traffic of children and exploitation of young girls, without exceptions allowed on the basis of social or cultural constraints (Hamilton 1995: 56). Nonetheless, on occasion Western courts have been inclined to enforce child marriages entered into according to foreign law on the basis that the cultural and ethnic context sees such a marriage as normalised. This leads to the question whether it is right for a state to tolerate underage marriages acceptable to and performed under the auspices of the parties' religious norms and customs if they are considered highly undesirable for their own citizens.[29] Taking a sociological stance, it may be justifiable for a first generation of immigrants to be provided with legal status according to the factual situation created by the application of their customs, but this does not require states to adapt their general legislation to these customs, including second-generations of immigrants settled in the land. It is one thing to grant legal effects to foreign practices or enforce foreign norms in particular cases, and another to amend legal policy against international human rights standards so as to leave room for rules of minorities settled permanently in the land. At any rate, under current social circumstances, the minimum age of marriage should be seen in light of changes in the social perception of adolescent social interactions, including the practice of sex and the assumption of undesired side-effects like teenage pregnancy or the contraction of diseases. To this end, even though these limits seem to be highly ineffective, they may be justified in order to avoid parental or familial pressure on adolescents in certain environments to marry and enter into a permanent cohabitation that is likely to severely curtail his or her development.

---

[27] In the sense that religious or ethnic codes do not promote same-sex stable relationships, but usually condemn them: see Wardle (2010: 315ff). Marriage between two men or two women may, however, be recognised by certain religious denominations or within some ethnic subcultures and the question of whether such unions must be recognised and enforced as marriage by state law will arise. See already Hamilton (1995: 53ff). Traditional practices of transgender parenting in Polynesia are indeed challenging the prevailing stance of metropolitan French adoption law: Zanghellini (2010: 651–77).

[28] This possibility is found in a number of Western legal systems and accords minimum age rules laid down in international conventions in force.

[29] In these terms, see Hamilton (1995: 56).

Another ambit of disagreement is the prohibited degrees of marriage, where the extent of prohibition based on consanguinity (blood relations) and affinity (through marriage) varies a great deal between state and religious norms. This problem usually arises on occasion of the application of foreign law as the personal law dealing with the substantive requirements of marriage. The question is whether a marriage entered into within the prohibited degrees laid down in state law should be avoided. A critical trend against these rules is visible in many countries, and in a number of them the prohibition of marriage for affinity reasons has been abolished. Moreover, dispensation of the prohibition of marriage between blood relations for 'grave reasons' has been introduced by canonical law within certain degrees (Harding 2008: 160). Tensions also appear with minority cultures characterised by endogamy practices, like the Irish Travellers (Harding 2008: 179–80).

Endogamy practices – but also non-registered religious marriages or marriages having entered into without the preliminaries stipulated by civil law being met – pose the more general problem of whether state law can simply close its eyes to the reality of irregular marriages. In practice, considerations of legal certainty and the fact that recognising any form of living arrangement is seen as impracticable are the most usual grounds for leaving these situations in the margins of the law. It seems, nevertheless, that some may merit specific consideration from family law.[30] They cannot simply be left to contractual rules or other remedies, like tort law or actions based on unjustified enrichment. Underneath these relations there may be an imbalance of economic and social power with personal and family elements that only family law is able to level out. Focusing on *status* only and disregarding the situation of the parties facing, for instance, the breakdown of their relationship or the death of a partner, may bring about unfair results with which family law must be concerned.

C Enforcement of Marital Duties and Rights

As is well known, over recent decades the trend in many Western legal orders has been to withdraw the attention of the law away from how individuals handle their own personal choices in issues held to be concerned exclusively with their moral codes. Many examples can be found such as, among others, the repeal of laws punishing adultery and other infringements of marital duties, the development of systems of no-fault divorce that grant divorce regardless of who is to blame for the marriage breakdown or the growing recognition of legal effects to unmarried couples.

Minorities or even religious groups of greater power in a given society may claim to uphold stricter moral standards than those currently enforced by the law

---

[30] See Estin (2004: 217) (referring to American courts' response to irregular marriages).

of the land.[31] Against this background, the position of state law may be unclear with regard to family arrangements – linked to the personal law applicable to a given case or flowing from an agreement freely entered into by the parties – which subjects them to harsher consequences than those stipulated by the default rules on marriage and marriage dissolution. A paradoxical outcome may result from recognition and enforceability of diverse family arrangements in settings from which state family law has withdrawn its regulation. Rules agreed to by the parties, often based on their cultural, ethnic or religious background, mean in fact a backlash towards traditional values that contemporary family law decided no longer to uphold. Cultural voluntarism may have a difficult time here justifying that these arrangements should not be legally enforceable.

D Divorce

Integration of cultural or religious practices could mean that divorce is granted with immediate legal effect by following the internal ways established by these groups according to their own codes, either as to the grounds for divorce or its consequences. This possibility may give rise to two different issues. First, whether the celebration of a religious marriage implies that parties are not allowed to have recourse to state law if any of them wishes to divorce. The second issue is whether and up to what point the religious divorce norms are to be recognised and enforced by state law.

The first issue recalls the problems of the so-called 'Millet system', whose practical limitations are evident in India and elsewhere. The issue has arisen in the context of Catholic countries with regard to the status of canonical marriage and its effects, but also where minority Muslim communities are allowed to settle family matters according to their own rules, as in West Thrace in Greece.[32] It is submitted that claiming forced adherence to the prescriptions of a special personal law on the basis of the type of marriage that the parties were allowed to celebrate overstates the scope of the recognition by state law. In fact, such a position would entail the complete abstention of the state from regulation of the rights and duties of the parties, which requires some additional assessment of the interests at stake. Accordingly, the two issues should not be mixed and recognition of the solemnisation of marriage does not necessarily require, for instance, submitting to religious or community bodies to decide on divorce according to the corresponding non-official set of rules.

---

[31] Hamilton (1995: 94) stressed that 'many minority religious groups have a rather stricter attitude towards morality than the exhibited by the civil system of family law, and fear that their standards of morality will decline if their members are subject only to the requirements and values of the civil system'.

[32] For a recent account of the situation of Muslims in West Trace see Tsaoussim and Zervogianni (2008: 223ff).

It is well known that neither Jewish law nor Islamic law offer divorce on an equal basis to men and women (Hamilton 1995: 95). Accordingly, direct recognition of these religious divorces poses intractable problems that seem to make civil divorce proceedings unavoidable. However, these divorces have been recognised on occasion in order to avoid so-called limping marriages (Hamilton 1995: 112). In my view, deconstructing the situation and separating the question of how to obtain a divorce decree and the decision about the financial and personal consequences of divorce could help handling this issue. In fact, as Ayelet Shachar has stressed, 'women who turned to [religious councils] expressed no interest in (and, indeed, some explicitly rejected) the idea of delegating control over the distributive components of their fractured marriage' (2010: 128). And one of the most interesting findings of the research conducted by the team lead by Gillian Douglas is that practice of religious bodies is centered on the grant of the religious annulment/divorce to enable the parties to remarry within the faith. It is thus concluded that 'the focus is on the marriage itself, not the ancillaries' because 'for adherents, being able to remarry within the faith serves both to enable them to retain their standing within their faith community and to regularise their position with the religious authorities' (chapter eleven, this book).

The evident gender bias that most important religious divorces connote makes them abhorrent, but this rule may be less questionable if compared with the current system that prevails in most Western legal systems.[33] With the progressive withdrawal of substantive and procedural requirements that divorce has undergone in many Western legal systems, *talaq* divorces and other analogous privileges held by men in Muslim countries under Islamic law become less questionable.[34] Gender discrimination evident in the regulation of religious divorce, and especially Islamic *talaq*, could be overcome both at national level, in new legislation developed by Islamic jurisdictions, but also by applying the rules of conflicts of law. The Spanish legal system, for instance, tried to circumvent the difficulties created by gender limitations to accessing divorce under Islamic law by allowing wives to choose the *lex fori* as the governing law of divorce proceedings. The result is that both parties have now the possibility of obtaining a decree of divorce in Spain, without prejudice to the resulting personal or financial consequences.[35]

---

[33] See also Estin (2004: 222).

[34] See also Douglas, ch 11 in this book (divorce law moving towards an administrative process allowing 'registered repudiation' diminishes substantive and procedural objections to religious divorces).

[35] Art 107.2 II c) Spanish Civil Code, as amended by the Organic Act 11/2003, of 29 September. Until then courts had on occasion rejected divorce petitions filed by Moroccan wives resident in Spain arguing that Moroccan family law denied them such a possibility. For instance see Provincial Court of Barcelona, judgments of 15 September 1998 (Aranzadi Civil 1998\1564) and 6 April 2000 (Aranzadi Civil 2000\1088). In the same vein, an *attenuated public order* would be applicable to uphold the petitions filed by repudiated Muslim women living in Spain to get divorce recognized by state courts in order to clarify their legal status and enhance their autonomy. See Fernández-Coronado (2009: 150).

E Financial Consequences of Divorce

In religious norms and cultural practices, divorce and the consequences of it for husband and wife are completely intertwined. Indeed, this was also the case in Western laws until very recent legal developments took place. As is well known, the decline of fault as a ground for divorce led to uncertainty as to what the foundations of financial relief on divorce are.

The withdrawal of fault went along with the irrelevance of who took the initiative to dissolve the marriage. Only grossly reprehensible conduct against the other party remains as having certain influence.[36] Besides that, the growing incidence of divorce has brought into question the matrimonial property regimes in force in many Western countries. Community property regimes – although still prevalent across Europe and in many parts of the world – are being subject to equitable adjustments to avoid unfair results[37] and parties also substitute the default community rules by a separation of property regimes before or after marriage by means of marriage contracts.

These trends have stressed the role of courts in reviewing the imbalance produced to the parties on marriage dissolution, especially in those situations leading to seriously detrimental consequences for one of the parties that make the outcome unfair. In the case of marriage agreements – even if these are broadly recognised and enforced across Europe – procedural as well as substantive requirements allow courts to review and amend the proceedings of the divorce to grant a fair relief to the party most in need.[38]

These developments could be useful in examining institutions such as Islamic *mahr* and other parallel institutions known in Judaic law.[39] Although these derive their legal force from religious marriages and belong to the regulation laid down in sacred texts and clerical interpretation and application of them, this does not mean that their nature as a civil remedy can be disregarded. In fact, the whole relationship of the married parties appears to be seen as merely civil in nature according to the mentioned religious laws. Functionally, *mahr* serves the basic aim of providing the wife with a bargaining tool that protects her against the repudiation of her husband. It is also seen in a positive light as long as it may effectively deter husbands from marrying more wives if the wife is allowed to demand divorce and the payment of the deferred *mahr* in the case of a second marriage.[40] The counterpoint, however, is that in the absence of serious grounds for divorce attributable to him, if the husband is not interested in divorcing her, the wife who wants to divorce should either try to force her husband to divorce her or to forfeit her rights to *mahr* (Sayed 2008: 195–96).

---

[36] For instance, see s 1579 BGB and art 270 III French Civil Code.
[37] See the outline provided by Pintens (2009: 273–74).
[38] See recently, Dethloff (2011: 94).
[39] On this topic see extensively, Fournier (2010) *passim*.
[40] See Sayed (2008: 199ff).

Note that the distance between *mahr* and financial relief on divorce is apparently great. First, it is a remedy available to one party only, namely the (innocent) wife. In addition, its substantive requirements do not include taking into account the claimant's needs or economic means, or the defendant's. As a result, indiscriminate enforcement of marriage contracts, including *mahr*, risks being unfair because of either over or under-compensation.[41] Nonetheless, reading it contextually, *mahr* appears to be a protective device for women, if properly tailored according to the economic status of the husband. It is not gender biased in the sense of diminishing women's condition. It may be seen as paternalistic in light of a highly discriminatory divorce law, but it is not in itself discriminatory. Historically, Western legal systems have also been familiar with institutions aimed at providing security to wives, mainly against the risks of widowhood.[42] If, as Fournier has emphasised, '*mahr* cannot travel through either recognition or non-recognition' (2010: 135) its treatment by state law must focus on its basic functions and give up those preconditions linked with the privileges that men enjoy in divorce actions according to Islamic law. Subsequently, the enforcement of *mahr* should be granted only on controlling the procedural and substantive requirements that civil law imposes to marriage contracts. To this end, factors that are to be taken into account are, among others, those that courts regularly apply to decide on equitable adjustment of the financial consequences of divorce.[43] This result does not mean imposing state law values overriding any religious or cultural element inherent in *mahr*: the remedy is not disqualified as totally alien to the tradition of the land or as exclusively religious in nature. In practice, the likely outcome of its reception is better described as a hybrid construct where possible imbalances of power are necessarily adjusted according to the fairness assessments expressed in judicial adjudication of marital property cases.[44]

F Custody Arrangements

Facing disputes involving a dilemma posed by the religious or the ethnic adscription of any of the parties, state law is not allowed to surrender to practices that deny children of age and mature judgement any voice on issues relevant to them, or that apply biased criteria grounded on religious or cultural norms to adjudicate over custody. Accordingly, no faith or cultural heritage is to prevail in cases where parents belong to different communities.

---

[41] See for instance, Wilson (2007: 1379–80).
[42] On this point see especially, Fournier (2010: 131ff) (quoting case law tracing parallel lines between *mahr* and dower).
[43] See also Estin (2004: 226ff).
[44] Sayed (2008: 207) (stressing that *mahr* shall be treated as an institution of its own in the process of qualification of a subject-matter in conflict of laws rules).

Keeping the child in his or her cultural, ethnic or cultural environment is, however, a factor to be taken into account even if the decision shall not be determined exclusively by it. In particular, it is relevant whether the environment where custody is to be exercised deprives, as a matter of fact, children of any contact with the wider society, where the group's ideas could be challenged by exposure to external influences. Conversely, a culturally contextualised analysis may confer prima facie validity to agreements entered into by the parents, before birth or before separation, about the future of the children's religious upbringing or education. Provided that these agreements do not objectively harm the children, the fact that they clearly tend to favour raising the child within a minority culture does not prevent them from being enforced. Alternative arrangements that take into account the child's wider cultural community and that improve the chances of his or her successful upbringing beyond the parental conflict, may also represent a more nuanced view of how to define the children's best interests (Goolam 1998: 374–75).

G Inheritance Matters

Religious norms and cultural practices, some of them embedded in customary laws, may also deal with inheritance matters. In Western societies, although the testator's freedom is paramount, many countries lay down provisions in their law books that impose limitations regarding how and to whom one may leave one's estate (*imperative inheritance law*). Two main problems may arise when trying to integrate culture and religious norms in the area of succession law.

The first problem concerns the position of the surviving spouse. Traditionally the wife's position has been very weak and the assets left by her husband are often taken by children or returned to the husband's relatives. In Western law, improving the position of the surviving spouse has been a clearly ascertainable trend shared by all legal systems. This trend conforms to the demographic and social change of conditions in which succession on death now takes place. Foreign personal law or wills made according to religious or cultural contexts whereby the spouse's interests are not taken into account are likely to pose problems. State law needs to have regard to the position of the surviving spouse in the whole system of non-state law and provide for relief if leaving him or her with nothing is deemed an unfair result (Wilson 2010: 943–46).

The second problem arises when state law proceeds to regulate the distribution of the estate in a manner that reduces the scope of self-determination recognised by customs or religious practices, or produces an outcome that does not match with the traditional way of dividing the estate on death by members of the religious or ethnic group. In this area it is pretty clear that legal systems differ widely between each other. It is therefore difficult to say that a certain distribution is intrinsically fair. From the point of view of cultural voluntarism, upholding the testator's decision would be paramount unless we can find an overruling justification in the interest of the would-be beneficiary that deems it unreasonable to accommodate the cultural tradition. In this vein, a minimal protective net would require that dependants on the deceased person be granted a right against the estate allowing them to have the means to afford their needs and eventually reach financial autonomy. These protective measures, moreover, should be based on their relative fairness in relation to the relationship that linked the parties and their past conduct and relationship.[45] Otherwise, state law on the distribution of the estate may easily be seen as a mere imposition of the majority views on the minorities. Conversely, if according to personal law or cultural rules the freedom of the testator is limited to favouring some relatives or the community, the state is not compelled to provide legal remedies to make these moral or cultural requirements real, unless the outcome is deemed unfair according to the criteria summarised above.

V BY WAY OF CONCLUSION: THE CASE FOR CULTURALLY CONTEXTUALISED FAMILY LAW

Instead of imposing top-down solutions based on some morality standards or policy guidelines, family law should provide a framework within which individual choice is maximised, thereby according its fundamental goal of pursuing fairness in family relationships. Mavis Maclean called this model of family law a 'facilitative rights-based' model, which sits well with increasing experiences of multiculturalism in a global society (2000: 2).

First, however, this option is limited by the constraints of protecting individual human rights.[46] When setting the internal values to which any family relationship shall be accommodated, the paramount concern is enhancing the protection provided to individuals as basic human rights.[47] Human dignity and self-determination, as well as gender equality, are of overriding relevance here. On occasion, the deconstruction of the interests of the parties at stake will show that a balance must be struck between equally relevant rights. But this fact does not deprive human rights of the deference that they demand.

Secondly, fairness should also be addressed *within the relationship*. To my mind, this assessment can be made of family law rules that cannot be set aside by the individuals involved (*imperative family law rules*) and also of private arrangements in a broad sense (*agreements and practices*). In both cases, the entitlements of the parties are to be subject to scrutiny so as to find out whether or not the resulting consequences properly express the social internal values

---

[45] See Foqué and Verbeke (2009: 219) on the trend towards more open and flexible inheritance law aimed at protecting the weaker instead of providing an automatic forced share of the estate.

[46] As long as it can be said that 'neither is there a true private law existing in total autonomy, where each intervention of the State requires justification, nor can all law be based entirely on the state': Jansen and Michaels (2008: 11).

[47] See Roca (2010: 89).

that private family law wants to enhance. Such a standpoint may provide the flexible common ground for analysing family practices and arrangements and for assessing whether reasonable accommodation within family law is feasible or not. State family law often expresses not only value judgements enshrining human rights choices, but policy choices that have limited connection with these rights. Traditions reflected in legal rules have at times become obsolete and fallen into disuse. Some have even become at odds with values held by wider society and kept only by the political force of a minority. In addition, with a better understanding of religious, ethnic or cultural family practices, differences between the default rules will not be overstated.[48]

One should thus end by dealing with 'hybrid or reconstructed systems developed in the shadow of state law' (Davies 2010: 809), which are to fulfil the aspirations for respect for cultural values without endangering the individual's basic interests within the family relationship. Increasing the openness of family law to contractualisation should make it easier to accommodate different practices while setting limits to the involvement of state law in the enforcement of arrangements that jeopardise individual self-determination or result in gender discrimination.[49]

At the end of the day, broadening our standpoint from an analysis of cultural and religious practices to a parallel critical approach to the reach of state family law brings before us a wider panorama of institutions and subject-matters open to cross-cultural discussion.[50] In this setting, making the claim that private arrangements must be recognised and enforced brings us to consider also the proper limits of state interference.[51] This culturally contextualised analysis presupposes the positive reception of ethnic, cultural and religious diversity by the state, whose rules only override non-state normative matters insofar as accommodation would be unreasonable.[52] On the other hand, the communities should

---

[48] From different standpoints, a number of contributions to this book show that arguably rigid non-state normative systems are in fact much more flexible than imagined. See for instance, the outline provided both by Nazila Ghanea, ch 14 and Gillian Douglas, ch 11, in this book, on the so-called 'fatwa-shopping' inherent to decentralised adjudication of family matters in Muslim communities.

[49] In broader terms, Estin (2009: 480) concludes that 'this process balances the divergent values of families and groups, and helps preserve the vitality of religious communities and the cohesion of the state'.

[50] See also Waldron (2002: 33) and Prakash Shah, ch 3 in this book. On the chance of 'cultural transformative accommodation', understood as a change *from within*, see Shachar (2010: 130).

[51] But see the uncompromising stance held by Wilson (2010: 946ff) (arguing that states should be wary of ceding jurisdiction over family matters to bodies that may be unwilling or unable to vindicate women and children's rights). See also International Council on Human Rights Policy (2009: 68–70) (contending that non-state orders tend to put the burden disproportionately on women).

[52] The burden of proving that ethnic, cultural or religious practices cannot be accommodated would rest with the state. For instance, on accommodation of law to religious demands, see Woehrling (2010: 137). See also Wardle (2010: 354ff) (relying on the approach used by the rules on conflict of laws to ascertain how reasonable the accommodation of religious norms may be). Besides that, as Waldron (2010: 111) stresses, 'it seems unfair to hold the proposed accommodation to a higher level of justice than that established under the status quo'.

reciprocate by being open (Cotterrell 2006: 43) and align their practices[53] as to be able to grant the parties a result deemed fair both according to their own rules and to the culturally contextualised assessment of the conflict between their interests.[54]

This approach does not lead obviously to any *actual* family legal system, but only to a framework of analysis of the goals of family law that allows the internal validity of both cultural practices *and* state family law to be discussed.[55] According to this framework, we should be able to advance some steps in order to assess which religious or cultural practices or family arrangements must be overridden because they are deviant rather than diverse; but also to assess which of them can possibly be accommodated because they also follow the fairness goals that are expected from the legal processing of a private claim.[56]

Such a minimal approach, although closely linked with the actual protection of human rights within the private sphere, makes it possible to have different choices within the family. Insofar as many legal orders are still based on inherited legal traditions that plainly overlap with the rules followed by communities settled in a country, or even with family arrangements developed by the individuals, in the long run the process of hybridisation should entail that states will take steps to reduce the requirements imposed by family law rules and substitute them with basic contents aimed at warranting respect for individual human rights and interests.

---

[53] Reciprocity is a basic condition of the politics of recognition and means that communities shall be permeable and capable of change and evolution. This reciprocity may be predicated not only in communities settled in Western countries, but as part and parcel of the construction of shared values at global scale. In fact, encouraging bottom-up changes appears to be a successful strategy to root basic individual human rights within the traditional practices. See for instance the experience of Namibia in Hinz (1998: 139–52). Conversely, legislative movements bear the risk of bringing about severe setbacks for gender equality and a turn against women: see Mohamad (2011: 59ff).

[54] Entering a dialogue across the communities is possible when versions of common sense values are accepted by all participants in intercultural experience. See Freeman (2002: 350ff). In addition, to overcome the dichotomy between universalism and cultural relativism, a 'dialogue *within* the relevant ethno-cultural group, enabling the group's members to address the issue themselves' is required (International Council on Human Rights Policy (2009: 24). On instances of adaptation of practices and norms within cultural or religious groups see Estin (2004: 227–28).

[55] See also Estin (2009: 480).

[56] Waheeda Amien, in ch 6 of this book, concludes that secular regulation of Muslim marriages 'promises more protection for women's rights than mere recognition of Muslim marriages' and that 'regulation offers the opportunity for those discriminatory features to be constitutionally challenged, which could facilitate the gendered reform of Muslim marriages. In this way, the true objectives of Islamic law, which include equality, justice, freedom, fairness, the protection of human welfare and the condemnation of women being subordinated to men could find expression in a meaningful and significant way'.

REFERENCES

Adroher Biosca, S (2003) 'Desafíos del Derecho de familia en una sociedad intercultural' in D Borobio (ed), *Familia e interculturalidad* (Salamanca, Universidad Pontificia).

Agell, A (1998) 'Should and Can Family Law Influence Social Behaviour?' in J Eekelaar and T Nhlapo (eds), *The Changing Family: International Perspectives on the Family and Family Law* (Oxford, Hart Publishing).

Askola, H (2011) 'Cut–Off Point? Regulating Male Circumcision in Finland' 25 *International Journal of Law, Policy and the Family* 100.

Bainham, A (1995) 'Family Law in a Pluralistic Society' 22 *Journal of Law and Society* 234.

Carrasco Perera, Á (2006) *Derecho de familia. Casos, reglas, argumentos* (Madrid, Dilex).

Collins, JM, Leib, EJ and Markel, D (2008) 'Punishing Family Status' 88 *Boston University Law Review* 1327.

Cotterrell, R (2006) 'Legal Philosophy and Legal Pluralism' in *Law, Culture and Society. Legal Ideas in the Mirror of Social Theory* (Burlington, Ashgate).

Dagan, H (2008) 'The Limited Autonomy of Private Law' in N Jansen and R Michaels (eds), *Beyond the State. Rethinking Private Law* (Tübingen, Mohr Siebeck).

Davies, M (2010) 'Legal Pluralism' in P Cane and HM Kritzer (eds), *The Oxford Handbook of Empirical Legal Research* (Oxford, Oxford University Press).

Dethloff, N (2011) 'Contracting in Family Law: A European Perspective' in K Boele-Woelki, J Miles, and JM Scherpe (eds), *The Future of Family Property in Europe* (Cambridge, Intersentia).

D'Onofrio, E (2005) 'Child Brides, Inegalitarianism and the Fundamentalist Poligamous Family in the United States' 19 *International Journal of Law, Policy and the Family* 373.

Eekelaar, J (2000) 'Uncovering Social Obligations: Family Law and the Responsible Citizen' in M Maclean (ed), *Making Law for Families* (Oxford, Hart Publishing).

—— (2010) 'From Multiculturalism to Cultural Voluntarism: A Family-based Approach' 81 *The Political Quarterly* 344.

Eekelaar, J and Maclean, M (1994), *Introduction to Family Law* (Oxford, Oxford University Press).

Ellman, IM (2003) 'Why Making Family Law is Hard' 35 *Arizona State Law Journal* 699.

Estin, AL (2004) 'Human Rights, Pluralism, and Family Law' in P Lødrup and E Modvar (eds), *Family Life and Human Rights* (Oslo, Gyldendal).

—— (2004a) 'Toward a Multicultural Family Law' 38 *Family Law Quarterly* 501.

—— (2009) 'Unofficial Family Law' 94 *Iowa Law Review* 451.

Fernández-Coronado González, A (2009) 'Matrimonio islámico, orden público y función promocional de los derechos fundamentals' 85 *Revista Española de Derecho Constitucional* 125.

Foqué, R and Verbeke, A (2009) 'Towards an Open and Flexible Imperative Inheritance Law' in C Castelein, R Foqué and A Verbeke (eds), *Imperative Inheritance Law in a Late-Modern Society* (Antwerp, Intersentia).

Fournier, P (2010) *Muslim Marriage in Western Courts: Lost in Transplantation* (Farnham, Ashgate).

Freeman, M (1998) 'Cultural Pluralism and the Rights of the Child' in J Eekelaar and T Nhlapo (eds), *The Changing Family: International Perspectives on the Family and Family Law* (Oxford, Hart Publishing).

—— (2002) 'Human Rights, Children's Rights and Judgement – Some Thoughts on Reconciling Universality and Pluralism' 10 *The International Journal of Children's Rights* 345.

Goolam, N (1998) 'Constitutional Interpretation of the "Best Interests" Principle in South Africa in Relation to Custody' in J Eekelaar and T Nhlapo (eds), *The Changing Family: International Perspectives on the Family and Family Law* (Oxford, Hart Publishing).

Hamilton, C (1995) *Family, Law and Religion* (London, Sweet & Maxwell).

Harding, M (2008) '"To Affinity and Beyond": A Critical Analysis of the Law on Marriage within Prohibited Degrees of Relationship' in K Boele-Woelki and T Sverdrup (eds), *European Challenges in Contemporary Family Law* (Antwerp, Intersentia).

Hinz, MO (1998) 'Family Law in Namibia: The Challenge of Customary and Constitutional Law' in J Eekelaar and T Nhlapo (eds), *The Changing Family: International Perspectives on the Family and Family Law* (Oxford, Hart Publishing).

International Council on Human Rights Policy (2009) *When Legal Worlds Overlap: Human Rights, State and Non-State Law* report available at: www.ichrp.org.

Jansen, N and Michaels, R (2008) 'Beyond the State? Rethinking Private Law' Introduction to *Beyond the State. Rethinking Private Law* (Tübingen, Mohr Siebeck).

La Barbera, MC (2010) 'Mujeres, migración y Derecho penal: el trato jurídico de la "mutilación genital femenina"' 4 *Sortuz. Oñati Journal of Emergent Socio-legal Studies* 34.

Maclean, M (2000) 'Introduction: Making Law for Families: Studies in the Legislative Process' in M Maclean (ed), *Making Law for Families* (Oxford, Hart Publishing).

Malik, M (2000) 'Faith and the State of Jurisprudence' in P Oliver, SD Scott and V Tadros (eds), *Faith in Law. Essays in Legal Theory* (Oxford, Hart Publishing).

Mohamad, M (2011) 'Malaysian Sharia Reforms in Flux: The Changeable National Character of Islamic Marriage' 25 *International Journal of Law, Policy and the Family* 46.

Moreno Antón, M (2007) 'Libertad religiosa y salud' in I Martín Sánchez (ed), *Libertad religiosa y Derecho sanitario* (Madrid, Fundación Universitaria Española).

Pintens, W (2009) 'Ehegüterstände in Europa' *Zeitschrift für Europäisches Privatrechts* 268.

Roca, E (2010) 'Familia, formas familiares y economía. Dos ensayos sobre metodología del Derecho de familia' in *Patrimonio matrimonial en matrimonios no indisolubles* (Madrid, Fundación Coloquio Jurídico Europeo).

Sayed, M (2008) 'The Muslim Dower (Mahr) in Europe –With Special Reference to Sweden' in K Boele-Woelki and T Sverdrup (eds), *European Challenges in Contemporary Family Law* (Antwerp, Intersentia).

Shachar, A (2010) 'State, Religion, and the Family: The New Dilemmas of Multicultural Accommodation' in R Ahdar and N Aroney (eds) *Shari'a in the West* (Oxford, Oxford University Press).

Stacey, J and Meadow, T (2009) 'New Slants on the Slippery Slope: The Politics of Polygamy and Gay Family Rights in South Africa and the United States' 37 *Politics & Society* 167.

Tsaoussim, A and Zervogianni, E (2008) 'Multiculturalism and Family Law: The Case of Greek Muslims' in K Boele-Woelki and T Sverdrup (eds), *European Challenges in Contemporary Family Law* (Antwerp, Intersentia).

Van Houtte, J and Breda, J (2005) 'Maintenance of the Aged by their Adult Children: An Adequate Legal Institution?' in M Maclean (ed), *Family Law and Family Values* (Oxford, Hart Publishing).

Waldron, J (2002) 'One Law for All? The Logic of Cultural Accommodation' 59 *Washington & Lee Law Review* 3.

—— (2010) 'Questions about the Reasonable Accommodation of Minorities' in R Ahdar and N Aroney (eds), *Shari'a in the West* (Oxford, Oxford University Press).

Wardle, LD (2010) 'Marriage and Religious Liberty: Comparative Law Problems and Conflict of Laws Solutions' 12 *Journal of Law & Family Studies* 315.

Wilson, RF (2007) 'The Overlooked Costs of Religious Deference' 64 *Washington & Lee Law Review* 1363.

—— (2010) 'Privatizing Family Law in the Name of Religion' 18 *William & Mary Bill of Rights Journal* 925.

Woehrling, J (2010) 'Accords et dissonances à propos du concept de laïcité: le Quebec entre le modele français et le modele canadien' 68 *Études canadiennes/Canadian Studies* 127.

Zanghellini, A (2010) 'Queer Kinship Practices in Non-Western Contexts: French Polynesia's Gender-variant Parents and the Law of "La République"' 37 *Journal of Law and Society* 651.

Zimmermann, R (2007) 'Compulsory Heirship in Roman Law' in K Reid, M de Waal and R Zimmermann (eds), *Exploring the Law of Succession: Studies National, Historical and Comparative* (Edinburgh, Edinburgh University Press).

17

Variation and Change in Normative Parental Discipline: Persuasion or Legislation?

MARJORIE SMITH AND ANN PHOENIX[1]

In any discussion of child upbringing, the question of discipline must be at once the central and most controversial issue. It is central because it arises in some form at every turn of the child's daily life; it is controversial because human beings, whether parents or not, tend to have views on how parents ought to behave towards their children.

John and Elizabeth Newson (1968: 387)

I INTRODUCTION

INTEREST AND CONCERN about the physical punishment of children in the home emerged at the point when parenting and family life was still seen largely as a private domain, and not otherwise subject to public scrutiny or censure. Despite the multiple dimensions of parenting, parental discipline arguably continues to be the single most debated and controversial aspect of parenting. It is the focus of political and professional debate, as well as being the topic of an active and ongoing lay debate.

As Maccoby and Martin (1983: 1–101) identified, parental control is one of the key qualitative dimensions of parenting behaviour, along with warmth, associated with positive outcomes for children. The issue, however, is not about

[1] Marjorie Smith's studies were funded by the UK Department of Health, whose support is gratefully acknowledged. The views expressed, however, are not necessarily those of the Department of Health.

Ann Phoenix's research was funded by a Professorial Fellowship from ESRC (Award Number: RES-051-27-0181). Elaine Bauer and Stephanie Davis-Gill were the Research Fellows on the programme. Interviews with serial migrants were conducted by the three of them from the Thomas Coram Research Unit, Institute of Education, University of London, and by Leandra Box from the Race Equality Foundation. The programme was composed of three studies of adults who in childhood were: serial migrants; grew up in visibly ethnically different households and language brokers.

the importance or necessity of control, but rather whether it is necessary, appropriate or desirable for parents to physically discipline or punish their children, with physical punishment, defined (to borrow the definition of corporal punishment from Straus and Donnelly (2005: 3) as 'the use of physical force with the intention of causing a child to experience pain, but not injury, for the purpose of correcting or controlling the child's behaviour'. Historically, in Western cultures of Anglo-Saxon origin, 'reasonable' physical punishment has been viewed as necessary for the proper upbringing of children, with the biblical text, 'He that spareth the rod hateth his son, but he that loveth him chasteneth him betimes' (Proverbs 13:24), often used to support this belief.

Concerns about the use or extent of use of physical punishment have also been in evidence for a long time. Theorists differ in their identification of the reasons for the shift in attitudes away from physical punishment, and the date when they began to be evident. Donnelly (2005), taking an historical perspective on the physical punishment of children, distinguishes two different narratives that have been used to construct histories of the family and of childhood. He identifies these as the 'evolutionist track' and the 'contextualist track'. In the first, changes in parents' attitudes towards children and their perceptions of childhood are used to infer how children are likely to have been treated. Thus, by the mid-nineteenth century more psychological methods of discipline achieved greater prominence with the shift in family sentiments from a Calvinist tradition where original sin had to be expunged, and obedience cruelly beaten into the child, towards one of child nurturance, reflected in the emergence of toys and games for children. Changes in attitudes to, and the use of, physical punishment are seen as reflecting the 'smooth upward curve of social progress' (Donnelly 2005: 51).

In contrast, the contextualist track views the family as firmly embedded within its particular time and place, and thus best understood through a contemporary social and culturally constructed framework. Donnelly points out that the implications of this are that the phenomenon and meaning of corporal punishment will change over time, as will the evaluation and acceptability of interpersonal violence, and needs to be interpreted within a specific context. This suggests that there has been a series of discrete periods when there has been concern about physical punishment and violence, interspersed with others when it has not been an issue.

Most contemporary writers seeking to explain the current shift in attitudes to physical punishment adopt contextualist approaches, and tend to attribute the change to postwar events, such as the growing recognition of the phenomenon of physical maltreatment and abuse, with the publication in 1962 of *The Battered Child*, by Kempe and colleagues, and a number of high profile cases of child maltreatment. While early explanations of the phenomenon tended to adopt explanations based on individual characteristics, a number of theories were proposed to explain abusive parenting. The more persistent of these conceptualised parenting as multifactorial and multilayer, with individual, historical, social and contextual determinants combining to shape parenting (eg, Belsky, 1984, 1993). The quality of parenting is determined by the balance of stresses or sources of difficulty, which might include children who are fretful or non-responsive, and parenting supports, such as a supportive partner or good social supports. These theories suggested that harsh or abusive parenting could occur in 'ordinary' families when the stresses outweighed the supports, and was linked to the use of physical punishment.

The theorised links were explained by the 'continuum argument', proposing that there is a direct link between the 'normal' punishment of children (termed 'subabusive violence'), and child abuse. This was based on the observation that many cases of child abuse had originated as acts of punishment which had gone too far (Gil 1970; Graziano 1994). Links were also hypothesised as a result of the escalation of violence in families using physical means of disciplining in order to maintain its efficacy – the argument being that if physical punishment ceases to be effective, parents will resort to increasingly severe and punitive strategies in order to ensure that it is effective, and so 'normal' physical punishment may rapidly escalate into abuse.

In parallel with the concerns about parenting and what were perceived to be increases in family violence, have been developments in relation to the rights of the child. These led to movements to put a stop to the 'culturally sanctioned violence towards children' (Gil 1971) by outlawing the physical punishment of children. The initiative to legislate against smacking or the physical punishment of children was led by the Scandinavian countries: Sweden brought in legislation in 1979, so they have celebrated the thirtieth anniversary of the ban recently, followed by Finland in 1983 and Norway in 1987. Worldwide, a total of 32 states have now legislated against corporal punishment with the most recent (South Sudan, Republic of Congo, Poland, Tunisia and Kenya, which brought in legislation in 2010) including the first four countries on the African continent to ban smacking. Of the 27 EU Member States, 16 have now outlawed the physical punishment of children. Although a number of consultations have been conducted on the issue in the UK, and some changes have been initiated in the legislation as part of the Children Act 2004,[2] there is not yet any comprehensive legislation in the UK against the physical punishment of children by their parents. In part, this reflects the considerable resistance to legislation which interferes in the way parents behave with their children 'behind closed doors' in the home, but does mean that parents and others *in loco parentis* can use 'reasonable punishment' – including physical punishment – to discipline a child.

There is, however, a vociferous lobby which strongly supports the introduction of legislation. The most prominent campaigning movement was, and is, EPOCH – now the 'Global Initiative to End All Corporal Punishment of Children', launched in 2001, which 'aims to speed the end of corporal punishment of

---

[2] This Act removes any defence of 'reasonable chastisement' if a child is caused actual or grievous bodily harm. If no physical injury (eg, a bruise) is apparent, therefore, the defence could be used to a charge of common assault.

children across the world',[3] but within the UK there is also the 'Children are Unbeatable' alliance specifically campaigning 'for the UK to satisfy human rights obligations by modernising the law on assault to afford children the same protection as adults'.[4] The debate continues actively with websites both for and against anti-smacking legislation. One example of the latter[5] claiming to speak for the 'pro-families' lobby, also claims that many organisations which have publicly taken anti-smacking stances do not support legal reform to end smacking.

The purpose of this chapter is not, however, to discuss the current legal situation or debates, but to provide some descriptive background information on the pattern, nature and extent of different family disciplinary practices in England, and to raise some issues, such as the extent to which different disciplinary practices are 'normative' or not, factors associated with differences in patterns of parental discipline, and on the use of language. This contextual information is largely based on a study of parental control of children in the home, conducted some years ago now, by one of us (MS) with colleagues (Nobes et al 1999; Nobes and Smith 2002). The research – which involved a randomly selected community population of nearly 550 families – was conducted between 1990 and 1995, so the first necessary caveat is to point out that the data are already historical.

II THE PUNISHMENT STUDY

The study was distinctive in several ways. Most studies that have investigated the parental punishment of children have been limited in the types of punishment included. Many have been confined to studying physical punishment, usually interpreted only as smacking, and there has been little attempt to describe how the pattern of punishment changes with age. The terminology used has also imposed limitations on the developmental interpretation of the available data. That is, within a labelled punishment category the assumption has been made that the nature of the parental action does not change with the age of the child: a 'smack' to a one-year-old child was assumed to be the same as a smack to an older child.

The cross-sectional research investigated a randomly selected community sample drawn from health registers in two areas of the South East of England. Equal numbers of mothers of girls and boys aged (exactly) one, four, seven or eleven years of age were sampled. The mothers of these children were interviewed at home to obtain information on their use of a number of different punishments and control strategies (some fathers and all older children were also interviewed, but the data reported here are from mothers' accounts only). Parental disciplinary or control actions were divided into physical, non-physical and non-punitive, with a number of more specific categories and punishment

---

[3] See: www.endcorporalpunishment.org.
[4] See: www.childrenareunbeatable.org.uk.
[5] See: www.families-first.org.uk/art/epsur.html.

types within these broad divisions. Within each category, details were obtained on whether any of the types of punishment or control strategies had been used within the last year, or ever. For those used within the previous year, details of the frequency of use were obtained, as was information on the precise nature and 'quality' of the last incident. For physical punishments, details were also obtained of the most severe incident ever. From this detailed information an independent rating was made, based on all the information available, of the severity of the parental action. Severity was rated as mild, moderate or severe, where mild generally described incidents judged to have no intention to harm, including psychological harm, no use of implements, no repeated actions and no prolonged effect or actions; and incidents rated severe were those judged to have the intention or potential to cause injury or psychological damage, the use of implements, repeated actions or over long periods of time. For each category, parents were asked a standardised initial question. For example, for the category 'punishment by example' parents were asked, 'In order to stop their children from doing certain things, many parents show their children just how painful these things can be. Have you ever done anything like this?' If the parent's response was affirmative, they were asked questions about whether they had ever administered to the child each of the types of punishment in the category. The table below (table 1) shows the categories of punishment explored.

III CHILDREN'S EXPERIENCE OF PUNISHMENT

The large majority of children had experienced some form of physical punishment in the past year, with hitting or smacking being the most commonly experienced type of physical punishment – 91 per cent of children had at some time been smacked, and this was 97 per cent if one-year-old children were excluded; and 77 per cent had been hit in the last year. The upshot of this is that, at least when we conducted the research, physical punishment could be said to be normative. Smaller, but still considerable, numbers of children had also been subject to other types of physical punishment such as physical restraint or punishment by example (see table 2). Equally there was a wide variety of non-physical disciplinary strategies used by parents (see table 3) with the majority of children having experienced exclusions or time out, and the withdrawal of some privilege such as a favourite TV programme, or not being allowed out to play.

Approximately a quarter of children had experienced at least one disciplinary incident that was rated as 'severe' according to our ratings, but this did not include any one-year-old children. The large majority of severe incidents (88 per cent) involved hitting, but other sorts of physical and non-physical disciplinary incidents were rated as severe (figure 1). Disciplinary actions involving ingestions were relatively uncommon, but proportionally were most likely to be rated as severe. They included a seven-year-old child caught smoking, who was made to eat a cigarette, and a child forced to eat mustard as a punishment for swearing.

Table 1: Punishment/control strategies

Physical Control Strategies

Hitting/smacking:
included spanking, slapping and beating

Physical restraint:
included pushing, shaking, throwing and holding forcefully

'Punishment by example':
consisted of punishments such as hair pulling, biting and pinching, usually administered with the intention of demonstrating to children the consequences of their actions

Ingestion (not included for one-year-old children):
included washing the child's mouth out with soap and water and force feeding

Non-physical Control Strategies

Withdrawal of privileges:
included withholding TV/computer, pocket money; 'grounding' , treats

Exclusion/time out:
included being sent to bedroom, sent out of the room

Reparation/fining:
included doing something to make amends, payment/fines

Ignoring/emotional blackmail:
included verbal rejection, physical rejection

Verbal control:
included denigration or belittling, spiteful or nasty, 'talking to' , remind of rule, command, nagging, non-specific threats, threats of things not likely to happen, shouting

Table 2: Physical control strategies experienced by children (physical)

% experiencing	ever	(last yr)
Hitting	91	(77)
Physical restraint	42	(29)
Punishment by example (PBE)	42	(14)
Ingestion	12	(5)

Table 3: Non-physical control strategies experienced by children

% experiencing	ever	(last yr)
Exclusion/Time out	78	(72)
Withdrawal of privileges	54	(53)
Ignoring/emotional blackmail	31	(30)
Reparation/Fines	26	(24)

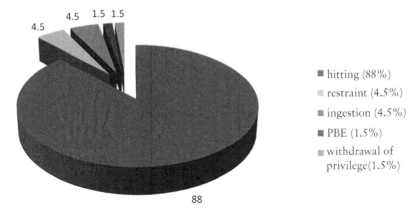

Figure 1: Severe incidents by punishment type (%)

Looking at the total experience for children, it was clear from the data that the concept of 'positive' or 'negative' parenting put forward by some writers was not a realistic one – most children experienced a wide variety of control strategies, including both physical and non-physical methods, and most mothers behaved in ways that were positive and loving – as well as in ways that could be described as negative (see figure 2).

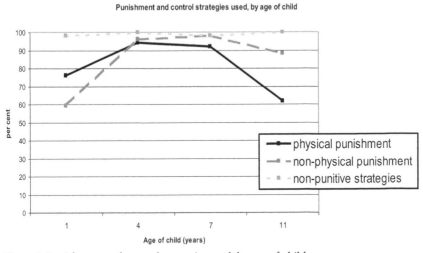

Figure 2: Punishment and control strategies used, by age of child

IV VARIABLES ASSOCIATED WITH DIFFERENCES IN PHYSICAL PUNISHMENTS

Both the pattern and types of punishments used differed with the child's age, and within a punishment or control category, the frequency and nature of the action differed with the age of the child. For both physical and non-physical punishments there was evidence that some mothers thought that these were inappropriate for one-year-old children. However, as children 'grew into' physical punishments, so they largely 'grew out' of them by the time they were 11 years of age. This did not happen as much with non-physical punishments, which once established as control or punishment mechanisms, continued to be used (see figures 3 and 4).

There were differences within punishment categories in relation to the 'quality' of punishment. For example, although most children had been hit or smacked by their mothers, younger children were more likely to be hit – or

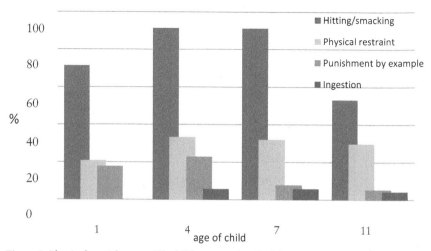

Figure 3: Physical punishments (% children experiencing) in past year

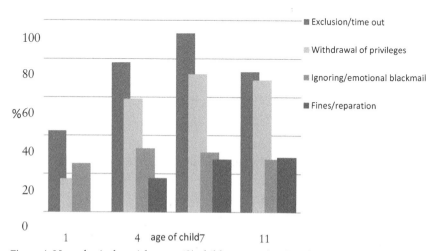

Figure 4: Non-physical punishments (% children experiencing) in past year

'tapped' as it was often described – on their hand, and older children to be hit on their clothed bottom or leg. There were also age-related differences in what children were hit with (younger children were hit with fingers and older children smacked with a whole open hand), the number of impacts, the rated severity of the action and the mothers' reported affect before hitting the child – generally the older the child, the more likely it was that the mother reported having lost her temper or been out of control. No implements were reported to have been used for hitting one-year-old children, but 10 per cent of older children had been hit with an implement, such as a hair brush or a fly swat. There were similar age-related differences in most of the types of punishment investigated, including verbal control of children.

In contrast, there were almost no differences in parental disciplinary practices related to the gender of the child, with the one exception that girls were more likely to be in the small minority of children who had never been hit according to their mothers' reports – 14 per cent were female compared with just four per cent of boys.

A number of family functioning and other family variables were associated with higher rates of physical punitiveness, and these were generally stronger predictors than demographic variables such as family type or social class. For example, parenting stress, the quality of the marital relationship and poor maternal mental health were all associated with higher rates of physical punishment (Nobes and Smith 2002). These findings are in line with those reported by Woodward and Fergusson (2002) based on over a thousand families from the Christchurch longitudinal study, in New Zealand. They propose a cumulative risk factors model where factors in the child, mother and environment all contribute, in line with the multilevel theories of parenting proposed by Belsky and others. Maternal factors that were implicated in higher rates of punishment included an early history of relationship difficulties and strict parenting in the mother's family of origin; drug and alcohol abuse, depression, family stress and marital conflict. Child factors included higher rates of conduct disorder and attention problems.

There were in our data, also differences in parental disciplinary practices and attitudes related to ethnicity. These were generally in line with those reported in Korbin (1981), with lower rates of physical punishment in families of South Asian origin, but higher rates of non-physical strategies such as threats; and more frequent use of physical punishment and more positive attitudes to it in families of African Caribbean and African origin. There are, however, some data from the United States that suggest that the relationship between the experience of physical discipline and negative child outcomes – in this case child aggression – may differ in different ethnic groups (Deater-Deckard et al 1996; 1997). Specifically, it was found that higher rates of physical punishment were associated with higher rates of conduct disorder in white American children, but not in black American children. It was suggested that more strict and disciplinarian methods of parenting were adaptive, and indeed protective, to black youths growing up in high risk environments. This is an important finding as it suggests that the cultural context and meaning of parental discipline may determine to some extent the outcomes of it – but more on this later.

V A NOTE ON TERMINOLOGY

Related to the differences associated with ethnicity, is the apparently trivial, but practically important, issue of terminology. This is rather well illustrated by an account from an eminent clinical colleague (of MS's), an expert in child abuse and neglect, of her experience many years ago with a black mother attending her clinic with her three-year-old daughter, as she was finding it difficult to manage her child's behaviour. On one occasion, the mother reported on a recent misdemeanour by her daughter. She also reported that as a result she 'had beaten her, and beaten her and beaten her'. My eminent colleague took a deep breath, before asking calmly, 'And what did you beat her with?', to which the mother replied, 'Oh words, words'.

There is an assumption, implicit in most studies, that there is consistency between parents, and between researchers and parents, in the usage of words to describe parental actions. The problem is common to all forms of parental punishment or control, but the most commonly measured physical punishment, that of hitting a child, is a good example. There are those who would argue that the act of hitting a child is wrong however it is done, and therefore the precise nature of the action is unimportant, but this fails to distinguish a gentle tap with the parent's fingers on the child's hand with no intention to hurt, from a repeated forceful hitting in anger and with intent to hurt.

The normative, and therefore more socially acceptable labels for hitting a child, are 'spanking', in the US (eg Straus 1994); or more usually 'smacking' in the UK and New Zealand (Newson and Newson 1968: 387–429; Ritchie and Ritchie 1981; Maxwell 1993; Nobes and Smith 2002). Many other labels have been used, such as slapping, thrashing and beating, with some authors describing a hierarchy of progressively more serious physical actions – for example, a beating is distinguished as more severe than spanking or smacking, or thrashing as more severe than strapping (Ritchie and Ritchie 1981; Maxwell 1993). What is less clear is whether there is a distinction between a slap, a smack, a spank or a beating, for example, and if so, what it is. It is also not apparent from the label where on the body the child was hit, whether it was a single or repeated action, and whether the impact was with the fingers, whole hand, fist or an implement (does a beating, as opposed to a spanking, imply that an implement was used, or that it was a repeated action)?

As well as national differences in the way hitting is described, there is evidence that black Caribbean parents are more likely to use the word 'beating' to describe the same action that a white parent would describe as smacking (or spanking) the child – and, as the quote above demonstrates, the generic description 'beating' can also be used for a much wider variety of disciplinary practices.

The difference in terminology is almost certainly relevant to interpreting some of the historical data relating to supposed ethnic differences in punishment practices. Pollak (1979: 94–99) asked mothers and their nine-year-old children in south London about their usual punishment. At the time, physical punishment was the most frequently reported punishment by both children and their mothers (the other options were reprimand, banished, no television, or none) but the white and 'West Indian' groups differed markedly in whether they reported they were smacked or beaten. The white children were more likely to say that they were smacked than beaten (65.6 per cent said they were smacked, versus 4.8 per cent who said they were beaten) while black children were more likely to report that they were beaten than smacked (53 per cent versus 31.8 per cent). Although mothers were less likely than children to report that physical punishment was the child's 'usual punishment', the differences were more marked, with 42.4 per cent of black mothers reporting beating as the usual punishment, against 9.1 per cent who said they smacked their children, in contrast to 8.2 per cent of white mothers, who reported beating and 32.8 per cent who said that they normally smacked their children.

VI CARIBBEAN SERIAL MIGRANTS AND GENERATIONAL SHIFTS IN NARRATIVES ON PUNISHMENT

Since the study reported above was completed, a variety of studies conducted in the US have documented differences in the use of physical punishment by parents from different ethnic groups. There has been much debate and disagreement about whether black parents are culturally predisposed to use harsh physical punishment as part of their repertoire of disciplinary practices, and whether or not this constitutes child abuse. As mentioned earlier, in the US, African-American parents have been found to be more likely than European-American parents to use physical punishment as a disciplinary strategy, and this relationship holds true even if socio-economic status and gender are controlled (Hill and Sprague 1999).

But the impact of physical punishment on children has also consistently been found to differ between ethnic groups. Deater-Deckard and colleagues' (1996; Gershoff et al 2010) influential longitudinal study found that white European American parents' use of physical discipline was predictive of higher levels of externalising (aggressive) behaviour among their children, but this relationship did not hold for African-American children. They argued that within African-American culture, physical discipline short of abuse is more acceptable than in European-American culture, so that white European Americans who use such practices may be erratic or do so because they lose control. From his review of the literature, Whaley (2000) also found that physical discipline was linked to disruptive disorders in European-American families, but not for African-American families. He suggests that in white families children's negative behaviours both lead to spanking and result from it, whereas for black families, spanking follows negative behaviour rather than producing it.

Similarly, Pachter et al (2006) found from a quantitative, longitudinal study in the US, that poverty has pervasive and deleterious effects for all ethnic groups and parenting is universally important, but that there are important differences between ethnic groups. For example, maternal depression and neighbourhood do not directly affect child behaviour for black families, but do for white families. They suggest that the findings may be explained by reference to differences in normative cultural values and processes that act as possible 'sociocultural buffers' against poor childhood outcomes. In keeping with this, Vendlinski et al (2006) suggest that ethnic differences may be accounted for by how normative family processes are considered to be, and the meaning that children of different ethnic backgrounds assign to these processes.

One difficulty with much of the research on ethnicity, parenting and punishment is that it assumes that parents from the same ethnic groups are likely to take the same approaches to disciplining their children. Yet, as is frequently shown with white majority ethnic parents, there are multiple approaches to parenting. A study of parenting in mainland China illustrates such differences in relation to parenting style. Xu et al (2005) found that both authoritarian and authoritative parenting styles could be positively related to endorsement of traditional Chinese values, and for mothers who endorsed traditional values, behaviours such as obedience and propriety may be important, regardless of parenting style. As Pachter et al (2006) argue, there is thus a need for studies that can help to clarify the underlying causes and mechanisms for such differences. Ponterotto (2003) recommends the use of qualitative methods to deepen understanding of ethnicity and parenting.

The next section briefly explores the complexity of issues of ethnicity and punishment by considering a few examples of differences in approaches to punishment for UK African-Caribbean parents and their own parents and grandparents.

VII CHANGING PARENTAL PUNISHMENT STRATEGIES

The few examples discussed here come from an interview study of 53 adults who were serial migrants from the Caribbean (39 women and 14 men), two of their mothers and three group discussions conducted with participants who had previously been interviewed after the participant feedback sessions. The study formed part of an ESRC-funded research programme on 'Transforming Experience' (conducted by AP). The term 'serial migration' is used in the literature in two ways. It describes repeated migrations (eg, Ossman 2004) as well as migrations where family members (or sometimes friends) migrate in series, following each other, rather than migrating at the same time; a process that is also referred to as 'chain migration'(Mayhew 2004). As a result, serial migration in this second sense entails (some degree of) family reunification over time. In the study reported here, 'serial migration' is used in this second sense and describes a situation where children follow their parents (or a parent, mostly a mother) who migrate first.

While many of the sample narrated experiences of having been 'beaten' in their childhoods, it is noteworthy that several reported that they had never received such physical punishments, with one woman saying that she had been disciplined through the quoting of proverbs. In the example below, a father explains that he had never been 'beaten' by his grandparents in the Caribbean, but was beaten by his parents when he joined them in the UK, particularly his mother since his father did shift work:

Lloyd: When I came in this country, the first beat I get is from my mother, yeah, so my mum is always moanin' . . . Yeah, (coughs) but um (3) I used to get beaten,

Q: You . . . you . . . how do you . . . how do you . . . do you discipline the kids?

Louisa: Well I . . . I don't beat, I might (.) shout and you shrug . . . try and (.) talk to them instead of thinkin' everythin' physically, you know what I'm sayin'. Sometimes I given em a little wallop but not anything t – to . . . to write home about . . . sometimes they want a good slap but (.) you see what I'm sayin', at the end of the day, I don't beat them, I don't. Even my grandkids . . . Lloyd is the one who would say it but he don't even really beat (.) he say '(inaudible)' but he doesn't, he don't. Don't think you have to beat, they're supposed to be able to listen and understand what you're sayin' to them without all the brutality.

Lloyd: I don't like it myself . . . I'll do it but I don't] like it, you know, I don't like it, [you know what I mean.

The above quote illustrates how punishment strategies are not passed unquestioningly down through generations. Lloyd suggests that his parents used physical punishments when his grandparents did not and, together with his wife Louisa, Lloyd reported himself to dislike using them. Louisa makes a strong distinction between what Lloyd has said (that his parents did 'beat') and her giving 'a little wallop'. The point is that it would be hard to see punishment as simply a traditional cultural practice since it changes across generations, partly in reaction to the parents' childhood experiences and partly in relation to the social context and inclination.

In the next two quotes Michael justifies the 'beatings' he received as never whimsical and contextualises them as Caribbean, while Claudette suggests that she has brought up her daughter (now in her twenties) in the 'West Indian' way, in smacking her if she needed it:

Michael: I had beatings, I mean I can remember think – I can remember when we were (inaudible) and you know, that was part of life, I mean even at school, you know, you didn't do anything wrong and the messages all got home long before you anyway, you know. So that was (.) that was just part of (.) part and parcel of being in the Caribbean. /. . . / I wouldn't say, I can't say that oh, they were destructive parents that you know, I was just beaten just for any reason and that, there was always something behind it and I you know, I personally, like I never did hit my children, yeah? But then maybe I didn't spend all the time with them but then even when I had them over two weeks and such like, I didn't. But I remember you know, and things and sorts of things that st make (.) that I might have done, do you know what I mean, sometimes it's (.) kind of gets me 'cos you know, I didn't (.) I didn't think it was really necessary. Some of my children will cry just mind me looking at them and being upset with them and shouting at them, so (laughs).

Claudette: Well no, well I've brought her up the West Indian way. How *I* know. To be polite. If she's out of order she'll get a good smack, although you're not allowed to smack them any more . . . No just brought her up the way I know and that worked out fine.

For Michael, experiences of physical punishment, however justified, produced discontinuity and the belief that it was not necessary to 'hit' children, while for Claudette, bringing her daughter up to be polite required her to do what her parents had done. Taken together, Lloyd, Louisa and Michael as Caribbean-born UK parents indicate that 'beatings' are not simply Caribbean, even though several participants speak in essentialist terms about Caribbean parents as 'strict' and likely to resort to physical punishments. They also indicate (as in the two accounts below) how generational change occurs in both resistance to, and complicity with, the childrearing practices they experienced:

Clementine: I did in the beginning, as I said . . . When you learn a pattern, the way of (.) doin' things, that's the way, even though if you didn't like it yourself, some people can opt from never doin' it and they manage it, some people just lash out because that's the quickest fing they know how to respond to. And I think that's what I did, I picked up – picked up some of his negative (.) pattern and behaviour which I knew that impacted on me in a way that I didn't like him so I didn't want that for my children so I had to sort of, as I said, knock it on the head very early. Um, you know, yeah, I – I can't even imagine like, you know, obviously I hit my ones when they were younger but I can never imagine even touchin' . . . my grandchild, [you know what I mean [faster]] how you change in your views. 'Cos I realise you don't have to hit children for them to listen t – you know, for them to um do (.) your commands. Um, but he ne – my dad never learned that 'cos he didn't know any different, that's what he knew, his parents did it to him, he did it to me 'cos I was rude and he had to beat me 'cos that's what (.) you know. So I don't really blame him anymore for it, I would have like to know that if I was given another chance to actually build my relationship a bit better with him, as an adult now, you know. 'Cos I – I was rude to him and (.) as I said, bein' a parent myself, I realise that, you know, if my children talk to me in a certain way, I would feel hurt.

David: You know. I never hit my kids. I smacked my daughter once. Looking back at it I was never happy with it. My son grew up I never smacked them . . . because I don't believe in it sorry that's my job, it's my job to discipline them and make sure they're on the right track . . . Sorry you can't do that, they're kids, you can't go beating the hell out of them. And people say oh my parents beat me so I beat my kids. That's rubbish, (laugh) I mean I got beaten by my grandmother but I don't beat my kids.

It was not the case that adults who had been smacked by their parents rejected all their parents' values. Many wanted to bring their own children up to adhere to the values with which they were raised:

Q: But can I ask something? From what you've said and we'll come to an end, but why are you bringing your children up in the same values, because you've said that you are, for which reasons?

Vadne: Because I, personally, am very, very proud of what my parents done for us . . . we're all supposedly settled, respectable, married homeowners, all in jobs. And when you look back at my mum who was a nurse, came over and joined the Health Service and dad who came, was a bus conductor, wanted to be a driver, wasn't allowed, but both my parents worked three jobs all of the time to keep us going. And as adults, when you suddenly look back and you think 'Wow, how did they do that?' And it's a huge pride when you think that they must have done something right, and I don't even think it was a conscious 'I must do that because it happened'. . . and actually the husband that I found, though he's white and English, has the very same kind of values, the 'traditional', to use that term, setting, and we've come together very, very strongly and maintained that. But like I say, I hit my children when they were young and I only mean hit not beat and I stopped by the time the oldest one was about five because he just had this attitude of 'You're not hurting me, hit me harder'. So you had to stop, I realised by the age of about five, you had to stop so then you try and negotiate with them but I'm very proud of what my parents achieved . . . though growing up, we resented it hugely.

Vadne's account nuances her feelings about her parents in ways that fit with the US literature that suggests that the impact of physical punishment is mediated by sociocultural circumstances, whether children see their family processes as normative and the meaning that children assign to these processes (Vendlinski et al 2006). Equally, she indicates that family values and practices are shared across ethnicised groups.

VIII CHANGES IN THE UK CONTEXT

Discussion of physical punishment is recursive in the UK because there are divisions about whether or not parents should be allowed to smack children. Nonetheless, as shown in the examples of African Caribbean parents above, there have been changes over the last 15 years in how the UK population views physical punishment. A survey was conducted by the UK Department of

Children, Schools and Families (as it was then) as part of the review of English legislation, which changed in 2004 to ban any smacking that led to a reddening of children's skin. The survey has tracked a decrease since 1998 in the number of parents agreeing that occasional use of physical discipline is acceptable and necessary, although just over half the people surveyed in the most recent round still thought it was acceptable (DCSF 2007). A recent report based on a study conducted in Northern Ireland (Bunting et al 2010) has suggested that these parental attitudes are not straightforward, and described considerable ambivalence in parents' attitudes to physical punishment, as parents did not see it is an optimal method of control, but acknowledged that they still use it when stressed or angry. (This would also be an accurate summary of the attitudes expressed in HS's original study.) While there may have been some attitudinal change in the UK, the changes are less marked than those reported to have taken place in countries where legislation banning smacking is in place (see, for example, Durrant 1996: 19–25 reviewing the impact of the anti-smacking ban in Sweden) where changes in parental attitudes have been tracked, but researchers have tended not to ask more direct questions about the use of physical punishments – partly because of the potential biases and problems in asking questions about illegal behaviour.

It is also relevant to report that in a number of studies conducted by one of us (MS) since the original punishment study, all involving community samples that are at least broadly comparable, directly comparable questions on smacking have been included. These suggest that the rates of physical punishment have shown a progressive and quite significant decline in the time since the original research was conducted. For example, comparison of the results of the original punishment study with data from a study conducted ten years later, investigating in a randomly selected community sample the normal experience of minor injuries to children, suggests that both the incidence, and particularly the frequency, of physical punishment had declined quite markedly (Smith 2008). There are a number of reasons to be somewhat cautious about these data, but the underlying trend and message is quite clear. The accounts from the serial migration study lend support to these findings. Despite the considerable debate about possible legislation and much campaigning to make it illegal physically to punish children, this decline has occurred in the absence of any effective legislation to outlaw the use of physical punishment.

REFERENCES

Belsky, J (1984) 'The Determinants of Parenting: A Process Model' 55 *Child Development* 83.

—— (1993) 'Etiology of Child Maltreatment: A Developmental–ecological Analysis' 14 *Psychological Bulletin* 413.

Bunting, L and Webb, MA (2010) 'In Two Minds? – Parental Attitudes Toward Physical Punishment in the UK' 24 *Children and Society* 359.

Deater-Deckard, K, Dodge, KA, Bates, JE and Pettit, GS (1996) 'Physical Discipline among African American and European American Mothers: Links to Children's Externalizing Behaviours' 32 *Developmental Psychology* 1065.

Deater-Deckard, K and Dodge, KA (1997) 'Externalizing Behaviour Problems and Discipline Revisited: Nonlinear Effects and Variation by Culture, Context and Gender' 8 *Psychological Inquiry* 161.

DCSF (2007) *Review of Section 58 of the Children Act 2004* (London, Department of Children, Schools and Families).

Donnelly, M (2005) 'Putting Corporal Punishment of Children in Historical Perspective' in M Donnelly and MA Straus (eds), *Corporal Punishment of Children in Theoretical Perspective* (New Haven, CT, Yale University Press).

Durrant, JE (1996) 'The Swedish Ban on Corporal Punishment: Its History and Effects' in D Frehsee, W Horn and KD Bussmann (eds), *Family Violence Against Children: A Challenge for Society* (Berlin and New York, de Gruyter).

Gershoff, ET, Grogan-Kaylor, A, Lansford, JE, Chang, L, Zelli, A, Deater-Deckard, K and Dodge, KA (2010) 'Parent Discipline Practices in an International Sample: Associations with Child Behaviors and Moderation by Perceived Normativeness' 81 *Child Development* 487.

Gil, D (1970) *Violence Against Children: Physical Child Abuse in the United States* (Cambridge, MA, Harvard University Press).

—— (1971) 'Violence against Children' 33 *Journal of Marriage and the Family* 637.

Graziano, A (1994) 'Why we should Study Subabusive Violence against Children' 9 *Journal of Interpersonal Violence* 412.

Hill, S and Sprague, J (1999) 'Parenting in Black and White Families: The Interaction of Gender with Race and Class' 13 *Gender and Society* 480.

Kempe, CH, Silverman, FN, Steele, BF, Droegemueller, W and Silver, HK (1962) 'The Battered-Child Syndrome' 181 *Journal of the American Medical Association* 17.

Korbin, JE (ed), (1981) *Child Abuse and Neglect: Cross-cultural Perspectives* (Berkeley, University of California Press).

Maccoby, EE and Martin, JA (1983) 'Socialization in the Context of the Family: Parent–child Interaction' in EM Hetherington (ed) and PH Mussen (series ed), *Handbook of Child Psychology (vol 4) Socialization, Personality and Social Development* (New York, Wiley).

Maxwell, G (1993) *Physical Punishment in the Home in New Zealand* (Wellington, NZ, Office of the Commissioner for Children).

Mayhew, S (2004) *A Dictionary of Geography* (Oxford, Oxford University Press): www.encyclopedia.com/doc/1O15-chainmigration.html.

Newson, J and Newson, E (1968) *Four Years Old in an Urban Community* (London, George Allen and Unwin).

Nobes, G, Smith, M, Bee, P and Heverin, A (1999) 'Physical Punishment by Mothers and Fathers in British Homes' 14 *Journal of Interpersonal Violence* 887.

Nobes, G and Smith, M (2002) 'Family Structure and the Physical Punishment of Children' 23 *Journal of Family Issues* 349.

Ossman, S (2004) 'Studies in Serial Migration' 42 *International Migration* 111.

Pachter, L, Auinger, P, Palmer, R and Weitzman, M (2006) 'Do Parenting and the Home Environment, Maternal Depression, Neighborhood, and Chronic Poverty affect Child Behavioral Problems Differently in Different Racial-ethnic Groups?' 117 *Pediatrics* 1329.

Pollak, M (1979) *Nine Years Old* (Lancaster, MTP Press).

Ponterotto, JG (2003) 'Qualitative Research Methods: The Fifth Force in Psychology' *Counseling Psychologist* 394.

Ritchie, J and Ritchie, J (1981) *Spare the Rod* (Australia, George Allen and Unwin).

Straus, MA (1994) *Beating the Devil out of Them: Corporal Punishment in American Families* (New York, Lexington Books).

Straus, MA and Donnelly, M (2005) 'Theoretical Approaches to Corporal Punishment' in M Donnelly and MA Straus (eds), *Corporal Punishment of Children in Theoretical Perspective* (New Haven, CT, Yale University Press).

Smith, M (2008) 'Ordinary Families? Learning about Families and Parenting from Normative Studies: Institute of Education Inaugural Professorial Lectures' (London, Institute of Education, University of London).

Vanderfaeillie, J, Van Holen, F, Trogh, L and Andries, C (2012) 'The Impact of Foster Children's Behavioural Problems on Flemish Foster Mothers' Parenting Behaviour' 17 *Child & Family Social Work* 34.

Vendlinski, M, Silk, J, Shaw, D and Lane, T (2006) 'Ethnic Differences in Relations between Family Process and Child Internalizing Problems' 47 *Journal of Child Psychology and Psychiatry* 960.

Whaley, A (2000) 'Sociocultural Differences in the Developmental Consequences of the Use of Physical Discipline during Childhood for African Americans' 6 *Cultural Diversity and Ethnic Minority Psychology* 5.

Woodward, LJ and Fergusson, DM (2002) 'Parent, Child, and Contextual Predictors of Childhood Physical Punishment' 11 *Infant and Child Development* 213.

Xu, Y, Farver, JM, Zhang, Z, Zeng, Q, Yu, L and Beiying, C (2005) 'Mainland Chinese Parenting Styles and Parent–child Interaction' 29 *International Journal of Behavioral Development* 524.

Index

Note: Only the names of authors who are not contributors to this book and who have been substantially cited or drawn on have been indexed.